Rights, Race, and Reform

In 1962, a 15-year-old Arizona boy named Gerald Gault may or may not have made a lewd phone call to a neighbor. Gerald was arrested, prosecuted, removed from his parents' custody, and sent to a juvenile prison, all without legal representation. Gerald's mother's outrage at the treatment of her son eventually propelled the case to the United States Supreme Court. With its sweeping 1967 decision in *In re Gault*, the Court revolutionized the American juvenile court system by finding that children charged with delinquency have a constitutional right to counsel.

This anthology, which commemorates the fiftieth anniversary of the Gault decision, blends, across its three parts, legal and historical analyses, oral history, and personal narrative to provide an overview of modern Supreme Court juvenile justice jurisprudence, the advocates and organizations that defend children in juvenile court, the role these lawyers have played in the fight for justice for accused children, and the contemporary challenges facing juvenile defenders and their clients. The authors are leading juvenile justice reformers, advocates, and scholars, all of whom have been deeply involved in shaping modern juvenile justice policy and practice and most of whom have represented children in juvenile court.

This book is for everyone concerned about justice in America. The personal narratives about children in the system will intrigue students and academics, engage lay individuals who are interested in children's rights, and guide professionals, legislators, and other policymakers involved in juvenile justice reform and criminology.

Kristin Henning is the Agnes N. Williams Research Professor of Law and Director of the Juvenile Justice Clinic and Initiative at Georgetown Law. Her scholarship on race, adolescence, and juvenile justice appears in journals such as the *Cornell Law Review*, *California Law Review*, and *NYU Law Review* and in books such as *Policing the Black Man* (Random House, 2017) and *Punishment in Popular Culture* (NYU Press, 2015). Henning was formerly the Lead Attorney for the Juvenile Unit of the D.C. Public Defender Service and worked closely with the Juvenile Indigent Defense Action Network to develop and co-author the Juvenile Training Immersion Program, a national training curriculum for juvenile defenders. She is the Director of the Mid-Atlantic Juvenile Defender Center and an Adviser to American Law

Institute's Restatement on Children and the Law. She has also served as an expert consultant to the U.S. Department of Justice's Civil Rights Division and as an investigator in several state assessments of access to counsel for accused youth. Henning has received several awards, including the Robert E. Shepherd, Jr. Award for Excellence in Juvenile Defense by the National Juvenile Defender Center.

Laura Cohen is Distinguished Clinical Professor of Law, the Justice Virginia Long Scholar, and Director of the Criminal and Youth Justice Clinic at Rutgers Law School. She also co-directs both the Rutgers Center on Youth Violence and Juvenile Justice and the Northeast Juvenile Defender Center, and has served as an expert consultant to the U.S. Department of Justice Civil Rights Division in its investigation of systemic due process violations in the St. Louis County, Missouri Juvenile Court. Previously, Cohen was a staff attorney and Director of Training for the New York City Legal Aid Society's Juvenile Rights Practice. Her scholarship explores topics ranging from juvenile justice and parole to legal ethics and lawyering theory, with a particular focus on the legal representation of adolescents. Cohen has received numerous awards for her work, including the MacArthur Foundation's Champion for Change Award and the National Juvenile Defender Center's Robert E. Shepherd Award for Excellence in Juvenile Defense.

Ellen Marrus is the Royce Till Professor of Law at the University of Houston Law Center, the founder and Director of the Center for Children, Law & Policy (CCLP), and the co-director of the Southwest Juvenile Defender Center (SWJDC). She teaches juvenile law, street law, children and the law, professional responsibility, and practice-related courses, and directs clinical programs, including child advocacy clinics and a lab component for her children and a law course where students receive hands-on experience in child dependency cases. In her capacity as Director of CCLP and SWJDC, Marrus has provided technical assistance to public defenders, court appointed juvenile attorneys, the U.S. Department of Justice, juvenile probation, and federal and state legislators. She concentrates her scholarship in the areas of juvenile law, children's rights, and professionalism, with a focus on representing children in various proceedings and the intersection of juvenile justice with race and gender.

Rights, Race, and Reform

50 Years of Child Advocacy in the Juvenile Justice System

Edited by
Kristin Henning, Laura Cohen and Ellen Marrus

Routledge
Taylor & Francis Group
LONDON AND NEW YORK

First published 2018
by Routledge
2 Park Square, Milton Park, Abingdon, Oxon OX14 4RN

and by Routledge
711 Third Avenue, New York, NY 10017

Routledge is an imprint of the Taylor & Francis Group, an informa business

British Library Cataloguing-in-Publication Data
A catalogue record for this book is available from the British Library

Library of Congress Cataloging-in-Publication Data
Names: Cohen, Laura, (Law teacher), editor. | Henning, Kristin, (Law teacher) | Marus, Ellen, editor.
Title: Rights, race, and reform : 50 years of child advocacy in the juvenile justice system / edited by Laura Cohen, Kristin Henning, Ellen Marus.
Description: New York, NY : Routledge, 2018. | Includes bibliographical references and index.
Identifiers: LCCN 2017053091 | ISBN 9781138094697 (hbk) | ISBN 9781351602556 (web pdf) | ISBN 9781351602549 (epub) | ISBN 9781351602532 (mobipocket)
Subjects: LCSH: Juvenile justice, Administration of--United States. | Children--Legal status, laws, etc.--United States. | Juvenile delinquency–United States.
Classification: LCC KF9779 .R54 2018 | DDC 345.73/08--dc23
LC record available at https://lccn.loc.gov/2017053091

ISBN: 978-1-138-09469-7 (hbk)
ISBN: 978-1-315-10590-1 (ebk)

Typeset in Galliard
by Taylor & Francis Books

Contents

Introduction vii
KRISTIN HENNING, LAURA COHEN AND ELLEN MARRUS
Acknowledgments xiv
List of contributors xv

PART I
Gault: then and 50 years later 1

1 The many stories of *In re Gault* 3
ZAWADI BAHARANYI AND RANDY HERTZ

2 Arizona before and after *In re Gault*: has Arizona realized the promises of *In re Gault?* 20
ELLEN MARRUS AND CHRIS PHILLIS

3 Toward equal recognition, authority, and protection: legal and extra-legal advocacy for black youth in the juvenile justice system 30
KRISTIN HENNING, JENADEE NANINI AND GEOFF WARD

4 A new juvenile jurisprudence: how adolescent development research and relentless defense advocacy revolutionized criminal law and jurisprudence 51
EDUARDO FERRER

PART II
Juvenile defense: models of representation 77

5 The due process revolution in juvenile court – New York and the early years after *Gault* 79
MARTIN GUGGENHEIM

6 *Gault*'s ripple effect: the founding of Juvenile Law Center 99
ROBERT SCHWARTZ

7 Specializing in juvenile defense: the D.C. Public Defender Service as a case study 114
KRISTIN HENNING, RANDY HERTZ AND HANNAH McELHINNY

8 The role of law school clinics in implementing the *Gault* decision 128
WALLACE MLYNIEC AND MEGHAN STRONG

9 Raising the bar: improving the model of defense representation for adolescents prosecuted in adult courts 154
NANCY GINSBURG

10 Building a national juvenile defense community: the National Juvenile Defender Center 169
PATRICIA PURITZ

PART III
Challenges and reform **185**

11 Being David: the future of juvenile defense and the Goliath of youth injustice 187
MARY ANN SCALI

12 Pride and prejudice: juvenile defenders for racial justice 50 years after *Gault* 199
KRISTIN HENNING AND ERIN KEITH

13 Gerald Gault meet Brendan Dassey: preventing juvenile false and coerced confessions in the twenty-first century 217
LAURA NIRIDER, MEGAN CRANE AND STEVEN DRIZIN

14 No more "desert Devil's Island": the right to counsel for incarcerated children 227
LAURA COHEN AND SANDRA SIMKINS

15 *Gault* at 50: what juvenile defenders can do to dismantle the youth prison model 252
LIZ RYAN AND CARMEN DAUGHERTY

16 Busting the "juvenile super-predator" myth 269
LAURA COHEN AND JANE SPINAK

Index 285

Introduction

Kristin Henning, Laura Cohen and Ellen Marrus

In 1962, a 15-year-old Arizona boy named Gerald Gault may or may not have made a lewd phone call to a neighbor. Gerald was arrested, prosecuted, removed from his parents' custody, and sent to a juvenile prison until he turned 21, all without legal representation. Gerald's mother's outrage at the treatment of her son eventually propelled the case to the United States Supreme Court.

With its sweeping 1967 decision in *In re Gault*, the Court revolutionized the American juvenile court system. In finding that children charged with delinquency have a constitutional right to counsel, the Court for the first time acknowledged the need for effective legal advocacy on behalf of a historically voiceless population that was overwhelmingly poor and consisted disproportionately of youth of color.

In the wake of the *Gault* decision, lawyers from across the country answered the call and became juvenile defenders. Many of these attorneys are skilled, fearless, and passionate advocates who have committed themselves to righting the many injustices that have plagued the system since its inception: racial bias, mass incarceration, denial of due process, wrongful convictions, dangerous and damaging conditions of confinement, prosecution of youth as adults, and – despite the Court's mandate – widespread lack of access to counsel for children. These advocates see, up close every day, the tragic circumstances, trauma, and challenges their young clients face. At their best, juvenile defenders are true champions for children, ensuring that their rights are protected, their voices are heard, and that whenever possible, they are extricated from a juvenile "justice" system that often does more harm than good. At the same time, these lawyers, and the organizations for which they work, have been on the front lines of every major systemic reform effort of the last half-century. Their stories provide a unique lens through which to view and evaluate our nation's juvenile courts.

This anthology, the publication of which is timed to coincide with the fiftieth anniversary celebration of the *Gault* decision from May 2017 to May 2018, tells these stories. It also reflects on the progress and setbacks young people have experienced in juvenile courts over the last 50 years. By looking back, the authors hope the anthology will move us forward.

The authors of the chapters in this anthology are leading juvenile justice advocates, reformers, and scholars, all of whom have been deeply involved in shaping modern juvenile justice policy and practice and most of whom have represented children in juvenile court. Blending legal and historical analyses, oral history, and personal narrative, the book offers an overview of modern Supreme Court juvenile justice jurisprudence, the advocates and organizations that defend children in juvenile court, the role these lawyers have played in the fight for justice for accused children, and the contemporary challenges facing juvenile defenders and their clients.

Part I of the book, "Gault: then and 50 years later," helps situate *In re Gault* in the social, legal, and political context of the 1960s. In Chapter 1, "The many stories *of In re Gault*," Zawadi Baharanyi and Randy Hertz explore the early Supreme Court cases that recognized and defined the contours of constitutional rights for children in juvenile court, including *Gault, Kent v. U.S.* (involving due process rights of children waived to adult court), and *McKeiver v. Pennsylvania* (involving jury trial rights for juveniles). By taking us behind the scenes with a compelling narrative about Jerry Gault, his mother, and his lawyers, this chapter sets the tone for the entire anthology by not just focusing on the cases and their rulings, but also on the children who are at the heart of the juvenile justice system. Baharanyi and Hertz also set the stage for later chapters by helping us understand the legal scope and the limits of *Gault.*

In the second chapter, "Arizona before and after *In re Gault*: has Arizona realized the promises of *In re Gault*?," Professor Ellen Marrus and Arizona juvenile defender Chris Phillis provide additional historical context by describing the legal landscape for children in Arizona in the years before and after *Gault* and by offering more insights into the lives of Jerry Gault and his family. Although their chapter starts with the history of the Arizona juvenile court, it also brings us forward by reminding us that the promise of *Gault* has not been fully realized in Arizona or throughout the country. Fifty years after *Gault*, youth still appear without the assistance of counsel and other due process protections necessary to ensure fundamental fairness in juvenile proceedings.

Part I also recognizes that the legacy of advocacy for black youth in the juvenile system requires a special telling. In the third chapter, "'Toward equal recognition, authority, and protection: legal and extra-legal advocacy for black youth in the juvenile justice system," Kristin Henning, Jenadee Nanini, and Geoff Ward remind us that from the inception of the first juvenile courts, white Progressive Child Savers often refused to engage in the rehabilitation of "Negro" children. As a result, the earliest advocates for black youth, including black women's clubs of the Progressive Era, had to fight for the basic recognition of black children as "children" and for access to resources and services to which they were entitled. Even when the Supreme Court guaranteed youth the right to counsel and other due process protections in *Kent v. US* and *In re Gault*, those protections did little to rid black youth of racial discrimination and to ensure black children received protection and rehabilitation in lieu of criminalization and incarceration. In the years after *Gault*, civil rights lawyers continued the fight for racial justice by relying on equal protection litigation to dismantle the legal system of Jim Crow juvenile justice. As the fight for racial justice continues today, this chapter reminds us of the need for legal and non-legal strategies for reform.

Part I concludes with a review of the Supreme Court's evolving recognition that children are different from adults. Although this is an intuitive, undisputed fact that the law has recognized for centuries, criminal law and jurisprudence have been slow to account for these differences. In "A new juvenile jurisprudence: how adolescent development research and relentless defense advocacy revolutionized criminal law and jurisprudence," Eduardo Ferrer recounts how youth advocates and juvenile defenders have prodded courts and legislatures for much of the last 120 years to meaningfully incorporate the differences between youth and adults into substantive law, while still recognizing that the Constitution guarantees youth many of the same procedural rights afforded to adults. Ferrer's chapter surveys adolescent research critical to the formation of the Court's current differential jurisprudence and traces the evolution of the Supreme Court jurisprudence from the eventual abolition of the juvenile death penalty under the Eighth Amendment to the acknowledgment of the importance of adolescence in the *Miranda* context. This chapter also helps us look forward by identifying ways juvenile defenders can push the courts and other justice system stakeholders to meaningfully incorporate the differences between youth and adults beyond the death penalty and sentencing of youth in adult court.

Part II of this anthology, "Juvenile defense: models of representation," focuses on the unique role of juvenile defenders and the various models for the delivery of juvenile defense services, including public defender offices, nonprofit organizations, and law school clinics. This section includes personal accounts of how juvenile defenders and other children's lawyers opened their doors, refined their practice, specialized in juvenile defense, and engaged in systemic reform after *Gault*. The authors in this section are brutally honest about the challenges they faced in setting up their offices in the years immediately after *Gault*, and many acknowledge the challenges they continue to face in the political and social climate of the twenty-first century. They consider ethical dilemmas, resource challenges, political opposition, lack of specialization, and the need for class action attacks on persistent patterns of injustice. All of these stories reveal the courage and conviction of young and seasoned lawyers who battled against extreme odds on behalf of indigent children arrested across the country.

Offices featured in Part II are the New York Legal Aid Society's Juvenile Rights Division, Juvenile Law Center in Philadelphia, the D.C. Public Defender Service, and the Adolescent Intervention and Diversion (AID) Project of the Legal Aid Society. Although this section profiles a few highly-regarded juvenile defender offices, this collection is by no means exclusive. There are many public defenders, private juvenile defense attorneys, and nonprofit defense offices that have provided creative, persistent, and transformative advocacy on behalf of accused youth. The offices highlighted in this volume represent only a small fraction of the many forms this work can take.

In "The due process revolution in juvenile court: New York and the early years after *Gault*," Martin Guggenheim tells the story of the Juvenile Rights Division in New York's Legal Aid office. As a juvenile defender who began practicing only four years after the Supreme Court held that youth were entitled to counsel in

Gault, Guggenheim recounts what it was like to practice in juvenile court when there was minimal due process and a great deal of Progressive Era paternalism. This oral history describes the disruption that vigorous, well-trained, and highly motivated juvenile defenders created in the courts and narrates the victories and precedent-setting decisions that new juvenile defenders were able to achieve.

Robert G. Schwartz tells a similar story about the evolving juvenile defense practice in Philadelphia. In "*Gault's* ripple effect: the founding of Juvenile Law Center," Schwartz shares inspiring and sometimes amusing details of the early days of Juvenile Law Center. Founded in 1975 by four third-year law students at Temple Law School, the new office was committed to giving children a voice (and a "guiding hand") in decisions affecting their lives. Schwartz and his comrades represented children in a range of legal settings, including delinquency, dependency, and special education cases, and struggled to define what it meant to be lawyers for children, especially in juvenile cases when the role of defense lawyers in juvenile court was not fully formed.

In "Specializing in juvenile defense: the D.C. Public Defender Service as a case study," former and current public defenders Kristin Henning, Randy Hertz, and Hannah McElhinny describe the evolution of juvenile court practice by looking at the changes in the District of Columbia's Public Defender Service (PDS). In the years immediately following *Gault*, lawyers assumed that the right to counsel meant providing youth with the best representation adults would receive in criminal court. Juvenile court lawyers, however, quickly realized that the unique needs of children and the unique nature of juvenile court practice demanded something more. These lawyers knew they needed specialized training in adolescent development, more contact with the youth's family and key supports in the community, and help from social workers who would identify resources and services to support their young clients. The authors of this chapter practiced at PDS in three different eras: Randy Hertz was a staff attorney in the office in the second half of the 1980s, handling both juvenile and adult criminal cases; Kristin Henning was the lead attorney in the office's newly-created juvenile unit in the second half of the 1990s; and Hannah McElhinny is currently a supervising attorney in the office's juvenile section.

The juvenile defender movement also has deep roots in the law school curriculum. In "The role of law school clinics in implementing the *Gault* decision," Wallace Mlyniec and Meghan Strong teach us about the birth of children's rights' clinics in law schools in the late 1960s and early 1970s. Before *Gault*, children's rights were hardly noticed in law schools or in society at large. If the legal needs of children were considered at all, they were discussed in terms of the responsibility owed to children by adults. As the civil rights movement gathered steam and the due process revolution spawned decisions like *In re Gault,* law schools began to open juvenile justice clinics to implement the right to counsel for accused adults and youth. Although the earliest clinics faced obstacles such as a dearth of experienced juvenile defense lawyers, prejudice against "kiddie clinics," and a lack of reliable funding, they provided valuable defense for accused youth. Today at least 55 law schools have clinics dedicated to defending children.

Part II also recognizes that legal advocacy for children who are tried as adults requires an expansion of the traditional criminal defense model. In "Raising the bar: improving the model of defense representation for adolescents prosecuted in adult courts," Nancy Ginsberg introduces readers to the specialized interdisciplinary team – the Adolescent Intervention and Diversion (AID) Team of the Legal Aid Society of New York. Comprised of lawyers, social workers, and investigators dedicated to the representation of youth aged 13–18 who are prosecuted in the adult criminal courts in New York City, the AID team employs a multi-pronged approach including litigation, mitigation, and policy advocacy. The team advocates for better outcomes for teenage clients, their families, and their communities by seeking to improve the quality and quantity of services available to court-involved youth.

Part II ends with one of the most important stories in the book – the evolution of a national juvenile defense community. In "Building a national juvenile defense community: the National Juvenile Defender Center," leading juvenile defense activist Patricia Puritz describes the development and emergence of a robust, national juvenile defense community demanding reform of juvenile indigent defense systems across the country. Emphasizing the critical need for a strong and specialized cadre of counsel for children in delinquency courts, Puritz highlights the strategies and tactics used to build and strengthen the capacity of the juvenile defense bar, examines some of the challenges juvenile defenders have faced within and outside of the courtroom, and, perhaps most important, discusses the substantial progress that has been made in the pursuit of the fair treatment of children enmeshed in the justice system. This chapter is critical to our understanding of children's advocacy in America since *In re Gault.*

Part III of this anthology, "Challenges and reform," identifies the challenges currently confronting juvenile defenders and the children they represent and explores strategies for reform. These challenges include, among others, widespread waiver of the right to counsel by youth, deficiencies in the quality of representation afforded children in juvenile court, juvenile wrongful convictions, deplorable conditions of confinement, and continued racial disparities in the system. The chapters in Part III are prescriptive. They offer guidance not only for defenders, but also for state and local legislators, judges, prosecutors, and any others who are committed to fairness and equity in the juvenile justice system.

In "Being David: the future of juvenile defense and the Goliath of youth injustice," Mary Ann Scali, Executive Director of the National Juvenile Defender Center, surveys the most pressing challenges facing juvenile defenders today. She considers overwhelming caseloads, dismal budgets allocated to publicly-funded defender offices, and the dearth of youth-specific training for defense counsel among others. As long as we live in a nation where children are not treated as children, the future of juvenile defense demands strength and courage to revolutionize juvenile defense systems, collaboration with the broader community to end systemic injustice, and fierce advocacy for every child in need of representation.

Fifty years after *Gault,* the overcriminalization of youth of color continues to be one of the greatest challenges facing the juvenile system. In "Pride and prejudice:

juvenile defenders for racial justice 50 years after *Gault*," Kristin Henning and Erin Keith issue a clarion call for juvenile defenders to be champions for racial justice. Decided in 1967, during the heart of the Civil Rights movement, *Gault* was implicitly – although not explicitly – concerned about the way black youth were being treated in the juvenile justice system and served as an important legal corollary to the socio-political fight against discrimination. This chapter empowers defenders with practical strategies to fight against the overcriminalization of minority youth by confronting their own subconscious prejudices, attacking racial injustices at every stage of their client's case, and participating in systemic reform.

The next chapter is written by the founder and co-directors of the Center on Wrongful Convictions of Youth, the first and only organization dedicated to representing children who falsely confessed to crimes they did not commit. In "Gerald Gault meet Brendan Dassey: preventing juvenile false and coerced confession in the twenty-first century," Laura Nirider, Megan Crane, and Steven Drizin breathe life into Justice Fortas' warning that *In re Gault* "has cast formidable doubt upon the reliability of 'confessions' by children." In 2011, the United States Supreme Court revived Fortas' prescient words when it concluded in *J.D.B. v. North Carolina* that the problem of false confession is "all the more acute" when the subject of custodial interrogation is a juvenile. Using the involuntary and false confession of 16-year-old, mentally limited Brendan Dassey as an illustrative case study, this chapter examines the most egregious of the psychologically coercive interrogation tactics regularly used on children across our country and proposes litigation strategies for reform.

In "No more 'desert Devil's Island': the right to counsel for incarcerated children," Laura Cohen and Sandra Simkins contend that 50 years after *Gault*, a yawning gap still persists between the rehabilitative ideals of the juvenile court and the dangerous reality of juvenile prisons. This chapter documents the brutality of the Arizona State Industrial School, where Gerald Gault served his sentence, and describes how incarcerated children continue to be held in solitary confinement, physically and sexually abused, and denied adequate educational programs, medical care, and mental health treatment. These abuses continue in part because youth in custody rarely have access to lawyers. Outlining the constitutional bases for a post-dispositional right to counsel, as well as national standards articulating that right, Cohen and Simkins advocate for the right to counsel throughout the duration of a child's incarceration.

Nearly 50,000 youth are placed out of home each day in facilities that are extensions of the unfulfilled promises of *Gault*'s rehabilitative ideals. In "*Gault* at 50: what juvenile defenders can do to dismantle the youth prison model," youth activists Liz Ryan and Carmen Daugherty examine the history of the failed youth prison model and discuss reform efforts that have disrupted and dismantled this system across the country. The chapter calls upon attorneys to join and lead new reform efforts and outlines the work needed to ensure true youth rehabilitation.

This anthology concludes with "Busting the 'juvenile super-predator' myth," a chapter by Laura Cohen and Jane Spinak, which considers the obligation of juvenile defenders to advocate for their clients in the media and the legislature and looks back on the efforts of the New York City Legal Aid Society's Juvenile Right's Division to do so during the late 1990s. The authors, who were the organization's Attorney-in-Charge and Director of Training, were deeply involved in the fight to protect children from the frenzied, media-fueled fear of escalating youth crime that gripped the country from the late 1980s through the 1990s. As state and federal legislators vied to out-do each other in cracking down on juvenile crime, the consequences were and continue to be catastrophic and lifelong for tens of thousands of children, especially black and brown children. The lessons learned from the policy wars that followed the 1990s frenzy continue to resonate in the current quest for a rational, unbiased, and compassionate youth justice system. In response, this chapter provides a blueprint for sustained system-wide policy advocacy and juvenile justice reform.

Ultimately, this book is for everyone concerned about justice in America. The personal narratives and stories about children in the system will intrigue academics, engage lay individuals who are interested in the juvenile justice system and children's rights, and be instructive for legislators and other policymakers who are concerned about juvenile justice reform and access to justice for accused youth. The advocacy described in this anthology should inspire a generation of graduate and undergraduate students to pursue a career in juvenile defense, children's advocacy, social work, or public policy. More important, it should spawn creative new strategies to reduce the footprint of the juvenile justice system on the lives of youth and their communities, eliminate the disparate treatment of youth of color, dismantle youth prisons, improve conditions of confinement in those facilities that remain, and ensure access to counsel and zealous legal representation for all youth and at all stages of the juvenile justice system.

Acknowledgments

This book would not have been possible without the hard work and commitment of many people. The editors are especially grateful to Jenadee Nanini for her extraordinary research and editorial assistance. We also thank Amy Boorer and the staff of the National Juvenile Defender Center for their support and encouragement throughout this process.

We are deeply grateful to Zawadi Baharanyi, Megan Crane, Carmen Daugherty, Steven Drizin, Eduardo Ferrer, Nancy Ginsberg, Martin Guggenheim, Randy Hertz, Erin Keith, Hannah McElhinny, Wallace Mlyniec, Jenadee Nanini, Laura Nirider, Chris Phillis, Patricia Puritz, Liz Ryan, Mary Ann Scali, Robert Schwartz, Sandra Simkins, Jane Spinak, Meghan Strong, and Geoff Ward for their extraordinary contributions to this book and for their tireless work to ensure fairness for all youth impacted by the juvenile justice system. This book is dedicated to the many lawyers, policy advocates, activists, and scholars who fight every day to minimize the instrusions of the juvenile justice system into the lives of youth and their communities, eliminate the disparate treatment of youth of color, dismantle youth prisons, improve conditions of confinement in those facilities that remain, and ensure access to counsel and zealous legal representation for all youth at all stages of the juvenile justice system.

Contributors

Zawadi Baharanyi is a recent graduate of New York University School of Law and an E. Barrett Prettyman Fellow in the Juvenile Justice Clinic at Georgetown Law. During law school, Baharanyi participated in the Criminal Defense and Reentry Clinic and represented children facing delinquency adjudications in the Juvenile Defender Clinic. Prior to law school, Baharanyi worked at the Equal Justice Initiative of Alabama (EJI), where she helped formerly incarcerated clients, many of whom were children when convicted, transition to life outside of prison, and bolstered EJI's public education work around racial bias and mass incarceration.

Laura Cohen is Distinguished Clinical Professor of Law, the Justice Virginia Long Scholar, and Director of the Criminal and Youth Justice Clinic at Rutgers Law School. She also co-directs both the Rutgers Center on Youth Violence and Juvenile Justice and the Northeast Juvenile Defender Center, and is an expert consultant to the United States Department of Justice Civil Rights Division in its investigation of systemic due process violations in the St. Louis County, Missouri Juvenile Court. Previously, Cohen was a staff attorney and Director of Training for the New York City Legal Aid Society's Juvenile Rights Practice. Her scholarship explores topics ranging from juvenile justice and parole to legal ethics and lawyering theory, with a particular focus on the legal representation of adolescents. Cohen earned her B.A. from Rutgers College and her J.D. from Columbia Law School. She has received numerous awards for her work, including the MacArthur Foundation's Champion for Change Award and the National Juvenile Defender Center's Robert E. Shepherd Award for Excellence in Juvenile Defense.

Megan Crane is the Co-Director of the Center on Wrongful Convictions of Youth (CWCY) at Northwestern Pritzker School of Law in Chicago. She represents individuals who were wrongfully convicted for crimes when they were children or teenagers and supervises second- and third-year law students as they co-counsel in various stages of post-conviction proceedings. Most recently, Crane represented Davontae Sanford, who was wrongfully convicted at age 14 of a quadruple homicide based on his false confession, and who was finally released from prison in the summer of 2016 after almost a decade in adult prison. Before joining CWCY, Crane represented individuals sentenced to death in California. In 2013, she was honored as a California Attorney of the Year for her work to exonerate George Souliotes, a man wrongfully convicted of arson and triple murder and sentenced to life without parole.

Carmen Daugherty is the Policy Director at Youth First Initiative, where she supports state-based campaigns by developing policy options, reviewing legislation and proposed budgets, and creating state and national reports on youth incarceration. Before coming to Youth First, she served as Policy Director for Campaign for Youth Justice, focusing on ending the prosecution and incarceration of youth in the adult criminal justice system. Daugherty also served as Deputy Director and staff attorney for Advocates for Justice and Education, a D.C.-based nonprofit formed to educate parents, youth, and the community about the laws governing public education, specifically for children with special needs. In 2008, Daugherty was appointed to the D.C. Mayor's Juvenile Justice Advisory Group, where she works with city stakeholders to provide recommendations on compliance with the Juvenile Justice and Delinquency Prevention Act. She also co-chairs the American Bar Association, Section on Civil Rights and Social Justice's Criminal Justice Committee. Daugherty received her undergraduate degree from Vassar College and her J.D. from Tulane University School of Law.

Steven Drizin is a Clinical Professor of Law at Northwestern Pritzker School of Law, where he has been on the faculty since 1991. He served as the Legal Director of the Clinic's renowned Center on Wrongful Convictions from March 2005 to September 2013. In 2008, Drizin founded the Center on Wrongful Convictions of Youth, the first innocence organization focused exclusively on righting the wrongful convictions of youthful defendants. At the Center, his research interests involve the study of juvenile justice and false confessions, and his policy work focuses on supporting efforts around the country to require law enforcement agencies to electronically record custodial interrogations. Drizin's scholarship in the area of interrogations and confessions has been cited by the United States Supreme Court and numerous federal and state appellate courts. He lectures frequently on interrogation and confession-related topics throughout the United States, Canada, and Japan. Drizin, with Laura Nirider, represents Brendan Dassey, a central figure in Netflix's docuseries *Making a Murderer*.

Eduardo Ferrer serves as the Policy Director of the Georgetown Juvenile Justice Initiative, advocating to improve the D.C. juvenile justice system, and as a Visiting Professor at Georgetown Law, supervising students in the Juvenile Justice Clinic. He is also a Certified Trainer in the National Juvenile Defender Center's Juvenile Training Immersion Program, conducting trainings for juvenile defense attorneys across the country. Ferrer was a founding member of D.C. Lawyers for Youth (DCLY), a D.C.-based action tank dedicated to making D.C.'s juvenile justice system the smallest and best system in the country. During his 10-year tenure at DCLY, Ferrer was chiefly responsible for carrying out the organization's research, advocacy, and direct representation work. In 2013, Eduardo was awarded the Mid-Atlantic Innocence Project's Defender of Innocence Award for his work securing the release of David Boyce, an innocent man wrongfully convicted of murder in Virginia in 1990.

Nancy Ginsburg is the director of the Adolescent Intervention and Diversion Project in the Criminal Practice of the Legal Aid Society in New York City. The project represents adolescents, aged 13–18, who are prosecuted in the adult court system of the five counties, providing advocacy to obtain foster care, mental health, and educational services. Ginsburg was co-counsel in *J.G. vs. Mills*, a federal lawsuit addressing the school re-entry rights of court-involved youth. She is responsible for supervising and training lawyers throughout the five borough offices of the Legal Aid Society in adolescent practice and educational advocacy, and for legislative and policy issues concerning court-involved adolescents in the adult criminal system. She testifies frequently before the New York City Council, is a member of the Mayor's Leadership Team on School Climate and Discipline, and was a member of the New York City School Justice Partnership Task Force, the New York City Council Gun Violence Task Force, and the Task Force on the Future of Probation in New York State.

Martin Guggenheim is the Fiorello LaGuardia Professor of Clinical Law at New York University School of Law. He has worked in the field of juvenile justice since 1971 as a public defender, a scholar, and a law teacher. He began representing youth in 1971 upon graduating from New York University (NYU) School of Law, when he became a staff attorney at the famed Juvenile Rights Division of New York City's Legal Aid Society. Guggenheim has taught at NYU School of Law since 1973, variously serving as Director of Clinical and Advocacy Programs and the Executive Director of Washington Square Legal Services, Inc., teaching the Juvenile Rights Clinic, and creating the Family Defense Clinic. His research has focused on the role of counsel for children in court proceedings, empirical research in child welfare practice, juvenile justice, and family law.

Kristin Henning is the Agnes N. Williams Research Professor of Law and Director of the Juvenile Justice Clinic and Initiative at Georgetown Law. Her scholarship on race, adolescence, and juvenile justice appears in journals such as the *Cornell Law Review, California Law Review,* and *NYU Law Review* and in books such as *Policing the Black Man* (Random House, 2017) and *Punishment in Popular Culture* (NYU Press, 2015). Henning was formerly the Lead Attorney for the Juvenile Unit of the D.C. Public Defender Service and worked closely with the Juvenile Indigent Defense Action Network to develop and co-author the Juvenile Training Immersion Program, a national training curriculum for juvenile defenders. She is the Director of the Mid-Atlantic Juvenile Defender Center and an Adviser to American Law Institute's Restatement on Children and the Law. She has also served as an expert consultant to the United States Department of Justice's Civil Rights Division and an investigator in several state assessments of access to counsel for accused youth. Henning has received several awards, including the Robert E. Shepherd, Jr. Award for Excellence in Juvenile Defense by the National Juvenile Defender Center.

Randy Hertz is the Vice Dean of NYU School of Law and the Director of the law school's clinical program. He has been at the law school since 1985, and teaches the Juvenile Defender Clinic. Before joining the NYU faculty, Hertz worked at the D.C. Public Defender Service in the juvenile, criminal, appellate, and special litigation divisions. He writes in the areas of criminal and juvenile justice and is the co-author, with Professor James Liebman, of *Federal Habeas Corpus Law and Practice* (Michie, 2017), the co-author, with Professor Anthony G. Amsterdam, of *Trial Manual for the Defense of Criminal Cases* (American Law Institute, 2016), and the co-author, with Professors Amsterdam and Martin Guggenheim, of *Trial Manual for Defense Attorneys in Juvenile Delinquency Cases* (American Law Institute, 2015).

Erin Keith is the Juvenile Defense and Policy Fellow in Georgetown Law's Juvenile Justice Clinic. She graduated *summa cum laude* from Howard University in 2013 with her B.A. in Political Science and from Georgetown Law in 2016 with her J.D. While in law school, Keith taught a human rights course at a local public high school and created a Know Your Rights canvassing initiative in her capacity as Attorney General for Georgetown's Black Law Students Association. She also served as a student attorney in the Georgetown Juvenile Justice Clinic, where she represented youth in delinquency and school disciplinary proceedings. Keith served as a judicial intern for a juvenile judge in D.C. Superior Court and interned with the NAACP Legal Defense Fund, the United States Department of Justice's Public Integrity Section, and the D.C. Public Defender Service's Juvenile Services Program. In 2017, she was selected as one of ten fellows nationwide for the National Juvenile Justice Network's Youth Justice Leadership Institute.

Ellen Marrus is the Royce Till Professor of Law at the University of Houston Law Center, the founder and Director of the Center for Children, Law & Policy (CCLP), and the co-director of the Southwest Juvenile Defender Center (SWJDC). She teaches juvenile law, street law, children and the law, professional responsibility, and practice-related courses, and directs clinical programs, including child advocacy clinics and a lab component for her children and the law course where students receive hands-on experience in child dependency cases. In her capacity as Director of CCLP and SWJDC, Marrus has provided technical assistance to public defenders, court appointed juvenile attorneys, the United States Department of Justice, juvenile probation, and federal and state legislators. She concentrates her scholarship in the areas of juvenile law, children's rights, and professionalism, with a focus on representing children in various proceedings and the intersection of juvenile justice with race and gender.

Hannah McElhinny is the Deputy Trial Chief, Juvenile Section, at the D.C. Public Defender Service (PDS). She joined PDS in 1999, after clerking for the

Honorable Warren Matthews, Chief Justice of the Alaska State Supreme Court, and has been representing juvenile and adult clients in delinquency and criminal cases ever since. In her capacity as Deputy Trial Chief, McElhinny manages the Juvenile Section at PDS. She is responsible for the training and supervision of all PDS attorneys practicing in juvenile court. McElhinny serves on several D.C. Family Court committees and is a member of the District's Juvenile Detention Alternatives Initiative Executive Committee. She is a graduate of the University of California at Santa Cruz and earned her J.D. from Yale Law School.

Wallace Mlyniec is the Lupo-Ricci Professor of Clinical Legal Studies and former Associate Dean for Clinical Education and Public Service Programs at Georgetown Law. He is the founding Director of Georgetown's Juvenile Justice Clinic and now serves as its Senior Counsel. Mlyniec is the author of several books and many articles on children's rights, family law, criminal justice, and clinical education. He has been a consultant to schools of social work and law, to the American Bar Association Center for Children's Rights, and to the National Council of Juvenile and Family Court Judges. Mlyniec received a Bi-Centennial Fellowship from the Swedish government to study comparative law regarding children's issues and was a Visiting Scholar in Pediatric Law at Loyola University Law School's Child Law Program. He has spoken on the topics of juvenile and criminal law and clinical education throughout the nation, and has litigated criminal, juvenile, and family law issues in the District of Columbia for over 40 years. Mlyniec is past Chair of the American Bar Association Committee on Juvenile Justice and is a Board member and the former Board Chair of the National Juvenile Defender Center.

Jenadee Nanini is an attorney with the D.C. Affordable Law Firm and is currently earning an LLM. Her research for Professor Kristin Henning has focused on race and juvenile justice. Nanini was a student attorney with the Georgetown Juvenile Justice Clinic in 2016–2017. Her work, which has appeared in the *Georgetown Journal of Modern Critical Race Perspectives* and the *Georgetown Law Technology Review*, focuses on Native American issues, one piece specifically on Native American youth and the right to counsel in the multiple youth systems. Prior to earning her J.D., Nanini taught middle school and high school math for three years in West Dallas, Texas, her first two years through Teach for America. Nanini received her B.S. and B.A. from Washington State University and her J.D. from Georgetown Law.

Laura Nirider is a Clinical Assistant Professor of Law and Co-Director of the Center on Wrongful Convictions of Youth (CWCY) at Northwestern Pritzker School of Law in Chicago. Nirider represents individuals who were wrongfully convicted of crimes when they were children or teenagers. Her clients have included Brendan Dassey, whose case was profiled in the Netflix Global series *Making a Murderer*, and Damien Echols of the West Memphis Three, whose case was profiled in the documentary *West of Memphis*. In addition to her courtroom work, Nirider regularly publishes scholarly and practitioner-focused articles on interrogations and post-conviction relief. In partnership with the International Association of Chiefs of Police, she has co-authored one of the only existing juvenile interrogation protocols. She is also a frequent presenter on interrogations at defender and law enforcement training conferences around the country and has been featured in film and television programs as an expert on interrogations. Recently, Nirider co-authored an *amicus curiae* brief that was cited by the United States Supreme Court in *J.D.B. v. North Carolina* for the proposition that the risk of false confession is "all the more troubling … and all the more acute … when the subject of custodial interrogation is a juvenile."

Chris Phillis is the Director of the Public Defense Services constellation of Maricopa County, Arizona. She spent the first 15 years of her career representing youth in delinquency matters as a Deputy Public Defender for the Maricopa County Office of the Public Defender. In 2008, Phillis was selected to head a new indigent representation office dedicated to the representation of youth in delinquency matters. Under her directorship, in addition to advocating for juveniles in delinquency proceedings, the Maricopa County Office of Public Advocate grew to include a division that represents parents in dependency proceedings, a unit that protects the rights of individuals in mental health court, and a division that handles capital post-conviction relief matters. Phillis also provides attorney training seminars, sits on numerous advisory boards, and serves on committees that promote policy change and community outreach.

Patricia Puritz has worked as a child advocate in the juvenile justice system for over 40 years. She founded the National Juvenile Defender Center (NJDC) in 1997 and served as its executive director until she stepped aside in 2015. Puritz now serves as the President and CEO of Patricia Puritz & Associates LLC, a justice and policy consulting firm, and as an Adjunct Professor at American University's Washington College of Law. Prior to founding NJDC, Puritz was the Director of the American Bar Association's Juvenile Justice Center. For decades, she has been involved in designing, implementing, managing, and monitoring programs to reform the nation's juvenile justice system, with a targeted focus on enhancing juvenile defense delivery systems and strengthening the capacity of the juvenile defense bar. Puritz has served on the Virginia Board of Juvenile Justice, and has played a significant role in advising and assisting federal government agencies on matters related to improving the nation's juvenile indigent defense systems. She has served on numerous national and local boards of directors and advisory committees, and has received recognition from several organizations, including being honored in 2017 with the Gault at 50 Award presented by NJDC.

Liz Ryan is President and CEO of Youth First Initiative. She is the founder and former CEO of the nationally recognized Campaign for Youth Justice (CFYJ), which leads the national effort to end the practice of trying, sentencing, and incarcerating youth in the adult criminal justice system. Since CFYJ was launched in 2004, nearly half of U.S. states have reduced the prosecution of youth in adult court. Ryan has worked on many campaigns, including spearheading the launch of the Act 4 Juvenile Justice campaign to overhaul the main federal law on youth justice, the Juvenile Justice & Delinquency Prevention Act, and the No More Oak Hills campaign to successfully close the notorious Oak Hill Youth Detention Center for D.C.'s youth. An author of numerous opinion editorials, articles, and reports, Ryan frequently serves as an expert resource to reporters and national media outlets.

Mary Ann Scali became Executive Director of the National Juvenile Defender Center in January 2017, after serving more than 16 years as Deputy Director. She manages the overall strategic, operational, and programmatic advancement of NJDC's mission to promote justice for all children by ensuring excellence in juvenile defense. Scali leads a team of ten advocates in the national office and nine regional juvenile defender centers fighting for the rights of youth in the juvenile court system. Prior to joining NJDC, she worked in the Juvenile Division of the Office of the Public Defender in Baltimore City, Maryland. After graduating from Holy Cross, Scali spent two years teaching English and math at a boys' trade school in Pohnpei, Micronesia. She then served as an assistant to the Director of the Jesuit Refugee Service in Rome, Italy and as a middle school teacher for boys from Baltimore City at the Baraka School in Nanyuki, Kenya. Scali received her J.D. and MSW from Loyola University Chicago, where she was a Civitas ChildLaw Scholar.

Robert Schwartz is a co-founder of Juvenile Law Center (JLC) and served as its executive director from 1982 to 2015. In his career at JLC, he represented dependent and delinquent children in Pennsylvania juvenile and appellate courts, brought class-action litigation, and testified in Congress. Schwartz chaired the American Bar Association's Commission on Youth at Risk from 2011–2013, and the Juvenile Justice Committee of the American Bar Association's Criminal Justice Section from 1992–1998 and 2006–2008. In 1993, Schwartz co-authored the American Bar Association's report, *America's Children at Risk*, and in 1995 he co-authored a follow-up report on youths' access to quality lawyers, *A Call for Justice*. From 1996–2006, he was a member of the MacArthur Foundation Research Network on Adolescent Development and Juvenile Justice. In 2005, Schwartz became Chair of the Advisory Committee to the Children's Rights Division of Human Rights Watch.

Sandra Simkins is the Director and co-founder of the Children's Justice Clinic at Rutgers Law School. Prior to joining the Rutgers faculty in 2006, she spent 15 years working in criminal and juvenile defense, including serving as Assistant Chief of the Juvenile Unit at the Defender Association of Philadelphia. Simkins co-directs the Northeast Region Juvenile Defender Center, a subsidiary of the National Juvenile Defender Center, where she consults with and trains child advocates in Delaware, New Jersey, New York, and Pennsylvania, and she is the Due Process Monitor for the settlement agreement between the Department of

Justice and the Juvenile Court of Shelby County, Tennessee. Simkins has been involved in a wide range of national and statewide policy reform for children and, in 2008, was selected by the MacArthur Foundation to participate in the Models for Change Juvenile Indigent Defense Action Network. Her areas of expertise include post disposition representation, conditions of confinement, and solitary confinement.

Jane Spinak is the Edward Ross Aranow Clinical Professor of Law at Columbia Law School. She co-founded the school's Child Advocacy and Family Advocacy Clinics, and currently directs the Adolescent Representation Clinic, which represents adolescents and young adults aging out of foster care. During the mid-1990s, Spinak served as Attorney-in-Charge of the Juvenile Rights Division of the Legal Aid Society of New York City. In 2002, she became the founding Chair of the Board of the Center for Family Representation, an advocacy and policy organization dedicated to ensuring the procedural and substantive rights of parents in child-welfare proceedings. Spinak is a member of the New York State Permanent Judicial Commission on Justice for Children. She has served on numerous task forces and committees addressing the needs and rights of children and families, and has trained and lectured widely on those issues to lawyers, social workers, and other mental health professionals. Spinak has authored books and articles for child advocates, lawyers, and judges on child welfare and family court matters. Her current scholarship focuses on the history and effectiveness of the family court.

Meghan Strong is a third-year J.D. candidate at Georgetown Law, where she is a student attorney with the Georgetown Juvenile Justice Clinic for the 2017–2018 academic year. During her second year of law school, Strong worked at the D.C. Children's Law Center in their Policy Group, where she helped draft recommendations for updating D.C.'s laws on child abuse and neglect to better protect child victims of human trafficking. Strong is an Executive Editor of the *American Criminal Law Review* and serves as a research assistant to Wallace Mlyniec, focusing on children's rights and clinical legal education. She graduated *summa cum laude* from Ursinus College in 2015 and will graduate from Georgetown Law in 2018.

Geoff Ward is an Associate Professor in Criminology, Law & Society, Sociology, and the School of Law at the University of California-Irvine. His scholarship focuses on socio-historical relationships between race, crime, and justice, with particular interests in racial violence, youth justice, and democratic social control. His book *The Black Child Savers: Racial Democracy and Juvenile Justice* (University of Chicago Press, 2012), examining the rise, fall, and lasting remnants of Jim Crow juvenile justice, received the prestigious Hindelang Award from the American Society of Criminology, and Outstanding Book Prize of the History of Education Society. His current project, the Racial Violence Archive, is a research, education, and advocacy initiative to advance understanding of historical racial violence, its contemporary legacies, and implications for redress.

Part I

Gault: then and 50 years later

1 The many stories of *In re Gault*

Zawadi Baharanyi and Randy Hertz

A book celebrating the fiftieth anniversary of *In re Gault* naturally begins with a description of the case itself. But, as is perhaps inevitable for a case as pathbreaking and profoundly important as *Gault*, there is not just a single story to tell but a mosaic, made up of the many different strands of stories that came together to produce the landmark ruling.

The story of Jerry Gault

Although casebooks, treatises, and law review articles understandably focus on the legal rules the Supreme Court announced in *Gault* and the transformation they brought to juvenile court law and practice – and these are certainly subjects we will take up, although a bit later in this chapter – a book like this one starts most appropriately with the child at the center of the case: 15-year-old Gerald Francis Gault.

Jerry, who lived with his parents and older brother in Globe, Arizona, had been arrested for making a lewd phone call to a neighbor. In the Supreme Court's opinion, the content of the call was decorously described as being "of the irritatingly offensive, adolescent, sex variety."[1] Although the maximum possible sentence for such an offense by an adult would have been imprisonment for not more than two months or a fine of $5 to $50,[2] the judge who presided over the case and convicted Jerry of being a "juvenile delinquent" sentenced him to placement in "the State Industrial School 'for the period of his minority (that is, until 21), unless sooner discharged.'"[3]

The conviction and sentence were the products of two abbreviated court hearings at which Jerry was not represented by counsel.[4] The complaining witness did not testify at either of these hearings; her account apparently was presented in hearsay form by a probation officer who had spoken with her once by telephone. Jerry was questioned by the juvenile court judge without notice of his Fifth Amendment rights. Jerry may or may not have admitted making the lewd remarks. (This was an issue on which the judge's and other participants' recollections differed, and there was no transcript of the proceedings to show what actually was said at the hearings.) After the conviction and sentence, Jerry's parents petitioned the Arizona Supreme Court for a writ of habeas corpus, arguing that the juvenile court judge had violated a number of constitutional requirements, including the rights to notice of the charges, counsel, confrontation and cross-examination, and the privilege against self-incrimination. The Arizona Supreme Court denied the writ, and the case was appealed to the United States Supreme Court.

The story of Jerry's lawyers

Cases like Jerry Gault's – in which a child was convicted as a juvenile delinquent in a summary proceeding and sentenced to the industrial school for a term grossly out of proportion to the offense – were commonplace in that era.[5] What was so unusual about this case was that it went first to the state supreme court and then to the United States Supreme Court, and that it did so with a broad-based attack on the propriety of practices employed in juvenile courts across the United States. These events, and the transformational ruling they produced, came about because of the vision and perseverance of three lawyers.

The first of these was Amelia Lewis, an Arizona lawyer who had practiced law in New York City for 33 years and then moved to the Phoenix area and opened a law practice there.[6] She filed and litigated the state habeas corpus petition in a state trial court and then, after the judge ruled against the Gaults, handled the appeal to the Arizona Supreme Court with the assistance of the Northern Arizona chapter of the American Civil Liberties Union (ACLU). When the state supreme court ruled against her, she consulted with the ACLU and then sent a package of materials from the case to Professor Norman Dorsen of New York University (NYU) School of Law, who had created a Project on Social Welfare at the Law School, and was on the ACLU board of directors; the cover letter said: "Here is a case that may interest you."[7]

Dorsen requested that Gertrud Mainzer, who worked with him as a research consultant at the Project on Social Welfare Law, review the materials.[8] Mainzer, the second of the lawyers in our story, was born in Germany, survived years in a concentration camp, came to the United States and attended NYU Law School after World War II, and, after working with Dorsen and in other positions as a children's advocate, was later appointed to the New York City Family Court bench.[9] Mainzer recognized the importance of the *Gault* case and recommended to Dorsen that they take the case. They reached out to the director of the ACLU, and filed pleadings in the United States Supreme Court.[10]

The third of the lawyers was Dorsen himself. He served as Jerry's lawyer in the United States Supreme Court, writing the briefs and presenting the oral argument. Dorsen was in many ways the ideal person for this job. His expertise as a constitutional scholar positioned him perfectly for grappling with the thorny constitutional issues in the case. As Dorsen later recounted in reflections on his brief-writing process in *Gault*, he had to navigate between the Justices' varying views of incorporation of constitutional rights and come up with a compromise that could provide relief in this case, set the juvenile court on the right path, and command at least five votes on the Court.[11] Dorsen's experience with law reform as the head of NYU's Project on Social Welfare and as a member of the Board of the ACLU (which he later headed as President of the organization for 15 years) provided him with an important perspective on how to frame and argue the case. When a lawyer who was assisting Dorsen strongly pressed for focusing primarily on one of the constitutional claims in order to improve the chances of success, Dorsen made the crucial decision – which turned out to be precisely the right call – to pursue all of the claims rather than sacrifice any of the important constitutional claims in the case.[12]

The story of the Supreme Court and its ruling

In re Gault reached the United States Supreme Court in the heyday of the Warren Court. It was a heady time for civil liberties. The Court had been handing down landmark rulings reforming the criminal justice system, including *Mapp v. Ohio*[13] in 1961, *Gideon v. Wainwright*[14] in 1963, and *Miranda v. Arizona*[15] in 1966.

Equally important as a foundation for what would become the *Gault* decision, the Court decided a juvenile rights case, *Kent v. United States*,[16] in 1966, the Term immediately preceding *Gault*'s. The *Kent* case concerned the procedural safeguards that are required when a judge decides whether to waive or transfer a child from juvenile court to adult criminal court for prosecution as an adult. Morris Kent, a 16-year-old, had been arrested for burglary and rape, and, in an interrogation that went on for seven hours, confessed to having committed this crime and other burglaries, robberies, and rapes.[17] The juvenile court judge waived the case to adult criminal court without holding a hearing or providing an opportunity for Kent's counsel to address the court, even though the attorney had filed a motion seeking a hearing and appending a psychiatrist's affidavit certifying that Kent suffered from serious mental illness and needed hospitalization for psychiatric observation.[18] Kent was indicted, tried in criminal court, and the jury convicted him of six counts of housebreaking and robbery, but found him not guilty by reason of insanity on the rape counts. He was committed to a mental hospital "until his sanity is restored," with a follow-up prison sentence of 30–90 years (with the time in the mental hospital counting as part of the term of imprisonment).

Upon *certiorari* review in the United States Supreme Court, the Court held that the order of waiver to adult court violated the applicable statute and remanded the case for a new waiver hearing, specifying that if the waiver is found to have been inappropriate, the conviction must be vacated.[19] Construing the D.C. waiver statute, the Court held that waiver of a juvenile to adult court requires the following procedural safeguards: a hearing must be held; the juvenile is entitled to representation by counsel at such a hearing; counsel must be afforded access to the juvenile's social records on request; and the judge must state the reasons in support of the transfer order.[20] Although these rulings technically involved the interpretation of the waiver statute, it seemed apparent that the analysis was rooted in the Court's view of what due process requires. Indeed, at one point in the discussion of the new rules, the Court observed that a waiver hearing "must measure up to the essentials of due process and fair treatment."[21]

In a passage foreshadowing the upcoming ruling and analysis in *Gault*, the *Kent* majority opinion questioned the longstanding premise of juvenile court jurisprudence that children "cannot complain of the deprivation of important rights available in criminal cases" because "the State is supposed to proceed in respect of the child as *parens patriae* and not as adversary," and thus juvenile court "proceedings are 'civil' in nature and not criminal."[22] Observing that:

> [t]here is much evidence that some juvenile courts, including that of the District of Columbia, lack the personnel, facilities and techniques to perform adequately as representatives of the State in a *parens patriae* capacity, at least with respect to children charged with law violation,

the Court stated that "there may be grounds for concern that the child receives the worst of both worlds: that he gets neither the protections accorded to adults nor the solicitous care and regenerative treatment postulated for children."[23]

In the Term immediately following *Kent*, the Supreme Court addressed this aspect of juvenile court head-on in *Gault*. The author of the *Gault* majority opinion was the very same Justice who had written the majority opinion in *Kent*: Abe Fortas. Elaborating upon his previous discussion in *Kent* of the fallacies of the traditional *parens patriae* rationale for denying rights to juveniles, Justice Fortas observed that the term "juvenile delinquent" "has come to involve only slightly less stigma than the term 'criminal' applied to adults"; the claim of protective confidentiality of juvenile court records "is more rhetoric than reality"; and "however euphemistic the title, a 'receiving home' or an 'industrial school' for juveniles is an institution of confinement in which the child is incarcerated for a greater or lesser time."[24] Pointing out that "[i]f Gerald had been over 18," "the maximum punishment [for his offense] would have been a fine of $5 to $50, or imprisonment in jail for not more than two months" rather than "commit[ment] to custody for a maximum of six years," and that "he would have been entitled to substantial rights under the Constitution of the United States," Justice Fortas stated that "[s]o wide a gulf between the State's treatment of the adult and the child requires a bridge sturdier than mere verbiage, and reasons more persuasive than cliché can provide."[25] "[T]he condition of being a boy," he declared, "does not justify a kangaroo court."[26]

The *Gault* Court therefore held that the Due Process Clause requires that a juvenile court delinquency trial "'measure up to the essentials of due process and fair treatment.'"[27] Cautioning that this should not be taken to mean that a delinquency trial necessarily "'must conform with all of the requirements of a criminal trial,'"[28] the Court applied its new due process rubric to the specific issues presented by the trial in Jerry Gault's case. Addressing each of the aspects of the trial challenged by Jerry's counsel, the Court held that juveniles were entitled to the following:

Notice

Juveniles in delinquency proceedings, like adults in criminal cases, are entitled to notice of the charges, and such notice must "'set forth the alleged misconduct with particularity,'" and "must be given sufficiently in advance of scheduled court proceedings so that reasonable opportunity to prepare will be afforded."[29] The State of Arizona violated this due process requirement because the only written notice ever provided to Jerry's parents was "a note on plain paper" from the probation officer on a Thursday or Friday that a hearing "on Gerald's delinquency" would take place on the following Monday. The charging paper filed in court said nothing more than that the probation officer believes Gerald to be "'a delinquent minor and that it is necessary that some order be made by the Honorable Court for said minor's welfare.'"[30]

Counsel

Juveniles charged with a delinquency offense have a right to counsel just as do adult criminal defendants, and "the child and his [or her] parents must be notified of the child's right to be represented by counsel retained by them, or if they are unable to afford counsel, that counsel will be appointed to represent the child."[31] Although Jerry's mother testified at the habeas corpus proceeding that "she knew that she could have appeared with counsel at the juvenile hearing," the Supreme Court found that "[t]his knowledge is not a waiver of the right to counsel which she and her juvenile son had, as we have defined it," because they were never expressly advised of their rights, including the right to court-appointed counsel if they could not afford to retain a lawyer, and afforded an opportunity for "specific consideration of whether they did or did not choose to waive the right."[32] In the course of discussing the guarantee of counsel, the Court also made clear that the proper role of defense counsel in a delinquency proceeding is the same as in an adult criminal case: to assist the client in "cop[ing] with problems of law, to make skilled inquiry into the facts, to insist upon regularity of the proceedings, and to ascertain whether [the client] … has a defense and to prepare and submit it."[33]

Privilege against self-incrimination

"[T]he constitutional privilege against self-incrimination is applicable in the case of juveniles as it is with respect to adults."[34] The Court explained that "special problems may arise with respect to waiver of the principle … depending upon the age of the child and the presence and competence of parents," and these circumstances may call for "differences in technique" – but "not in principle" – from what is done in adult criminal cases.[35] Demonstrating a keen understanding of the kinds of questions that inevitably arise whenever the state obtains a confession from a youth, the Court stressed that:

> the greatest care must be taken to assure that the admission was voluntary, in the sense not only that it was not coerced or suggested, but also that it was not the product of ignorance of rights or of adolescent fantasy, fright or despair.[36]

In *Gault*, Jerry's conviction rested on a confession obtained from him by the probation officer. There may also have been admissions by Jerry at the two hearings before the judge, although the record was unclear about what transpired at those hearings because there was no transcript or other record, and there were differing recollections about whether the admissions were made or not and, if so, what Jerry actually said in court.[37] The Court found that these alleged confessions were insufficient to support the conviction because the statement to the probation officer occurred "out of the presence of Gerald's parents, without counsel and without advising him of his right to silence," and the courtroom admissions were not "reduced to writing, and, to say the least, the process by which the[se] 'admissions,' were obtained and received must be characterized as lacking the certainty and order which are required of proceedings of such formidable consequences."[38]

Confrontation and cross-examination of witnesses

In delinquency cases, as in criminal cases, the accused has the right to "confrontation and sworn testimony by [prosecution] witnesses available for cross-examination."[39] The complainant was not called to the witness stand at Jerry's hearing even though his mother requested that she appear so that she could listen to the voices of Jerry and his friend and then say which of them spoke to her on the telephone. To the extent that any facts obtained from the complainant were recited at the hearing, they would have been presented in hearsay form by the probation officer, who had spoken to the complainant once on the telephone. The Court summarily rejected such hearsay as a basis for a delinquency adjudication.

The final claim that Dorsen raised was a challenge to the Arizona statute on the ground that it neither provided for appeal as of right nor transcription or recording of the proceedings so as to make an appeal possible. The Court declined to resolve these claims, explaining that it had not yet held that appellate review is required by the Federal Constitution and that the issue need not be reached in *Gault* because the lower courts' ruling was being reversed on the above-described grounds. But the Court sent a clear signal to the lower courts by stating that the proceedings in the *Gault* case "illustrate[]" that "the consequences of failure to provide an appeal" and "to record the proceedings" "saddle" the habeas corpus process "with the burden of attempting to reconstruct a record, and to impose upon the Juvenile Judge the unseemly duty of testifying under cross-examination as to the events that transpired in the hearings before him."[40]

Undergirding the specific rulings described above, as well as the overarching holding that juvenile court trials must conform to the "essentials of due process and fair treatment," was a central narrative that the *Gault* majority presented about the origins and evolution of the juvenile court. Looking back to the end of the preceding century, the Court told a grand tale about the "early reformers" who established a system of juvenile courts throughout the United States, starting with the first juvenile court in Illinois in 1899, because they were "appalled" that juveniles were being tried in adult criminal court and "could be given long prison sentences and mixed in jails with hardened criminals."[41] As the Court told the tale, these reformers set out to help children by creating a court system that would treat and rehabilitate children, focusing on their needs. To that end, these early reformers "discarded" the "apparent rigidities, technicalities, and harshness which they observed in both substantive and procedural criminal law," so that juvenile court judges could focus instead on who the child is, "'how has he [or she] become what he [or she] is, and what had best be done in his [or her] interest and in the interest of the state to save him [or her] from a downward career."[42] Thus, as the Court put it, "the highest motives and most enlightened impulses led to a peculiar system for juveniles, unknown to our law in any comparable context."[43] The failures of the resulting juvenile court system, so graphically illustrated by the *Gault* case itself, thus were an unexpected and entirely unpredictable product of good intentions gone awry. In abandoning the formalities of the criminal process, the reformers had gone too far by eliminating "the fundamental requirements of due process," thereby opening the door to "instances, which might have been avoided, of unfairness to individuals and inadequate or inaccurate findings of fact and unfortunate prescriptions of remedy."[44] With the problem thus defined, the remedy was self-evident: to inject due process into the system, thereby righting the balance, while preserving those features of the juvenile court system that appropriately and effectively furthered the founders' goal to rehabilitate children.

In line with this framing of juvenile court history and the Court's own role in refashioning that court, the Supreme Court emphasized in *Gault* that the due process requirements it was announcing – which would "introduce a degree of order and regularity to Juvenile Court proceedings to determine delinquency, and in contested cases will introduce some elements of the adversary system" – would not "require that the conception of the kindly juvenile judge be replaced by its opposite."[45] The Court pointed out that it was not "rul[ing] upon the question whether ordinary due process requirements must be observed with respect to hearings to determine the disposition of the child."[46]

As some legal commentators pointed out in the wake of the *Gault* decision, the historical evidence raises serious questions about the rosy picture the Court painted of the early days of the juvenile court. The Court accepted the published statements of the early reformers at face value, and took it on faith that their actions matched their lofty rhetoric. Digging more deeply into the historical data, these commentators portrayed the early juvenile courts as merely another stage in a centuries-long exercise of social control over the poor, driven by prevailing stereotypes about the lower classes.[47]

But whatever the truth may be about the words and deeds of the founders of the juvenile court, there could be no doubt that the juvenile court system that came before the Supreme Court in *Gault* was broken. That message emerged powerfully and incontrovertibly from the *Gault* opinion, from beginning to end. The Statement of Facts, presented in the neutral, objective manner of any such Statement, told a chilling tale of state control and arbitrariness. The Court wrote:

> On Monday, June 8, 1964, at about 10 a.m., Gerald Francis Gault and a friend, Ronald Lewis, were taken into custody by the Sheriff of Gila County … . At the time Gerald was picked up, his mother and father were both at work. No notice that Gerald was being taken into custody was left at the home. No other steps were taken to advise them that their son had, in effect, been arrested. Gerald was taken to the Children's Detention Home. When his mother arrived home at about 6 o'clock, Gerald was not there. Gerald's older brother was sent to look for him at the trailer home of the Lewis family. He apparently learned then that Gerald was in custody. He so informed his mother. The two of them went to the Detention Home. The deputy probation officer, Flagg, who was also superintendent of the Detention Home, told Mrs. Gault "why Jerry was there" and said that a hearing would be held in Juvenile Court at 3 o'clock the following day, June 9.[48]

The core of this account, which is told from the perspective of the parents, is a classic "missing child" story: every parent's worst nightmare. That this anguish was inflicted by representatives of the state, who felt free to sweep up a child with no word to the parent, is evident but merely implicit: Indeed, several of the sentences were constructed in passive voice ("[a]t the time Gerald was picked up"; "[n]o notice … was left"; "[n]o other steps were taken to advise"), enabling an alert reader to fill in the subject of each of these damning independent clauses (*i.e.*, "the police") but refraining from pointedly and overtly casting the police as the villains in the piece.

After reciting the rest of the facts and procedural history of the *Gault* case and presenting its perhaps overly generous account of the founding of the juvenile court, the Court cited numerous studies and extensive data documenting the many failings of the current-day juvenile court.[49] With the foundation thus amply laid for the need for major changes, the Court announced its due process remedy with its various specific rules to prevent the types of abuses that occurred in Gerald Gault's case.

Whether one views the *Gault* decision as a resetting of a good system gone awry, or as a transformation of a system that was tainted from the start, it was (and is) readily apparent that *Gault* was a desperately-needed corrective for a deeply flawed juvenile court system. It was clear, however, that this was merely the first step in the cleansing of those flaws. The *Gault* Court expressly announced that its rulings would be limited to those aspects of the juvenile court system that were directly presented by the case itself:

> We do not in this opinion consider the impact of these constitutional provisions upon the totality of the relationship of the juvenile and the state. We do not even consider the entire process relating to juvenile "delinquents." For example, we are not here concerned with the procedures or constitutional rights applicable to the pre-judicial stages of the juvenile process, nor do we direct our attention to the post-adjudicative or dispositional process … . We consider only the problems presented to us by this case.[50]

Thus, to see the rest of the story, we need to turn to subsequent decisions of the United States Supreme Court.

The story of what came after: *McKeiver v. Pennsylvania*

The next juvenile delinquency case to reach the Supreme Court after *Gault* – *In re Winship*[51] in 1970 – provided reason to believe that the Court would use the *Gault* precedent to continue reshaping problematic aspects of the juvenile court system. The Court held in *Winship* that the "'essentials of due process and fair treatment'" require that the prosecution prove the charges beyond a reasonable doubt.

Just one year later, however – in *McKeiver v. Pennsylvania*[52] – *Gault*'s transformation of the juvenile court came to a screeching halt. This was actually not so much of a surprise because the Court itself had undergone a transformation in the few years since *Gault* was handed down in 1967. In 1969, both Chief Justice Earl Warren and Justice Abe Fortas left the bench (the former in retirement, the latter resigning due to a disclosure that he had long been receiving an annual retainer from a family foundation run by an individual who was under investigation for stock fraud), thus presenting Richard Nixon (who had been elected President in 1968) with the first two of the four appointments he would ultimately make to the Court. Nixon's first appointee, Chief Justice Warren Burger was on the Court by the time it decided *Winship* in 1970. Nixon's second appointee, Harry Blackmun, was on the Court when *McKeiver* was decided, and he wrote the plurality opinion.

The issue in *McKeiver* was whether the right to a jury trial, already clearly established in criminal cases, also applies to juvenile delinquency trials as one of the "essentials of due process and fair treatment" required by *Gault*. The Court split in various ways, not only on the ultimate issue, but also on the resolution of the cases that had been joined for Supreme Court review. Justice Blackmun joined by fellow Nixon appointee Chief Justice Burger and by Justices Stewart and White (the former of whom had dissented in *Gault* and the latter of whom had written a separate concurring opinion in *Gault*) stated in a plurality opinion that they categorically rejected the argument that the Due Process Clause entitles juveniles to a jury trial. Justice Brennan, concurring in one of the cases but dissenting in the other, expressed a more nuanced view that due process does not require jury trials so long as some other aspect of the process safeguards the interests that the Sixth Amendment jury trial guarantee serves. Justice Harlan concurred in the rejection of the youths' claims in both cases because he disagreed with the Court's 1968 ruling in *Duncan v. Louisiana*[53] that the Sixth Amendment jury trial right applies to the States in criminal cases, and thus was unwilling to consider its extension to delinquency trials. The remaining three Justices – Douglas, Black, and Marshall – dissented in an opinion authored by Douglas.

Although Blackmun's plurality opinion followed the by-now familiar rubric of assessing whether the procedural feature being sought by the child was an "essential[] of due process and fair treatment," it was abundantly clear that the four signatories of this opinion had embraced a new narrative that was directly antithetical to *Gault* and its reform of the juvenile court. After reiterating the

Gault Court's praise of the founders of "the juvenile court concept" and acknowledging the Court's previously-expressed concerns about "the disappointments of the system's performance and experience," Blackmun obliquely introduced the new narrative by stating:

> The Court has insisted that the[] successive decisions [in *Kent, Gault*, and *Winship*] do not spell the doom of the juvenile court system or even deprive it of its "informality, flexibility, or speed." *Winship*, 397 U.S., at 366. On the other hand, a concern precisely to the opposite effect was expressed by two dissenters in *Winship. Id.*, at 375–376.

Given that the two *Winship* dissenters referenced here were Chief Justice Burger and Justice Stewart, two of the four signatories of the plurality opinion, it was readily apparent which of these conflicting views the plurality would embrace. In the ensuing analysis, Blackmun did precisely that, rejecting the claim of a jury trial right for juveniles because it could "remake the juvenile proceeding into a fully adversary process and … put an effective end to what has been the idealistic prospect of an intimate, informal protective proceeding" and would "bring with it … the traditional delay, the formality, and the clamor of the adversary system and, possibly, the public trial."[54] The plurality opinion concluded with the following *coda*:

> If the formalities of the criminal adjudicative process are to be superimposed upon the juvenile court system, there is little need for its separate existence. Perhaps that ultimate disillusionment will come one day, but for the moment we are disinclined to give impetus to it.[55]

Blackmun's plurality opinion in *McKeiver* warrants a detailed examination here because it illustrates the degree to which the myths of the child-protective juvenile court and the compassionate juvenile court judge can blind even judges at the highest level to distortions in the system and manifest abuses in a particular case.

In developing his central thesis that a jury trial right would not enhance accurate fact-finding and would too severely erode desirable qualities of the juvenile court, Blackmun noticeably relies on unsubstantiated assertions about the juvenile court system, loading one on top of the other in a march to his desired conclusion.

In his explanation of the plurality's conclusion that "trial by jury in the juvenile court's adjudicative stage is not a constitutional requirement," Blackmun begins by declaring:

> There is a possibility, at least, that the jury trial, if required as a matter of constitutional precept, will remake the juvenile proceeding into a fully adversary process and will put an effective end to what has been the idealistic prospect of an intimate, informal protective proceeding.[56]

This assertion is made with no supporting citations of any sort or even further explanation. Although it is difficult to contest a statement framed in terms of the existence of "a possibility, at least," one would have expected a proposition so important to the plurality's conclusion to come with at least some support. This is especially so given that the dissenting Justices cited specific data showing that the use of jury trials in delinquency cases in some states did not give rise to the types of problems that Blackmun hypothesized.[57]

Blackmun next asserts: "The imposition of the jury trial on the juvenile court system would not strengthen greatly, if at all, the fact-finding function, and would, contrarily, provide an attrition of the juvenile court's assumed ability to function in a unique manner."[58] The first of the two dependent clauses in this sentence – the summary dismissal of the potential benefits of the jury trial guarantee – is crucial to Blackmun's conclusion and yet here again we have no supporting citations whatsoever. This is so even though there are compelling reasons to believe that juries are in fact better and fairer decision makers than judges.[59] The second of the two dependent clauses is merely a repetition of Blackmun's first assertion, again presented with no supporting documentation.

Having thus presented the twin pillars of the plurality's reasoning for rejecting a jury trial right, Blackmun addresses the counter-arguments in a single paragraph near the end of the opinion. He states:

> Finally, the arguments advanced by the juveniles here are, of course, the identical arguments that underlie the demand for the jury trial for criminal proceedings. The arguments necessarily equate the juvenile proceeding – or at least the adjudicative phase of it – with the criminal trial. Whether they should be so equated is our issue. Concern about the inapplicability of exclusionary and other rules of evidence, about the juvenile court judge's possible awareness of the juvenile's prior record and of the contents of the social file; about repeated appearances of the same familiar witnesses in the persons of juvenile and probation officers and social workers – all to the effect that this will create the likelihood of pre-judgment – chooses to ignore, it seems to us, every aspect of fairness, of concern, of sympathy, and of paternal attention that the juvenile court system contemplates.[60]

Having (albeit somewhat obliquely) acknowledged at the beginning of this passage that the "arguments advanced by the juveniles here" undergird the Sixth Amendment and have caused the United States Supreme Court and the lower courts to treat this guarantee as vital in criminal cases, Blackmun summarily dismisses the value of this guarantee in the juvenile court context on the (apparent) reasoning that a juvenile court judge's inherent "fairness, ... concern, ... sympathy, and ... paternal attention" will necessarily ensure procedural integrity and guard against any possible problems. Of course, if judges could be counted on to function in such a consummate manner, there would be no need for juries in the adult criminal context either. But, as the Supreme Court had previously recognized in *Duncan v. Louisiana* in 1968, the jury trial guarantee in adult criminal cases is an essential protection of the accused from "'the compliant, biased or eccentric judge.'"[61]

Blackmun's blithe confidence in the wisdom and ideal behavior of juvenile court judges is particularly baffling given the facts of the cases that were before the Court in *McKeiver v. Pennsylvania*. In describing Joseph McKeiver's case, Blackmun skips lightly over the facts – stating that they are set forth in the Pennsylvania Supreme Court's opinion "and need not be repeated at any length here"[62] – but even the few facts that Blackmun presents are sufficient to raise questions about the judge's conduct. Blackmun mentions in a footnote that:

> At McKeiver's hearing [*i.e.*, the trial of guilt or innocence] his counsel advised the court that he had never seen McKeiver before and "was just in the middle of interviewing" him. The court allowed him five minutes for the interview. Counsel's office, Community Legal Services, however, had been appointed to represent McKeiver five months earlier.[63]

Even if the Community Legal Services office was remiss in doing what it should have to prepare the case, one would expect that a reasonable judge would safeguard the child's right to a fair trial by affording the defense lawyer more than five minutes to hear the client's account for the first time and prepare for trial.

Blackmun's brief account of the facts adduced at Joseph McKeiver's trial acknowledges that the courts below described the testimony of the two prosecution witnesses "as somewhat inconsistent and as 'weak,'"[64] but it is only by looking at the Pennsylvania Supreme Court's opinion that one can appreciate the magnitude of the problem. The opinion's detailed account of the evidence at trial makes it readily apparent that any reasonable judge should have acquitted on the ground that the prosecution failed to prove the charges beyond a reasonable doubt. Although the "essence of the [robbery] charge was that he [Joseph] and some twenty or thirty other youths had taken some twenty-five cents from three young teenagers," the two complainants who testified at trial said that a single "boy on a bicycle demanded money" from them and then rode off on his bicycle; one of the two complainants "described the robbery as a gang effort while the other testified that the thief acted alone"; "[b]oth stated that the robber did not have on glasses, but McKeiver has worn them since childhood"; "[b]oth said that the robber rode a bicycle throughout the event, and yet one stated that he identified the boy by his distinctive walk."[65]

The Pennsylvania Supreme Court recounted that defense counsel gave a closing argument "similar to that usually made to a jury: [that] the story of the alleged victims was incredible, the eyewitness identification of children is unreliable, and the facts had not been proved beyond a reasonable doubt."[66] Although such an argument likely would have prevailed with a jury or a reasonable judge, the juvenile court judge in this case was – as the Pennsylvania Supreme Court put it – "apparently unimpressed."[67]

The North Carolina case joined with McKeiver's in the United States Supreme Court, *In re Barbara Burrus*, was an even starker and graver example of judicial bias and impropriety. Here again, Blackmun's account of the facts is problematically incomplete. Blackmun wrote:

> Barbara Burrus and approximately 45 other black children, ranging in age from 11 to 15 years, were the subjects of juvenile court summonses issued in Hyde County, North Carolina, in January 1969. The charges arose out of a series of demonstrations in the county in late 1968 by black adults and children protesting school assignments and a school consolidation plan. Petitions were filed by North Carolina state highway patrolmen[,] ... charg[ing] the respective juveniles with wilfully impeding traffic.[68]

What is omitted from this paragraph (and from the remainder of Blackmun's account of the facts and also from his entire plurality opinion) is that, as Justice Brennan stated in his dissent from the Court's rejection of Burrus' claim, this was a civil rights protest by "black adults and juveniles who believed that the Hyde County, North Carolina, school system unlawfully discriminated against black schoolchildren."[69] This was hardly an insignificant omission, especially in a case asking whether juries are needed as a bulwark against judicial bias. As Justice Brennan observed, a case such as this "present[ed] a paradigm of the circumstances in which there may be a substantial 'temptation to use the courts for political ends.'"[70] If there were any doubt about that, any such questions would have been dispelled by the opinion below by the North Carolina Court of Appeals. In its opinion affirming the trial judge's adjudications of delinquency, the Appellate Court stated:

> All of the cases stem from what may be classified as a concerted demonstration by Negroes of Hyde County to assert their definance [sic] of law and order and to disrupt the normal economic and social life of Hyde County by a wilful, intentional and flagrant disregard and violation of laws duly enacted by the governing bodies of the State for the public welfare and orderly conduct of human affairs for all citizens of the State.[71]

It seems unfathomable that Blackmun could fail to perceive these gross instances of judicial bias in the very cases that were before the Court. Assuming that this was indeed a misperception rather than a willful blindness, the explanation may lie in a passage of Blackmun's opinion in which he reveals the deep-rooted assumptions and preconceptions that are shaping his views of the juvenile court, judges of that court, and the issues before the Supreme Court. After reciting the *Gault* version of juvenile court history that cast the court's founders as reformers with the best of intentions, and then acknowledging the *Kent* and *Gault* opinions' descriptions of the "disappointments of the system's performance and experience and the resulting widespread disaffection," Blackmun stated:

> There have been, at one and the same time, both an appreciation for the juvenile court judge who is devoted, sympathetic, and conscientious, and a disturbed concern about the judge who is untrained and less than fully imbued with an understanding approach to the complex problems of childhood and adolescence.[72]

Of course, what is missing from this taxonomy are the conviction-prone judges who reflexively rule for the prosecution despite the existence of reasonable doubt (like the judge in Joseph McKeiver's case) and judges who suffer from biases of various sorts, including racial bias (like the judges in Barbara Burrus' case). Under Blackmun's conception of the world, at least as articulated in the above paragraph, all judges are inherently well-intentioned and capable of ruling in a fair and just manner, even if some of them need some additional "training" in order to better understand "the complex problems of childhood and adolescence." This rosy picture of the situation is evident again later in Blackmun's opinion when, after acknowledging that "[o]f course there have been abuses" in the juvenile court system, he declares that such abuses "relate to the lack of resources and of dedication rather than to inherent unfairness."[73] If one accepts on faith that Blackmun actually believed these things and that he was not merely using rhetoric to reach a predetermined conclusion, then he was operating with cognitive blinders that made it impossible for him to see (or perhaps to accept) the degree of arbitrariness and injustice that were plaguing the juvenile courts.

Whatever the explanation may actually be, *McKeiver* put an end to *Gault*'s transformation of the juvenile court. It would be many years before the defense would win another delinquency case in the United States Supreme Court. When Richard Nixon appointed his next two Justices, Lewis Powell and William Rehnquist, in 1971, the Court became even more resistant to juvenile rights claims. The Court rejected such claims in various cases, including *Schall v. Martin*,[74] which is discussed in Chapter 5 by Martin Guggenheim, who litigated the case and argued it in the United States Supreme Court. It was not until the current century, after the composition of the Court had changed again (due to appointments to the Court by Presidents Clinton and Obama), that the Court once again was open to juvenile rights claims. As Chapter 4, written by Eduardo Ferrer, describes, it was at this point that a whole new phase of Supreme Court jurisprudence emerged, in which the Court reshaped legal requirements to account for new developments in adolescent brain science.

Returning to the children

Victory in the Supreme Court came only after Jerry Gault spent more than two years at the Arizona Industrial School for Boys, a reformatory known as "desert Devil's Island."[75] Similarly, denouncement of the unconstitutional treatment in Morris Kent's case did not spare him from six years in St. Elizabeth's Psychiatric Hospital after being tried and convicted as an adult.[76] The Supreme Court cases discussed in this chapter, no matter their outcome, represented the culmination of a legal process that left a heavy imprint on the lives of society's most vulnerable members – children – mostly poor, many of color.

We hoped to end this chapter with a reflection on the lives of the children behind the cases but found little public information on Morris Kent, Terry Edwards, Joseph McKeiver, Barbara Burrus or any of the hundreds of children whose cases built the foundation of modern juvenile law. From the silence, we hopefully infer quiet yet fulfilling lives for the adults whose childhoods proved so influential to the juvenile law landscape.

As a result of Jerry Gault's occasional appearances at conferences and programs commemorating the anniversary of *In re Gault*, we know a little about his life after Fort Grant. Mr. Gault married, spent 23 years in the military, and became a grandfather.[77] His experience in the juvenile delinquency system imparted an important wisdom about the punitive treatment of children. Forty years after the Supreme Court's decision in his case, Jerry Gault commented, "People in this society need to realize that these children that we are putting behind bars ... are our next leaders."[78] This statement perfectly recognizes adolescents' unique potential for change and growth. Mr. Gault's wisdom embodies principles and truths the United States Supreme Court has taken decades to meaningfully embrace.

Notes

1 In re Gault, 387 U.S. 1, 4 (1967). By modern standards, the allegedly lewd statements were quite mild. According to the interview notes of the probation officer, Jerry stated that the friend of his who made the phone call together with him said: "Are your cherries ripe? Do you have big bombers? Do you give any away?" DAVID S. TANENHAUS, THE CONSTITUTIONAL RIGHTS OF CHILDREN: *IN RE GAULT* AND JUVENILE JUSTICE 30 (University Press of Kansas, 2011).

2 387 U.S. at 8–9.

3 *Id.* at 7.

4 The trial court proceedings are described in *id.* at 5–7.

5 *See, e.g.*, PRESIDENT'S COMM'N ON LAW ENF'T AND ADMIN. OF JUSTICE, TASK FORCE ON JUVENILE DELINQUENCY, TASK FORCE REPORT: JUVENILE DELINQUENCY AND YOUTH CRIME 7 (1967).

6 For further details about Amelia Lewis's background and her role in the *Gault* case, *see* TANENHAUS, *supra* note 1, at 33–45; David S. Tanenhaus, *Pursuing Justice for the Child: The Forgotten Women of In re Gault*, 13 WHITTIER J. CHILD & FAM. ADVOC. 36, 41–46 (2014) [hereinafter *Pursuing Justice*].

7 Norman Dorsen, *Reflections on In re Gault*, 60 RUTGERS L. REV. 1, 2 (2007).

8 *Id.* at 2–3.

9 For further details about Gertrud Mainzer's background and her role in the *Gault* case, *see* TANENHAUS, *supra* note 1, at 49–50, 68; TANENHAUS, *Pursuing Justice, supra* note 6, at 46–48.

10 Dorsen, *supra* note 7, at 3.

11 *See* Dorsen, *supra* note 7, at 5–6.

12 *Id.* at 4–5.

13 Mapp v. Ohio, 367 U.S. 643 (1961).

14 Gideon v. Wainwright, 372 U.S. 335 (1963).

15 Miranda v. Arizona, 384 U.S. 436 (1966).

16 Kent v. United States, 383 U.S. 541 (1966).

17 *Id.* at 543–44.

18 *Id.* at 545–46.

19 *Id.* at 564–65. On remand, the federal district court, sitting as a juvenile court, found that the waiver to adult court was proper, but the D.C. Circuit Court of Appeals reversed, holding that "Morris Kent should not have been waived in 1961, [and therefore] the subsequent criminal proceedings were invalid and must be vacated." Kent v. United States, 401 F.2d 408, 412 (D.C. Cir. 1968). The court stated, however, that the government can institute civil commitment proceedings to continue holding

Kent in Saint Elizabeth's Hospital, and the court expressed its view that civil commitment proceedings should be pursued. *Id.* The court stayed its mandate to afford the government time to initiate civil commitment proceedings before Kent's release. *Id.*

20 383 U.S. at 561–63 (1966).

21 *Id.* at 562.

22 *Id.* at 555.

23 *Id.* at 555–56.

24 387 U.S. at 23–24, 27.

25 *Id.* at 29–30.

26 *Id.* at 28.

27 *Id.* at 30–31, quoting Kent, 383 U.S. at 562.

28 *Id.* at 30, quoting Kent, 383 U.S. at 562.

29 387 U.S. at 33.

30 *Id.* at 31.

31 *Id.* at 41.

32 *Id.* at 41–42.

33 *Id.* at 36 (footnotes omitted).

34 *Id.* at 55.

35 *Id.*

36 *Id.*

37 *See id.* at 6–7 (recounting that "at the June 9 hearing Gerald was questioned by the judge about the telephone call" but "[t]here was conflict as to what he said," with "[h]is mother recall[ing] that Gerald said he only dialed Mrs. Cook's number and handed the telephone to his friend," the probation officer recalling that "Gerald had admitted making the lewd remarks," and the judge testifying that "Gerald 'admitted making one of these (lewd) statements'"; and the witnesses also "differed in their recollections of Gerald's testimony at the June 15 hearing," with his parents "recall[ing] that Gerald again testified that the he had only dialed the number and that the other boy had made the remarks," the probation officer "agree[ing] that at this hearing Gerald did not admit making the lewd remarks," but the judge "recall[ing] that 'there was some admission again of some of the lewd statements'").

38 *Id.* at 56.

39 *Id.*

40 *Id.* at 58.

41 *Id.* at 14–15.

42 *Id.* at 15 (quoting Julian Mack, *The Juvenile Court*, 23 HARV. L. REV. 104, 119–20 (1909)).

43 *Id.* at 17.

44 *Id.* at 19–20.

45 *Id.* at 27.

46 *Id.*

47 *See, e.g.*, Sanford J. Fox, *Juvenile Justice Reform: An Historical Perspective*, 22 STAN. L. REV. 1187, 1187–88, 1238 (1970); Douglas R. Rendleman, *Parens Patriae: From Chancery to the Juvenile Court*, 23 S.C. L. REV. 205, 255–56 (1971).

48 387 U.S. at 4–5.

49 *See* Gault, 387 U.S. at 18–27.

50 *Id.* at 13.

51 In re Winship, 397 U.S. 358 (1970).

52 McKeiver v. Pennsylvania, 403 U.S. 528 (1971).

53 Duncan v. Louisiana, 391 U.S. 145 (1968).

54 403 U.S. at 545, 550 (1971).

55 *Id.* at 551.

56 *Id.* at 545.

57 *See id.* at 561–62 & n.2 (Douglas, J., dissenting).

58 *Id.* at 547 (plurality opinion).
59 This point is developed at great length in Martin Guggenheim & Randy Hertz, *Reflections on Judges, Juries, and Justice: Ensuring the Fairness of Juvenile Delinquency Trials*, 33 WAKE FOREST L. REV. 553 (1998).
60 403 U.S. at 550.
61 391 U.S. at 156.
62 *Id.* at 536.
63 *Id.* at 535 n.2.
64 *Id.* at 536.
65 In the Matter of Edward Terry and Joseph McKeiver, 438 Pa. 339, 342 n.1, 265 A.2d 350, 352 n.1 (1970), *aff'd sub nom.* McKeiver v. Pennsylvania, 403 U.S. 528 (1971).
66 *Id.*
67 *Id.*
68 403 U.S. at 536 (footnote omitted).
69 *Id.* at 556 (Brennan, J., concurring and dissenting). For a detailed discussion of the Burrus case, *see* Robin Walker Sterling, *Fundamental Unfairness: In re Gault and the Road Not Taken*, 72 MD. L. REV. 607 (2013).
70 *Id.*
71 In re Barbara Burrus (and 43 other cases), 4 N.C. App. 523, 528, 167 S.E.2d 454, 457 (1969), *aff'd sub nom.* McKeiver v. Pennsylvania, 403 U.S. 528 (1971).
72 403 U.S. at 534.
73 *Id.* at 548.
74 Schall v. Martin, 467 U.S. 253 (1984).
75 *See* Tanenhaus, *Pursuing Justice*, *supra* note 6, at 39; Wallace J. Mlyniec, *In re Gault at 40: The Right to Counsel in Juvenile Court – A Promise Unfulfilled*, 44 CRIM. L. BULL. 371, 22 n.5 (2008).
76 *See* O.W. Ketcham, *Kent Revisited*, 2 JUV. JUST. UPDATE 1, 11 (1996).
77 *See* TANENHAUS, *supra* note 1, at 122–23.
78 *Id.* at 123.

2 Arizona before and after *In re Gault*: has Arizona realized the promises of *In re Gault?*

Ellen Marrus and Chris Phillis

In 1966, Arizona was an arid desert that travelers passed through to reach the sunny beaches of California. A true Wild West state where commerce was based upon the five Cs – cattle, copper, cotton, citrus, and climate – Arizona was a collection of mining towns and farming communities, with the exception of two urban cities, Phoenix and Tucson, that were separated by vast open spaces. It was also the birthplace and home of Barry Goldwater, a U.S. Senator and 1964 presidential candidate who helped redefine the Republican Party as the fiscal conservative party.[1] Goldwater placed the constitution and its protections above all other laws, stressed small government, and rejected collectivism, placing individual rights over group rights. Goldwater's acceptance speech for the Republican Presidential nomination reflected the political climate in Arizona in the 1960s: "I would remind you that extremism in the defense of liberty is no vice. And let me remind you also that moderation in the pursuit of justice is no virtue."[2] Arizonans' Wild West roots and belief in individual rights led to courageous attorneys being willing to challenge the criminal justice system.

Arizona had already leapt onto the front pages of newspapers with the United States Supreme Court's decision *Miranda v. Arizona* in June 1966.[3] But, while the nation turned its attention to the due process rights of adults during police interrogations, the children of Arizona were being subjected to the whims of local law enforcement. Arizona's 1.6 million residents[4] had accepted the state's claim that *parens patriae*, parent of the state, allowed local magistrates and probation officers to punish mischievous children without the benefit of constitutional legal proceedings and due process protections. This was the attitude in Arizona, as in much of the United States, in spite of Arizona's general attitude that government needed to stay out of private citizens' lives.

Children accused of wayward activities were unceremoniously brought before a magistrate by a probation or police officer, often without the benefit of family or counsel being present, a trial, the ability to confront the accuser, the right to remain silent, or any other due process protections.[5] The magistrate leveled judgment and punishment based upon the accusations of the officers, as the children stood defenseless. Magistrates placed children, often for minor offenses, at the Arizona State Industrial School at Fort Grant, an 1872 abandoned army post.[6] The court shipped children hundreds of miles from their communities and families to this juvenile prison in the middle of the desert, without any consideration for the psychological damage this alienation would cause. This happened throughout Arizona, including Gila County, one of the state's 15 counties, which was comprised of small mining towns. Prior to 1967, the only individuals who knew of Gila County were mining company executives and miners. That was about to change.

Arizona's juvenile system pre-*Gault*

On June 8, 1964, Gerald Gault, a 15-year-old boy living in Gila County, Arizona, experienced the paternalistic process of the Arizona juvenile court.[7] Gerald and a friend, Ronald Lewis, were spending a hot summer afternoon lolling around Gerald's home. Gerald's parents were at work and the boys were home on summer vacation. A sheriff came to speak to the boys about a complaint from a neighbor, Mrs. Cook, who called police because she claimed to have received a lewd prank call from Gerald and Ronald. Despite the boys' denial that they had placed the call, they were taken into custody and placed in the Children's Detention Home. No note was left for Gerald's parents, and no one attempted to reach either of them at work. When Mrs. Gault arrived home after work, a neighbor told her that Gerald had been taken to the detention home. She went to the detention home, where she was not allowed to see Gerald, but she was told there would be a hearing the next day.

Gerald and his mother appeared before the judge the next day, without having received formal charges or appointed counsel. The judge questioned Gerald about the offense, even though Gerald had no idea what was happening and was given no time to prepare, and Mrs. Cook was not present at the hearing. After the proceeding, Gerald was returned to the detention home. A few days later, he was released to his parents and ordered to return to court on June 15, 1964.[8] At that hearing, despite Mrs. Gault's request to have Mrs. Cook present, the court found, without the testimony of any witnesses, that Gerald had made a lewd phone call and that he was "habitually involved in immoral matters."[9] Upon the recommendation of the probation officer, the court sentenced Gerald to the Arizona State Industrial School for six years, until he reached the age of majority, 21. Had Gerald been 18 years old, he would have been formally charged, provided with counsel,[10] entitled to face his accuser, and eligible to receive a maximum sentence of two months in jail and a $50 fine.[11]

As a juvenile, Gerald was not entitled to appeal the court's decision. His only recourse was to file a motion for habeas corpus, unlawful detainment, with the Arizona Supreme Court. The Arizona Supreme Court sent Gerald's habeas request down to the Superior Court to rule on the motion. Not surprisingly, the Superior Court dismissed the habeas petition, and the Arizona Supreme Court affirmed that decision. Arizona held that these were not criminal proceedings, and, therefore, Gerald was not promised the due process protections an adult would receive in criminal court. The goal of the juvenile court was to help the youth, and the judge had a great deal of discretion. Gerald, with the assistance of an attorney, took his case to the United States Supreme Court.[12]

The United States Supreme Court, in an 8–1 decision, held that Gerald's commitment to the Arizona State Industrial School was a violation of the Due Process Clause of the Fourteenth Amendment.[13] At that time, Arizona, and all other states, considered juvenile proceedings to be civil in nature, and therefore, children were not provided with the due process protections guaranteed to criminal defendants. The Court found that Arizona's "parent of the state" juvenile court system had not meant that "children receive[d] careful, compassionate, individualized treatment … [nor that it] always produced fair, efficient, and effective procedures."[14] The court held that, although there are legitimate reasons for treating juveniles and adults accused of crime differently, juveniles facing an adjudication of delinquency and incarceration are entitled to certain procedural safeguards under the Due Process Clause of the Fourteenth Amendment,[15] including timely and specific notice of the charges,[16] the right to an attorney,[17] and the right to confront accusers and call witnesses.[18] The Court held that children are also protected by the privilege against self-incrimination guaranteed under the Fifth Amendment, and could not be forced to testify against themselves.[19] The Court stated that "[u]nder our Constitution, the condition of being a boy does not justify a kangaroo court."[20]

This decision released Gerald Gault from confinement after more than two years at the Arizona State Industrial School. Gerald's case and the Supreme Court decision that bears his name would forever change the due process rights of juveniles.

Arizona's response to the *Gault* decision

The *Gault* decision forced Arizona to respond. Three years after the decision, the Arizona state legislature created a new juvenile code to address the due process rights that were mandated or implied by the Supreme Court in *Gault.* The Arizona Juvenile Code was amended to require that parents and children be provided with timely, written notice of the specific charges, parents be informed of hearing dates and times, children be provided with counsel, and children be permitted to appeal.[21]

As the juvenile system was undergoing changes, so, too, was the adult criminal system. In 1963, four years prior to the *Gault* decision, the Supreme Court had decided *Gideon v. Wainwright*, holding that individuals charged with a criminal offense were entitled to counsel not just in federal court, but also in state court.[22] In 1965, Arizona's first county-funded public defender office opened in Maricopa County. In the following years, nine more counties created public defender offices, while counties without such offices created contract lists from which to appoint attorneys. After the *Gault* decision, many of the public defender offices created special units to represent children in juvenile court. However, the juvenile unit was often used as a training ground for new attorneys, and the assignment of experienced attorneys to the juvenile unit was perceived as punishment.

The appointment of counsel for children in delinquency court appreciably changed the landscape of juvenile justice in Arizona. Providing counsel for children helped protect children's statutory and constitutional rights to trial, to remain silent, and to call, confront, and cross examine witnesses. Additionally, new rules of juvenile court procedure ensured that courts provided children with the due process rights granted under *Gault* and subsequent Supreme Court decisions. With counsel representing youth and courts following new rules of procedure, due process rights were better protected. And when children were denied due process, they could now appeal their case.

Through the appellate process, attorneys challenged juvenile court practices, and every appellate victory further defined Arizona's juvenile law and children's due process rights. Appellate attorneys successfully challenged the use of deferred detention without providing the child an opportunity to contest the alleged bad behavior,[23] the detention of a child for more than 48 hours without a hearing,[24] the filing of petitions beyond the required timeframe,[25] unconstitutional criminal statutes (many which only applied to children),[26] the use of juvenile confessions due to the coercive nature of police interrogations,[27] and the illegal extension of probation beyond the statutory period.[28] The work of appellate attorneys also convinced Arizona courts to require that juvenile defendants, like adults, be competent to stand trial.[29] Without the advocacy of attorneys dedicated to juvenile issues, due process rights afforded to children in *Gault* would have gone unrealized.

Arizona also made several structural changes to its juvenile system. Juvenile courthouses and juvenile dockets began to spring up in many of the fifteen counties. Jurisdictions with more than one Superior Court judge dedicated a juvenile court docket, and judges and commissioners assigned to the juvenile docket began to receive specialized training. Many jurisdictions created juvenile probation departments, and eventually the Arizona Office of the Courts, a division of the Arizona Supreme Court, created a special juvenile justice division to address youthful issues and oversee juvenile probation. As Arizona became more populous, presiding juvenile court judges began to meet quarterly at the Committee on Juvenile Courts to discuss issues impacting the welfare and rights of children statewide.

Progress and setbacks post-*Gault*

By the mid-1990s, perceptions of the juvenile justice system began to change. Public hysteria around the myth of the juvenile superpredator changed the way children and juvenile courts were viewed.[30] Citizens feared that Arizona's youth were becoming increasingly more violent and that juvenile court was no longer a suitable venue to handle these young supposed predators. A voter-approved referendum empowered county attorneys to directly charge children who were at least 14 years old and accused of a dangerous felony offense in adult criminal court.[31] Arizona children were thrown into an arena where rehabilitative services were replaced with retribution and long prison terms.

At the same time, Arizona's juvenile courts were also changing: children were brought to court in shackles and handcuffs, metal detectors appeared at court entrances, and detention centers were overflowing with children. Seemingly overnight, the juvenile court changed its perception of children, no longer viewing them as inexperienced, immature young people who acted impulsively, but as smaller adults with years of life experiences. For the next two decades, juvenile attorneys fought valiantly to free children from detention, shackles, and the harsh consequences for adolescent lapses of judgment.

Another, different change occurred in 2005, when the United States Supreme Court ruled that the imposition of the death penalty for a crime committed while under the age of 18 is unconstitutional.[32] The Court's focus on the juvenile brain and adolescent development led to specialized training for attorneys assigned to represent children: a specific track for juvenile defense was added to the yearly training program sponsored by the Arizona Public Defender Association, and an additional two-day training was added that focused on juvenile defense. In 2008, Arizona's first county-funded juvenile public defender office, the Office of the Public Advocate, was created in Maricopa County and dedicated to the representation of youth charged with delinquent acts.[33] Other juvenile public defender offices soon followed.

As time passed and the juvenile superpredator did not materialize,[34] juvenile public defenders began to have conversations with juvenile court judges, community leaders, and legislators, using the sociological and brain science research from *Roper v. Simmons*[35] to remind them of what every parent knows: children act recklessly, lack maturity and a sense of responsibility, are unduly influenced by peer pressure, and often do not consider the consequences of their actions. Children are not capable, physically or mentally, of analyzing situations in the same manner as adults, and therefore should not be held to the same standards.

One of these conversations led to the first statutory change of the new millennium, the elimination of the unfettered discretion of county attorneys to charge a child as an adult without an opportunity for a court to review the appropriateness of that decision.[36] A pathway back to the juvenile system was created: children charged in the adult court were now allowed to request a transfer to juvenile court. At that transfer hearing, the child, represented by an attorney, would be allowed to call experts, such as psychologists, to assist the judge in deciding whether the child could be rehabilitated in the juvenile system before their eighteenth birthday. Children's fates were no longer at the sole discretion of the prosecuting attorney.

Another significant advance in Arizona juvenile law entitled detained children to be taken before a hearing officer within 24 hours of a petition being filed, even on weekends and holidays.[37] For decades, the statutory requirement that detained children be taken before a judicial officer within 24 hours was ignored, in order to allow court staff and judicial officers to spend time with their families on weekends and holidays. Unlike adults, who were always taken before a judicial officer within 24 hours of confinement, children brought to a detention center on Friday were in limbo for three or four days, not knowing what offense they were accused of or when they might go home. Juvenile defenders, appalled at this disparity of treatment and violation of the law, successfully challenged the unsanctioned practice of stopping the 24-hour clock on weekends and holidays.[38] Detained children are now provided with written notice of the charges and afforded an opportunity, through counsel, to argue for their release within 24 hours of a petition being filed. Children can now be released to enjoy holidays with their families and be in school Monday morning.

In the past few years, Arizona has joined the growing number of states that participate in the Juvenile Detention Alternatives Initiative, a reform model rooted in the philosophy that the incarceration of children, which has traumatic and long-lasting effects, should be used sparingly, and only children who pose a true threat to the community should be detained. Nearly every county in Arizona has created a juvenile court working group, including juvenile defenders, to assist in creating policies regarding the use of detention. The reduction in the number of detained children has resulted in the closing of five detention centers, without an increase in the risk to the community.[39]

In 2016, through the persistent work of juvenile public defenders statewide, Arizona children were freed from indiscriminate shackling. A new Rule of Procedure for Juvenile Court now requires that children appear in court free of restraints unless there have been recent acts or threats of violence or escape. Courts have also begun to reconsider the programs they utilize for correcting children's behavior, sending children to programs that deliver a positive message, rather than focusing on children's mistakes.

Next steps to meet the promise of *Gault*

Fifty years after the landmark decision of *In re Gault*, the Wild West state of Arizona has grown up. Arizona's economy is no longer based upon the five Cs, but on health care, transportation, and tourism. Arizona's population has quadrupled, to 6.9 million residents.[40] The Wild West towns have grown into metropolises, many farms and citrus groves are now housing developments, and most small mining towns have become either tourist destinations or ghost towns. Residents of Maricopa and Pinal counties take refuge from the desert heat in cabins among the pines of Gila County, whose population has grown from 28,000 to more than 50,000 in those 50 years.[41] The cabin-goers travel the numerous paved highways and freeways, an option not available 50 years ago. The state has three universities with a combined enrollment of more than 115,000 students, and four professional athletic teams. Arizona is no longer a state people pass through when traveling to their final location, it is a destination for millions of people every year.

As Arizona has grown up, so, too, has its juvenile court system. In the years since *Gault* was decided, due process protections for youth in Arizona have made important inroads, yet children still face many obstacles to obtaining due process in the system.[42]

Arizona still allows youth to waive their right to counsel before the child has had an opportunity to meet with a defense attorney to discuss their case and rights. Children often rely on the guidance of their parent when deciding whether to waive counsel, and many parents, fearing they will be responsible for compensating the attorney, encourage their child to waive their right to an attorney. Often, parents and children are told if they ask for an attorney they will have to come back on a future date for the hearing, further encouraging waiver. In some instances, the first person who discusses the right to counsel with the child and parents is not a juvenile defender, but a probation officer or county attorney, who emphasizes that there really is not a need for an attorney and the matter can be disposed of more quickly if no defense attorney is involved. If the court does not adequately inform the youth and parent of the benefit of counsel and the potential negative impacts of being adjudicated delinquent, the child may believe they are capable of self-representation. Extreme caution should be taken by the judiciary to ensure the child clearly understands the constitutional right they are about to waive, but this does not always occur.[43]

As the birthplace of *Gault*, Arizona has an obligation to guarantee due process rights for children. State legislators should adopt legislation that precludes children from waiving their right to counsel unless they have first consulted with qualified juvenile defense counsel about their rights. Arizona should also ensure that youth receive counsel at all critical stages of the system, including police interrogation. Requiring an attorney to be present for police interrogations will ensure children understand the right to remain silent and will serve as a child's best defense against wrongfully admitting to misconduct based on confusion or despair.

Not all public defender offices in Arizona have attorneys exclusively dedicated to the representation of youth in juvenile court. While the criminal offenses children are charged with are the same offenses charged to adults, the juvenile court process, sentencing structure, and case law are significantly different. Many defense attorneys believe that juvenile matters are insignificant compared to adult criminal matters; being incarcerated for a month as opposed to years seems inconsequential. However, a month out of a child's life can derail their future: a child who misses a month of school is more likely to drop out, forever changing the course of their life.[44]

Arizona needs to take steps to ensure that juvenile defense is a recognized, respected, specialized practice of law throughout the state, not just in some counties. All juvenile defenders, along with juvenile judges and county attorneys, should receive training in adolescent development, communicating with and advocating for children, and juvenile court practice and procedure. And juvenile defenders must be provided with adequate resources and support staff, including specialized social workers, to zealously represent their clients, investigate cases, and identify appropriate treatment options for their child clients.

Reminiscent of pre-*Gault* days, Arizona children convicted of a felony offense can be imprisoned for significant amounts of time, until the child's eighteenth birthday. Fortunately, children are no longer shipped to the middle of the desert to be rehabilitated; the Arizona Department of Juvenile Corrections (ADJC) is located just north of downtown Phoenix, off a major freeway. However, although incarcerated children receive treatment and are able to maintain contact with their families via weekly visits and phone calls, it is still a prison. Children live behind walls, adhere to strict regimens, and are policed by guards. And many of their families struggle to maintain face-to-face contact, as getting to the facility can be challenging for a family with limited resources and transportation. Children incarcerated at ADJC lose their youth and just as much freedom, if not more, than adults sent to prison.

ADJC has not been without its issues. The United States Department of Justice conducted an investigation of ADJC facilities from October 2002 through January 2003, in response to a number of suicides at the facility.[45] The investigation revealed that incarcerated children were being denied federal and state constitutional and statutory protections, and that the facility did not provide appropriate supervision, education, treatment, or health services. Inappropriate supervision led to suicide and the sexual and physical victimization of incarcerated children by other children and staff.[46] Children receiving educational services at ADJC were far behind children in the community[47] and were unable to pass Arizona's standardized tests. Treatment services were non-existent or being provided by untrained staff. Children's physical and dental needs were not being addressed, and their general health was compromised by the lack of services. The Department of Justice filed a complaint against ADJC on September 14, 2004,[48] giving ADJC three years to correct the identified issues.

Under the guidance of a then-new director, ADJC made significant changes to the facility in 2004 and the following years. The new director hired a licensed psychologist to run the treatment programs, brought in doctors and a dentist to address the children's health issues, hired licensed educators, employed a safety and compliance director to oversee the training of new staff, and remodeled the facilities. The number of suicides and physical and sexual assaults declined significantly, children's standardized testing scores increased, and some children began taking community college courses. Unfortunately, Arizona soon learned that the progress of the facility was largely dependent upon the vision of the director, when a subsequent director ended many of the advances.

Ultimately, placement at ADJC should be the last alternative. Services should be provided in the child's community before the child is removed from their home. As the justices in *Gault* noted, "it is of no constitutional consequence – and of limited practical meaning – that the institution to which [children are] committed" is not called a prison.[49]

The state legislature must also curtail the number of offenses for which the county attorney may directly charge a child in the adult criminal system or, ideally, eliminate direct file entirely. Since 1996, when direct file was passed by a citizen referendum, the list of offenses eligible for direct file has expanded, and too many Arizona children are lost to the criminal justice system for incidents that do not warrant being locked away for years. Instead, children should be entitled to an evidentiary hearing before they are transferred to adult criminal court, allowing a judge who is better trained in adolescent development to determine if juvenile court is the appropriate arena to address the child's misbehavior. Although allowing for reverse transfer of a juvenile who faces automatic transfer to adult criminal court was a constructive improvement for Arizona, it is not enough to ensure the due process rights of children are protected. Having a hearing prior to any transfer of a child to criminal court will better protect the rights and interests of children.

Arizona has come a long way in 50 years, but much work still needs to be done for its juvenile justice system to reflect the state's proud history as the Wild West, full of independent, strong-willed people who value their rights. The fiftieth anniversary of the *Gault* decision is a fitting time for Arizona to remember native son Barry Goldwater's proclamation that "moderation in the pursuit of justice is no virtue," and to ensure that every Arizona child is fully protected by the constitution and the promises of *Gault.*

Notes

1 Barry Goldwater – Biography, Biography.com, https://www.biography.com/people/barry-goldwater-9314846 (last visited Oct. 16, 2017).
2 Robert Andrews, Famous Lines: A Columbia Dictionary of Familiar Quotations 159 (Columbia University Press, 1997).
3 Miranda v. Arizona, 384 U.S. 436 (1966) (holding that the Fifth Amendment requires law enforcement to inform suspects of their right to remain silent and their right to an attorney prior to interrogation).
4 U.S. Bureau of the Census, *Intercensal Estimates of the Total Resident Population of States*, (released Aug. 1996), https://www2.census.gov/programs-surveys/popest/tables/1980–1990/state/asrh/st6070ts.txt.
5 In re Gault, 387 U.S. 1, 4–8 (1967).
6 Arizona Department of Corrections, *ADC History*, https://corrections.az.gov/adc-history (last visited Oct. 16, 2017).
7 *See* Gault, 387 U.S. 1 (1967).
8 *Id.* at 4–8.
9 *Id.* at 9.
10 In Arizona, indigent defendants receive counsel for both misdemeanors and felonies if the defendant faces any jail time. Ariz. Const. art. II, § 24.
11 Gault, 387 U.S. 1, 8–9 (1967).
12 *Id.* at 8–10.
13 *Id.* at 31–57.
14 *Id.* at 18–19.
15 *Id.* at 13–14.
16 *Id.* at 33.
17 *Id.* at 41.
18 *Id.* at 57.
19 *Id.* at 44–57.
20 *Id.* at 28.
21 *See* Ariz. Rev. Stat. Ann., Title 8, Chapters 2–3.
22 Gideon v. Wainwright, 372 U.S. 335, 344–45 (1963).
23 *See, e.g.*, In re Jeffrey W., No. 1 CA-JV 08–0198, 2009 WL 2168689, at ¶ 26 (Ariz. Ct. App. July 21, 2009).
24 Maricopa County Juv. Action No. JV-111701, 786 P.2d 998, 1004 (1989).
25 *Id.*
26 *See, e.g.*, In re Marxus B, 13 P.3d 290 (2000); In re Cesar R., 4 P.3d 980 (1999).
27 In re Andre M., 88 P.3d 552 (2004).
28 In re Andrew G., 165 P.3d 182 (2007).
29 State ex rel. Dandoy v. Superior Court, 12 Ariz. 184, 619 P.2d 12, 14 (1980); *see also* Ariz. Rev. Stat. Ann §§ 8–291 *et seq.*, which were enacted after Dandoy was decided.
30 John J. Dilulio, Jr., *The Coming of the Super-Predators*, The Weekly Standard (Nov. 27, 1995), http://www.weeklystandard.com/the-coming-of-the-super-predators/article/8160.

31 Children's Action Alliance, Prosecuting Juveniles in the Adult Criminal Justice System, Key Issues and Recommendations for Arizona (June 2003), http://azchildren.org/wp-content/uploads/2013/01/Prosecuting-Juv-as-Adult-2003.pdf.

32 Roper v. Simmons, 543 U.S. 551, 578 (2005).

33 In 1993, Christina Phillis was hired by the Maricopa County Public Defender Office and assigned to represent children in delinquency proceedings, making her the first Juvenile Public Defender in Arizona, a position she held for 15 years. In 2008, Maricopa County established a separate office to represent delinquent children, the Office of the Public Advocate, and appointed Phillis to lead the office.

34 Dilulio, *supra* note 30.

35 543 U.S. 551 (2005).

36 Ariz. Rev. Stat. Ann. § 13–504 (2011).

37 Juv. Action No. JV-111701, 786 P.2d at 1004.

38 *Id.*

39 Detention Regionalization Work Group, Arizona Office of the Courts (forthcoming). Draft on file with author.

40 U.S. Census Bureau, *Quick Facts Arizona*, https://www.census.gov/quickfacts/AZ (last visited Oct. 16, 2017).

41 U.S. Census Bureau, *Fact Finder*, https://factfinder.census.gov/faces/tableservices/jsf/pages/productview.xhtml?src=bkmk (last visited Oct. 12, 2017).

42 Children's access to counsel in Arizona is undergoing an assessment based upon protocols from the National Juvenile Defender Center. Site visits were performed during the summer of 2017, and a full report of the assessment is forthcoming. When published, the report will be available at njdc.info/our-work/juvenile-indigent-defense-assessments.

43 The observations in this paragraph are based upon the authors' juvenile defense practice in Arizona, court observations, and conversations with juvenile defenders across the state.

44 *See* Ellen Marrus, *Education in Black America: Is It the New Jim Crow?*, 68 Ark. L. Rev. 27, 38–39 (2015).

45 U.S. Department of Justice, Civil Rights Division, Letter from R. Alexander Acosta, Assistant Attorney General, to The Honorable Janet Napolitano, Governor of Arizona (Jan. 23, 2004), https://www.justice.gov/sites/default/files/crt/legacy/2011/04/13/ariz_findings.pdf.

46 *Id.*

47 *See* Johnson v. Upchurch, Consent Decree (D. Ariz. May 6, 1993) (No. CIV-86–195-TUC-RMB), https://www.clearinghouse.net/chDocs/public/JI-AZ-0002–0002.pdf.

48 Arizona Department of Corrections, *Agency History*, https://adjc.az.gov/about-adjc/agency-history (last visited Oct. 16, 2017).

49 Gault, 387 U.S. at 27.

3 Toward equal recognition, authority, and protection: legal and extra-legal advocacy for black youth in the juvenile justice system

Kristin Henning, Jenadee Nanini and Geoff Ward

This book documents the critical role of advocacy for youth in America's juvenile justice system. Opening with a retrospective of *In re Gault* and *Kent v. United States*, the book highlights *Gault*'s lineage within the Warren Court's due process revolution.[1] Viewed from this lens, the authors recognize defense counsel's important role in ensuring that children have a meaningful opportunity to be heard and confront evidence against them. However, because black youth have faced a unique set of challenges in the juvenile system, the legacy of legal and non-legal advocacy for black youth requires a special telling. Advocacy for black youth has necessarily extended beyond these fundamental due process protections to include struggles for the right of black youth to be recognized as "children" in the juvenile courts, the recognition of black adults as authorities in youth justice, and the right of black communities to enjoy equal protection, including access to juvenile justice services and resources.

Although *Gault* was decided in the heart of the civil rights movement and may be viewed as a due process victory for black defendants, the reality is that cases like *Gault* and *Kent* did little to rid black youth of racial discrimination and hyper surveillance by law enforcement. Nor did they secure equal protection for black youth in court, or otherwise ensure black children are treated *as children* with all the attendant benefits of protection and rehabilitation in lieu of criminalization and incarceration. Before *Gault*, white Progressive Child Savers ignored or outright denigrated black youth in their quest to assimilate poor white youth, including newly arrived European immigrants, into a white-dominated and idealized society.[2] These early juvenile justice reformers did not contemplate the rehabilitation of "Negro" children, whom they saw as morally and intellectually irredeemable, and whom they politically excluded from the citizen-building agenda of the rehabilitative ideal.[3] When reformatories did admit black children, they often relegated these youth to the "colored section," where they were "trained" for futures in menial labor (e.g., as servants), denied rehabilitative services comparable to those afforded white youth, and excluded from civic engagement. Black men who were confined in Florida's Jim Crow reformatory for boys have likened the ordeal to enslavement: "On the white side, it was more roomy, you had the industrial shops, the woodworking shop – places the white boy was able to get a certificate," 61-year-old John Bonner recalled, "[but] the black side was the slave side."[4]

From slavery through the Progressive Era, the civil rights movement, and the contemporary era of mass incarceration, black youth have been plagued by narratives casting them as violent, immoral, degenerate, and undeserving of child welfare and social services, perhaps especially education.[5] Whereas these early moral and political arguments were articulated in explicitly racialized terms, over time they have evolved into facially race-neutral claims about the "realities" of inner-cities, family failure, and crime rates.

These narratives are deeply ingrained. Today, the cultural stereotype of blacks as violent, hostile, aggressive, and dangerous is so pervasive that the mere thought of "crime" activates a racial stereotype.[6] Unfortunately, contemporary research in implicit racial bias demonstrates that these stereotypes have a particularly harmful impact on the assessment of adolescent innocence and culpability in delinquency cases. Although the period of time when middle class white boys are not held fully responsible for their actions can extend well into their late twenties,[7] black children may be viewed as adults as soon as age 13, with the public and law enforcement overestimating the average age of black youth by more than 4.5 years.[8] These distorted perceptions mean that black children are more likely to be regarded and treated as adults much earlier than other youth, and less likely to receive the benefits and special considerations typically granted to youth. Couple this with evidence of racial bias in culpability assessments demonstrating that black youth and adults are perceived as more responsible and more dangerous than whites, it is easy to see how generations of black youth have been neglected as juvenile defendants and punished more severely in the criminal legal system, notwithstanding *Gault*.[9]

Against this tortured landscape, the right to counsel and other due process guarantees afforded in *Gault* are certainly important, but have not and will not be enough to ensure justice and equality for black youth. Advocates for black children have always understood that strategies to secure fundamental legal rights and protections for these youth would have to be paired with non-legal strategies contesting society's persistent disregard for black children, their development, and the well-being of the black community. As W.E.B. Du Bois often noted in his discussion of the "immortal child," at stake in this legal and extra-legal struggle were *collective* black social, economic, and political interests, linked to the fates of black youth.[10]

In the decades leading up to and immediately following *Gault*, the fight for racial equity in the juvenile justice system preceded on three over-lapping fronts. The movement began with self-help efforts and public outcry for institutional reform led by Progressive Era black women's clubs. These early and vital representatives of black youth and community interests in American youth justice insisted upon the recognition of black children as children and advocated for their related developmental rights and interests. These efforts continued and expanded in the 1930s as northern migration, voting rights, greater access to education and the professions, and other changes altered movement strategies and resources. These included the earliest cohorts of black officials who challenged unjust juvenile court systems and sought to expand black recognition, authority, and protection from within. Civil rights legislation and litigation would eventually join this mix, resulting in the dismantling of formal "Jim Crow" juvenile justice, if not separate and unequal treatment.

In our reflection on the fiftieth anniversary of the right to counsel for accused youth, we should pay special attention to the needs and challenges of black children, in part because they have borne a disproportionate share of the burden of the system's failures, historically and today.[11] To that end, this chapter begins with a discussion of the success and limits of *In re Gault* for black youth and then examines the efforts and successes of black activist leaders, including black court actors and civil rights lawyers, who were both explicit and intentional in their challenge to racial discrimination. We hope to draw insights from this history that will inform our contemporary fight for racial equity for all accused youth and help advocates fully implement the due process and equal protection victories of the Warren Court era.

Black children and the Warren Court

In 1963 and 1967, the Supreme Court under the leadership of Earl Warren guaranteed accused adults and youth the right to appointed counsel in criminal and juvenile courts in two seminal cases, *Gideon v. Wainwright*[12] and *In re Gault*,[13] respectively. Decided at the peak of the civil rights period, these cases arguably served as an important legal corollary to the civil rights struggle against racial discrimination as they appeared to be concerned about the way black defendants were being treated in the criminal and juvenile justice systems.[14] Collectively, the Court's school desegregation, criminal procedure, and juvenile justice decisions reflected a shift in constitutional jurisprudence to protect individual rights – especially the civil rights of racial minorities.[15] Thus, the Court's due process revolution appeared to be an intentional effort to protect minorities from state officials, impose procedural restraints on official discretion, and infuse governmental services with greater equality.[16] As such, the Warren Court is often remembered as a crusader of minority rights.[17] While we cannot wholly disagree with this assessment, the narrative warrants further scrutiny.

Although the Warren Court significantly reshaped the juvenile and criminal justice systems and seemed to share a genuine respect for the rights of accused defendants,[18] race was almost never explicitly discussed in its criminal procedure and juvenile justice opinions.[19] Moreover, in practice, many of the Warren Court's rulings provided only marginal benefit to black defendants, while others were outright harmful. For example, notwithstanding its locus in the backlash against blacks in Cleveland during the civil rights era,[20] the Court's 1968 ruling in *Terry v. Ohio* never explicitly discussed race and arguably pronounced one of the most harmful legal outcomes for black males of all time. In *Terry*, the Court was asked to decide whether the Fourth Amendment's prohibition on unreasonable searches and seizures is violated when a police officer stops and frisks a suspect on the street for investigatory purposes without probable cause to arrest. In permitting the officer's intrusion, the Court issued a broad ruling that now permits officers to engage civilians in an "investigatory stop" based on "reasonable articulable suspicion" – a standard much lower and arguably even more ambiguous than probable cause.[21]

Ironically, the Court in *Terry* explicitly acknowledged the tenuous relationship between police, youth, and minorities when it conceded in a footnote that

> [t]he frequency with which "frisking" forms a part of the field interrogation practice … cannot help but be a severely exacerbating factor in police-community tensions[,] … particularly … in situations where the "stop and frisk" of youths or minority group members is "motivated by the officers' perceived need to maintain the power image of the beat officer."[22]

The Court further acknowledged that the "degree of community resentment aroused by particular practices is clearly relevant to an assessment of the quality of the intrusion upon reasonable expectations of personal security caused by those practices."[23]Notwithstanding these acknowledgments, the Court quickly dismissed these considerations – still in a footnote, stating that

> the abusive practices which play a major … role in creating this friction are not susceptible of control by means of the exclusionary rule, and cannot properly dictate our decision with respect to the powers of the police in genuine investigative and preventive situations.[24]

Unfortunately, the Warren Court and the Courts thereafter have been consistently unwilling to use the Fourth Amendment to address abusive and discriminatory police conduct and have persisted with a reasonable articulable suspicion standard that exacerbates the disproportionate contact between police and black Americans.[25]

Even more relevant to our discussion here are *Gideon v. Wainright* and *In re Gault*, which together gave indigent defendants the right to appointed counsel in criminal and delinquency proceedings, but made no mention of the unique needs of racial minorities – maybe because the defendants in both cases were white, maybe because the Court was not wholly committed to racial equality in the criminal justice context, or maybe because the pressure from whites to suppress violent black protest during the civil rights era was too great. Regardless of its motives, the Court took no opportunity to articulate a commitment to rooting out discrimination "root and branch" from the criminal justice system as it had done in *Brown v. Board of Education.*[26] The Court's failure to address racial discrimination head on left a significant gap in the fight for racial equality in the juvenile justice system.

The limits of the Court's due process revolution were arguably even more apparent for black youth than black adults since children did not benefit from the full array of procedural protections afforded by jury trials in adult cases.[27] As Professor Sara Sun Beale notes:

> Although the Warren Court was well aware of the problems of racial oppression and its effects in the criminal justice system, it did not respond directly to

> those problems. Instead, the Court adopted race-neutral procedural mechanisms to increase the general fairness of the criminal justice process, and it imposed no real check on the discriminatory exercise of prosecutorial discretion. The Court recognized the possibility that the discriminatory exercise of law enforcement authority could violate the Equal Protection Clause, but made it virtually impossible to prove such a claim. The Warren Court did extend the right to trial by jury to a wide range of cases in the state systems, and it enforced the right to a jury drawn from a cross-section of society from which the prosecutor could not exclude individual jurors on the basis of their race. To some extent the right to a jury trial serves as a check on racial bias or discrimination by the prosecutor, but that check is not available in the juvenile court system. Thus ... juvenile defendants have no real means of challenging the prosecutor's exercise of discretion in their cases.[28]

The limits of *Gault* and other due process protections in the court were exacerbated by the lack of black political and legislative representation in American juvenile justice. While generations of activists had increased black dominion in this institutional context, the federalization and nationalization of crime control policy marginalized voices of black constituents, including their interests in delinquency prevention, gun control, and rehabilitative services, leaving black youth and their appointed counsel to contend with an increasingly punitive system.[29]

Within this context, *Gault* arguably imposed other – possibly unintended – harms on black youth. As Professor Barry Feld has argued, *Gault's* insistence on procedural safeguards legitimated a growing imposition of punitive sentences that fell disproportionately on minority offenders.[30] Scholars also worried that the Court's new emphasis on procedural due process would convert juvenile courts into replicas of the criminal courts and obscure the "real needs" of youth in the system.[31] Arguably, while black youth were granted more procedural rights in the due process revolution, the new system facilitated the increased criminalization of black youth and limited their already tenuous access to what remained of the rehabilitative ideals.

For all of its good, and much like its noted predecessor *Brown,* the *Gault* ruling did not do enough to free the juvenile justice system of racial discrimination. In the 50 years since *Gault*, due process protections have not only done little to reduce the hyper surveillance of black youth by police or to ensure that black youth enjoy the mitigating benefits of "childhood," but they have also arguably contributed to black youth being drawn deeper into the juvenile and criminal systems. As such, in remembering *Gault*, we must revisit both the flaws and the victories in the historical fight against racial injustice, in part to better inform strategies for advancing equal youth justice today.

The fight for recognition of black childhood

The recognition of black childhood as a legally relevant status and a basis for access to developmental opportunities and resources is fundamental to the struggle for equitable youth justice. While mainstream Progressive reformers were fighting in the early twentieth century to save white and immigrant children from adult penal institutions and provide them with rehabilitative services and treatment, marginalized black leaders fought for their youth to be recognized as children and adolescents, equally deserving of investments in their human potential.

From the inception of the first juvenile courts, mainstream reformers focused their efforts on "normaliz[ing]" poor white, particularly European immigrant youth they believed to be neglected and delinquent, and assimilating them into the white body politic. They did not often contemplate the rehabilitation and "citizen-building" of "Negro" and other nonwhite children.[32] Child welfare facilities that were opened in the Progressive era were typically restricted to white youth deemed salvageable in part because of their "racial stock."[33] Black children were often excluded on the grounds that their presence would "degrade" white youth and undermine their salvation, and on the basis of their own supposedly immutable depravity.[34] In popular culture, politics, and law, black children were routinely caricatured as a "perennial 'lost cause' … lacking the physical, moral, and intellectual capacity on which normalization would depend."[35]

Such claims and exclusions were often explicit before the 1960s. In a 1906 speech Mississippi's governor described, "a dollar invested in the development of the mind of a white child … the best investment the State ever made," but "every dollar invested on negro education … an indefensible and unwarranted prodigality of cash."[36] State and local leaders across the United States invested little in juvenile justice services for black youth before the courts forced them to. In 1943 Missouri's governor vetoed a planned appropriation of $5,000 for the over-crowded black-run reformatory for black girls in the state, claiming the funds "exceeded the girls' needs by $4,297.00"[37] When state reformatories accepted black children, they were assigned to the "colored section" not only bereft of many services, but also organized to reproduce white racial dominance and black subordination.[38] Although these homes educated white youth and trained them to be farmers and skilled artisans, contributing to their prospects for mobility, black boys received little if any recreation, education, and moral instruction, and were instead forced into agricultural and other manual labor.[39] Black girls were trained to be cooks, maids, and seamstresses.[40] Early institutions were in essence organized to reproduce racial-caste relations.

White juvenile justice reformers and other civic leaders in the North were scarcely more invested in citizen-building for black youth than their counterparts in the South. As blacks migrated from the rural South to the urban North during the Great Migration (1916–70), Northern whites reacted with fear and hostility that forced blacks into segregated urban ghettos.[41] Although Northerners were somewhat more willing than Southerners to accommodate black youth in segregated juvenile facilities, they were also hostile to black families who had migrated North in search of work and discriminated against black youth who might benefit from resources and apprenticeship opportunities available to other youth.[42] Even Jane Addams, a leading opponent of race discrimination and segregation in the Child Savers era seemed to accept stereotypes about working class black families when she suggested that immigrant parents were more capable than black parents of preventing sexual immortality and delinquency among their daughters and that colored girls did not have mothers who could serve as "true women" and moral instructors.[43] Addams ran one of the most prominent settlement houses in Chicago (the Hull House), but it too was marred by racial prejudice as white settlement workers and immigrant patrons sought to differentiate themselves from blacks, in part by excluding or discriminating against black youth.[44] As a result, black youth often languished in what were intended as short-term detention facilities, and were refused access to services prioritized for white youth. Chicago's chief probation officer, Harry Hill, lamented in 1927 that, "practically no institutions are to be found in the community to which [black] children may be admitted."[45]

Black leaders did not passively watch black children suffer exclusion from the benefits of the rehabilitative ideal and juvenile court movement, but rather, mobilized to counter threats to the black child and the collective interests of black communities. Efforts to address the lack of services for alleged delinquent and at-risk black youth manifested in three key ways: social and political advocacy by predominantly black women leaders, institutional reform efforts of black professionals (e.g., probation officers and judges), and equal protection litigation to dismantle the legal system of Jim Crow juvenile justice.

Black women's clubs: voluntary and vital representatives

During the half-century preceding *Gault*, black women's clubs were instrumental in organizing against ideological and institutional elements of "Jim Crow" juvenile justice. They challenged racist and sexist myths about black youth and contested policies and practices that denied black youth access to rehabilitative ideals and resources, such as vocational training.[46] When all else failed, as was typically the case, black women created and operated rehabilitative institutions themselves.

Black women railed against several prevailing racial stereotypes about black delinquents, including the "Jezebel" myth, the delinquent black mother stereotype, and the delinquent black community paradigm.[47] Black women resisted the portrayal of "delinquent" black girls as the modern Jezebel who symbolized lust, sexual immorality, "innate wickedness," and even "disobedience to God."[48] In particular, club women sought to prevent black girls from being sent to reform schools where they might be involuntarily sterilized and subject to physical and sexual abuse by staff and guards who saw them as sexually promiscuous.[49]

Black women also challenged the myth that black women were unable to raise moral and well-behaved children and resisted the stereotype that black families lived in degenerate neighborhoods that inherently bred delinquent children.[50] In response to a chief concern among white reformers that black women could not be home to control their children because they had to seek employment as cooks, housecleaners, laundresses, caretakers, and domestics to satisfy their basic economic needs,[51] black women's clubs began to fill the gaps in services for black youth who were abandoned, delinquent, or at risk.

Angered over lynching, convict leases, and work gangs that were common responses to perceived criminality among blacks during the Jim Crow era, organizations like the National Association of Colored Women (NACW) made criminal and juvenile justice issues a significant part of their civil rights agenda from 1899–1930.[52] Black women's clubs brought food and clothing to incarcerated black youth, opened and operated several rehabilitative homes and schools for black children, fought for juvenile rights through social work, raised money for legal campaigns, and became probation officers in order to extend services to black children.[53]

The national, regional, and local networks of black club women became a primary means of establishing black child welfare protections.[54] To fill the gaps left by white institutions, black women across the South and the North started settlement houses, kindergartens, orphanages, and other institutions, including juvenile courts and reformatories. Frances Joseph-Gaudet, a prison reformer and founder of the Colored Industrial Home and School in New Orleans, Louisiana, worked tirelessly to save black youth who were poor, homeless, and neglected.[55] After hearing about a black woman's child who had been jailed, Gaudet started a prison ministry. These efforts, along with those of the Prison Reform Association and the Era Club of New Orleans led to the establishment of the first juvenile court in New Orleans in 1903.[56] Gaudet worked to rehabilitate young blacks arrested for misdemeanors or vagrancy and became the first woman to support young black offenders in Louisiana, even arranging to take custody and care of court-involved youth in her home.[57]

Janie Porter Barrett was the leading advocate for black dependents and delinquents in Virginia.[58] In 1907, Barrett helped organize the Virginia State Federation of Colored Women's Clubs and made juvenile justice reform a top priority for the organization.[59] With Barrett's impetus and support, Virginia club women raised money and purchased land for a rehabilitation center for delinquent girls – The Industrial Home for Wayward Colored Girls, which later became the Virginia Industrial School for Colored Girls.[60] The school opened with two girls in 1915 and was the first home for delinquent black girls in the South.[61] When girls were released from the home at the age of 17, Barrett and her staff supervised their reintegration into community placements because there were no parole officers for these youth. Barrett dedicated 25 years of her life to the Virginia Industrial School for Colored Girls and was its superintendent until about 1940.[62]

Similar institutions were established in every Southern state and several Northern cities. In 1920, when most blacks still lived in the South, nearly 80 percent of blacks outside the South resided in urban settings.[63] Although the juvenile court movement was concentrated in cities, racial segregation left growing numbers of black city dwellers with few child welfare resources, notwithstanding interventions of black women's clubs and other civic leaders. Dynamics of exclusion were evolving and so too their opposition. Although social service efforts continued, black leaders increasingly looked to change juvenile justice policies and practices, leveraging growing access to voting rights and representation in positions of authority.

Fighting from within: black authorities weigh in

As discrimination persisted and related violence and inequality flourished, the predominantly black women leaders driving juvenile justice reform sought to infiltrate the justice system and fight for changes from within. This strategy was not entirely new or distinct, as it often coincided with ameliorative and voluntary social service work, yet it markedly altered the juvenile justice bureaucracies and policies over the middle-third of the twentieth century.

Many black women entered the social work profession in the 1920s.[64] While most were public health nurses, family welfare agents, and probation officers, a few women were hired by the courts, prisons, and parole offices.[65] Black women entered the system at a time when probation offices insisted that children could only be assigned to a probation officer of the same race. Taking advantage of the increasing need for black probation officers, many black women volunteered or accepted very low pay to serve in probation departments in the juvenile courts.[66] Eventually, black women waged campaigns for black probation officers to be hired and paid.

Elizabeth McDonald was the first black woman to serve as a juvenile court probation officer – as a volunteer – in 1901 in Chicago.[67] Because she was only allowed to visit children of her same race, she supervised all the black children in the department. As McDonald became increasingly troubled by the number of dependent youth who were put in jails for delinquency, she established the Louise Juvenile Home of Chicago in 1907 and the Louise Training School for Colored Boys in 1913.[68]

Similarly, in 1910, black citizens in Memphis noted disparities in services for black and white juvenile delinquents and raised funds to pay for a separate detention home for black youth. Eventually a Negro Probation Department was established as part of the juvenile court, and Julia Hooks, a black teacher and superintendent in the Memphis public school system, was named matron and chief probation officer for the new Department.[69] Memphis' white juvenile court judge Camille Kelley later invited Hooks to help with black juvenile cases.[70]

Black probation officers were vital in supporting black youth in the juvenile system. Although Ida B. Wells is widely remembered as a staunch advocate against lynching, founder of the National Association for the Advancement of Colored People (NAACP), and an advocate for women's suffrage,[71] she was also a juvenile probation officer. Working as a probation officer until 1916, Wells' relentless efforts against Jim Crow segregation and dedication to juvenile rehabilitation in Chicago were monumental. For example, Wells used her own money in 1910 to fund efforts to create and maintain the Negro Fellowship League and used the League office as a reporting station for her probationers.[72] She also created the first African-American kindergarten in her community, helped black men find employment, challenged the harassment of black youth in Chicago – including her own sons – by white gangs, and raised awareness for youth wrongly accused of crime and delinquency.[73]

From the early to mid-twentieth century, several black women were able to break through the proverbial glass ceiling of racial discrimination to become more powerful legal and government authorities, including lawyers and judges. Many of these women were effective in securing reforms for black youth in the juvenile justice system. In 1912, Gertrude E. Durden Rush, one of the first black women admitted to the bar in Iowa, organized the Charity League in Des Moines, which succeeded in having a black probation officer placed in the local juvenile court.[74] Rush also guided the league in founding the Protection Home for Negro Girls and later served as the case worker in the Associated Charities of the town.[75]

This professionalization of child welfare and other reform work was increasingly encouraged by black women leaders, including the National Council of Negro Women. The founding president of the council, Mary McLeod Bethune, helped elevate black youth issues to a national level. In 1935, Bethune became the first black woman appointed to a federal office when President Roosevelt appointed her as director of the Division of Negro Affairs of the National Youth Administration (NYA).[76] Bethune's concern was not to integrate youth programs, but to instead force NYA programs to train black youth for more rewarding services and occupations than were traditionally allowed under Jim Crow and to ensure black supervision of black programs and increase black participation in policymaking.[77] Later, Bethune participated in a conference on child welfare in President Calvin Coolidge's administration and served on a committee on child health for President Herbert Hoover.[78]

In 1931, Jane Bolin became the first black woman to graduate from Yale Law School, and in 1939, the first black woman judge in the United States.[79] In New York, Bolin was instrumental in serving youth from 1939–1979 as the judge of the Domestic Relations Court of the City of New York, which became the Family Court of the State of New York.[80] During her 40 years on the bench, Bolin fought tirelessly against discrimination in youth justice. For example, early on she realized that probation officer assignments and access to court services were segregated by race and religion. Her opposition to this practice before the City Council and the Board of Estimates of the City, in partnership with the NAACP, led to the passage of legislation barring public funding of institutions that denied services on the basis of race.[81]

Marjorie McKenzie Lawson and Elizabeth Davis Pittman also used their status and influence as judges to improve the plight of black youth in juvenile courts. Lawson served on the District of Columbia Juvenile Court from 1960–1965 and was the first black woman appointed to the bench by a President.[82] Lawson continued to work with President Kennedy after he signed a bill to create three juvenile courts in Washington, D.C., and in 1960 served on Kennedy's Democratic campaign by directing research and advice on civil rights and campaign issues.[83]

Pittman was the first black woman to graduate from Creighton University School of Law and was appointed to the bench in 1971.[84] Pittman was the first black and first female judge in Nebraska and was likely the first black woman in the nation appointed as judge by a governor.[85] Judge Pittman was tough on crime, but used her position to advocate and inform people about issues of particular concern to black communities, including juvenile justice.[86] She was also a strong advocate for parental accountability and believed that probation and rehabilitation, not incarceration, were appropriate to build productive members of society.[87]

Like reformers before them, Judge Pittman and other black professionals advanced equal justice in juvenile courts, yet their practical and policy interventions would not spare their own or later generations of black children from discrimination in the juvenile justice system. Further, there were growing signs that integration would not ensure equality. As Judge Bolin lamented at the end of her career, in the late 1970s, "the whole philosophy of the juvenile court was changed," encouraging greater treatment of children as adult criminals.[88] Black youth and communities gaining formal access to juvenile courts and reformatories would be distinctly subject to this newfangled yet long familiar ordeal of exclusion, which withheld recognition of black childhood, and limited black authority, ultimately denying black youth the equal protection of rehabilitative ideals.

Demanding equal protection: the civil rights enforcement cases

By the 1960s the struggle against anti-black racism in American juvenile justice as elsewhere was in full throttle, operating on multiple fronts. While black women's clubs and growing ranks of professionals were fighting to have black children recognized and treated as children through social protests, service provision, and institutional reform, civil rights lawyers used litigation to fight exclusion, segregation, and disparate provision of services in state juvenile justice facilities. Beginning in the early 1960s and continuing for at least a decade, lawyers launched a series of equal protection challenges to desegregate state juvenile justice institutions and reform schools. As is common in any effective campaign for reform, these legal strategies were an important complement to the extra-legal strategies advanced by other civic leaders.[89] Lawyers understood that equal protection victories would make the informal and geographically variable extra legal achievements legally binding and nationwide. These lawyers also likely understood that the due process victories secured in *Gideon v. Wainwright* and *In re Gault* would be insufficient to curtail blatant discrimination in the provision of services and treatment to black youth.

Following the framework of *Brown v. Board of Education*,[90] lawyers demanded access to white juvenile justice facilities, including equality of services for black youth in those facilities and black employment among system officials. For example, when an African-American youth, Robert Myers, was adjudicated delinquent in Maryland in 1961 and due to be committed to a reform school, lawyers moved to have Myers sent to the all-white reform school rather than the all-black school.[91] Contending that Maryland's facilities for the detention and training of delinquent minors were actually "schools," the youth filed a bill of complaint to have the system of racially segregated reform schools declared unconstitutional.[92] Lawyers further argued that the black school, Boys' Village, could not provide Myers with rehabilitation and educational training equal to that provided to white youth at the Maryland Training School.[93] The trial court ruled in Myers' favor, providing one of the first legal victories in the country for the equality of services for black youth in the juvenile justice system. In finding the system of racially segregated reform schools illegal, the court agreed with Myers' claims that the reform schools were more like schools than a detention facility and thus subject to the laws regarding the integration of public schools. Mimicking *Brown,* the court stated that in the field of public education, the doctrine of "separate but equal" has no place and separate educational facilities are inherently unequal.[94]

A few years after the Maryland litigation, four "Negro juveniles," aged 16–18, were arrested and charged with trespass for sitting in a segregated restaurant in St. Augustine, Florida. The ordeal was shared by many black children and youth who exercised their rights to advocate for change. In Mississippi, teenager Brenda Travis was given an indeterminate sentence to the segregated state training school after multiple arrests for peaceful protest, leaving her mother to lament the cruel irony that Brenda was labeled delinquent and "taken away ... because she was determined to get her rights."[95] In the St. Augustine case, Judge Charles C. Mathis of the Juvenile Court of St. Johns County, Florida, offered to let the youth off with probation if they stopped protesting, but they refused, as did their parents. In a class action claim filed when the youth were sent to reform schools, the plaintiffs sought to desegregate the Florida state reform schools. The plaintiffs sued on behalf of "all Negro juveniles committed or subject to commitment to the schools under the Board's jurisdiction."[96] The complaint alleged that "white and Negro inmates of the schools are separated; that certain courses and recreational facilities available to Whites are denied to Negroes; and that the assignment of staff members at the schools is based on race."[97] Ruling in support of the plaintiffs and requiring reform schools to desegregate, the United States Court of Appeals for the Fifth Circuit again relied on *Brown.*[98]

Shortly thereafter, lawyers in an Alabama prisoners' class action suit, *Washington v. Lee*, sought to have the practice of racially segregating all prisoners (including juvenile prisoners), and the state statutes requiring such practice, declared a violation of the prohibition on cruel and unusual punishment and of the Equal Protection Clause of the U.S. Constitution.[99] The case was filed on behalf of "one white and five Negro citizens" and on behalf of other persons similarly situated. In rejecting the prison officials' claims that racial segregation of prisoners was designed to maintain security and discipline, and thus did not violate the Equal Protection Clause, the court reiterated that federal law did not tolerate racial discrimination by governmental authorities in the use of public facilities. Although it declined to issue a formal injunction, the court ruled that the practice of racially segregating prisoners, and the statutes requiring it, violated the Equal Protection Clause, and ordered officials to desegregate all prisons and jails in Alabama within specified time periods.[100] Interestingly, although the Court did not require an immediate and total desegregation of state, county, and city adult penal facilities in the state (allowing instead for almost the same lag time allowed in *Brown*), it did order that the honor farms, educational programs, youth centers, and hospitals in the state system be completely desegregated immediately.[101]

In the same year as *Gault*, another desegregation case surfaced in Arkansas. A black mother and her minor son brought suit seeking relief under civil rights statutes, 28 U.S.C. § 1981 and § 1983.[102] This suit was brought as a class action against the respective Board of Managers of the Arkansas Training School for Boys at Wrightsville and at Pine Bluff for the maintenance of a separate "training school for white and Negro juveniles."[103] It was alleged that the plaintiffs were being deprived of their right to equal treatment, privileges, and opportunities by the State of Arkansas solely because of their race or color. Citing *Brown*, the court found that in the field of public education, "separate educational facilities are inherently unequal" and held that the statutes are clearly unconstitutional to the extent that they require commitment to and maintenance of segregated juvenile facilities.[104]

In the four years after *In re Gault*, three additional desegregation cases helped shape the landscape favorably for minority youth.[105] In 1969, in *Major v. Sowers*, lawyers filed a class action claim to desegregate the Louisiana state youth correctional institutions and declare the state statutes that required racial segregation at these institutions unconstitutional.[106] In a second case, *Crum v. State Training School for Girls* (1969), lawyers brought a class action for the desegregation of three reform schools: the Alabama Boys Industrial School, the State Training School for Girls, and the Alabama Industrial School for Negro Children, all in the state of Alabama.[107] The case was remanded in 1969 with an order for the three schools to coordinate their planning and present one plan for the system as a whole that would accomplish immediate and total desegregation of each school. In 1971, lawyers brought another class action suit seeking desegregation of the Alabama Industrial School for Negro Children (referred to as Mt. Meigs).[108] Advocates argued that the black facility was not only inferior to white facilities, but also that staff at the black facilities engaged in harmful practices, such as corporal punishment. The court ruled for the plaintiffs and issued a decree requiring that white facilities accept males regardless of race, prohibiting corporal punishment, and mandating a number of other program and facility improvements.[109]

This series of desegregation victories posed a direct and immediate challenge to institutional racism in the juvenile justice system, at least as it was formally organized. They also provided an important complement to other noted efforts to recognize and protect the developmental interests and rights of black youth. Collectively, the cases brought added attention to extreme racial disparities in the juvenile justice system, and, at least for a time, reaffirmed the idea that juvenile justice institutions should function like schools, with a rehabilitative and educational focus, for the benefit of all youth and community stakeholders. By challenging racial discrimination explicitly, the plaintiffs and their lawyers forced state courts to take sides on the question of racial justice. Even as doubt lingered about whether the Supreme Court was truly committed to eliminating racial discrimination in juvenile and criminal courts during the due process revolution, lawyers found at least a handful of state courts that were willing to tackle discrimination head on.

Ultimately, the Equal Protection Clause proved to be a more effective tool than the Due Process Clause in the fight against systemic discrimination and disparity, yet both proved limited in actually securing black recognition, authority, and protection in youth justice. While *Gault's* guarantee of access to counsel and other due process protections inadvertently legitimized punitive and disparate treatment of black youth, desegregation cases requiring integration of youth and institutional staff did not ensure either equal access to rehabilitative services or community control over institutional resources. In 1967, as the fight for reformatory desegregation was being waged and won, President Lyndon Johnson's Commission on Law Enforcement and the Administration of Justice proposed a two-track approach to juvenile justice administration that was tailored to criminal and noncriminal jurisdictions. The noncriminal delinquency track still emphasized rehabilitative ideals, informal intervention such as diversion, and community-based strategies. The criminal track institutionalized the penal logic of just deserts in juvenile justice, subjecting boys and girls labeled as more serious delinquents to greater punishment and control. By the mid-1970s, state legislatures revised their statutes to stress juvenile culpability and accountability, with an emphasis on punishment and public safety over the best interests of the child, and prosecutors disproportionately imposed this "undeserving offender" label on black and brown youth.[110]

Further, while ordering the integration of professional and non-professional staff, the federal court held that race must be irrelevant to justice administration. By limiting the local influence and discretion of black juvenile justice authorities, these and other "color-blind" remedies, including the later introduction of mandatory sanctioning, automatic adult court transfer, and other "standardized decision-making," restricted possibilities for more inclusive racial politics, including the anti-racist advocacy demonstrated by generations of black activists and authorities. Integrated black authorities were expected to enlighten juvenile justice administration, contributing unique standpoints and leadership through more inclusive processes, but in key ways they remained estranged. Reorganization of juvenile justice by *Gault* and other legal and extra-legal developments, constrained and relocated discretion in ways that limited black community input and authority in juvenile justice law, policy, and practice.[111]

Conclusion

As we celebrate the legacy of lawyers who advocated for Gideon Wainwright and Gerald Gault, we cannot forget the broader legacy of legal and extra-legal advocacy for black children in the juvenile justice system. This history teaches us important lessons about the stakes and dynamics of institutional change. It reminds us that while white and immigrant children were seeking procedural protections such as the right to confront witnesses before services and sanctions could be imposed, black children were and are still fighting for the right to be recognized, represented, and protected as children, and thus the right to developmental ideals and resources traditionally reserved for white youth. Black youth have faced unique challenges of discrimination that could not wait for and were not resolved by procedural victories secured in *Gault* and other due process cases.

More important, this history reminds us that justice systems are contested institutions.[112] Advocacy for racial equity in the juvenile justice system has proceeded along a number of parallel and complementary tracks over a long span of time. There can be little doubt that the vocal protests of black club women in the years leading up to and during the civil rights movement laid the foundation for later interventions, including work to dismantle Jim Crow juvenile justice systems from within and, later, litigation in civil rights enforcement cases. Realizing that due process victories in the federal court would not translate into a clear mandate against racial discrimination in the states, lawyers turned to equal protection litigation in state courts to supplement other legal and non-legal strategies for reform.

Our celebration of the right to counsel for youth in the juvenile justice system should acknowledge the generations of predominantly black women leaders who fought for equal recognition, representation, and protection in the juvenile system, along with the cadre of civil rights lawyers who explicitly demanded desegregation of youth justice. Acting through extra-legal and legal means due to the gender and race constraints of the times, black women Child Savers helped shaped law and policy and were among the most effective advocates for black youth in the juvenile justice system. These social, professional, and legal movements, working in tandem from the inception of the juvenile courts through the Court's ruling in *Gault*, and beyond, deserve a great deal more credit for whatever "constitutional domestication" American juvenile justice has seen.[113]

Unfortunately, these victories were limited and the struggle must go on as race-based denials of recognition, authority, and protection persist in American juvenile justice. Neither the due process victories secured by *In re Gault* nor the equal protection victories of the desegregation cases have been sufficient to eliminate this discrimination. Implicit and explicit racial biases continue to deprive black youth of the right to be recognized and treated as children in the juvenile justice system. Centuries old notions that black youth are irredeemable, and undeserving of child-welfare services, endure today. Today juvenile courts across the country undermine the procedural guarantees of *Gault* by allowing children to waive counsel, imposing exorbitant attorney's fees on indigent youth, delaying appointment of counsel until after critical stages like arraignment, and failing to provide juvenile defenders with adequate training and resources.[114] Early equal protection victories have lost their vitality in the fight against disparity as police officers and prosecutors exercise tremendous discretion to arrest and prosecute blacks at disproportionately higher rates than white youth, and as public schools in poor, urban, predominately black communities deploy in-school police surveillance, judges allow black youth to penetrate more deeply into the juvenile and criminal legal systems, and state legislators allow youth in urban centers to reside in treatment facilities with deplorable conditions and little access to rehabilitative services.

Now, 50 years after *Gault*, advocates will need to identify new strategies to address the problem of racial injustice in the juvenile court. As new challenges arise and states continue to stumble in their implementation of due process and equal protection mandates, legal and non-legal advocates must continue to think creatively about how to address the unique needs of African American youth in the juvenile justice system. Here we can find both inspiration and direction from the past, drawing energy and ideas from the long movement on behalf of the besieged and still "immortal" black child.[115]

Notes

1 In re Gault, 387 U.S. 1 (1967); Kent v. U.S., 383 US 541 (1966). The Supreme Court's due process revolution is typically understood as the period between 1961 and 1969, during which the Court expanded the rights of criminal defendants under the leadership of Earl Warren, who was Chief Justice of the Supreme Court from October 5, 1953–June 23, 1969.

2 Geoff K. Ward, The Black Child-Savers: Racial Democracy & Juvenile Justice 39, 52–53, 60, 86–87 (The University of Chicago Press, 2012).

3 *Id.* at 38–39, 86–87.

4 *Id.* at 53–56; Michael Mechanic & Nina Berman, *It Was Kind of Like Slavery*, Mother Jones (Feb. 19, 2014), http://www.motherjones.com/politics/2014/02/returning-to-dozier-florida-school-for-boys (last visited Dec. 26, 2017).

5 Cheryl Nelson Butler, *Blackness as Delinquency*, 90 Wash. U. L. Rev. 1335, 1388–89 (2013); *see generally* James D. Anderson, The Education of Blacks in the South, 1860–1935 (University of North Carolina Press, 1988) (discussing racist opposition to black education in the South, from Reconstruction to the Great Depression, and black resilience and self-determination in education).

6 L. Song Richardson & Phillip Atiba Goff, *Implicit Racial Bias in Public Defender Triage*, 122 Yale L.J. 2630 (2013); Jennifer L. Eberhardt et al., *Seeing Black: Race, Crime, and Visual Processing*, 87 J. Personality & Soc. Psychol. 876, 890 (2004).

7 Michael Kimmel, Guyland: The Perilous World Where Boys Become Men 6, 8 (Harper Collins, 2008).

8 Phillip Atiba Goff et al., *Essence of Innocence: Consequences of Dehumanizing Black Children*, 106 J. of Personality and Soc. Psychology 4, 526–545 (2014).

9 *See, e.g.*, George S. Bridges & Sara Steen, *Racial Disparities in Official Assessments of Juvenile Offenders: Attributional Stereotypes as Mediating Mechanisms*, 63 Am. Soc. Rev. 554, 561 (1998) (discussing an empirical study in which probation officers' narratives about the youth they supervised were analyzed for attributions of character, likeliness to reoffend, and sentencing, resulting in a finding that officers view black youth as more personally responsible and likely to reoffend than white counterparts); Sandra Graham & Brian S. Lowery, *Priming Unconscious Racial Stereotypes About Adolescent Offenders*, Law and Human Behavior (2004), https://www.gsb.stanford.edu/faculty-research/working-papers/priming-unconscious-racial-stereotypes-about-adolescent-offenders (last visited Dec. 26, 2017) (finding that implicit racial biases of police and probation officers correspond to negative trait ratings, perceived culpability, expected recidivism, and endorsement of harsher punishments); *Investigation of the St. Louis County Family Court*, U.S. Dep't of Justice, Civil Rights Division 13 (July 31, 2015) (reporting inadequate legal representation and that "St. Louis County Family Court engages in conduct that violates the constitutional guarantee of Equal Protection. Even after controlling for other factors such as gender, age, risk factors, and severity of the allegation, we find that Black children are disproportionately represented in decisions to: formally charge youth versus handle matters informally; detain youth pre-trial; commit youth under existing Court supervision to Division of Youth Services custody; and place youth in a secure Division of Youth Services facility after conviction.").

10 W. E. B. DuBois, *The Immortal Child*, 12 The Crisis 267–71 (1916); Ward, *supra* note 2, at 71–72.

11 *See* Ward, *supra* note 2; Barry C. Feld, Bad Kids: Race and the Transformation of the Juvenile Court (Oxford University Press, 1999) [hereinafter Bad Kids].

12 Gideon v. Wainwright, 372 U.S. 335 (1963).
13 In re Gault, 387 U.S. 1 (1967).
14 Gabriel Chin, *Race and the Disappointing Right to Counsel*, 122 YALE L. J. 2236 (2013); Burt Neuborne, *The Gravitational Pull of Race on the Warren Court*, 2010 SUP. CT. REV. 59, 86 (2010) ("[T]he right to counsel cases from Gideon to Argersinger were driven, in part, by concern over a criminal justice system where white judges and prosecutors processed poor, unrepresented blacks and Hispanics.").
15 Barry C. Feld, *Race, Politics, and Juvenile Justice: The Warren Court and the Conservative "Backlash"*, 87 MINN. L. REV. 1447, 1451 (2003); *see also* Louis Michael Seidman, *Brown and Miranda*, 80 CALIF. L. REV. 673, 678 (1992).
16 Feld, *supra* note 15, at 1477.
17 *See generally* Gray A. Debele, *The Due Process Revolution and the Juvenile Court: The Matter of Race in the Historical Evolution of Doctrine*, 5 LAW & INEQ. 513 (1987).
18 *See* Joan Rapczynski, *The Legacy of the Warren Court*, YALE-NEW HAVEN TEACHERS INSTITUTE, http://www.yale.edu/ynhti/curriculum/units/2004/1/04.01.07.x.html (last visited Jan. 5, 2017); Sara Sun Beale, *You've Come a Long Way, Baby: Two Waves of Juvenile Justice Reforms as Seen from Jena, Louisiana*, 44 HARV. C.R.-C.L. L. REV. 511, 515 (2009).
19 *See, e.g.*, Heather Cobb, *Symposium Response: Separate and Unequal: The Disparate Impact of School-Based Referrals to Juvenile Court*, 44 HARV. C.R.-C.L. L. REV. 581, 587 (2009); Beale, *supra* note 18, at 524 (arguing that for all its groundbreaking decisions, the Warren Court neglected to discuss race when deciding the criminal procedure cases during the civil rights era).
20 *See* Renee Hutchins, *Stop Terry: Reasonable Suspicion, Race, and a Proposal to Limit Terry Stops*, 16 N.Y.U. J. LEGIS. & PUB. POL'Y 883, 886–92 (2013) (discussing the social and racial dynamics in Cleveland and the nation in the years leading up to Terry v. Ohio).
21 Terry v. Ohio, 392 U.S. 1 (1968).
22 *Id.* at 14 n.11 (quoting LAWRENCE P. TIFFANY ET AL., DETECTION OF CRIME: STOPPING AND QUESTIONING, SEARCH AND SEIZURE, ENCOURAGEMENT AND ENTRAPMENT 47–48 (Frank J. Reimington ed., Little, Brown, 1967).
23 *Id.* at 17 n.14.
24 *Id.; see also* discussion Mia Carpiniello, *Striking a Sincere Balance: A Reasonable Black Person Standard for "Location Plus Evasion" Terry Stops*, 6 MICH. J. RACE & L. 355, 355 (2001).
25 *See, e.g.*, Whren v. United States, 517 U.S. 806, 813 (1996) (holding that "the actual motivations of the individual officers" are irrelevant to the Fourth Amendment analysis and noting that these issues are better left to the Equal Protection Clause).
26 347 U.S. 483 (1954); *see also* Gabriel Chin, *Race and the Disappointing Right to Counsel*, 122 YALE L.J. 2236, 2238 (2013).
27 McKeiver v. Pennsylvania, 403 U.S. 528 (1971).
28 Beale, *supra* note 18, at 515.
29 WARD, *supra* note 2, at 248; nationalization and federalization refer to an increasingly national agenda to control juvenile crime and related changes to the political structure of juvenile justice policy and practice after 1950. The growing influence of federal and state governments marginalized local politicians, service professionals, and constituents. *See* LISE MILLER, THE PERILS OF FEDERALISM: RACE, POVERTY, AND THE POLITICS OF CRIME CONTROL 5–8 (Oxford University Press, 2008).
30 Barry C. Feld, *The Transformation of the Juvenile Court – Part II: Race and the "Crack Down" on Youth Crime*, 84 MINN. L. REV. 327, 350–79 (1999).
31 *Id.* at 350.
32 WARD, *supra* note 2, at 38–39, 86–87; *see* Robin Walker Sterling, *Fundamental Unfairness: In re Gault and the Road Not Taken*, 72 MD. L. REV. 607, 616–25

(2013) (describing the discrepancy in treatment and services between European youth and black youth).

33 Sanford J. Fox, *Juvenile Justice Reform: An Historical Perspective*, 22 STAN. L. REV. 1187, 1191 (1970); *see* WARD, *supra* note 2, at 86–87 (discussing claim that white youth were more amenable to rehabilitation by virtue of their "racial stock").

34 WARD, *supra* note 2, at 53.

35 *Id.* at 39, 52–53, 60, 86–87.

36 *Id.* at 82.

37 ETHEL BOWLES, BIENNIAL REPORT OF THE STATE INDUSTRIAL HOME FOR NEGRO GIRLS, IN BIENNIAL REPORT OF THE DEPARTMENT OF PENAL INSTITUTIONS, 1933–1934 435, 437 (Missouri Department of Penal Institutions, 1934); DOUGLAS E. ABRAMS, A VERY SPECIAL PLACE IN LIFE: THE HISTORY OF JUVENILE JUSTICE IN MISSOURI 106 (Missouri Juvenile Justice Association, 2003).

38 WARD, *supra* note 2, at 53–56; *see also* CTR. FOR CHILDREN'S LAW & POLICY, RED PRACTICE MANUAL 8 (2015), http://www.cclp.org/wp-content/uploads/2016/06/Introduction-and-Chapter-1-Beginning-or-Restarting-Work-to-Reduce-Racial-and-Ethnic-Disparities.pdf (last visited Dec. 26, 2017) ("In 1834 the first juvenile detention facility in the United States, the New York House of Refuge, excluded youth of color from rehabilitative services and consigned them to a 'colored' section, on the rationale that providing services to such youth was a 'waste of resources.'").

39 WARD, *supra* note 2, at 56–58, 74.

40 *Id.* at 56, 74.

41 FELD, *supra* note 30, at 340–45.

42 WARD, *supra* note 2, at 110–14.

43 WANDA A. HENDRICKS, GENDER, RACE, AND POLITICS IN THE MIDWEST: BLACK CLUB WOMEN IN ILLINOIS 56 (Indiana University Press, 1998); Butler, *supra* note 5, at 1389.

44 HENDRICKS, *supra* note 43, at 56 ("Even the YMCA, the YWCA, and the Salvation Army discriminated against blacks").

45 WARD, *supra* note 2, at 84; *see also* DAVID S. TANENHAUS, JUVENILE JUSTICE IN THE MAKING 37 (Oxford University Press, 2004).

46 Butler, *supra* note 5, at 1341.

47 *Id.*

48 *Id.* at 1385–87.

49 *Id.* at 1386.

50 *Id.* at 1388–89, 1393.

51 *Id.* at 1391–92.

52 *Id.* at 1340.

53 *See generally* BUTLER, *supra* note 5 (describing the variety of work black club women did for black youth and delinquent youth); *see* WARD, *supra* note 2, at 105–61.

54 HENDRICKS, *supra* note 43, at 56.

55 *See, e.g.*, SHIRELLE PHELPS, NOTABLE BLACK AMERICAN WOMEN 391–393 (Jessie Carney Smith, ed., Gale Research, 1992); WARD, *supra* note 2, at 132; *Francis Joseph Gaudet, Educator and Prison Reformer, 1934*, HOLY WOMEN, HOLY MEN BLOG (Dec. 30, 2010), https://liturgyandmusic.wordpress.com/2010/12/30/december-30-frances-joseph-gaudet-educator-and-prison-reformer-1934 (last visited Dec. 26, 2017).

56 WARD, *supra* note 2, at 132–33.

57 *Id.*

58 WARD, *supra* note 2, at 136–37.

59 WARD, *supra* note 2, at 138.

60 HENDRICKS, *supra* note 43, at 58.

61 FLORIS LORETTA BARNETT CASH, AFRICAN AMERICAN WOMEN AND SOCIAL ACTION: THE CLUBWOMEN AND VOLUNTEERISM FROM JIM CROW TO THE NEW DEAL, 1896–1936 72 (Greenwood, 2001).

62 *Id.* at 72; Phelps, *supra* note 55, at 57–58.
63 Hendricks, *supra* note 43, at 41.
64 Cash, *supra* note 61, at 130.
65 *Id.*
66 Anne Meis Knupfer, Reform and Resistance: Gender, Delinquency, and America's First Juvenile Court 64, n.91 (Routledge, 2001).
67 *See, e.g.*, Anne Meis Knupfer, *African-American Facilities for Dependent and Delinquent Children in Chicago, 1900 to 1920: The Louise Juvenile School and the Amanda Smith School*, 24 J. of Sociology & Soc. Welfare 3, 199 (2015); Tanenhaus, *supra* note 45, at 36; Ward, *supra* note 2, at 159.
68 Marcia Chatelain, The Most Interesting Girl of this Country is the Colored Girl: Girls and Racial Uplift in Great Migration Chicago, 1899–1950 48, n.84 (2008), https://repository.library.brown.edu/studio/item/bdr:262/PDF (last visited Dec. 26, 2017); *see also* Knupfer, *supra* note 66, at 49; Knupfer, *supra* note 67, at 199–202.
69 Jennifer Trost, Gateway to Justice: The Juvenile Court and Progressive Child Welfare in a Southern City 47 (The University of Georgia Press, 2005).
70 Ward, *supra* note 2, at 146; Phelps, *supra* note 55, at 511–13; African American Registry, *Julia Hooks, An Activist and Educator with Passion*, http://www.aaregistry.org/historic_events/view/julia-hooks-activist-and-educator-passion (last visited July 30, 2017).
71 Butler, *supra* note 5, at 1379–80.
72 Hendricks, *supra* note 43, at 58; Phelps, *supra* note 55, at 1232–38.
73 Butler, *supra* note 5, at 1379–80.
74 Phelps, *supra* note 55, at 575–76.
75 *Id.*
76 Ward, *supra* note 2, at 182; Phelps, *supra* note 55, at 86–92; Chatelain, *supra* note 68, at 185; Cash, *supra* note 61, at 142–43; Mary McLeod Bethune, Biography, http://www.biography.com/people/mary-mcleod-bethune-9211266#synopsis (last visited July 30, 2017).
77 *Id.* at 182.
78 Bethune, *supra* note 76 (additionally, she opened the Daytona Normal and Industrial Institute for Negro Girls in Daytona, Florida in 1904 that initially served black girls, but later also served black boys); *see also* Phelps, *supra* note 55, at 86–92 (Bethune was also active in the black women's movement in Florida, which opened a home in Ocala for delinquent girls, and helped black youth train and find jobs).
79 Virginia G. Drachman, The Reader's Companion to U.S. Women's History 321 (Houghton Mifflin, 1998).
80 Phelps, *supra* note 55, at 94–95; Ward, *supra* note 2, at 188–90.
81 Jane M. Bolin, Oral History Interview (by Jean Rudd and Lionel Bolin), June 4, 1990, 11, Jane Bolin Papers, Schomburg Center for Research in Black Culture, New York.
82 Phelps, *supra* note 55, at 661.
83 *Id.*
84 J. Clay Smith, Jr., *Elizabeth D. Pittman: Black Legal Pioneer in the Midlands*, 32 Creighton L. Rev. 511, 520 (1998) [hereinafter *Pioneer in the Midlands*].
85 *Making Invisible Histories Visible*, Student Projects, http://invisiblehistory.ops.org/StudentProjects/2016StudentProjects/JudgeElizabethPittman/tabid/291/Default.aspx (last visited Jan. 7, 2017).
86 Smith, Jr., *supra* note 84, at 517.
87 *Id.* at 523.
88 Bolin, *supra* note 81, at 45–46 ("Philosophy from the last century had been that children were not to be treated as adult criminals").
89 William N. Eskridge, Jr., *Some Effects of Identity-Based Social Movements on Constitutional Law in the Twentieth Century*, 100 Mich. L. Rev. 2062, 2072 (2002)

(stating that the lawyers of the civil rights movement "translated the social, moral, and political goals of the movement into constitutional discourse").

90 Brown v. Board of Education, 347 U.S. 483 (1954).

91 State Board of Public Welfare v. Myers, 167 A.2d 765, 767 (1961) (*see* case no. JI-MD-0002–7500).

92 *Id.* at 766.

93 *Id.* at 767.

94 *Id.* at 768.

95 Larry Still, *White Family in Ala. Gets Custody of Miss. Negro: Sit-In Student to Live, Study*, JET, May 10, 1962, at 16.

96 Singleton v. Bd. of Comm'rs, 356 F.2d 771, 772 (5th Cir. 1966) (Plaintiffs alleged that the State of Florida, through its Board of Commissioners of State Institutions, operated reform schools, particularly the Florida State School for Boys and the Florida School for Girls, on a racially segregated basis).

97 *Id.* at 773.

98 The court also relied on Johnson v. Virginia, 373 U.S. 61, 62 (1963) ("It is no longer open to question that a State may not constitutionally require segregation of public facilities").

99 Washington v. Lee, 263 F. Supp. 327, 328 (M.D. Ala. 1966).

100 *Id.* at 328, 331.

101 *Id.* at 332.

102 Bd. of Managers v. George, 377 F.2d 228, 12 (8th Cir. 1967) (holding that segregation is unconstitutional in training school facilities and orders them desegregated).

103 *Id.* at 229 (they also sought an injunction against Lincoln County, Juvenile Court Judge, E. G. Brockman and all other "juvenile court" judges similarly situated from assigning or sentencing minor Negro juveniles to the Training School at Wrightsville on the basis of race or color).

104 Washington v. Lee, Id. at 233 (citing Brown v. Board of Education, 347 U.S. 483, 495 (1954)).

105 Major v. Sowers, 298 F. Supp. 1039 (E.D. La. 1969); Crum v. State Training Sch. for Girls, 413 F.2d 1348 (5th Cir. 1969).

106 Citations for desegregation support include: Singleton v. Bd. of Comm'rs, 356 F.2d 771 (5th Cir. 1966); Washington v. Lee, 263 F. Supp. 327 (M.D. Ala. 1966) ("[t]he Alabama statutes requiring segregation by race in all state prison facilities including youth correctional centers were declared unconstitutional and immediate desegregation of reform schools was ordered"); Wilson v. Kelley, 294 F. Supp. 1005 (N.D. Ga. 1968) (similar Georgia statutes requiring racial segregation in prison facilities were declared unconstitutional); State Board of Public Welfare v. Myers, 167 A.2d 765, 767 (1961) (the Maryland statute requiring racial segregation in state training schools was held violative of the Fourteenth Amendment in 1961); Bd. of Managers v. George, 377 F.2d 228, 231 (8th Cir. 1967) ("invocation of a three judge court was not required to declare that the Arkansas statutes requiring racial segregation in the state's juvenile training schools were unconstitutional").

107 Crum v. State Training Sch. for Girls, 413 F.2d 1348, 1350 (5th Cir. 1969) (the court went on to order: the district court should require the plan to provide for integration of classrooms, dormitories, athletic programs, and all activities, and services; the faculty must be integrated without waiting for the filling of vacancies on a non-racial basis; the pattern of teacher assignment to any particular school should not be identified as tailored for a heavy concentration of either Negro or white pupils in the school; professional and non-professional members of the staff must be integrated).

108 Charles Jerome Stockton v. Alabama Industrial School for Negro Children (1971), https://www.clearinghouse.net/chDocs/public/JI-AL-0004–0003.pdf (last visited Jan. 5, 2017).

109 *Id.*

110 *See, e.g.*, President's Comm'n on Law Enf't & Admin. of Justice, The Challenge of Crime in a Free Society: A Report, Washington, DC: U.S. Government Printing Office (Feb. 1967), www.ncjrs.gov/pdffiles1/nij/42.pdf; Feld, Bad Kids, *supra* note 11, at 166–244; Ward, *supra* note 2, at 240.

111 *See generally* Ward, *supra* note 2, at 246–56.

112 Philip Goodman et al., Breaking the Pendulum: The Long Struggle Over Criminal Justice (Oxford University Press, 2017).

113 *See* 387 U.S. 1, 22 (1967) (discussing the notion of "constitutional domestication").

114 *See State Assessments*, The Nat'l Juvenile Defender Ctr. (NJDC), http://njdc.info/our-work/juvenile-indigent-defense-assessments (last visited Jan. 8, 2017). For example, the Illinois Assessment finds that nationally children of color are severely overrepresented at every stage of the juvenile justice process. The Children & Family Justice Ctr. et. al., Illinois: An Assessment of Acess to Counsel & Quality of Representation in Delinquency Proceedings 73 (2007), http://njdc.info/wp-content/uploads/2013/11/Illinois_Juvenile_Defense_Assessmen-t_Report_FINAL.pdf (last visited Dec. 26, 2017). Moreover, the Kentucky Assessment finds that minority children and youth with disabilities tend to suffer the most severe consequences in school disciplinary actions and that minority youth are overrepresented in nearly every aspect of Kentucky's juvenile justice system, from arrest to transfer to incarceration. American Bar Ass'n Juvenile Justice Ctr. et. al., Kentucky – Advancing Justice: An Assessment of Access to Counsel and Quality of Representation in Delinquency Proceedings 5 (2002), http://njdc.info/wp-content/uploads/2013/11/Kentucky_Assessment-FINAL.pdf (last visited Dec. 26, 2017). The Missouri Assessment found that in the state, similar to many other states, disproportionately transfers African American youth to adult court. The Nat'l Juvenile Defender Ctr. (NJDC) et. al., Missouri: Justice Rationed: An Assessment of Access to Counsel and Quality of Representation in Juvenile Delinquency Court (2013), http://njdc.info/wp-content/uploads/2013/11/Missouri-Assessment.pdf (last visited Dec. 26, 2017). The Ohio Assessment found that minority youth were much more likely to be waived to adult criminal court than white youth in all offense categories. American Bar Ass'n Juvenile Justice Ctr. et. al., Ohio – Justice Cut Short: An Assessment of Access to Counsel and Quality of Representation in Delinquency Proceedings 45–48 (2003) http://njdc.info/wp-content/uploads/2013/11/Final-Ohio-Assessment-Report.pdf. The Virginia Assessment found that countless numbers of children are waiving the right to counsel and proceeding unguided through a sometimes harsh and uncaring system that offers little opportunity for meaningful guidance and rehabilitation. American Bar Ass'n Juvenile Justice Ctr et al., Virginia: An Assessment of Access to Counsel and Quality of Representation in Delinquency Proceedings 43–45 (2002), http://njdc.info/wp-content/uploads/2013/11/Final-Virginia-Assessment-Report.pdf (last visited Dec. 26, 2017).

115 DuBois, *supra* note 10, at 267–71.

4 A new juvenile jurisprudence: how adolescent development research and relentless defense advocacy revolutionized criminal law and jurisprudence

Eduardo Ferrer

Introduction

Children are different from adults. This is an intuitive, undisputed fact that the law generally has recognized for centuries.[1] However, criminal law and jurisprudence have been slow to account for these differences. Indeed, for much of the last 120 years, youth advocates and juvenile defenders have pushed and prodded courts and legislatures to meaningfully incorporate the differences between youth and adults into substantive law while still recognizing that the Constitution guarantees youth many of the same procedural rights afforded to adults.

At the turn of the twentieth century, youth advocates secured a major victory regarding the manner in which youth accused of crimes would be treated under the law with the creation of the first juvenile court in Illinois. Founded on the beliefs that delinquent and ungovernable youth needed guidance and rehabilitation from a court acting *in parens patriae* rather than the punishment common in traditional criminal courts,[2] the first juvenile court formalized the notion that youth were not miniature adults and should not be treated as such.[3] Unfortunately, although the juvenile courts in the early twentieth century were well intentioned, the courts were overly paternalistic and generally omitted the checks on power afforded by an adversarial due process system.[4] Indeed, juvenile courts often saw themselves more as social services agencies working in the best interests of youth, thereby obviating the need for the youth to have any rights or due process.[5] As a result, juvenile court generally devolved into a system that presented the worst of both worlds for children ensnared by the system – children received neither meaningful services nor effective due process.[6]

Beginning around the mid-century mark, defense attorneys representing youth began pushing back against this status quo by seeking the assistance of the Supreme Court to address the lack of procedural rights afforded to children. First, in *Haley v. Ohio* (1948), advocates convinced the Supreme Court to suppress the confession of a 15-year-old boy,[7] holding both that the Due Process Clause protected the boy and requiring that the boy's young age be considered an important factor when analyzing the voluntariness of his confession.[8] Second, in *Kent v.*

United States (1966), the Court found that Due Process protections afforded a youth waived from juvenile court to adult court the right to a hearing, the right to access records and reports considered by the Court in its decision, and the right to a statement of the court's rationale for the waiver sufficient in detail to enable appellate review of the decision.[9] Finally, in *In re Gault* (1967), the seminal case whose fiftieth anniversary this book celebrates, the Court confronted the case of a young boy accused, convicted, and sentenced to a term of commitment with the state for the high crime of making a prank phone call despite having never received formal notice of the charges, an attorney to represent him, the ability to see the evidence or confront witnesses, or a record of the limited proceedings that did exist.[10] The Supreme Court reaffirmed that although children are different from adults, they are nevertheless entitled to many – though not all – of the due process rights afforded to adults in criminal proceedings.[11] Having secured a level of procedural protections for youth through *Gault* and its progeny, youth defenders would spend the next 50 years pressing courts and legislatures to finally meaningfully incorporate the underlying premise of juvenile court – that youth are different from adults – into substantive criminal law and jurisprudence.

This chapter will focus on the struggles and successes youth advocates and juvenile defenders experienced in pursuing substantive protections for youth in the justice system. In particular, this chapter will focus first on the defenders' initial failures to convince the Supreme Court to abolish the juvenile death penalty. The chapter will then review a number of key studies from adolescent development research published in the 1990s and 2000s that highlight the biological and psychological reasons that youth, when compared to adults, are less adept decision-makers and more capable of change. The chapter will next discuss how juvenile defenders and youth advocates used this emerging research to convince the Supreme Court and legislatures across the country not only to abolish the juvenile death penalty, but also to meaningfully embed the fact that youth are different from adults into criminal law and jurisprudence. Finally, this chapter will offer some ideas about what the future may hold for creating a more research-driven, developmentally appropriate approach to youth who become involved in the juvenile and criminal justice systems.

Failed attempts at abolishing the juvenile death penalty

Between the reinstatement of the death penalty in 1976 and the abolition of the death penalty for youth in 2005, 22 individuals were executed for crimes they were found guilty of committing during their adolescent years.[12] During this period, juvenile defenders tried and failed multiple times to convince courts across the country to recognize that youth had a substantive right under the Eighth Amendment to be free from imposition of the death penalty. Indeed, between 1980 and 1990 alone, juvenile defenders argued the constitutionality of the death penalty as applied to crimes committed during childhood in the United States Supreme Court three times.[13] Although juvenile defenders ultimately fell short of their goal of convincing the Court that it should abolish the death penalty for all youth under age 18 in all three cases,[14] the trio of cases produced two important results. First, the lives of the individual youth involved in these three cases were ultimately spared.[15] Second, the cases inspired a new strategy for attacking the juvenile death penalty that would result not only in the abolition of that ultimate penalty, but also in the recognition of additional constitutional substantive protections for youth grounded in the notion that the law must meaningfully accommodate the differences between youth and adults.

The 1980s: a trio of supreme defeats

In the first case of the trio – *Eddings v. Oklahoma* (1982) – the Court sidestepped the question of the constitutionality of the death penalty for a 16-year-old boy convicted of murder.[16] Relying on the *Lockett* rule[17] instead of the Eighth Amendment, the Court held that the lower court erred by not accounting for Eddings' emotional disturbance and a traumatic upbringing, including physical abuse at the hands of his father, as mitigating circumstances in sentencing. The Court further reasoned that

> youth is more than a chronological fact. It is a time and condition of life when a person may be most susceptible to influence and to psychological damage … . Particularly "during the formative years of childhood and adolescence, minors often lack the experience, perspective, and judgment" expected of adults.[18]

The move of the *Eddings* court – in holding that youthfulness, not just as a number but with all the attendant implications, must be meaningfully taken into account during the sentencing *process* – further affirmed the notion that children are fundamentally different from adults in a manner that must be taken into account in criminal cases. However, the case provided little clarity as to whether youth as a class must be spared the most serious punishments.

In the second case of the trio – *Thompson v. Oklahoma* (1988) – the Court did squarely confront the issue of whether the Eighth Amendment prohibited the execution of a youth convicted of a murder the youth committed when he was 15 years old.[19] However, a majority of the justices failed to reach consensus on the legal justification for setting aside the sentence. The four justices in favor of setting aside the conviction concluded that the Eighth Amendment barred the execution of any child for a crime committed prior to the child's sixteenth birthday. In its reasoning, the plurality recognized that youth, by their very nature, are less culpable, less experienced, more impulsive, more susceptible to peer pressure, and have a greater capacity for growth than adults.[20] As a result, the plurality found that the social purposes served by the death penalty – retribution and deterrence – were inapplicable in the case of youth who committed capital offenses under the age of 16 and that evolving standards of decency prohibited its imposition.[21] In contrast, the dissenting justices objected to the categorical rule created by the plurality that no child under the age of 16, regardless of the individual circumstances of the child or the case itself, could be deemed mature enough to be punished with a death sentence.[22] Justice O'Connor, who concurred in judgment only, agreed with both the plurality and the dissenters on different points and crafted a compromise position. Specifically, Justice O'Connor agreed with the plurality that evolving standards of decency favored a prohibition on the imposition of the death penalty for offenses committed before a youth's sixteenth birthday and agreed that Thompson himself should not be executed. However, Justice O'Connor ultimately found that she could not adopt a categorical rule abolishing the death penalty for *all* youth under 16 absent additional evidence that youth as a class are different from adults.[23] Thus, although the *Thompson* court seemed to be moving in the direction of recognizing that youth as a class should be treated differently from adults when it comes to capital punishment, the plurality decision left little precedential clarity with regard to what degree courts should accommodate youthfulness in their sentencing decisions.[24]

That clarity would come less than a year later in the third case in the trio – *Stanford v. Kentucky* (1989). Unfortunately for juvenile defenders pushing for a more developmentally appropriate approach to sentencing, a divided Court rejected a categorical prohibition under the Eighth Amendment to the imposition of the death penalty for youth who commit capital offenses while 16 or 17 years old.[25] Justice O'Connor again cast the deciding vote – this time concurring in part and concurring in judgment with the dissenting judges in the *Thompson* case – to form a majority whose reasoning rested on the finding that there was no national consensus forbidding the imposition of capital punishment on 16- and 17-year-olds. Importantly, despite disagreeing on whether the Court should conduct a proportionality analysis, the majority rejected the dissenters' central argument – that the available scientific evidence regarding adolescent psychosocial development supported a constitutional prohibition on the imposition of the death penalty on youth under 18 *as a class*. Instead, Justice Scalia and his concurring colleagues suggested that advocates of more developmentally appropriate sentencing take their arguments to the "citizenry of the United States."[26]

The 1990s: the super-predator myth reigns supreme

The 1990s, however, would not provide fertile ground for convincing the "citizenry of the United States" of the need for developmentally appropriate sentencing. Indeed, quite the contrary, rising youth crime rates between the mid-1980s and early-1990s led one researcher to predict that the United States was on the verge of being overrun by a generation of "severely morally impoverished juvenile super-predators" that are "perfectly capable of committing the most heinous acts of physical violence for the most trivial reasons … ."[27] Although time would reveal that youth crime rates had actually peaked prior to the popularization of the super-predator myth,[28] policy-makers wholeheartedly adopted the super-predator narrative.[29] This led to the passage of more draconian, not more developmentally appropriate, transfer and sentencing laws for youth.[30] Additionally, as the myth of the super-predator gained steam, the "machinery of death"[31] began to accelerate. While three youth were executed in the decade leading up to the decision in

Stanford, states executed ten more youth in the decade following that decision.[32] As a result, at the end of the twentieth century, the movement to treat kids as kids in the eyes of the law did not look promising.

Lessons learned from losing

Facing a number of looming executions scheduled for the first few months of the new century,[33] juvenile defenders realized that a new approach was urgently needed and that their voice and advocacy alone would not be sufficient.[34] Inspired by a series of high-level symposia during which staff members were first exposed to the research regarding the developing brain of the adolescent, organizers at the American Bar Association's (ABA) Juvenile Justice Center began reaching out to a host of other professional communities and affinity groups – including doctors, psychologists, victims of crime, clergy, and international human rights advocates – to gauge their interest in supporting the work of abolishing the juvenile death penalty.[35] Through this work, juvenile defenders at the ABA, which had adopted a resolution in 1983 opposing the juvenile death penalty,[36] hoped to both accelerate a developing national consensus against the imposition of the juvenile death penalty and directly answer Justice O'Connor's skepticism regarding the creation of a categorical rule with additional scientific evidence demonstrating that youth as a class were different from adults. The relationships developed with neurologists studying the development of the adolescent brain and psychologists studying the process of adolescent maturation would prove particularly fruitful.

The emerging science of adolescence development

In the years following the Supreme Court's decision in *Stanford* upholding the juvenile death penalty for 16- and 17-year-olds, researchers across a variety of disciplines explored not only the many differences between adolescents and adults with respect to decision-making, but also the reasons why those differences exist. Behavioral science research in particular shed substantial light on the developmental processes that explain the manner in which the mind of a youth functions differently from that of an adult. Specifically, the research documented that youth, relative to adults, are more likely to take risks, more susceptible to peer pressure, more impulsive, more sensation-seeking, and more focused on the short term, thereby, resulting in diminished decision-making abilities relative to adults. Moreover, advances in brain imaging technology enabled researchers to identify a biological basis for these differences in behavior and decision-making abilities. Increased knowledge of the development of the brain also led to the recognition that the brains of youth are still malleable well into their twenties, meaning that youth have an increased capacity for change relative to adults. It is this body of adolescent development research that juvenile defenders would later use to finally successfully attack the constitutionality of the juvenile death penalty in the Supreme Court.

Diminished decision-making defines adolescence

One of the central ideas undergirding the "national consensus" evaluated by the Supreme Court in *Stanford*, as well as the "tough on crime" policies of the 1990s, was the popular, but mistaken, belief that adolescents have similar decision-making capabilities to adults. At the time, this central premise was based on two key pillars. The first was the belief that decision-making capabilities derived primarily from an individual's cognitive abilities (i.e., the ability to learn, think, process information, and reason). The second pillar was research that supported the notion that a young person's reasoning abilities began to approximate the abilities of an adult by mid-adolescence.[37] However, these pillars failed to account for a key piece of the puzzle needed to fully understand the differences between adolescent and adult decision-making – *context*. Indeed, much of the research supporting the conclusion that adolescents have similar decision-making abilities to adults was done in a sterile, laboratory setting that did not adequately account for the stressful, group settings in which adolescents often make decisions.[38] Moreover, by focusing primarily on cognitive capacities as a proxy for decision-making capabilities, researchers ignored the influence that psychosocial factors (i.e., peer influence, risk-taking, impulsivity, and future orientation) have on decision-making.[39] Indeed, as the research discussed below demonstrates, when psychosocial factors and context are taken into account, the average youth tends to have diminished decision-making capacity compared to the average adult even though the average youth may have approximately the same cognitive capacity.

Critical research published in the first decade of the twenty-first century demonstrated the critical influence that psychosocial maturity has on decision-making. Cauffman and Steinberg (2000) released the results of a study examining the influence that three different psychosocial factors – responsibility, perspective, and temperance – have on the "way that the process of decision-making changes with development."[40] The study sampled over 1,000 individuals between the ages of 12 and 48 and administered an assessment tool measuring antisocial decision-making by presenting hypothetical situations that involved selecting between pro-social and anti-social alternative courses of action. First, Cauffman and Steinberg found that "psychosocial maturity significantly predicted decision-making within each of the five age groups considered."[41] Second, the results of the study demonstrated that antisocial decision-making decreased as psychosocial maturity increased.[42] Third, the study indicated that, although psychosocial maturity influenced antisocial decision-making more than age, age was also a significant predictor of pro-social decision-making.[43] More specifically, Cauffman and Steinberg concluded that "psychosocial characteristics continue[d] to develop during late adolescence, and that these changes resulted in declines in antisocial decision-making."[44] Finally, Cauffman and Steinberg were able to identify the particular manner in which the average adolescent's psychosocial functioning was less developed compared to the average adult. Specifically, they concluded that youth were less self-reliant, more impulsive, more focused on the short term, and less likely to consider someone else's perspective.[45]

Further research using behavioral tasks and improved self-report instruments confirmed these findings, specifically evaluating whether age differences impacted individual psychosocial factors. For example, studies by Gardner and Steinberg (2005)[46] and Steinberg and Monahan (2007)[47] specifically examined whether risk taking, risk preference, and risky decision-making varied by age and whether age determined susceptibility to peer influence. In the Gardner and Steinberg (2005) study, 306 participants across various age groups completed two self-report questionnaires measuring risk preference and risky decision-making. Participants also completed a behavioral task designed to measure risk taking *in the moment* rather than the more deliberative form of risk taking measured by more traditional assessment tools that involve hypothetical situations.[48] Additionally, in order to measure the effect of peer influence on risky decision-making, the questionnaires and behavioral task were administered to some participants in individual settings and other participants in group settings.[49] An analysis of the data revealed two key findings. First, risk taking and risky decision-making decreased significantly between adolescence and adulthood.[50] Second, adolescents (age 22 and under) were "more susceptible to the influence of their peers in risky situations" relative to adults (24 and over).[51]

Steinberg and Monahan (2007) found similar effects regarding adolescents' relatively greater susceptibility to peer influence. However, for this study, Steinberg and Monahan combined data from three different studies that used a new self-report tool designed to "separate[] susceptibility to peer influence from willingness to engage in antisocial acts."[52] With a sample size of over 3,600 participants between the ages of 10 and 30, the study concluded that adolescents were more susceptible to peer influence than adults.[53] Specifically, the data revealed that resistance to peer influence improved significantly during mid-adolescence (between ages 14 and 18), and did not improve in a significant manner either before or after this time period.[54]

Using common data from the MacArthur Juvenile Capacity Study,[55] several sets of researchers also evaluated whether age differences existed with regard to sensation seeking, impulsivity, future orientation, and overall cognitive and psychosocial maturity.[56] For instance, Steinberg, Albert, Cauffman, Banich, Graham, and Woolard (2008) concluded that sensation seeking and impulsivity develop along different timetables.[57] The data, which was derived from the results of self-report measures and a computerized driving task similar to the one used in the Gardner and Steinberg (2005) study, demonstrated that sensation seeking increases between ages 10 and 15 before stabilizing or declining while impulsivity declined steadily after age 10.[58] These findings supported the research team's hypothesis "that sensation seeking and impulsivity have different biological underpinnings and follow different developmental trajectories."[59] These findings also provided additional support for the view that risky decision-making in adolescence was the result of the interplay between two different neurobiological systems – the social-emotional system and the cognitive control system[60] – thereby resulting in a normative "vulnerability to heightened risk taking in middle adolescence."[61]

In addition, Steinberg, Graham, O'Brien, Woolard, Cauffman, and Banich (2009) found age differences with regard to future orientation (i.e., the ability to think ahead, plan accordingly, and delay gratification).[62] Using a self-report questionnaire and a delay discounting task to measure future orientation, Steinberg *et. al.* (2009) concluded that adolescents were more oriented to the present than adults.[63] Specifically, adolescents were less likely to plan ahead, to think about the future, and to think about the consequences of their actions before making a decision.[64] Additionally, younger adolescents were more likely than older adolescents and adults to prefer smaller, more immediate rewards than larger, more distant rewards.[65]

Building upon the research collected through the MacArthur Juvenile Capacity Study and the findings in the aforementioned studies, Steinberg *et. al.* (2009) then examined age differences in cognitive capacity and overall psychosocial maturity – a composite measure that included risk perception, sensation seeking, impulsivity, susceptibility to peer influence, and future orientation.[66] Not surprisingly, the findings confirmed the earlier research. First, an analysis of the data revealed significant age effects relating to psychosocial maturity. Specifically, the study indicated that there were no significant differences in psychosocial maturity through mid-adolescence (16–17 years old), but that significant age differences existed between those in mid-adolescence and young adults (22 and older) and those in late adolescence (18–21) and adulthood (26 and older).[67] Second, the study confirmed that cognitive development seemed to follow the opposite pattern, with age differences existing through the first part of adolescence but ceasing after age 16.[68] Taken together, the study confirmed that "[b]y age 16, adolescents' general cognitive abilities are essentially indistinguishable from those of adults, but adolescents' psychosocial functioning, even at age 18, is significantly less mature than that of individuals in their mid-20s."[69]

In light of these findings as well as previous research in the field, the authors emphasized the importance of examining the context in which adolescents make decisions when determining policy. Specifically, the authors concluded that adolescents as young as 16 can likely make decisions in a manner similar to adults when the situation allows time for deliberate thought, is divorced from emotional or social pressures, and provides for the opportunity to consult with an individual who can provide information about the costs and benefits associated with a particular decision. In contrast, when the situation calls for a quick decision, involves excitement or peer pressure, or does not permit consultation with someone more experienced, adolescents under the age of 18 are likely to display less mature decision-making capabilities than adults.[70] As this latter set of circumstances better describes the context in which adolescents engage in criminal activity, the research on the relative psychosocial immaturity of adolescents provided clear lessons for criminal justice law and policy.

A biological basis for adolescent behavior

The research after the turn of the century did not stop with observing the differences in decision-making capacity between adolescents and adults, but also identified a biological basis for those differences. With the aid of new technology that allowed researchers to look at the brains of adolescents and adults over time and in real-time,[71] researchers were able to establish a neurobiological basis for the observed differences between the psychosocial maturity of children and adults. The neurological basis for those observed differences is rooted in three key concepts derived from the research.

First, using MRI technology, researchers confirmed that the brain continues to change significantly during childhood and adolescence despite the fact that the brain does not grow in size much past the age of five.[72] During the period of adolescence in particular, there are two simultaneous processes underway that fundamentally alter the composition of the adolescent brain in preparation for adulthood. First, the "white matter" of the brain increases significantly during childhood and adolescence due to the process of myelination, which is essentially the wrapping of the brain's connections with a form of insulation.[73] This process follows a pattern, moving from the bottom of the brain to the top and the back of the brain to the front.[74] Second, the "gray matter" of the brain increases during childhood but decreases significantly during adolescence, resulting in a net decrease of "gray matter" in the brain prior to adulthood.[75] This decrease is due to the process of synaptic pruning, which is the elimination of connections in the brain that are either underutilized or unnecessary.[76] Importantly, the manner in which both of these processes unfold is driven substantially by an individual's experiences and environment.[77] As a result of these neurological processes taking place at this time, the period of brain development during adolescence is defined by its heightened ability (relative to adults) to change, adapt, and respond to experience and environment.[78]

Second, the research revealed important lessons regarding the order and timing of brain development, specifically finding that the different regions of the brain develop and mature at different times.[79] Using MRI images of the brains of 13 youth taken every two years over the course of 8–10 years, researchers were able to track the maturing of the various regions of the brain by tracking gray matter density in those regions.[80] The images taken revealed that the "parts of the brain associated with the more basic functions matured early," while the parts of the brain associated with "executive functioning, attention, and motor coordination" were among the last to develop.[81] Additional research around this time further confirmed this finding, specifically highlighting that the parts of the brain most associated with incentive-processing, risk-taking, and sensation-seeking develop earlier than the parts of the brain most responsible for regulating impulses and behavior.[82]

Third, building upon the aforementioned knowledge of brain development and with the assistance of functional MRI (fMRI) technology, researchers were able to demonstrate very specific ways in which the brains of youth work differently from the brains of adults, thus validating the earlier observations and hypotheses regarding youth's different psychosocial capacities and diminished decision-making capabilities.

For instance, Chein *et. al.* (2010) were able to pinpoint a neurological basis for increased risk-taking by adolescents when in the presence of their peers.[83] In their study, Chein *et. al.* (2010) revisited the driving simulation task used in many of the previous studies to measure risk-taking and the effect of peer influence. However, this time, researchers measured the brain activities of the sample of 40 participants while the participants completed the driving simulation task alone or in the presence of peers.[84] The goal of the study was to measure the differences across age in the activation of two brain systems – the incentive processing system and the cognitive control system[85] – to determine whether "adolescents' especially heightened propensity to take risks when with peers may derive from the maturational imbalance between these competing brain systems."[86] The study's key findings validated this hypothesis. The study found that adolescents "demonstrated significantly greater activation" of the incentive processing system than adults, but only when they were in the presence of peers.[87] In contrast, adults showed little difference in their engagement of the incentive processing system when in the presence of peers compared to alone.[88] Moreover, the study found that adults activated their cognitive control system "more robustly than adolescents" and did so irrespective of whether or not peers were present.[89] Adolescents, in contrast, only weakly recruited their cognitive control system when making decisions.[90] As such, the data confirmed the imbalance in terms of maturity between the incentive processing and cognitive control system of adolescents. The data also added a new piece to the puzzle – that the heightened susceptibility to peer influence observed during adolescence is likely due to the presence of peers stimulating the incentive processing system of the adolescent brain rather than suppressing the cognitive control system of the brain.[91]

Viewed as a whole, the body of research relating to adolescent development since the Supreme Court's decision rejecting a categorical ban on the juvenile death penalty for 16- and 17-year-olds in *Stanford v. Kentucky* has clear implications for criminal justice law and policy. First, the research strongly supports the conclusion that, when compared to adults, youth have diminished decision-making capabilities as a result of their psychosocial immaturity. Second, the diminished decision-making capacity of youth is most dramatic in the same types of situations where adolescents are most likely to engage in risky or criminal behavior – situations requiring quick decisions in the presence of peers. Third, while variability in psychosocial and cognitive maturity among adolescents exists, the difference in decision-making abilities between youth and adults has its basis in normative neurobiological development and processes. As such, psychosocial immaturity and diminished decision-making are traits that should be considered to apply to youth as a class.

The influence of adolescent development research on law and jurisprudence

As this body of adolescent development research evolved at the start of the century, juvenile defenders continued to fight executions and sought another chance to convince the Supreme Court to abolish the juvenile death penalty.[92] That opportunity would present itself on May 28, 2002, though the victory was bittersweet.

Indeed, with the execution of one youth and a stay of execution granted for another, May 28, 2002 would prove to be a fateful day in the fight against the juvenile death penalty that would come to "embody the disparities and the changing debate concerning the juvenile death penalty."[93] On that day, the state of Texas executed Napoleon Beazley, a 25-year-old black man who killed the father of a federal judge during a carjacking when he was just 17 years old.[94] The United States Supreme Court refused to block the execution pending its upcoming decision in *Atkins v. Virginia*,[95] an opinion released less than a month later holding that the execution of individuals with diminished decision-making abilities due to intellectual disability was unconstitutional.[96] The Texas Board of Pardon and Paroles also rejected Beazley's appeal to stay the execution despite receiving pleas for clemency from tens of thousands people and six Nobel Peace laureates.[97] In contrast, on that same day, the Missouri Supreme Court granted Christopher Simmons, a 26-year-old white man, a stay of his execution, which was scheduled for the following week.[98] Like Beazley, Simmons was 17 years old when he committed the murder for which he was sentenced to death. Additionally, like Beazley, Simmons argued that the execution should be stayed pending the United States Supreme Court's upcoming ruling in *Atkins*.[99] Tragically, Napoleon Beazley was executed while, fortunately, Christopher Simmons would move closer to having the Supreme Court reconsider not only his sentence of death but also the constitutionality of the death penalty as a punishment for youth generally.

Armed with the precedent set in *Atkins* and the emerging research concerning the psychosocial and neurological differences between children and adults,[100] juvenile defenders made the most of the opportunity in the Simmons' case, finally convincing a majority of the Supreme Court to abolish the juvenile death penalty. Simmons' case was just the start of a revolution. Over the course of the next dozen years, juvenile defenders convinced the Court to radically alter sentencing and substantive legal jurisprudence to make it more developmentally appropriate. During this 12-year span, the Court considered five cases reaffirming the fact that youth are different from adults and establishing a jurisprudence that meaningfully accommodates these differences. These cases were accompanied by several legislative trends relating to juvenile and criminal justice that also reflect an increased awareness and adoption of the relevant research regarding adolescent development.

Substantive sentencing jurisprudence: recognizing that children are categorically and constitutionally different from adults

The first case – *Roper v. Simmons* (2005) – abolished the juvenile death penalty. In a reversal of its previous decision in *Stanford*, the United States Supreme Court affirmed the Missouri Supreme Court's holding that the Eighth and Fourteenth Amendments to the Constitution prohibited the execution of individuals for crimes committed prior to their eighteenth birthday.[101] The majority opinion, written by Justice Kennedy, based its reversal on three key findings. First, the Court found that national standards of decency as demonstrated by the pronouncements of state legislatures had so evolved since the time of *Stanford* that the death penalty could no longer be considered a proportional punishment for juveniles. Specifically, the Court found that the majority of states already prohibited the imposition of the death penalty on youth and that the trend was heading toward abolition. Second, the majority found that, in its own estimation, the death penalty was a disproportionate punishment for juveniles. Specifically, the majority pointed to three key differences between youth and adults – a youth's "objective immaturity, vulnerability, and lack of true depravity" – that demonstrate that a youth cannot be classified reliably with those offenders deserving of the death penalty, despite the youth's commission of a capital offense.[102] Finally, the majority recognized that the United States was the only country in the world that officially sanctioned the death penalty for youth, and, as result, the "overwhelming weight of international opinion" supported the abolition of the practice.

Interestingly, although Justice O'Connor appeared primed to be the swing vote in favor of a prohibition on the death penalty for youth based on her concurrences in *Thompson* and *Stanford*, it was Justice Kennedy who flipped from upholding the death penalty in *Stanford* to authoring the majority's decision in *Roper*. Justice Kennedy's move from pro-discretion to pro-abolition was influenced heavily by the wealth of adolescent development research published since the decision in *Stanford*.[103] Although Justice Kennedy recognized that the trend toward abolition of the death penalty in the states was not dramatic and that international opinion did not control the Court's decision, he found the research detailing the differences between youth and adults so compelling that it required a categorical rule prohibiting the imposition of the death penalty on youth.[104] Indeed, Justice Kennedy reasoned that "[t]he differences between juvenile and adult offenders are too marked and well understood to risk allowing a youthful person to receive the death penalty despite insufficient culpability."[105] In doing so, *Roper* laid the foundation for a new jurisprudence requiring that criminal courts also give meaningful accord and accommodation to the fact that youth *as a class* are different from adults.

The far-reaching implications of this new, more meaningful, developmentally-appropriate jurisprudence would begin to shine through less than five years later in *Graham v. Florida* (2010).[106] In *Graham*, the Supreme Court faced the question of whether sentencing a youth who committed a non-homicide offense to life without the possibility of parole violated the Eighth Amendment's prohibition on cruel and unusual punishment. Justice Kennedy again wrote for the majority and again the research regarding adolescent development played a central role in the Court's decision. Recognizing that the research "continue[s] to show fundamental differences between juvenile and adult minds,"[107] the majority concluded that a youth's immaturity and capacity for change required the imposition of a *categorical* rule prohibiting life without parole for non-homicide offenses and required states to provide a youth with a realistic opportunity for release.[108]

The impact of *Roper* and the centrality of the adolescent development research to this burgeoning jurisprudence are revealed through a comparison of the different opinions concurring in judgment. Chief Justice Roberts, who concurred with the judgment of the *Graham* majority that the sentence imposed in this specific case was disproportional, agreed with the fundamental premise that youth are less culpable than adults because they are less mature, more vulnerable, and more amenable to change.[109] However, Chief Justice Roberts objected to the creation of a new categorical rule that would prohibit the imposition of life without parole on any youth who commits a non-homicide offense. In many ways Chief Justice Roberts mirrored the approach taken by Justice O'Connor in *Thompson*, believing that judges could determine in individual cases whether a particular youth was indeed less culpable as most youth are or was instead among the "worst offenders" for whom the most serious punishment are reserved.[110] In contrast, the majority found that this type of sorting proposed by Chief Justice Roberts – between which youth fit the normative path of development and which youth are more culpable because they are both more advanced and more depraved than the course of normative development would suggest – was not a function that the system could perform reliably and accurately.[111] Pointing back to *Roper* and the body of adolescent development research that formed the foundation of the reasoning in the *Roper* decision, the Court emphasized that the differences between youth and adults were too stark and now too well-accepted to allow for any risk that a youth with diminished culpability could be sentenced to life in prison without the possibility of earning parole.[112] Indeed, the majority's holding in *Graham* revealed that the precedential value of *Roper* was not a narrow rule that youth cannot be sentenced to death, but a broad recognition that youth as a class are different from adults and that the law must accommodate those differences when considering the proportionality of punishment.[113]

Two years later, in *Miller v. Alabama* (2012), the Supreme Court would continue to build on the foundation laid by *Roper* and cement its legacy as a jurisprudence separate and apart from traditional Eighth Amendment jurisprudence. In *Miller*, the Court faced the issue of whether a sentencing scheme that mandated the imposition of a sentence of life without parole for all capital offenses, even those committed prior to turning 18 years of age, was cruel and unusual punishment in violation of the Eighth Amendment. In holding that such a scheme ran afoul of the Constitution, the majority departed from historical Eighth Amendment analysis, which typically looked to the laws and practices in the states for guidance as to whether standards of decency had evolved to the point where the challenged practice was now cruel and unusual.[114]

Instead, the *Miller* majority moored its holding on two complementary lines of precedent. First, the majority affirmed that *Roper* and *Graham* stood for the broad proposition that children are categorically and constitutionally different from adults for purposes of sentencing. After again outlining the key differences between youth and adults – immaturity, vulnerability, and amenability to change – and re-acknowledging the strength of the scientific and social scientific research supporting the existence of these differences, the majority reasoned that these distinguishing factors between youth and adults were not crime-specific. As such, the reasoning in *Roper* and *Graham* teaches that youth matters when determining whether the sentence of life without parole is appropriate.[115]

Second, having established that youthfulness must be taken into account when determining whether a sentence of life without parole for a youth is proportional, the majority reasoned that the holding of *Eddings* should be broadened accordingly. Specifically, while *Eddings* originally required that a court meaningfully account for youthfulness as part of its individualized inquiry into whether a youth should be sentenced to death, the *Miller* majority extended the holding to require the same type of individualized inquiry when the possible penalty was life without parole.

Combining these two lines of precedent, the court concluded that a statutory scheme that mandated the imposition of life without the possibility of parole violated both the *Graham/Roper* rule that youth are different from adults for sentencing purposes and the *Eddings* rule that the sentencing process itself must meaningfully account for the mitigating factors of youth. Taken together, the majority demonstrated the importance of the jurisprudence emerging from *Roper* and progeny – accounting for youthfulness and its attendant mitigating characteristics during sentencing is of such constitutional importance that no legislature can override its consideration, even in the most serious of cases.[116]

Indeed, four years after *Miller*, the Supreme Court put a punctuation mark on the importance and reach of the *Roper* jurisprudence. In *Montgomery v. Louisiana* (2016), the Supreme Court considered whether *Miller*'s prohibition on mandatory life without parole for offenses committed prior to the age of 18 announced a substantive rule of constitutional law that should be applied retroactively in state collateral review cases.[117] In holding that *Miller* announced a substantive rule that did apply retroactively, the majority found that *Miller* was more than just a procedural rule. Although it did have a procedural component in that it required courts to account for youthfulness during the sentencing process, the *Miller* majority went further and "established that the penological justifications for life without parole collapse in light of the distinctive attributes of youth."[118] The majority in *Montgomery* thus found that, while *Miller* specifically invalidated statutory schemes that required the mandatory imposition of life without parole on youth, its rule was actually broader and more substantive. Specifically, the majority found that the full rule of *Miller* was that it "bar[red] life without parole …for all but the rarest of juvenile offenders, those whose crimes reflect permanent incorrigibility."[119] As such, it announced a substantive rule of constitutional law that state courts must apply retroactively on collateral review.

In sum, in the span of just over a decade, juvenile defenders pushed the Supreme Court to reverse its previous course and established a new, far-reaching, and retroactive constitutional rule requiring courts not only to meaningfully account for the differences between youth and adults when fashioning appropriate punishment in criminal cases, but also to reserve the most serious of sentences for only those rare youth whose crimes reflect permanent incorrigibility. Remarkably, although traditional Eighth Amendment jurisprudence formed the foundation for *Roper* itself, as *Roper* and its progeny continued to develop, it became clear that the true foundation of this new sentencing jurisprudence was the exhaustive scientific and social scientific research demonstrating the psychosocial and neurological differences between youth and adults. Practically, a majority of the court, once confronted with this evidence, knew that the courts and the Constitution itself could not continue to ignore what common sense and experience had always told us – that kids are different from adults.

Substantive legal jurisprudence: affirming the "reasonable child" standard

The impact of adolescent development research did not only result in the creation of a new sentencing jurisprudence. The developmental research also played a fundamental role in affirming the need to account for youthfulness in other aspects of criminal jurisprudence as well. In *J.D.B. v. North Carolina* (2011), for example, which was decided during the same time period as *Roper* and its progeny, juvenile defenders convinced the Court to apply the fundamental foundation of the sentencing jurisprudence – the finding that youth *as a class* are different from adults – to Fifth Amendment jurisprudence. In doing so, the Court created a "reasonable child" standard that will likely have far-reaching implications.

In *J.D.B.*, the Supreme Court faced a question very similar to the one it faced over 60 years earlier in Haley – to what extent, if any, should age be considered when evaluating whether the confession of a youth was voluntary or was extracted in violation of the youth's due process rights. Just as in *Haley*, the majority in *J.D.B.* concluded that age was a factor that must be considered as part of the Court's due process analysis. However, because *Haley* pre-dated *Miranda v. Arizona* (1966), the Court's due process analysis in *J.D.B.* occurred within a different framework. Specifically, in order to find a violation of J.D.B.'s due process rights, the Court had to consider whether J.D.B. was even in state custody when interrogated in the first place. Per the dictates of *Miranda* and progeny, the Court was therefore required to conduct two discrete inquiries. First, the Court had to consider the totality of the circumstances surrounding the setting of the interrogation. Second, the Court had to determine *whether a reasonable person* in those circumstances would have felt free to leave or otherwise end the interrogation.

After describing the facts of the interrogation of J.D.B., the Court turned to the central question – what impact did J.D.B.'s age have on the Court's inquiry into whether a reasonable person would have felt free to leave given the facts of the interrogation. In holding that age is a factor that a court must take into account when determining whether a suspect would have felt free to leave for *Miranda* purposes if the suspect's age was either known to the officer or readily apparent, the majority relied on three key findings that would lay the foundation for a broad "reasonable child" jurisprudence.

Harkening back to cases such as *Haley, Eddings, Roper*, and *Graham*, the majority first affirmed that youth are different from adults in ways that are constitutionally relevant and significant. Specifically, the majority found that youth are less mature, less responsible, more susceptible to outside pressures, and "often lack the experience, perspective, and judgment to recognize and avoid choices that could be detrimental to them."[120] Additionally, the Court recognized "that events that 'would leave a man cold and unimpressed can overawe and overwhelm a lad in his early teens.'"[121]

The Court's second finding was perhaps its most consequential. Instead of explicitly focusing on the adolescent development research as other decisions had done to justify that the differences between youth and adults were both stark and well-accepted, Justice Sotomayor writing for the *J.D.B.* majority put that knowledge in the hands of lay persons. Instead of cloaking the Court's findings within the provenance of experts, Sotomayor noted that stark differences between youth and adults were "commonsense conclusions" that merely "restate what 'any parent knows' – indeed, what any person knows – about children generally."[122]

From these two findings flowed the majority's third conclusion – that the age of the suspect was an *objective*, not subjective, factor in the *Miranda* custody analysis. The finding that youth *as a class* share the common characteristics of immaturity and vulnerability (among others) eliminated any need to engage in a subjective analysis of whether the suspect youth necessarily shared these characteristics. Additionally, the finding that all people – not just experts in adolescent development – understood these differences by virtue of having been children themselves meant that all stakeholders, including police officers and judges, could accommodate these differences in the course of their work without specialized training.[123]

Taken together, these three findings underpinning the holding in *J.D.B.* laid the foundation for an emerging jurisprudence – a "reasonable child" jurisprudence – that recognizes that youthfulness and its attendant characteristics is an objective factor that juvenile and criminal courts must accommodate, arguably wherever they apply a reasonable person standard. This emerging "reasonable child" jurisprudence should have broad, sweeping implications for a host of substantive issues in criminal law.

State legislation: reversing the failures of the 1980s and 1990s

Inspired by the same body of adolescent development research that formed the foundation for *Roper* and its progeny, legislatures across the United States over the last 15 years have begun to reverse the tough-on-crime approach of the 1980s and 90s that led to far more youth being treated as adults in the criminal justice system.[124] Between 2005 and 2014, 11 states passed laws limiting the housing of youth in adult jails; 5 states raised the age of their juvenile court jurisdiction to some degree; 15 states reformed their transfer laws; and 12 states changed their "sentencing laws to take into account the developmental differences between youth and adults."[125] Additionally, since 2014, at least three other states have made significant changes to their statutory schemes to make them more developmentally appropriate. Both Louisiana and New York raised the age of juvenile court jurisdiction to some degree, thereby significantly reducing the number of youth charged in adult court,[126] and the District of Columbia passed a comprehensive reform package that implemented developmentally appropriate reforms across a range of issues.[127]

Considerations for the future

Recent research regarding the normative differences between adolescents and adults has already had a significant impact on criminal jurisprudence and law. However, these changes should only be the beginning. The research and reasoning undergirding the foundation of the Supreme Court's recent quintet of cases involving adolescents has implications that reach far beyond the areas of sentencing and evaluating custody for *Miranda* purposes. Areas of likely reform include the reconsideration of the age at and manner in which youth are treated as fully culpable adults for purposes of the criminal justice system; the extension of a robust "reasonable child" jurisprudence that meaningfully accounts for the differences between youth and adults and makes the law more developmentally appropriate; and the continued incorporation by legislatures and courts of the scientific research into policy and jurisprudence. However, it is up to attorneys, advocates, and researchers to continue to learn more about how youth develop and push courts and legislatures to make criminal justice jurisprudence, policy, and practice more responsive to the developmental needs and realities of adolescence.

Transfer, age of jurisdiction, and accommodations for young adults

Informed by the developmental research regarding the differences between youth and adults and spurred by the leadership of the Supreme Court, courts and legislatures across the country are re-examining what "adulthood" means for the purposes of justice system involvement. Based on the research demonstrating that key developmental milestones relating to executive functioning and decision-making are not reached until around age 25, court systems, prosecutors, and legislatures are looking at ways to treat young adults (typically within 18–25 age range) more like youth in the juvenile justice system.[128] Examples of programmatic initiatives include young adult courts, targeted probation or parole programs, prosecutor-led initiatives, and community-based partnerships, among others.[129] Most of these initiatives pair case management with intensive individualized services relating to education, employment, behavioral health, and housing tailored to support the unique needs of the young adult.[130] The overall approach of these programs tends to be more akin to social work rather than traditional supervision with a more punitive focus.[131]

Legislatures have also sought to improve the manner in which the criminal justice system responds to young adults. These legislative initiatives "generally f[a]ll under three main categories: (1) raising the age of juvenile court jurisdiction; (2) mitigating circumstances, especially in sentencing; and (3) expungement of records."[132] The goals of these types of legislative initiatives are to provide young adults with more developmentally responsive services, to better account for the developmental immaturity of young adults during the sentencing process, and to mitigate the long-term harm caused by a mistake during late adolescence.[133]

The "reasonable child" standard

Although the holding of *J.D.B.* – that age must be taken into account when determining whether a reasonable person would feel free to leave for purposes of determining custody under *Miranda* – is based on "common-sense conclusions" regarding youth, adolescent development research strongly supports a broadened application of *J.D.B.*'s holding and the creation of a "reasonable child" standard that permeates through all areas of criminal jurisprudence, not merely the *Miranda* custody doctrine.[134] For instance, a study by Grisso *et al.* (2003) compared the adjudicative competence abilities of 927 youth to those of 466 young adults.[135] The study sought to measure a variety of psychosocial factors that might influence the participants' ability to make sound legal decisions.[136] Key findings of the study include: 1) that age is significantly related to the decision to choose to confess in response to police questioning and to take a plea; 2) youth age 15 and below were significantly more likely to demonstrate compliance with authority; 3) younger adolescents were relatively less likely to recognize risks, the likelihood of risks, or the seriousness of risks; and 4) youth under 14 were significantly less likely to identify the long-term consequences of their choices.[137] Thus, as youth are significantly more likely to comply with authority while at the same time demonstrating impaired decision-making capacities, these findings have clear implications for other areas of criminal law and procedure – in particular those areas involving voluntariness and reasonableness determinations.

Specifically, the research supports the creation of a rule that age be a meaningful factor when determining voluntariness across a host of areas, including voluntariness of a *Miranda* waiver, of the statement itself, or of one's consent to be searched. Historically, the test for determining voluntariness was whether a decision was "the product of [one's] free and rationale choice" or whether one's will was "simply overborne."[138] However, as the research demonstrates, youth's relative propensity to comply with authority makes their decisions in these contexts inherently less free. Moreover, the diminished decision-making capacities of youth also make their choice less rationale. As such, the threshold for what courts find as involuntary with respect to youth should be lower than the threshold that is applied to adults.

The research also supports the extension of the "reasonable child" standard outlined in *J.D.B.* to all "areas of the criminal law in which an assessment of the 'reasonableness' of the offender's conduct or an assessment of how a 'reasonable person' would have acted or reacted under similar circumstances bears directly on criminal responsibility."[139] Such an extension should apply not only to other areas of criminal procedure such as whether a reasonable person felt free to leave for purposes of a Fourth Amendment seizure,[140] but also to issues of duress, self-defense, *mens rea*, and foreseeability.[141] However, the incorporation of age into these analyses cannot merely be given lip service. As the notion of a "reasonable child" standard has taken root, courts have often given short shrift to the full scope of the manner in which age significantly impacts a youth's ability to make decisions and have relegated age to being one co-equal factor among others that they are required to consider in their analysis.[142] Instead, in order that the "reasonable child" standard meaningfully reflect all that society knows about childhood both from the research and from experience, juvenile defenders must continue to push courts to view age *as the prism* through which all other factors in the analysis are viewed. Only then will criminal jurisprudence be developmentally responsive.

Notes

1 *See* Goss v. Lopez, 419 U.S. 565, 590–91 (1975) (asserting that "the court ignores the experience of mankind, as well as the long history of our law, recognizing that there *are* differences which must be accommodated in determining the rights and duties of children as compared with those of adults. Examples of this distinction abound in our law: in contracts, in torts, in criminal law and procedure, in criminal sanctions and rehabilitation, and in the right to vote and to hold office.") (dissenting opinion); *see also* J.D.B. v. North Carolina, 131 S. Ct. 2394, 2403–04 (2011) ("The law has historically reflected the same assumption that children characteristically lack the capacity to exercise mature judgment and possess only an incomplete ability to understand the world around them. Like this Court's own generalizations, the legal disqualifications placed on children as a class – *e.g.*, limitations on their ability to alienate property, enter a binding contract enforceable against them, and marry without parental consent – exhibit the settled understanding that the differentiating characteristics of youth are universal." (internal citations omitted).)

2 Kent v. United States, 383 U.S. 541, 554–55 (1966).

3 *See id.* at 554 ("The Juvenile Court is theoretically engaged in determining the needs of the child and of society, rather than adjudicating criminal conduct. The objectives are to provide measures of guidance and rehabilitation for the child and protection for society, not to fix criminal responsibility, guilt and punishment.").

4 *See id.*

5 *See id.* at 554–56.

6 *See id.* at 556 ("There is evidence, in fact, that there may be grounds for concern that the child receives the worst of both worlds: that he gets neither the protections accorded to adults nor the solicitous care and regenerative treatment postulated for children.").

7 Haley v. Ohio, 332 U.S. 596, 600–01 (1948) ("The age of petitioner, the hours when he was grilled, the duration of his quizzing, the fact that he had no friend or counsel to advise him, the callous attitude of the police towards his rights combine to convince us that this was a confession wrung from a child by means which the law should not sanction. Neither man nor child can be allowed to stand condemned by methods which flout constitutional requirements of due process of law.").

8 *See id.* at 559 ("What transpired would make us pause for careful inquiry if a mature man were involved. *And when, as here, a mere child – an easy victim of the law – is before us, special care in scrutinizing the record must be used.* Age 15 is a tender and difficult age for a boy of any race. He cannot be judged by the more exacting standards of maturity. That which would leave a man cold and unimpressed can overawe and overwhelm a lad in his early teens. This is the period of great instability which the crisis of adolescence produces.") (emphasis added).

9 *See generally* Kent, 383 U.S. 541.

10 In re Gault, 387 U.S. 1 (1967).

11 *See generally id.*

12 *Execution of Juveniles in the U.S. and other Countries*, Death Penalty Information Center, https://deathpenaltyinfo.org/execution-juveniles-us-and-other-countries (last

visited Aug. 12, 2017). Of the 22 individuals executed for crimes committed before their eighteenth birthday, 13 were executed by the state of Texas, 3 by the state of Virginia, 2 by the state of Oklahoma, and 1 each by the states of South Carolina, Missouri, Georgia, and Louisiana. *Id.* All but 1 were 17 years old at the time of their crime. *Id.*

13 Stanford v. Kentucky, 492 U.S. 361, at 380–81 (1989); Thompson v. Oklahoma, 487 U.S. 815 (1988); Eddings v. Oklahoma, 455 U.S. 104 (1982).

14 *See id.*

15 *See* Kim Stott, *Slain Trooper's Family Upset at Overturning of His Killer's Death Penalty*, The Oklahoman (Aug. 1, 1984), http://newsok.com/article/2076622 (noting that the Oklahoma Court of Criminal Appeal modified Monty Lee Eddings' death penalty to life in prison); *see* Thompson, 487 U.S. 815 (1988) (finding that the execution of William Wayne Thompson would be unconstitutional because of the age at which he committed the offense); Andrew Wolfson, *Killer Stanford Seeks New Sentence – or Release*, Courier-Journal (Jan. 27, 2017), http://www.courier-journal.com/story/news/crime/2017/01/27/killer-kevin-stanford-seeks-release/97137350.

16 Eddings v. Oklahoma, 455 U.S. 104 (1982).

17 *See* Lockett v. Ohio, 438 U.S. 586, 605 (1978) (holding that the Eighth and Fourteenth Amendments require that sentencers in capital cases have the opportunity to consider all mitigating evidence related to the "defendant's character and record").

18 Eddings, 455 U.S. at 115–16 (citations omitted).

19 487 U.S. 815 (1988).

20 *See id.* at 835–37, ns. 42 and 43.

21 *See id.* at 836–38.

22 *See id.* at 859 ("It is whether there is a national consensus that no criminal so much as one day under 16, after individuated consideration of his circumstances, including the overcoming of a presumption that he should not be tried as an adult, can possibly be deemed mature and responsible enough to be punished with death for any crime.").

23 *See id.* at 857–59.

24 In *Stanford v. Kentucky*, Justice O'Connor clarified her approach in *Thompson* and, thus, explained the holding of *Thompson*: "a criminal defendant who would have been tried as a juvenile under state law, but for the granting of a petition waiving juvenile court jurisdiction, may only be executed for a capital offense if the State's capital punishment statute specifies a minimum age at which the commission of a capital crime can lead to an offender's execution and the defendant had reached that minimum age at the time the crime was committed. As a threshold matter, I indicated that such specificity is not necessary to avoid constitutional problems if it is clear that no national consensus forbids the imposition of capital punishment for crimes committed at such an age." Stanford v. Kentucky, 492 U.S. 361, 380–81 (1989).

25 *Id.* at 365–74.

26 *Id.* at 378.

27 John. R. Dilulio, *The Coming of the Super-Predators*, The Weekly Standard (Nov. 27, 1995), http://www.weeklystandard.com/the-coming-of-the-super-predators/article/8160.

28 *Juvenile Arrest Rate Trends, Law Enforcement & Juvenile Crime*, OJJDP Statistical Briefing Book, http://www.ojjdp.gov/ojstatbb/crime/JAR_Display.asp?ID=qa05200 (last visited Mar. 27, 2017) (according to data from the Bureau of Justice Statistics, total juvenile arrests peaked in 1996 before dropping 68 percent prior to 2015).

29 *See* Kristin Henning, *Criminalizing Normal Adolescent Behavior in Communities of Color: The Role of Prosecutors in Juvenile Justice Reform*, 98 Cornell L. Rev. 383, 395–96 (2013) (explaining that state legislatures in the 1980s and 1990s chose to pass more punitive laws to address criminal conduct by youth, including transferring youth to adult court).

30 *Id.*

31 The "machinery of death" is the term used by Justice Blackmun to refer to the death penalty. *See* Callins v. Collins, 510 U.S. 1141 (1994) (cert. denied, Blackmun, J. dissenting) (renouncing the death penalty as inherently unconstitutional).

32 *Execution of Juveniles in the U.S. and Other Countries*, DEATH PENALTY INFORMATION CENTER, https://deathpenaltyinfo.org/execution-juveniles-us-and-other-countries (last visited Aug. 12, 2017).

33 *Id.* In total, states would execute nine youth in the first three-and-a-half years of the new century, almost as many as they had executed in the preceding ten years.

34 Telephone interview by Eduardo Ferrer, conversation with Patricia Puritz, Founder, National Juvenile Defender Center, and former Director, American Bar Association Juvenile Justice Center (July 28, 2017).

35 *Id.*

36 *Juvenile Death Penalty Resolution*, AMERICAN BAR ASSOCIATION (1983), https://www.americanbar.org/content/dam/aba/uncategorized/Death_Penalty_Representation/juvenile_dp_0883.authcheckdam.pdf (last visited Aug. 12, 1017).

37 Laurence Steinberg & Elizabeth Scott, *Less Guilty by Reason of Adolescence: Developmental Immaturity, Diminished Responsibility, and the Juvenile Death Penalty*, 58 AM. PSYCHOLOGIST 1009, 1011–12 (2003).

38 *See id.*

39 *See id.* at 1012 ("Whereas cognitive capacities shape the *process* of decision making, psychosocial immaturity can affect decision making *outcomes*, because these psychosocial factors influence adolescent values and preferences in ways that drive the cost-benefit calculus in the making of choices. In other words, to the extent that adolescents are less psychosocially mature than adults, they are likely to be deficient in their decision-making capacity, even if their cognitive processes are mature.") (emphasis in the original); *see also* Elizabeth Cauffman & Laurence Steinberg, *(Im)maturity and Judgment in Adolescence: Why Adolescents May be Less Culpable Than Adults*, 18 BEHAV. SCI. & L. 741, 741–45 (2000) [hereinafter *(Im)maturity and Judgment in Adolescence*].

40 Cauffman & Steinberg, *(Im)maturity and Judgment in Adolescence, supra* note 39, at 741–43 (Drs. Cauffman and Steinberg refer to this as "maturity of judgment.").

41 *Id.* at 756 (The five age groups considered were 8th graders, 10th graders, 12th graders, young adults, and older adults.).

42 *Id.* at 756.

43 *Id.* at 755, 758.

44 *Id.* at 758. Cauffman and Steinberg also concluded that although the differences between adolescents and adults in terms of decision-making were "*appreciable* enough to warrant drawing a legal distinction[,]" the variation within and among age groups in the study did not allow them to conclude that the differences between adolescents and adults were "*consistent* enough" to draw a legal distinction.

45 *Id.* at 759.

46 Margo Gardner & Laurence Steinberg, *Peer Influence on Risk Taking, Risk Preference, and Risky Decision Making in Adolescence and Adulthood: An Experimental Study*, 41 DEV. PSYCHOL. 625 (2005). [hereinafter *Peer Influence on Risk Taking*].

47 Laurence Steinberg & Kathryn C. Monahan, *Age Differences in Resistance to Peer Influence*, 43 DEV. PSYCHOL. 1531 (2007). [hereinafter *Age Differences in Resistance*].

48 Gardner & Steinberg, *Peer Influence on Risk Taking, supra* note 46, at 625–27.

49 *Id.*

50 *Id.* at 629–32.

51 *Id.*

52 Steinberg & Monahan, *Age Differences in Resistance, supra* note 47, at 1531. Steinberg and Monahan combined data from the MacArthur Juvenile Competency Study, the MacArthur Juvenile Capacity Study, and the Research on Pathways to Desistance. All three studies administered the Resistance to Peer Influence (RPI) measure.

53 *Id.*

54 *Id.*

55 The MacArthur Juvenile Capacity Study "was designed to examine age differences in a variety of cognitive and psychosocial capacities that are relevant to debates about the relative maturity of adolescents and adults, especially as they affect judgments of criminal blameworthiness." Laurence Steinberg et al., *Are Adolescents Less Mature than Adults? Minors' Access to Abortion, the Juvenile Death Penalty, and the Alleged APA "Flip, Flop"*, 64 AM. PSYCHOLOGIST 583, 587 (2009). [hereinafter *Are Adolescents Less Mature than Adults?*]. Data collected for the study came from five sites across the United States and included a sample of 935 individuals between the ages of 10 and 30. *Id.* Participants in the study completed an interview that involved three sets of measures: (1) computerized tasks designed to assess cognitive functioning; (2) questionnaires designed to measure psychosocial capacity; and (3) tests used to determine basic intellectual functioning. *Id.* The MacArthur Foundation, after whom the study is named, played a significant role in funding a significant amount of research relating to juvenile justice reform through various initiatives, including the MacArthur Foundation Research Network on Adolescent Development and Juvenile Justice.

56 Laurence Steinberg *et. al.*, *Age Differences in Sensation Seeking and Impulsivity as Indexed by Behavior and Self-Report: Evidence for a Dual Systems Model*, 44 DEV. PSYCHOL. 1764 (2008) [hereinafter *Age Differences*]; Laurence Steinberg *et. al.* (2009), *Age Differences in Future Orientation and Delay Discounting*, 80 CHILD DEV. 28; Steinberg *et. al.*, *Are Adolescents Less Mature than Adults?*, *supra* note 55.

57 Steinberg *et. al.*, *Age Differences in Sensation Seeking and Impulsivity, supra* note 56. Whereas previous research often conflated the concepts of sensation seeking and impulsivity, Steinberg *et. al.* (2008) made clear that "they are not the same thing. Impulsivity refers to a lack of self-control or deficiencies in response to inhibition; it leads to hasty unplanned behavior. Sensation seeking, in contrast, refers to the tendency to seek out novel, varied, and highly stimulating experiences, and the willingness to take risks in order to attain them." *Id.* at 1765. Thus, in their study, Steinberg *et. al.* (2008) sought to evaluate each psychosocial factor on its own to gauge the development path of each factor.

58 *Id.* at 1774.

59 *Id.* at 1776.

60 *Id.* at 1764.

61 *Id.* at 1776.

62 Steinberg *et. al.*, *Age Differences, supra*, note 56. Future orientation "has been used to refer to a collection of loosely related affective, attitudinal, cognitive, and motivational constructs," including, but not limited to, whether one thinks about the future, whether one thinks about the outcomes of one's actions before making a decision, and whether one plans before one acts. *Id.* at 28–30.

63 *Id.* at 39.

64 *Id.*

65 *Id.* The result of the delay discounting task indicated that significant differences between adolescents and adults in terms of delay discounting was limited to the differences between 13 years old and younger compared to 16 years old and older, indicating that the period between 13 and 16 years old is likely critical for the development of skills that support an individual's preference for larger, more distant rewards. *Id.*

66 Steinberg *et. al.*, *Are Adolescents Less Mature than Adults?, supra* note 55, at 587–88.

67 *Id.* at 591.

68 *Id.*

69 *Id.* at 592.

70 *Id.*

71 *See* Sarah Durston et al., *Anatomical MRI of the Developing Brain: What Have We Learned?*, 40 J. Am. Acad. Child Adoles. Psychiatry 1012, 1016 (2001) (discussing the lessons learned from MRI technology and the promise of functional MRI technology).
72 *Id.* at 1014.
73 *Id.; see also* Jay N. Giedd et al., *Brain Development during Childhood and Adolescence: A Longitudinal MRI Study*, 2 Neuroscience 861 (1999).
74 Durston et al., *supra* note 71, at 1014.
75 *Id.; see also* Giedd et al., *supra* note 73, at 861–62.
76 *Id.*
77 *See* Bruce D. Perry, The Neurodevelopmental Impact of Violence in Childhood, Textbook of Child and Adolescent Forensic Psychiatry 4 (Diane Schetky & Elissa P. Benedek eds., American Psychiatric Publishing, 2001).
78 *See* Laurence Steinberg, Age of Opportunity: Lessons from the New Science of Adolescence 25 (Eamon Dolan/Mariner Books, 2014). This time concept is now commonly referred to as developmental plasticity and "refers to the malleability of the brain during periods in which the brain is being built." *Id.*
79 Nitin Gogtay et al., *Dynamic Mapping of Human Cortical Development during Childhood through Early Adulthood*, 101 PNAS 8174 (2004).
80 *Id.*
81 *See id.* at 8177; Steinberg, *supra* note 78, at 76–78.
82 Jason M. Chein et al., *Peers Increase Adolescent Risk Taking by Enhancing Activity in the Brain's Reward Circuitry*, 14 Developmental Sci. F1, F2 (2010) (discussing the research regarding the different timetables on which the incentive processing and cognitive control systems mature).
83 *Id.*
84 *Id.*
85 *Id.* at F1–F2.
86 *Id.* at F1–F2.
87 *Id.* at F7–F8.
88 *Id.*
89 *Id.*
90 *Id.*
91 *Id.*
92 Telephone interview by Eduardo Ferrer, with Patricia Puritz, Founder, National Juvenile Defender Center, and former Director, American Bar Association Juvenile Justice Center (July 28, 2017).
93 Adam Ortiz, *Overview of the Juvenile Death Penalty Today*, Am. Bar Ass'n, Criminal Justice Section, Juvenile Justice Cntr. at 1 (Spring 2003).
94 *Texas Executes Beazley*, CNN (May 29, 2002), http://www.cnn.com/2002/LAW/05/28/beazley.execution/index.html.
95 *USA: Killing Hope, Confirming Hypocrisy – Texas Executes Another Child Offender*, Amnesty International (May 29, 2002). [hereinafter *USA*]. Justices Souter, Scalia, and Thomas all recused themselves from the decision as the victim's son had worked for all of them. *See Texas Executes Beazley*, *supra* note 94.
96 Atkins v. Virginia, 536 U.S. 304, 318 (2002).
97 *See USA*, *supra* note 95.
98 *Id.*
99 *Id.*
100 *See, e.g.*, Adam Ortiz, *Adolescence, Brain Development, and Legal Culpability*, Am. Bar Ass'n, Criminal Justice Section, Juvenile Justice Cntr. (Jan. 2004).
101 *See* Roper v. Simmons, 543 U.S. 551, 578 (2005).
102 *See id.* at 569–73 ("The differences between juvenile and adult offenders are too marked and well understood to risk allowing a youthful person to receive the death penalty despite insufficient culpability.").

103 *See generally* Aliya Haider, Roper v. Simmons*: The Role of the Science Brief*, 3 Ohio St. J. Crim. L. 369 (2006).

104 543 U.S. at 573.

105 *Id.*

106 560 U.S. at 89 (concurring in judgment only: "Today, the Court views *Roper* as providing the basis for a new categorical rule that juveniles may never receive a sentence of life without parole for non-homicide crimes. I disagree.") (Roberts, J.).

107 *Id.* at 68 (2010) (citing amicus briefs by the American Medical Association and American Psychological Association).

108 *See id.*

109 *Id.* at 89.

110 However, as Justice Sotomayor had replaced O'Connor and Chief Justice Roberts had replaced Chief Justice Rehnquist by the time Graham was considered, the decision resulted in a 6–3 decision with a 5-justice majority opinion as opposed to the 5–4 decision with a 4-justice plurality in Thompson.

111 560 U.S. at 77–78.

112 *Id.* at 67–69, 77–79.

113 Miller v. Alabama, 132 S. Ct. 2455, 2464 (2012) (finding that "*Roper* and *Graham* establish that children are constitutionally different from adults for purposes of sentencing.").

114 *Id.* at 2469–73.

115 *Id.* at 2463–69.

116 *Id.*

117 Substantive rules create "categorical constitutional guarantees that place certain criminal laws and punishments altogether beyond the State's power to impose." Montgomery v. Louisiana, 136 S. Ct. 718, 729–30 (2016).

118 *Id.* at 734 (citations omitted).

119 *Id.*

120 *See* J.D.B. v. North Carolina, 131 S. Ct. 2394, 2403 (2011).

121 *Id.* (quoting Haley).

122 *See id.*

123 *See id.*, 131 S. Ct. 2394, 2403 (2011) ("A child's age is far more than a chronological fact. It is a fact that generates commonsense conclusions about behavior and perception. Such conclusions apply broadly to children as a class. And, they are self-evident to anyone who was a child once himself, including any police officer or judge." (internal citations omitted)).

124 *See* Henning, *supra* note 29, at 395–97.

125 *See* Campaign for Youth Justice, State Trends: Updates from the 2013–2014 Legislative Session 2–3 (2014), http://www.campaignforyouthjustice.org/images/nationalreports/state_trends-_updates_from_the_2013-2014_legislative_session.pdf (last visited Dec. 15, 2017). Typically, the age of juvenile court jurisdiction is the age at which cases against delinquent youth automatically originate in juvenile court. *See id.* at 4–5. Transfer statutes provide a mechanism for youth in the juvenile justice system to be transferred to adult court. *See id.* at 5.

126 Jesse McKinley, *"Raise the Age," Now Law in New York, Is Still a Subject of Debate*, N.Y. Times (April 10, 2017), https://www.nytimes.com/2017/04/10/nyregion/raise-the-age-new-york.html?_r=0; Kevin Litten, *"Raise the Age" Bill Passes the House of Representatives*, The Times-Picayune (Aug. 9, 2016), http://www.nola.com/politics/index.ssf/2016/06/raise_the_age_bill_passes.html.

127 Comprehensive Youth Justice Amendment Act of 2016, http://lims.dccouncil.us/Legislation/B21-0683 (last visited Sept. 2, 2017).

128 Connie Hayek, *Environmental Scan of Developmentally Appropriate Criminal Justice Responses to Justice-Involved Young Adults*, Nat'l Inst. of Justice, U.S. Dept. of

JUSTICE (July 2016), https://www.ncjrs.gov/pdffiles1/nij/249902.pdf (last visited Dec. 15, 2017).

129 *See id.* at 6–15.

130 *See id.*

131 *See id.* at 13–15.

132 *See id.* at 17.

133 *See id.* at 17–19.

134 *See generally* Marsha L. Levick & Elizabeth-Ann Tierney, *The United States Supreme Court Adopts a Reasonable Juvenile Standard in J.D.B. v. North Carolina for Purposes of the Miranda Custody Analysis: Can a More Reasoned Justice System for Juveniles Be Far Behind?*, 47 HARV. C.R.-C.L. L. REV. 501 (2012).

135 Thomas Grisso et al., *Juveniles' Competence to Stand Trial: A Comparison of Adolescents' and Adults' Capacities as Trial Defendants*, 27 LAW & HUMAN BEHAVIOR 333, 337–38 (2003).

136 *Id.* at 338–41.

137 *Id.* at 356.

138 Mincey v. Arizona, 437 U.S. 385, 402 (1978).

139 Levick & Tierney, *supra* note 134, at 518.

140 *See, e.g.*, Hunt v. Dept. of Safety and Homeland Sec., 69 A.3d 360, 366 (Del. 2013) (finding that a child's age is one of the circumstances to be considered in evaluating the reasonableness of a seizure).

141 Levick, *supra* note 134, at 518–27.

142 *See, e.g.*, People v. N.A.S., 2014 WL 2957719 (Colo. June 30, 2014).

Part II

Juvenile defense: models of representation

5 The due process revolution in juvenile court – New York and the early years after *Gault*

Martin Guggenheim

In re Gault[1] revolutionized juvenile justice. Before *Gault*, children accused of delinquency were brought before "courts" presided over by judges who possessed virtually unchecked power to act as they saw fit. In most juvenile courtrooms before *Gault*, no lawyers appeared; neither prosecutors nor defense counsel. Probation officers or other court personnel filed the petition or other document that placed the matter on the court's docket. Judges had full access to everything in the file that was written about the accused, including the child's interview with the probation officer, the police, and others, as well as social and other information that may have been obtained from family members, teachers, or others in the community. Judges would read these files, interrogate the children before them, and fashion an order according to the judge's sense of what was best for the child and for society. The Supreme Court unflatteringly called this a "Star Chamber."[2] Such disapprobation was, of course, deeply insulting to the professionals who toiled in juvenile court. But to the majority on the Court, the criticism was meant as a thorough rejection of the exercise of near absolute power by state officials, even when they wear robes and are called judges.

What *Gault* stood for, above all else, is the simple principle that to ensure even a modicum of a fair system requires meaningful checks on the exercise of power. Such checks are, of course, the meat and potatoes of a regime characterized by due process. *Gault* was entirely about procedural due process; thus the "revolution" was of a particular kind. Juvenile justice may be discussed as having two major components: the specialized procedures that attend the court system and the unique sentencing or dispositional powers accorded to the judges. *Gault* only addressed the court process in the juvenile justice system. It ignored entirely the *substance* of the system, by which I mean the power to *do* something to a child as the consequence of the child getting into trouble with the law.

The disposition, or sanction, is, of course, an extremely important feature of the entire system. What are the proper limits of sanctions on juveniles for their misconduct? When is it appropriate to inflict adult-like sentences on young people? Is it just to subject children to longer periods of loss of liberty than could be imposed on adults based on criminal-like conduct? None of these questions were even touched upon by *Gault*. Even more interesting, the Court would not impose any meaningful restrictions on juvenile sentencing (with the sole exception of

Thompson v. Oklahoma when the Court held in 1989 that children under 16 may not be sentenced to death) for nearly 40 years, when it held in 2005 that the Constitution forbids the death penalty for a crime committed before the person's eighteenth birthday.[3]

Focusing solely on the procedural flaws of juvenile justice was a sound strategy, deliberately employed by Norman Dorsen, the American Civil Liberties lawyer who argued *Gault*. Not too many years after *Gault* was decided, Professor Dorsen had occasion to describe some of the give and take in the Supreme Court during oral argument. As he wrote,

> Toward the end of the oral argument in the *Gault* case, Justice Tom Clark leaned forward and inquired of counsel, "if you win, what will be left of the juvenile court system?" The response, which seemed apt at the time, was "the best part," by which was meant the dispositional phase of the juvenile proceeding, with its promise of sensitive and individualized rehabilitation of delinquents. By providing juveniles with a right to counsel, notice of charges, the right to confront witnesses and the privilege against self-incrimination, the Supreme Court would leave undisturbed, and perhaps enhanced, the process by which delinquent youths are treated and returned to society, hopefully prepared to lead law-abiding and productive lives.[4]

"*The best part*" was meant to describe a system that was characterized by two very different qualities: an aspirational goal of tailoring an individual plan for each child found to have committed a crime by linking them with child services meant to help them thrive as adults and a virtually lawless arrangement by which judges could send children to prison-like facilities for up to ten years after finding them guilty of acts that would not even authorize a term of imprisonment for an adult. Dorsen's acceptance (and seeming praise) of the standardless disposition power to be exercised by low level judges was entirely strategic. Professor Dorsen well understood that the Court would be far more inclined to impose procedural limitations on *how* decisions were made than to interfere with the discretion accorded to judges to impose the sanction they thought was appropriate. Writing only a few years after *Gault* was decided, Professor Dorsen was well aware of

> the widely conceded failure of "the best part" of juvenile justice. In some jurisdictions, there was little attempt to implement the rehabilitation or treatment process; in others, concerned professionals were frustrated by lack of political support or community resources. And, in many states, there were unduly long detentions and even solitary confinements.[5]

Gault held that accused delinquents were entitled to a system operated with "the essentials of due process and fair treatment."[6] But even though the Court made no effort to change the "best part" of juvenile justice, it very plainly criticized it. It described the dispositional hearing process Gault endured: a "'referral report'" made by the probation officers was filed with the court, although not disclosed to

Gerald or his parents."[7] After the hearing, which lasted no more than a few minutes, Gault was committed to the State Industrial School for up to six years.[8] In Justice Fortas's words:

> [O]ne would assume that in a case like that of Gerald Gault, where the juvenile appears to have a home, a working mother and father, and an older brother, the Juvenile Judge would have made a careful inquiry and judgment as to the possibility that the boy could be disciplined and dealt with at home, despite his previous transgressions.[9]

But, Justice Fortas explained:

> except for some conversation with Gerald about his school work and his "wanting to go to … Grand Canyon with his father," the points to which the judge directed his attention were little different from those that would be involved in determining any charge of violation of a penal statute.[10]

Having concluded that children were poorly treated in the dispositional phase of the juvenile justice system, the Court ruled that juveniles are entitled to at least four essential rights in juvenile court: the right to notice of charges, the right to remain silent, the right to counsel, and the right to cross-examine adverse witnesses.[11] It saved for the future the task of deciding whether any additional changes to juvenile court practice were constitutionally required.[12]

No case has had a greater impact on juvenile justice or the broader field of children's rights in the United States than *Gault*. Still, it is curious that *Gault* chose to say nothing about the substantive unfairness of juvenile justice other than that it required procedural modifications to the adjudicative phase. In this chapter, I will describe my work in the early years immediately after *Gault* was decided. As I will recount, the new corps of juvenile defenders in New York City that began practicing in juvenile court in the wake of *Gault* meaningfully impacted how the court practiced. We won many of our cases and successfully challenged long-established practices that were declared unlawful when we brought them to a higher court's attention. We forced the powers that be to invest more heavily in better trained prosecutors. We helped upgrade the quality of the judges as the system became more rooted in law and legal analysis. But our successes also led to changes outside the courtroom. As we helped make the juvenile justice system fairer, as we helped make it more difficult to convict accused juvenile delinquents, prosecutors and legislators came up with a powerful response: they changed the terms under which young people would be prosecuted as juveniles.

Within a decade of *Gault* being decided, states began changing their laws to lower the age of criminal responsibility, in effect abandoning the juvenile justice experiment for older children and for youth accused of serious offenses. As it happened, the state in which I began practicing – New York – was the first in the country to make these changes.[13] Over the next two decades, every state followed New York's lead, either by making it easier to transfer children from juvenile to adult criminal court or by initiating prosecutions in criminal court directly, thereby bypassing juvenile court entirely.[14] By 1999, youth could be tried as adults in criminal court in every state.[15] As a result, an ever-growing number of persons under 18 are prosecuted as adults.[16] Today, a very substantial number of young people who would have been prosecuted as juveniles before *Gault* was decided are prosecuted as adults. In adult criminal court, these young people receive the identical procedural protections afforded adults, but they also receive the identical sentences imposed on adults.

The modern juvenile defender system in New York City began before *Gault* in 1962, when the Legal Aid Society created the Juvenile Rights Division, a unit founded and headed by Charles Schinitsky. Before that office was created, juvenile delinquency cases were handled mostly without prosecutors or defense lawyers. I practiced in the court that Charles Schinitsky helped create and, more importantly, in the law office that he designed. Schinitsky was ahead of his time and advocated for forceful and meaningful representation of children accused of delinquency in the late 1950s and early 1960s. An important organization that focused on children's interests in the 1950s, the Citizens' Committee for Children, persuaded the Association of the Bar of the City of New York to undertake a study of the Domestic Relations Court (in which juvenile delinquency cases were prosecuted). The job ultimately fell to Schinitsky.

For most of 1960, Schinitsky and a small team of lawyers from the Young Lawyers Committee of the Association of the Bar observed more than 1,000 cases, the vast majority of which involved unrepresented parties. But even in the 1950s in New York City, some children were represented by counsel. Altogether, Schinitsky and his team of observers saw more than 100 cases in which youth were represented by counsel, approximately 8 percent of the cases they observed.[17]

What Schinitsky saw, he did not like. In an extensive interview conducted by Peter Prescott, a journalist who wrote *The Child Savers*, a book on New York City's juvenile justice system in the 1970s, Schinitsky reminisced about his experience as an observer of Children's Court. "What we saw," Schinitsky told Prescott, "was an abundance of practices which were not consonant with notions of fundamental fairness."[18] As Prescott reported it, judges always had before them the child's entire previous record.[19] New cases were never decided on the merits of the facts and circumstances of the event that immediately brought the case to court. Instead, the previous claims were added to everything already said about the child, an accumulation that commonly led the court to an adjudication and placement without ever bothering to hold any kind of evidentiary hearing. In these circumstances, of course, lawyers were not needed. All they would do, from the judges' perspective, is interfere with their way of life – a life characterized by maximum judicial discretion to do what they wanted. This breadth of discretion ran from choosing whether to hold or forgo any kind of factual inquiry into the events alleged in the petition to the full range of dispositional options from dismissal of the case to placement in the state training school. Only once in the entire time Schinitsky and his team observed the court did they ever see an unrepresented child object to any testimony on any ground.[20]

Schinitsky's ultimate conclusion about Children's Court was straightforward: it was built on the premise "that a kid is not a full individual with constitutional rights. You did with him what you wanted because he was a kid."[21] Schinitsky's goal became to change this. As a direct result of his work, the New York legislature revamped the juvenile justice system in New York in 1962 by creating the state-wide Family Court in which accused delinquents were to be prosecuted and tried.[22] In addition, the legislature enacted the country's first law requiring that judges appoint counsel for indigent accused young people.[23]

In New York City, an office was established to represent children in the newly created Family Court. It would have the responsibility of being the attorney of record on behalf of all indigent accused juvenile delinquents. It was called the Juvenile Rights Division of the Legal Aid Society. And its head was Charles Schinitsky. This happened five years before *Gault* was decided.

I first became a juvenile defender in 1971, when I was hired as part of a class of six new attorneys in the Juvenile Rights Division (the largest class the Division had ever had to that point). The role of a juvenile defender has long been debated, beginning even before *Gault* held that accused delinquents had a constitutional right to court-assigned counsel. And that debate persisted long after *Gault* was decided, even if many of us had little doubt that our role was to strive to achieve the objectives of our clients, a role virtually indistinguishable from that of any criminal defense attorney.

There were not many lawyers who appeared in juvenile court before *Gault* was decided. In the rare states that even allowed counsel, few practitioners believed that counsel should function like a defender in an adult criminal case. The occasional articles or treatises that discussed the role of counsel for juveniles at the time argued that defenders should refrain from an adversarial stance on behalf of their juvenile clients and should instead work with the Family Court to obtain rehabilitative services for the client.[24] As Kristin Henning has explained, even after *Gault* was decided scholars continued to argue that juvenile defenders "should reflect the paternalistic philosophy of juvenile courts."[25] For some, this meant advocating for what the lawyer perceived to be in the child's best interests, rather than by the child's explicit instructions.[26] Sadly, even today, there are many remaining examples of paternalistic advocacy that bear little resemblance to client-directed advocacy.[27]

This may seem surprising since the Court in *Gault* rather unambiguously defined the child's counsel's role in a straightforward fashion: "to ascertain if he [the accused delinquent] has a defense and to prepare and submit it."[28] The Court left no room for juvenile defenders to trouble themselves with determining what would be the "best" outcome for their clients or with taking on the unfamiliar role of determining the client's best interests before choosing what kind of defense to mount. Justice Fortas gave an elegant instruction: investigate the facts, determine if there is a defense, prepare and submit it. It does not get more straightforward than that.

From the first day I joined the Juvenile Rights Division, there was never even the slightest ambiguity regarding the role I was expected to perform. Schinitsky, the office's founder, was truly a believer in client-centered lawyering and in the right of young people to have lawyers who are expected to strive to achieve the result desired by the client. That was the simple principle on which Schinitsky founded the office. As Peter Prescott explained it, when the Juvenile Rights Division first opened in 1962, it employed three lawyers, including Schinitsky. According to Prescott, the first thing Schinitsky did was to define the role he and the lawyers in the office would perform. In his words,

> [T]here were two ways in which we could operate. One was to decide the best interests of the child. We took a look at that and we quickly discarded it. For two reasons. First, the legislature was clearly not happy with that theory. It hadn't worked for sixty years. Second, when it comes to determining what really is a child's "best interest," everyone's an expert. If you have a child, you're an expert. If you have fifteen different people in a courtroom, you have fifteen opposing expert points of view. I thought, with a room full of experts there ought to be one person who would stand up and say, "I don't have any idea what the best interest of this child is. I'm here to tell you what he wants. I'm here to look out for his rights."[29]

In 1976, Schinitsky sat down with Peter Prescott to reiterate his simple concept of being a juvenile defender:

> The attorney has been injected into the system not primarily because of expertise in the behavioral sciences but because he is trained in law. Counsel for the child provides the primary check on abuse of judicial power. If counsel adopts a "best interests" posture, he undercuts that check and denies to his client his statutorily and constitutionally mandated right to have someone to protect his legal interests and articulate his side of the case as persuasively as possible. Those few children who are able to retain private counsel do so for this precise reason. They would fire an attorney who abrogated his duties in this regard and replace him with one who would not. If assigned counsel failed to assert a child's rights, in the common effort to advance the child's best interests, he would be in essence participating in the creation of a separate class of youthful citizens – second-class citizens.[30]

Part of what I have been asked to do in this chapter is reminisce about my job as a juvenile defender in the very early days after *Gault* was decided. Trying to remember what it was like to practice law more than 45 years ago, when we were newly-hired and struggling to learn how to be effective lawyers in a nascent system is, to say the least, challenging. I do have personal memories and recollections but am reluctant to commit them to writing, concerned that I would, however faithfully, be reporting false memories or exaggerations or ones that were only mine, and not reflective of what other lawyers remember. Thus, for example, I recall an odd combination of feelings: winning a high percentage of our cases and deeply disliking the court system and the judges who presided in it. I recall that our defender office was, by far, the superior legal office in the courthouse. We were better trained and considerably more highly motivated. We outmatched and outgunned the prosecutors we were up against. But are those recollections fantasy? To help me recall those days better, I re-read THE CHILD SAVERS, which carefully studied the same Family Court in which I practiced only a few years after I changed positions from being a staff lawyer at the Legal Aid Society to a clinical law teacher at New York University (NYU). Its author, Peter Prescott, spent an entire year observing court proceedings and interviewing the court players, including judges, prosecutors, defense lawyers, and probation officers, among many others. I was pleasantly surprised to discover that my memory comports with what the principal actors were quoted as saying by Prescott.

The court I recall first practicing in was largely populated by lazy professionals unused to working hard. My adversaries rarely prepared their cases with any vigor. They were mostly weak lawyers who could not get a better job. The budget for their office was low; they were poorly trained and understaffed. But they did not have to be very good to win most of their cases. The judges, too, were poorly trained and, more often than not, bad lawyers who ended up on the bench by buying their seats through political contributions. The going rate for this was half a year's salary.[31]

As I recall, many of the judges before whom we appeared were weak thinkers who rarely bothered to look up the law. They were well used to doing what they wanted to do. Few matters were appealed and in that environment judges rarely worry about whether the orders they want to enter are technically legal. If they are not challenged on appeal, duly entered court orders are by definition lawful.

My recollections of the judges fit well with what Schinitsky told Prescott in 1976. He explained that the overriding characteristic of the judges was their "ignoran[ce] of the law and of the appellate process. You can cite a Supreme Court decision to them and they will say they don't care."[32] According to Schinitsky, the majority of judges before whom I appeared in the early 1970s were "political hacks who came up by the clubhouse route."[33] Thus, among the judges before whom I appeared was Mayor Abraham Beame's wife's mahjong partner. According to Prescott, near the end of 1977 when his term as mayor expired, Beame filled eight vacancies on the Family Court bench with people so manifestly unsuited to such a sensitive post that the press and Mayor-elect Edward Koch let out a cry of rage. Koch called the appointments "abominations." Judge Justine Wise Polier, in a letter to the *New York Times*, agreed and said that "they demonstrated once more the lack of concern for justice to the poor and minority groups whose lives are disposed of in these courts."[34]

If we were disadvantaged by appearing before weak judges, our greatest advantage was appearing against weak, poorly trained, and paid prosecutors. A new juvenile prosecutor's office was started in 1971, the same year I began working at Legal Aid. The New York City Corporation Counsel added a new Family Court branch to its practice. It took over from police counsel, an especially weak version of prosecutors that could usually prevail when they were prosecuting unrepresented children, but were getting the worst of it as Legal Aid grew in size and talent. By the early 1970s, the Legal Aid staff had grown from three lawyers to more than 50 attorneys and almost as many social workers.

The other divisions of the Corporation Counsel's office staffed well-trained, good lawyers. But the lowest rung in the office was Family Court. The weakest hires by the Corporation Counsel were assigned to Family Court and few of them wanted to be there. As a result, we were often able to outmaneuver the newly fashioned Corporation Counsel's staff. They complained about us regularly, and one of the themes of Prescott's study is the jealousy of the prosecutors. Here is what the supervising prosecutor in the Bronx Family Court told Prescott in 1976:

> We have only five trial attorneys here, and me: I have to go into court myself. One of my people is actually assigned to Staten Island, but he's here to replace an absentee. Another has had exactly one week's experience. A third has been admitted to the bar for six months. A fourth, for a year and a half. Our fifth lawyer is experienced. We have no clerk, no typist, no one to answer the phone. Our attorneys have to do their own clerical work. Not too long ago, we had eight lawyers, but one was transferred, another quit, and the third quit under less-than-honorable conditions. We cover three thousand delinquency cases a year in the Bronx, never mind the PINS. We also have four thousand support cases, which, because they're disputes between adults, Legal Aid doesn't get involved in.[35]

Corporation Counsel also was jealous that Legal Aid was more aggressive and more successful at securing grants to enhance their staff. As the chief prosecutor in the Bronx told Prescott,

> Legal Aid is always getting [grants]. We don't because our boss is not a strong administrator. We've never had a strong administrator. The job doesn't lead anywhere, so we've just not had them. We could use more support staff, too. We need access to a stenographer to take a statement from someone. We need an investigator to go to the scene. We could use a police car for two hours a week to bring in reluctant witnesses. The worst of it is that we have no administrative control. I do things my way, the guy in Queens does it another. We have no memos, no standard procedures for ordering evidence, no reliable statistics.[36]

So what was an average month like in the mid-1970s in Family Court? In June 1976, according to Prescott, the Bronx Corporation Counsel's office

> adjourned 445 delinquency and Persons in Need of Supervision (PINS) cases, dismissed 93 more, and achieved 84 guilty verdicts, most of them through admissions. Opposing the five prosecutors in the Bronx were ten Legal Aid trial attorneys, two supervisors, a lawyer in charge of writs and stays, and eleven supporting staff.[37]

The chief prosecutor in the Bronx complained:

> We're trying cases right now with five minutes' preparation. We're trying cases without knowing what's supposed to happen. We can't contact people. We can't follow up. We haven't got the complainant's address. We have no time. And we get a lot of dismissals for this. Dismissals are almost always our fault. We have to take an ACD – an adjournment in contemplation of dismissal, which means that if a kid doesn't get in more trouble within a specified period of time his case will be dismissed – when we could have forced the issue. There are other kinds of dismissal. If a kid has a lot of petitions, we go for one – a delinquency finding – and let the others go, it makes no difference. If we can get a case to trial, we generally win; we're 80 percent sure of a finding. If we can get them to trial. A judge has, say, forty cases on his calendar any given day. Only two or three of these can be tried. Now if twelve of these cases, say, are ours, we may have ten ready for trial. That means we have in the waiting room nine cops, some medical examiners, witnesses, the complainants, parents, but the judge can't possibly hear these cases. Legal Aid knows that if ten cases are ready it can play them against each other before the judge. Maybe none will be tried. Each will be used to adjourn another. One day I saw six cases not tried, just through this maneuver. Everyone has so much to do that their combined hopes that some will be adjourned result in all being adjourned.

These sentiments came not only from the prosecutors. The leading state senator overseeing Family Court practice and the chief judge of the Family Court all agreed. In 1977, at a hearing on Family Court practice state senator Donald H. Halperin complained that "sending Corporation Counsel into court against Legal Aid is like sending the Lithuanians to fight the Russians."[38] And Joseph Williams, the Chief Judge of the Family Court told Prescott:

> The [Legal Aid attorneys] are not only better than their adversaries, but they got all the money. And all the support. The City of New York supplies the Corporation Counsel, and they have Corporation Counsel that are just as skillful, but they don't have any investigators, no appeals bureau, no support staff.[39]

In the meantime, the Juvenile Rights Division was thriving. By the mid-1970s the staff had grown even more, to 70 attorneys and more than 30 social workers. Schinitsky had, from the beginning, a vision of meaningful representation of juveniles that included a rigorous commitment to challenge regularly the rulings made by Family Court judges. He insisted that the office include a Writ and Stay Unit, which brought special appeals in the general jurisdiction court that could review detention orders or in the intermediate appellate court that could review interim court orders. Similarly, the organization included a specialized and acclaimed appeals unit, comprised of lawyers who had practiced in juvenile court, understood the special rules and procedures used there, but were also fluent in criminal law. Thus it was, for example, that *In re Winship*,[40] in which the United States Supreme Court first held that the standard of proof in juvenile delinquency (and, by extension, criminal) cases is proof beyond a reasonable doubt, was successfully prosecuted by Legal Aid. At the trial level in a delinquency proceeding in 1969, the Legal Aid lawyer who represented Samuel W. argued in her closing argument that the evidence was insufficient to prove him guilty beyond a reasonable doubt and urged the trial judge find that, although the prosecution had proved the case by a preponderance of the evidence, the evidence would have been insufficient under the higher standard. Legal Aid lawyers appealed the case unsuccessfully to the New York Appellate Division and New York's highest court, the Court of Appeals.[41] They then brought the case to the United States Supreme Court, winning a major victory in 1970.

To give the reader a sense of how much law there was to be made around the time I began practicing, I will describe some of the litigation I was involved in as a staff attorney in the Juvenile Rights Division starting in February 1972, when I was admitted to the bar. Between 1972 and 1974, I was involved in perhaps as many as 40 trials in which my clients were accused of committing various crimes, ranging from routine candy-store theft to homicide. I won many of these cases, including two within the first two days I was admitted to practice. In my very first case, we really had no defense. But the judge, knowing this was my first trial, acquitted my client at the end of the case. When I was leaving the courtroom, the judge told me that was his present to me, but not to expect more of the same going forward. Thus, in my very first case, I was introduced to a lawless system in which the judge recognized his awesome power and exercised it to impress me.

Over time, defending cases one at a time became less interesting to me than challenging aspects of practice that we came up against on a regular basis and that struck me as unfair. After appearing in juvenile court for several weeks, I began to question a routine practice in the court. Juvenile clients were often ordered into pre-trial custody pending their trial whenever the judge found them to be a flight risk or pose a danger to society, based solely on the statements in the petition that was the basis for commencing the proceeding. Youth, under this practice, were denied entirely an opportunity for a probable cause hearing and the right to cross-examine witnesses. Even worse, the petitions used to bring cases against juveniles in New York were almost always signed by someone lacking personal knowledge of the underlying facts. These petitions were sworn to "upon information and belief." Rarely was even the source of the information provided. This practice had been going on since the Family Court Act was enacted in 1962. I believed it could not be upheld if challenged.

With the support of my officemates, we started challenging the legality of this practice by seeking writs of habeas corpus on behalf of our clients who were detained pending trial. The challenge claimed that children had a due process right to a probable cause hearing whenever they were detained for more than three days without trial. Filing these writs was exceedingly easy. It took me a day to learn what a writ looked like. Our office had a full-time attorney working in the

Writ and Stay Unit. She explained to me the few steps one had to take to file the writ, including the parties that needed to be served. In New York, writs of habeas corpus seeking the release of someone allegedly illegally detained were heard in the court of general jurisdiction (oddly named in New York "the Supreme Court").

These courts existed in every county and, almost always, were literally across the street from the Family Court. Thus, all we had to do was go across the street to challenge various practices in Family Court. Even better, we did not need to wait until we lost the case to challenge the result on appeal. Appeals are considerably more ambitious undertakings, requiring the filing of the record from the court below and a formal brief. Writs could be filed merely by attaching the Family Court documents and pleading that they were legally deficient. The rest of the case could be argued orally before a judge in Supreme Court when the case was called. And, because writs were assigned to a special part of the Supreme Court designated to hear special proceedings, the case could be heard within days of filing the writ. Thus, after only a few weeks of filing my first such writ, a judge in Special Term of the Supreme Court heard the matter. Altogether, I brought perhaps ten of these challenges over a three-month period in my first year of practice. In most of the cases, the child was either released from custody before the writ was decided or the trial began in Family Court, mooting the legal issue because the client was no longer detained.

Finally, after several months, the Supreme Court ruled against one of my clients and denied the writ while he was still in pre-trial detention. In my third year of law school at NYU, I took a course that most students took in those days if they intended, as I did, to take the New York Bar. The course was called New York Procedure. The entire purpose of the course was to give students a leg up in knowing technical features of New York civil practice that were commonly covered on the bar exam. I paid close attention when the teacher taught us about a little known provision in the New York Civil Practice Law and Rules (CPLR) (Rule 5601(b)(2)). Pursuant to that rule, a party had the *right* to appeal an order directly to the Court of Appeals (New York's highest court) without having to seek intermediate appellate review when the only question involved was a challenge to the constitutionality of a statutory provision. For this rule to be applicable, there could be no disputed facts in the case.

These writs met those criteria perfectly. The writ challenged directly the constitutionality of a provision in the Family Court Act that authorized judges to detain children pretrial without holding a probable cause hearing and the undisputed facts in these cases were that children had been so detained. All the writs sought was a declaration that the statute was unconstitutional insofar as it did not require that judges conduct probable cause hearings. As a result, in December 1972, ten months after being admitted to practice, I had the opportunity to argue before the New York Court of Appeals in a case that I had tried and lost in the Supreme Court in October 1972.

That first case in the Court of Appeals was dismissed on mootness grounds.[42] Though technically a loss, it really was a victory. Through that time, New York law rigidly required the dismissal on mootness grounds of all challenges by writs of habeas corpus once the person bringing the writ was no longer in custody. The straightforward reasoning was that the writ's only purpose was to secure the release of someone from custody. Once that person was no longer in custody, no remedy was available. Hence the matter was moot. But in dismissing the appeal as moot, the Court of Appeals wrote:

> [t]he serious constitutional question raised by this direct appeal from Special Term turning on the protracted detention of the juvenile relator without hearing, plenary or for probable cause, has been rendered moot by the release on parole of the juvenile.[43]

We now had powerful language from New York's highest court that the challenge raised a "serious constitutional question." That got people's attention. Over the next several months, I brought several more writs. But now, on each occasion, just as Special Term was about to decide the writ, the prosecutor either requested that the child be released from detention or accelerated the time of trial. In either situation, these actions made the case moot – either because the child was no longer in detention of any kind or was no longer in *pretrial* detention. Nonetheless, by March of 1973, another trial court denied the writ and I again had the opportunity to appeal directly to the Court of Appeals. The prosecutor again used the tactic of accelerating the trial in Family Court and then filed a motion to dismiss the appeal as moot. I responded to the motion by appending a list of approximately 20 cases that we had brought over the past year, demonstrating the tactic of evading a ruling on the merits by deliberately mooting the case before it could be decided by the Court of Appeals. I argued that this situation fitted classically the paradigm of a matter of importance that was capable of repetition yet evading review and that the familiar ground of deciding a technically moot matter also needed to be applied to the field of habeas corpus. Thus, it was very satisfying when the Court of Appeals denied the motion to dismiss the appeal on mootness grounds and set the case for oral argument.[44]

I then had a second chance to argue before the Court of Appeals in the spring of 1973. This time, the court ruled on the merits. Although the challenge brought to the court was to the constitutionality of the statutory scheme, the Court of Appeals chose to avoid reaching the constitutional question by holding that the legislature implicitly intended to include such a requirement. In Judge Breitel's words, "[i]t would take a distorted view to believe that adult felony criminal proceedings were designed to be more tender of the rights of detained adults than the Family Court proceedings are of juveniles."[45] Therefore, the court held, the statutory scheme implicitly required such a hearing. Thus, the court held that before Family Court may detain an accused juvenile delinquent for longer than three days, "there must be presented to the court facts to show both probable cause to hold the juvenile and such facts, including reliable hearsay, to justify the adjournment of the full fact-finding hearing."[46]

As I continued practicing in Family Court and representing children accused of delinquency in the years between 1973 and 1975, I continued bringing challenges to various aspects of practice through writs of habeas corpus and direct appeals from losing trials.[47] Winning the procedural challenges proved to be easy. Although there had been very few challenges to the procedural peculiarities in juvenile court through the 1960s (with *In re Winship* being the huge exception), the new staff of Legal Aid lawyers hired in the early 1970s, after *Gault* was decided, brought many cases challenging procedural and substantive features of Family Court practice as well as major federal lawsuits challenging the conditions of confinement of sentenced juvenile offenders and PINS. In addition to the cases referenced in the preceding footnotes, I or other teammates in the Juvenile Rights Division continued to bring writs of habeas corpus when our clients were detained under circumstances we believed were illegal.[48] Our Special Litigation Unit, which I joined in 1973, also prosecuted civil rights cases in federal court. Among the cases the office brought in the 1970s was *Lollis v. New York State Dept. of Social Services*[49] and *Pena v. New York State Division for Youth*,[50] class action federal civil rights suits which challenged the use of solitary confinement in the state training schools and other claimed Eighth Amendment violations, such as hogtieing inmates and leaving them in isolation rooms for up to 24 hours a day. In 1976, after an extended trial, Judge Constance Baker Motley declared New York's practice of punishing inmates at the state training schools in violation of the Eighth Amendment and issued an injunction preventing state officials from continuing their practices. I was co-counsel in that trial. The Special Litigation Unit also successfully prosecuted *Martarella v. Kelley*,[51] a federal class action civil rights suit challenging the confinement of PINS in secure detention facilities.

One last affirmative challenge to Family Court practice that I brought in the mid-1970s serves as an appropriate coda to this period. After a long string of successes, not all of which have been described, there had to be some disappointments. The biggest one for me was *Schall v. Martin*,[52] a case decided by the Supreme Court in 1984 which upheld against a challenge of unconstitutionality New York's statutory scheme of allowing accused juvenile delinquents to be detained before trial for the purposes of preventing them from committing imagined future crimes if they were released. I first began the challenge to New York's preventive detention scheme in 1974, after winning the earlier cases holding that juveniles have the right to probable cause hearings when they are detained before trial for longer than three days.

This next challenge was to the substantive grounds for their detention. New York, like all states, authorized judges to detain accused delinquents when the judges concluded that they were a flight risk or would not return to court for the next scheduled appearance. But New York law also permitted judges to detain children who posed no risk of flight whenever the judge concluded that there was "a serious risk that he may, before the return date, do an act which if committed by an adult would constitute a crime."[53] It would be one thing if judges exercised the power to preventively detain youth when they had a substantial criminal record. But New York's scheme was entirely standardless. Judges locked children up for preventive purposes even when they had never before been arrested and even when they were accused of low level misdemeanors. *Gault*, of course, said nothing about this aspect of juvenile court practice.

Of all the practices in Family Court involving my clients, the arbitrary power exercised by judges to lock juveniles up when they first came to court struck me as the most egregious. But it was not merely the arbitrariness of this practice that I found so unfair; it was how crucial this judge-made decision proved to be in my cases. If my clients were released pending trial, we were in pretty good shape. We had the luxury of time to plan and investigate the defense. And we had the opportunity to help the client prepare for sentencing in the event we lost the trial or strategically chose to plead guilty. We could find a program for the client or otherwise show the court that the client could safely be kept in the community. When my clients were detained, we had very little time to prepare for trial and those clients ran a much higher risk of being sentenced to a term of placement far from their homes. And yet these dramatically different outcomes were often the consequence of a decision made by the judge after a five-minute appearance in which the judge had the full power to do whatever struck the judge as appropriate. If the judge uttered the statutory language that the child was being detained because he posed a risk of committing a crime before the trial date, that was the end of the matter.

Building on my experience in bringing writs of habeas corpus when my clients were allegedly in illegal detention, I began challenging the constitutionality of preventive detention through the filing of these writs. By now, I was working in the Special Litigation Unit and met with staff lawyers in the Juvenile Rights Division to plan challenges to the preventive detention statute. The plan called for all staff lawyers to object to the detention order of their clients whenever the court ordered the detention to prevent a future crime. The staff lawyers were instructed to raise the claim that the Constitution forbids such detention. The staff lawyers would then alert me when one of their clients was detained preventively. Then we went into action and filed a writ of habeas corpus "across the street." Before too long, we brought a case before a Supreme Court justice who agreed with our claim that preventive detention of juveniles violated the Constitution. In 1974, in *People ex rel. Wayburn v. Schupf*,[54] the court granted the writ of habeas corpus brought on behalf of a child who was in preventive detention. The court held that the statutory scheme violated the equal protection rights of juveniles. The court reasoned:

> Not only is the effect of preventive detention identical for juveniles and adults, but the purpose of it is the same. The purpose is the protection of society. There can be no compelling State interest in prohibiting preventive detention for adults while allowing it for juveniles. Subdivision (b) of section 739 must be declared unconstitutional.
>
> Even under the traditional standard of equal protection analysis, this scheme must fall. As has already been stated, the purpose behind preventive detention is always the same – to protect society. If the classification is not

> rationally related to the purpose of the law, it offends our Constitution. It is irrational to conclude that persons under the age of 16 – who are found to have a propensity to commit crime – need to be kept from society while persons over 16 who are found to have an equal (or greater) propensity to commit crime may not, by virtue of that fact alone, be confined. Preventive detention is irrational when applied if it is imposed because of age and not the danger to society.[55]

Once again, a direct appeal lay from this order to the Court of Appeals because the only issue raised in the case was the constitutionality of the statute with no facts in dispute. But, this time the court upheld the statute, rejecting our claim that the scheme violated the Constitution. In the oral argument, I stressed that the court had only recently explained that juveniles were at least entitled to the same rights as adults when it came to pre-trial liberty. The court, however, explained that it was referring to *procedural* rights: in that instance, the right to a probable cause hearing. But this challenge involved a substantive claim: an equal right to pre-trial liberty.

Instead of taking *Gault* in this new direction, stressing the right of juveniles to be free from confinement on grounds that would be prohibited for adults (something *Gault* itself never suggested), the Court of Appeals relied upon the characteristics of youth as a justification for locking them up more easily than is permissible for adults. "For the same reasons that our society does not hold juveniles to an adult standard of responsibility for their conduct," the court said, "our society may also conclude that there is a greater likelihood that a juvenile charged with delinquency, if released, will commit another criminal act than that an adult charged with crime will do so."[56]

Thus, by 1976, some of the bloom of *Gault* was beginning to fade in New York. Juveniles, New York's highest court explained, need to be protected from their own folly by being locked up in a pre-trial detention facility, even if they never have been convicted of any wrongdoing, whenever a judge concludes there is some chance they will break the law if released from court upon the arraignment for their first-ever arrest.

Many reading this story will be familiar with the ultimate outcome of this issue. In 1984, in *Schall v. Martin*,[57] the Supreme Court of the United States, agreeing with the Court of Appeals in *Wayburn*, upheld New York's preventive detention scheme for juveniles as constitutional. But there was a long eight years between these two decisions and a fair amount of litigation that continued along the way.

Wayburn was a big loss, in terms of pushing juvenile rights beyond gaining procedural protections for accused youth. But the New York Court of Appeals was not necessarily the last voice on the subject. Direct review in the Supreme Court from the loss in *Wayburn* was unavailable because the case was moot for federal purposes. *Wayburn* was not a class action. It sought relief on behalf of an individual who was detained in 1974 and who had been released from pre-trial detention for several years by the time the Court of Appeals issued its ruling. Under any reading, there no longer was a case or controversy for Article III purposes in a federal court.

How might one seek federal review of the constitutionality of preventive detention of juveniles? The device I chose was to file a federal class action habeas corpus petition in the Southern District of New York, which we did in 1978. In order to be able to bring a federal habeas corpus action, the petitioner needs to allege two things: that they are in state custody in violation of the federal Constitution *and* that the detainee has exhausted state remedies challenging the constitutionality of the confinement.[58] The first requirement was obviously met: we claimed that any preventive detention of a young person violated the federal Constitution's prohibition against punishing someone before proving that they committed a crime. We also claimed that the exhaustion requirement was met because, since New York's highest court had recently and definitively upheld the law against a challenge that it violated the federal Constitution, it would be futile to raise the claim in a state court.

This was sufficient to persuade the federal District Court that the case was properly before it. Our next strategy was to try the case in federal court by calling witnesses to show how the preventive detention decisions were reached in Family Court. This proved to be an enjoyable undertaking for me. I was able to call as fact witnesses friends of mine at Legal Aid who had practiced in Family Court for many years and could explain what the process was like. During the contested trial, judges and defense lawyers who practiced daily in Family Court told federal District Court Judge Robert Carter how the system operated. In 1981, Judge Carter ruled in our favor, finding the New York scheme to violate the federal Constitution.[59] Among his findings were as follows:

> The judge has no opportunity to interview the juvenile. Whatever he hears in opposing remand comes from counsel for the juvenile. If counsel is court appointed, and this is the typical case, he takes on responsibility for the proceedings only moments before convincing reasons must be presented to the court for not ordering pretrial detention. The judge has roughly 5 to 15 minutes to determine whether there is the likelihood that the juvenile would commit another crime before the return date if released.[60]

The Attorney General of New York, whose office defended the statutory scheme, appealed to the Second Circuit Court of Appeals. In 1982, that court unanimously affirmed Judge Carter's holding that the statute was unconstitutional.[61] Unfortunately, from our perspective, the Supreme Court granted the Attorney General's Petition for Certiorari, and in 1984, in *Schall v. Martin*,[62] reversed in a 6–3 decision written by then-Justice Rehnquist. *Schall* was widely regarded as a repudiation of the central tenet of *Gault*: that whatever differences the law may tolerate in the operation of juvenile justice as compared with criminal justice, juveniles possessed the same liberty interest as adults. But Justice Rehnquist, writing for the Court, stressed that juveniles have a decidedly less robust liberty interest because "juveniles, unlike adults, are always in some form of custody."[63]

The retrenchment in the Supreme Court in *Schall* was hardly the first blow to juvenile justice advancement in the post-*Gault* era. Despite our many victories in the New York Family Court in the early 1970s, and occasionally *because* of them, things began moving backwards towards the end of the decade. As a result, the complete picture in Family Court throughout the seventies is hardly a cause for celebration. Even if juvenile defenders were winning a lot of cases in Family Court, the system fought back in a variety of ways, often with judges exercising their power directly to undermine the principle of providing all children with excellent legal representation. Judges were notorious for calling cases when the child's lawyer was not present and insisting that anyone from the office stand in for the attorney-of-record. Schinitsky, the only children's lawyer who had been around since the beginning of the new era, complained to journalist Peter Prescott in 1976 about how common it was that judges were the enemy of the children's lawyers. "The courts are worse now than they were a year ago," he reported.[64] Prescott's own observations led him to observe that many of the judges "still think of the [children's lawyers] as obstacles."[65]

One of the unintended – and most consequential – repercussions of our successes was a pushback by the Legislature. In 1976, New York enacted the Juvenile Justice Reform Act of 1976,[66] which authorized courts to consider "protection of the community" in deciding juvenile delinquency cases (because juvenile defenders had taken what some regarded as excessive advantage of a statutory scheme that theretofore only mentioned "the needs and best interests of the respondent" when deciding what disposition to impose).[67] The 1976 Act also enhanced the punishment for certain juveniles accused of specific felonies. But perhaps the greatest, albeit perverse, tribute shown to the strength and abilities of the juvenile defenders in the early to mid-1970s was the Legislature's decision in 1977 to replace some of the regular juvenile court prosecutors (from the Corporation Counsel's Office) with lawyers from the District Attorney's Office, bringing criminal prosecutors into juvenile court for the first time. This was a remarkable shift.

But the ultimate blow to juvenile justice reform in New York occurred in 1978 when the legislature (in a matter of days) substantially amended the law to create one of the harshest juvenile justice systems in the country. The new statute introduced mandatory sentencing for adults, made 14- and 15-year-olds criminally responsible for 14 different crimes and made 13-year-olds responsible for murder. The "Juvenile Offender Law" also exposed children aged 13 and up to mandatory minimum prison sentences in adult criminal court.[68] Thus, New York helped lead the nation in turning its back on juvenile justice. As mentioned at the beginning of this chapter, the country soon followed, making it easier than at any time since the 1800s for young people to be tried, convicted, and sentenced as adults for misdeeds.

It would be going too far to suggest that these punitive responses were enacted because of the success of the juvenile defenders in Schinitsky's shop. But neither does this mean there was no relationship between these two phenomena. A high caliber defender office that unflinchingly advocated for dismissal of charges based on "technical" grounds unrelated to the underlying criminal allegation helped contribute to the notion that even young offenders might deserve to be locked up for longer periods than Family Court allowed. The logical connection between these very different inquiries may be fuzzy, but there is little doubt that there is some connection.

In the pre-*Gault* (or pre-Schinitsky) world in which courts had unfettered discretion to deal with any child who came before them, everyone connected with juvenile justice was comfortable with the organizing principle that children deserve to be treated differently from adults. They deserved to be treated less harshly but, because judges would exercise power over them benignly, they also "deserved" a less contentious and adversarial process. That pre-*Gault* process meant that no child could escape the judge's reach for technical reasons or even because the evidence was sparse. Since judges could send children for "treatment" whenever they thought it would be appropriate to do so, state officials were comfortable limiting the length of time for which children could lose their liberty.

But for most of the 1970s, Schinitsky's minions were whipping the other side, ensuring that children who would once have certainly been placed in a training school were now being sent home without any intervention because the evidence was secured in violation of the Constitution or because the eyewitness was unable to attend the court proceeding.

Thus, a mere 11 years after the great promise of *Gault*, a promise that led many lawyers to go into the field of juvenile justice to advance the rights of young people, New York began a retrenchment that helped lead the nation away from the bright hope that young people would be well treated when they became involved with the justice system. In this retrenchment, states simply gave up the experiment of having a separate juvenile justice system for children that it preferred to prosecute as adults. That led, in turn, to a vast increase in incarceration rates of young people, most of whom were black or brown, because as states like New York abandoned juvenile justice for these young people they became subject to adult sentences. And from the end of the 1970s, when New York led this retrenchment, until the mid-2000s, when the Supreme Court finally ruled that juveniles have the constitutional right *not* to be sentenced as if they were adults,[69] the long trail of juvenile justice reform took a sad detour.

Notes

1 In re Gault, 387 U.S. 1 (1967).
2 *Id.* at 18–19 n.25.
3 Roper v. Simmons, 543 U.S. 551 (2005).
4 Douglas J. Besharov, Juvenile Justice Advocacy, Practice in a Unique Court xvii (Practicing Law Institute, 1974) (Foreword by Norman Dorsen).
5 *Id.*
6 *Id.* at 30 (quoting Kent v. United States, 383 U.S. 541, 562 (1966)).
7 *Id.* at 7
8 *Id.* at 7–8.
9 *Id.* at 28.
10 *Id.* at 28–29.
11 *Id.* at 33–34, 55–57.

12 *Id.* at 58.
13 Act of July 28, 1978, ch. 481, 1978 N.Y. Laws 1.
14 *See* Franklin E. Zimring & Stephen Rushin, *Did Changes in Juvenile Sanctions Reduce Juvenile Crime Rates? A Natural Experiment*, 11 OHIO ST. J. CRIM. L. 57, 60 (2013) ("[F]orty-seven states across the country passed various legislative measures in the 1990s designed to deter youth violence by enhancing criminal penalties on juvenile offenders. These new laws took three primary forms: (1) forty-five states expanded juvenile eligibility for adult criminal court proceedings, (2) thirty states expanded sentencing authority in juvenile cases, and (3) forty-seven states removed traditional confidentiality provisions by making previously sealed juvenile records more open to public scrutiny.").
15 *See Juvenile Justice: A Century of Change*, U.S. DEP'T OF JUSTICE, OFFICE OF JUSTICE PROGRAMS 13 (1999) (showing how "[a]ll states allow juveniles to be tried as adults in criminal court under certain circumstances").
16 *See* Neelum Arya, *Using* Graham v. Florida *to Challenge Juvenile Transfer Laws*, 71 LA. L. REV. 99, 108 (2010) (finding that "an estimated 200,000 youth are prosecuted, sentenced, or incarcerated as adults across the United States" (footnote omitted)).
17 Charles Schinitsky, *The Role of the Lawyer in Children's Court*, 17 REC. N.Y.C.B. ASS'N 10 (1962).
18 PETER S. PRESCOTT, THE CHILD SAVERS 60 (Alfred A. Knopf, 1981).
19 *Id.*
20 *Id.* at 61.
21 *Id.* at 59.
22 N.Y. Sess. Laws 1962, ch. 686.
23 N.Y. Fam. Ct. Act § 249.
24 *See, e.g.*, Jacob L. Isaacs, *The Role of the Lawyer in Representing Minors in the New Family Court*, 12 BUFF. L. REV. 501, 507 (1963); Richard Kay & Daniel Segal, *The Role of the Attorney in Juvenile Court Proceedings: A Non-Polar Approach*, 61 GEO. L.J. 1401, 1410 (1973); Elyce Zenoff Ferster et al., *The Juvenile Justice System: In Search of the Role of Counsel*, 39 FORDHAM L. REV. 375 (1971); Anthony Platt & Ruth Friedman, *The Limits of Advocacy: Occupational Hazards in Juvenile Court*, 116 U. PA. L. REV. 1156, 1179 (1968).
25 Kristin Henning, *Juvenile Justice after Graham v. Florida: Keeping Due Process, Autonomy, and Paternalism in Balance*, 38 WASH. U. J.L. & POL'Y 17, 48 (2012).
26 As an early treatise on juvenile court work observed, "this cooperative, nonadvocate model often mandates encouraging an admission by the juvenile and avoiding the presentation of an available defense in order not to obstruct the rehabilitative goals of the juvenile court." *See* PAUL PIERSMA ET AL., LAW AND TACTICS IN JUVENILE CASES 47 (3d ed., 1977).
27 *See* Wallace J. Mlyniec, In re Gault *at 40: The Right to Counsel in Juvenile Court–A Promise Unfulfilled*, 44 CRIM. L. BULL. 371 (2008).
28 In re Gault, 387 U.S. 1, 36 (1967).
29 PRESCOTT, *supra* note 18, at 65.
30 *Id.* at 65–66.
31 *Id.*
32 *Id.* at 68.
33 *Id.*
34 *Id.*
35 *Id.* at 109.
36 *Id.* at 110.
37 *Id.* at 109.
38 *Id.* at 110.
39 *Id.* at 234–35.
40 In re Winship, 397 U.S. 358 (1970).

41 Matter of Samuel W., 30 App.Div.2d 781, 291 N.Y.S.2d 1005 (1968) (aff'd no opinion); 24 N.Y.2d 196, 247 N.E.2d 253 (1969) (affirmed).
42 People ex rel. Guggenheim v Mucci, 31 N.Y.2d 957, 293 N.E.2d 251 (1972).
43 *Id.*
44 People ex rel. Guggenheim v. Mucci, 32 N.Y.2d 647 (1973) (motion to dismiss appeal as moot denied).
45 People ex rel. Guggenheim v. Mucci, 32 N.Y.2d 307, 313, 298 N.E.2d 109, 110 (1973).
46 *Id.* at 111 (1973).
47 *See, e.g.*, People ex rel. Guggenheim v. Mucci, 77 Misc.2d 41, 352 N.Y.S.2d 561 (N.Y. Sup. Ct. 1974) (juvenile released after detained based solely on hearsay evidence in probable cause hearing); People ex rel. Guggenheim v. Mucci, 46 A.D.2d 683, 360 N. Y.S.2d 71 (N.Y. App. Div. 1974) (due process requires that something more than uncorroborated hearsay be presented before a finding of probable cause may be made); Matter of James H., 34 N.Y.2d 814, 316 N.E.2d 334 (1974) (trial court erroneously denied juvenile's motion to conduct a *voir dire* after the hearing when counsel first learned that the witness for the prosecution had been shown a photographic array as part of a pre-trial identification).
48 *See, e.g.*, People ex rel. Wayburn v. Davis, 52 A.D.2d 932, 383 N.Y.S.2d 624 (N.Y. App. Div. 1976); People ex rel. Wayburn v. Schupf, 47 A.D.2d 79, 365 N.Y.S.2d 235 (N.Y. App. Div. 1975); People ex rel. Wayburn v. Schupf, 80 Misc.2d 730, 365 N.Y. S.2d 110 (N.Y. Sup. Ct. 1974); People ex rel. Wayburn v. Schupf, 39 N.Y.2d 682, 350 N.E.2d 906 (1976).
49 Lollis v. New York State Dept. of Social Services, 322 F.Supp. 473 (S.D.N.Y. 1970); Lollis v. New York State Dept. of Social Services, 328 F.Supp. 1115 (S.D.N.Y. 1971).
50 Pena v. New York State Division for Youth, 419 F.Supp. 203 (S.D.N.Y. 1976).
51 Martarella v. Kelley, 349 F.Supp. 575 (S.D.N.Y. 1972).
52 Schall v. Martin, 467 U.S. 253 (1984).
53 New York Family Court Act § 739(a)(ii) (1976) (repealed and superseded New York Family Court Act 353 McKinney's 1983).
54 80 Misc.2d 730, 365 N.Y.S.2d 110 (N.Y. Sup. Ct. 1974).
55 80 Misc.2d at 733–34; 365 N.Y.S. at 113–14.
56 People ex rel. Wayburn v. Schupf, 39 N.Y.2d 682, 688; 350 N.E.2d 906, 909 (N.Y. 1976).
57 467 U.S. 253 (1984).
58 28 U.S.C. 2254.
59 U.S. ex rel. Martin v. Strasburg, 513 F.Supp. 691 (S.D.N.Y. 1981).
60 *Id.* at 701–02.
61 U.S. ex rel. Martin v. Strasburg, 689 F.2d 365 (2d Cir. 1982).
62 467 U.S. 253 (1984).
63 *Id.* at 265.
64 Prescott, *supra* note 18, at 69.
65 *Id.* at 70.
66 Juvenile Justice Reform Act, ch. 878, 1976 N.Y. Sess. Laws at 1755 (West).
67 Amending New York Family Court Act § 711 to add, "[i]n any juvenile delinquency proceeding under this article, the court shall consider the needs and best interest of the respondent as well as the need for protection of the community."
68 1978 N.Y. Laws ch. 481. The bill was introduced on July 14, 1978, passed the state assembly by a vote of 125–10 and was signed into law six days later. It has no legislative history. *See* Mara Thorpe, *Juvenile Justice Reform*, 15 Trial 22 (1979).
69 *See* Roper v. Simmons, 543 U.S. 551 (2005); Graham v. Florida, 560 U.S. 48 (2010); Miller v. Alabama, 567 U.S. 460 (2012).

6 *Gault's* ripple effect: the founding of Juvenile Law Center

Robert Schwartz

The United States Supreme Court decided *In re Gault* during a time of rapid growth of legal services in the United States. The National Association for the Advancement of Colored People (NAACP) Legal Defense Fund and an emerging activist bar had helped the civil rights movement gain momentum and success. The women's rights movement was emerging. There was new attention to the environment. Legal aid lawyers were challenging government regulation of poor people.

Gault's initial trickle of lawyers for children became a tributary that, by the mid-1970s, was merging with a larger river of lawyering in the public interest. Indeed, we who founded Juvenile Law Center attended law school precisely because we were caught in the flow. By the mid-1970s, legal services were flourishing, and there were about 90 public interest law firms in the country.

It was then, during our third year at Temple Law School in 1975, that three classmates– Judy Chomsky, Marsha Levick, and Phil Margolis – and I decided that it would be fun to practice law together. We were not inclined to go into private practice, so we discussed ways in which we could develop a practice that would serve disenfranchised populations, that is, groups of people who lacked power, whose voices were rarely heard, and who were generally overlooked by the legal community. We discussed forming a practice to represent either old people or children. This was around the time that senior citizens were beginning to organize, and we had some interest in having a client base that would have political and economic power.

For a variety of reasons, though, we turned to children. One reason was philosophical. We were vestiges of the 1960s. Judy, who was a few years older than the rest of us, had been very active in the anti-war movement. I was on the staff of the Main Line Peace Center before turning to law school, and I had also run a youth center and taught at an alternative high school modeled on the early twentieth century philosophy of John Dewey. Part of our sense of the world was that children ought to have a voice in decisions affecting their lives – that was certainly our own view as students in the 1960s – and that a voice was something that lawyers were well suited to offer.

We felt strongly that lawyers could help make the world more democratic. We believed that the law could prevent harm and promote opportunities for children;

that it could level the playing field of civil society by creating opportunities for healthy development, employment, and citizenship.

A second reason we turned to children was inspirational. Two Philadelphia judges, Lois Forer and Lisa Richette, had passionately fought for children in the 1960s. Judge Forer's book, *"No One Will Lissen": How Our Legal System Brutalizes the Youthful Poor,*[1] described her experiences in Philadelphia representing delinquent children after *Gault.* Judge Richette's book, *The Throwaway Children,*[2] was a bestseller that related her experience in the district attorney's (DA) office, where she dealt with cases of street children, abused and neglected children, and runaways. Judge Richette had taught the four Juvenile Law Center founders during our last year at Temple.

Another reason that we turned to children was pragmatic. We had a source of referrals of children who needed legal help. We had contacts with Barbara Fruchter and Connie Voynow, sisters who lived in nearby Montgomery County. Barbara and Connie ran the Juvenile Justice Center of Pennsylvania. They were leading a citizens' movement to prevent the construction of a large new juvenile detention center to replace the county's small, antiquated building, known as Montgomery Hall. They were also promoting a state-wide movement to remove "status offenders" from the delinquency jurisdiction of juvenile court. Status offenders were then – and are today – children who were deemed "delinquent" because of conduct that would not be criminal if committed by an adult. Status offenses included "ungovernability" or "incorrigibility" – the most explicit evidence of which was running away from home.

The Juvenile Justice Center did not provide legal representation, but it regularly received calls from children who wanted help with the courts. There was thus a ready pool of clients for us (by March, 1976, the Juvenile Justice Center would refer over two dozen youth to us). Barbara and Connie had also been in touch with Harry Swanger, Director of the National Juvenile Law Center in St. Louis. We met Harry in the summer of 1975, during one of his visits to Philadelphia, when Barbara and Connie hosted a meeting at which he discussed legal options to changing state law. He also addressed abusive conditions in Pennsylvania institutions. Harry strongly supported our effort to create a public interest law firm for children. That summer, when we found a lawyer to draw up incorporation papers, we paid tribute to Swanger's work by calling ourselves The Juvenile Law Center of Philadelphia. (Ten years later we would legally change our name to the more manageable "Juvenile Law Center.")

We were inspired and influenced by the civil rights lawyers of the 1960s, and by the new public interest law firms that were springing up around the country. There were only a few such firms in Philadelphia, and some of the leaders with whom we spoke discouraged us. They thought, correctly, that we knew very little about the practice of law or about running a law firm.

Nevertheless, Judy, Marsha, Phil, and I were enthusiastic when we opened our doors in 1975. We imagined that empowering our clients would be a constant theme of our work. We had a sense that each child's case offered an opportunity for reform. We envisioned class actions, of course, since the law school case study method had described such cases in glamorous ways. But even in juvenile court we could be lawyers who would seek court orders, directed to child-serving systems, that would put services in place and create opportunities for our clients. We might be those lawyers who asked courts to order out-patient mental health treatment as a less restrictive alternative to a mental hospital, or the lawyers who would petition for community-based services for delinquent clients. If judges failed to grant those petitions, we would appeal to higher courts. We dreamed that we could build, brick by brick, a common law of child well-being.

At the time, there were almost no lawyers for children – for the most part, representation was limited to post-*Gault* delinquency work and some inchoate efforts on behalf of abused and neglected children. The primary question for us was whether children would be better off with no lawyer, or with us. We were reasonably cocky, and believed that we *had* to be better than nothing. (I soon learned that there were many in the "helping" professions who disagreed, who saw lawyers as "counter-therapeutic." They accused us of getting in their way, and they made heart-felt arguments that we were, indeed, worse than nothing.)

So, it was when we opened Juvenile Law Center in 1975, even before we were admitted to the bar. We imagined ourselves as Clarence Darrows or William Kunstlers raising the clenched fist of the law on behalf of our clients. In our other fist we held Dr. Spock, or a recent volume by Yale Child Study Center academics, *Beyond the Best Interest of the Child.*[3] There was a sense that while we would promote rights, those rights would be in the service of children's naturally developing needs. To help us understand those needs, we envisioned adding social workers or psychologists to our staff. It would be a year before we hired a psychiatric social worker, but we had ties with several area child psychologists, and we confidently, and correctly, predicted that Juvenile Law Center would soon become a multi-disciplinary service for our clients.

We were incorporated as a non-profit Pennsylvania corporation in August, 1975. Interestingly, three days after our incorporation, San Francisco attorney Carole Brill founded Legal Services for Children. Like Juvenile Law Center, Legal Services for Children served Bay area children and youth who sought legal help. Both offices began similarly, taking on virtually any case of any child. In the following years, both offices had financial problems – at Juvenile Law Center we solved those problems by cutting back on individual representation to focus more on policy work. Legal Services for Children managed to obtain a mix of funding that has enabled it to continue as a legal aid office. It would be a couple of years before we learned of each other's existence.

We also needed an office. We had no funding, but we were in luck. Judy Chomsky's husband, David, was a cardiologist who only used his Center City Philadelphia office two mornings a week. We had his office the rest of the time. It consisted of a waiting room – it got pretty crowded on Tuesday and Thursday mornings, when we tried to do our work while patients waited for their exams – and an examining room. We were the only law office in Philadelphia with our own X-ray machine, blood pressure equipment, and EKG. When Dr. Chomsky wasn't in, we used each of the three rooms – the reception area, the doctor's office, and the examining room as an office. When we rotated the X-ray machine to be parallel to the floor, we found we could use it as a desk.

The doctor's office had a telephone with a couple of lines. So, we had a roof and a phone, and a law office does not need much more than that. The Philadelphia Bar Association's law library was a few blocks away, and we could also use area law school libraries. To produce reasonably professional correspondence and pleadings, we used my portable electric Smith Corona typewriter. (It would be another couple of years before we could acquire the magical IBM Correcting Selectric typewriter.) In the meantime, we used lots of white out and carbon paper.

In June and July we had to prepare for the Pennsylvania bar exam, but later in the summer and early fall we met with people whom we thought it was important to know, or who might be a source of referrals. We divided the meetings among us, going in pairs as often as possible. We also had no source of income, so to earn money we had odd jobs, one of which, for me, was working nights writing briefs for other lawyers.

We learned that we passed the bar in mid-October, 1975. It was a heady time, and we were eager to get going. Around then we also received our non-profit tax exempt status from the Internal Revenue Service (IRS). We qualified as a particular kind of non-profit organization, that is, a "public interest law firm." The IRS deemed it to be in the public interest for lawyers to take cases that the marketplace spurned. Our kind of work – representing children – was especially suited for the tax exemption, since there were few fee-paying clients in the world we were entering. The receipt of our tax-exempt status meant that we could begin fund-raising, of which we had little experience. But now we had everything we needed for our practice: an office, a phone, a typewriter, a license to practice, and a tin cup authorized by law.

There were many philosophical issues to resolve, some related to the way we ran the office, some tied to how we represented children and youth. We decided to operate the office as a collective. We were four partners, nurtured by a 1960s notion of participatory democracy. Even when we had volunteer staff – and paid staff, a year later – everyone had an equal say on every issue. (One of our summer law students half-joked that if the mailman entered while we were discussing an issue, we would give him a vote.)

We met often during our first couple of years, forging an office philosophy on the anvil of debate. Each week we had both "business" meetings and case conferences. At the former, we dealt with the routine of fund raising, purchases, and outreach. In the latter we discussed every case, and rehashed it again, to ensure a consistent approach to our work, and to avoid overlooking too many issues. (We continued as a collective until 1982.)

There were many ways that cases came to us. Sometimes children's relatives brought them in, sometimes youth came on their own. Who was our client? Eight years after *Gault,* this was still a gray area. In 1972, Lee Teitelbaum and W. Vaughan Stapleton published *In Defense of Youth: A Study of the Role of Defense Counsel in American Juvenile Courts.*[4] Teitelbaum and Stapleton argued that lawyers for youth charged with crimes had the same ethical obligations as lawyers for adults. Teitelbaum would later be the Reporter for the Institute for Judicial Administration-American Bar Association (IJA-ABA) Juvenile Justice Standards Relating to Counsel for Private Parties, which incorporated the Stapleton-Teitelbaum argument.

In 1975, however, the role of defense lawyers in juvenile court was not fully formed. The role of counsel was even murkier outside of juvenile court, in areas such as child abuse, or special education. What if a parent or relative approached us to represent a child? Who would pull our strings?

Judy, Marsha, Phil, and I endlessly debated this issue, as we did so many other issues. We decided that we could only have one master, and we decided that our client would be the child. We made this point clear at every first interview, letting adults and children in the room know that we would talk with everyone, but at the end of the day our loyalty would be to our child-client, to whom the lawyer-client privilege would flow. The first person with whom we would speak – if the client was old enough to talk – was the child herself. We would then get the child's permission to bring in the parent.

We wondered about charging our clients for our services. Many of our friends in social work advised us that children would be more "invested" in our representation, and be more responsible, if they paid for our services. It seemed awkward, but we arranged with some of our first clients to pay "fees" of two dollars or five dollars, depending on their ability to pay. It turned out that money became an obstacle. Just as patients with outstanding bills might not return to their dentist, even if they suffered a tooth ache, children were less likely to call us if they hadn't paid their two dollars. We wanted children to feel free to call. Instead, those we charged had an adult's embarrassment of debt, and several early clients avoided calling us just when we might have been most helpful.

One way we decided who we were as lawyers was by developing a core fund-raising proposal. As a collective, we had to agree on a common document that would establish a mission and goals for the new Juvenile Law Center. Our first grant application noted the large numbers of children and youth who came into contact with the legal system. We spoke of children who were accused of delinquency, as well as those involved with the child welfare system, which handled the cases of children who, at the time, were described as "deprived" (Pennsylvania law, like laws elsewhere, eventually referred to these children as "dependent"). In our state they included children who were abused and neglected, or who were ungovernable or truant. Indeed, in 1974 Congress had passed the Child Abuse Prevention and Treatment Act to encourage states to respond more appropriately to reports of child abuse. Pennsylvania's new Child Protective Services Law was passed in November of 1975, shortly after Juvenile Law Center opened for business, and we anticipated that more children would be arriving in Family Court through the child abuse door.

Our generic proposal added that we would represent children who were in institutions and foster care, or who were eligible for adoption. We also included, in Juvenile Law Center's mission, children involved in custody and child support hearings.

We added a number of miscellaneous categories that were congenial to our self-image. Even though we were beginning to recognize the complexities of cases involving children who were arrested or abused, we still envisioned a core of our work that would be tied to the expansion of children's rights. In the prior couple of years this idea had been gaining currency. In 1973, Marian Wright Edelman founded the Children's Defense Fund, arguing that children should have the same kind of lawyering that had served blacks during the prior 30 years. In 1974, the *Harvard Education Review* devoted a celebrated issue to "The Rights of Children." The *Review* included a seminal piece by Hillary Rodham, who reviewed substantive and procedural rights that were accruing to children, as well as other articles by some of the leading children's rights exponents of the day.

Our 1975 generic application thus spoke of "eliminating arbitrary age barriers which restrict the freedom of minors to engage in certain activities, or undertake certain responsibilities, with or without parental consent." We had the certainty of recent law school graduates, arguing that "those restrictions completely lacking in any rational justification should be eliminated." We were particularly interested in helping youth overcome barriers to obtaining medical and psychiatric treatment.

Our early documents reveal the tension in representing children that still exists in the field. Some of the rights we asserted were based on a notion of human dignity and autonomy – as youth matured, we believed, they should be able to participate in – and in many cases decide – important decisions affecting their lives. We also asserted a complementary notion of rights, one that grew out of children's needs. Drawing on Goldstein, Solnit and Freud's *Beyond the Best Interest of the Child*, we argued for stability in the lives of children.

Even more influential were the burgeoning mental health and special education movements. All of us had studied the literature on mental patients' right to treatment – mental health advocates argued that the state could not deprive patients of their liberty in order to treat them, and then fail to provide treatment. We understood the corollary to the right to treatment: patients had a right to be treated in the least restrictive setting necessary to accomplish the treatment goals. The combined notions of "right to treatment" and "least restrict alternative" led to the deinstitutionalization of mental patients that swept the country in the early 1970s. The language of Pennsylvania's Juvenile Act, passed in 1972, was consistent with the treatment language of mental health statutes, and we felt that we could transplant mental health case law into the garden of children's rights. We would argue, in particular, that youth in the juvenile justice system – which in Pennsylvania promoted "treatment, rehabilitation and supervision" – had a right to that treatment in the least restrictive setting.

The year we opened our doors, Congress also passed the Education for All Handicapped Children Act (then known as the EHA, now known as the Individuals with Disabilities Education Improvement Act). The new law required states to provide "free and appropriate" public education to children with disabilities. The law also included provisions for educating children in the least restrictive environments, and had a preference for "mainstreaming" disabled children with non-disabled children to create as normal an educational setting as possible for every child. With EHA in mind, we Juvenile Law Center attorneys also announced that we would be doing special education work.

Though we had not yet set foot in a courtroom or a classroom, we knew that we had a unique opportunity. As a private office, there were few restrictions on who we represented or how we represented them. Whereas public defenders might be limited to juvenile court representation of children accused of crime, we could represent the same child in more than one setting. For example, we felt comfortable representing a delinquent child in a special education hearing or a mental health client in juvenile court after he was arrested. We had an early inkling that the way public officials labeled our clients should not restrict our ability to represent them. Later, we would learn to fight the labels themselves.

As part of our outreach to potential donors, we declared that Juvenile Law Center would represent children *before* petitions were filed that brought them to court. We asserted that we would thus function like lawyers for corporate clients who did preventive lawyering. We would help prevent problems from developing, and we would help divert children from court. We thought that our comprehensive representation offered the best chance for preventive lawyering, since we could provide advocacy that would change the ways our clients were perceived. Without realizing it, we were singing our own version of West Side Story's "Officer Krupke." We wanted to be the ones who defined our clients, who declared their needs and their rights, and we wanted to do it *before* the formal system did.

Shortly after we were incorporated, we paid Baker the Sign Man 75 dollars to put "The Juvenile Law Center of Philadelphia" and our names below that of Dr. Chomsky on the opaque glass office door. I was thrilled to see our names on the door. Soon we were listed in the telephone book, and then the Bar Association's legal directory. The listings confirmed our identity as lawyers, the way publication of a first short story supports a young person's claim to be a writer.

Clients were the ultimate validation. If we had clients, we must be lawyers. It was amazing how quickly children and youth found their way to us. By the end of 1975 we had done our outreach. Referrals flowed, not exactly like a mighty stream, but steadily enough to be encouraging.

We first had to resolve, for ourselves, the issue that had plagued children's lawyers since the beginning of time, which was 1967, when the United States Supreme Court decided *Gault.* The Teitelbaum-Stapleton argument, mentioned above – that lawyers for children had the same ethical obligations as lawyers for adults – did not have deep roots. Lawyers for children in 1975 were still trying to locate ethical boundaries. Would we argue for what we thought was best for our clients, or would we counsel them and then, no matter their decision, serve as the child's "mouth piece" or "hired gun" in court? Early on we settled for the latter, believing that our clients had a right to expect the same kind of representation that a paying adult client would receive.

It was pretty easy to be a hired gun in delinquency cases, even if the judges didn't like it. In one of my first cases, Philadelphia Family Court Judge Jerome O'Neill called me to a sidebar to complain about the motion we had filed to suppress illegally seized evidence in the case. The judge was a kind old man who believed in the virtues of confession. He would bend over backwards to help any youth who confessed. Denizens of Family Court called him "Father O'Neill."

"You know," the judge said,

> a few weeks ago a famous defense attorney appeared before me, and he stood where you're standing. He said to me, "Judge, I can beat this case, but that won't help my client. He needs to be sent away, and you should lock him up for his own good."

There was silence while I tried to figure out a response. I was appalled, but it was early in my career, and I did not feel I had the stature to be appalled publicly. I nodded and renewed my motion, which was denied. I heard the judge's message. He was trying to train a lawyer who was new to his court.

If they involved Philadelphia children, dependency cases – those involving abuse, neglect, truancy, or ungovernability – usually came to us through referrals from the Young Lawyers Committee of the Philadelphia Bar Association. The Committee chairs would receive referrals from area hospitals. The chairs would then refer the cases to volunteer lawyers, including, on occasion, the lawyers at Juvenile Law Center. (A couple of years later, the Committee would reinvent itself by incorporating as the Support Center for Child Advocates.)

In 1975 – before child abuse reporting laws created a rapidly growing volume of cases that turned the field into an industry – a volunteer lawyer called by the Philadelphia Bar Association Committee would do some investigation and then file two petitions with Philadelphia Family Court. One petition – based on a form provided by the Young Lawyers – asked that the child be adjudicated dependent because of the legally sufficient reasons that followed. The second petition sought a court order appointing the volunteer lawyer to represent the child. The order would also give the lawyer access to the child and to various medical, educational, mental health, or other records thought to be necessary for effective representation.

My first dependency case involved Donna, a 12-year-old African American girl who was seen at Children's Hospital of Philadelphia (CHOP). CHOP's social workers reported that Donna lived in an unsafe home. It lacked windows and electricity. The social workers approached the Young Lawyers Committee, which recruited me. Without consulting Donna, I filed a dependency petition and a petition to be appointed as her lawyer in the dependency proceeding. It turned out that Donna very much wanted to be home with her parents, but this was before the days of "reasonable efforts to prevent placement," which a later federal law would require, and I had not yet learned how to use the law to get Donna or her family windows or electricity. The children and youth agency and the hospital social worker were adamant that Donna should be placed in foster care. They declared that if I followed my client's lead – if I offered evidence in court that would lead the judge to return Donna home – whatever harm that came to her would be on my head.

I did not know any better. I certainly did not want to be responsible for harm to anyone, especially my client. I was just beginning to develop clarity in representing delinquent youth. Post-*Gault* ethics had not yet spilled over to dependency cases – indeed, the field remains split today. In 1975, I had neither considered that there was a judge who was supposed to decide the case; nor had I developed an articulate view of how a lawyer might give voice to a child's concerns.

So, I went to court and I argued for foster care. I learned then, much to my surprise, that the judge listened to my opinion as though I knew what I was talking about. That autumn day, the judge listened to me, and he ordered Donna into foster care. That was my first "win." It was also my first exposure to something I had never been taught in law school – only in children's law will a lawyer's opinion routinely be treated as evidence in a case, without the possibility of cross examination.

After a week in foster care, Donna ran home and the system and I just ignored her. The case was closed. It became clear that I had failed to use the law to further Donna's goal of being with her parents in a way that would enable her to remain with them safely. It was also plain that after I sold her down the river, from her perspective there was no need for Donna to return to me for my sage legal advice. That was before the days of regular court reviews, and I never saw her again.

Meanwhile, new cases were coming our way. Some of them were to be expected. Parents brought children who were accused of crime. We were particularly interested in children whom prosecutors were petitioning to have "transferred" (also called "certified" or "waived") to adult criminal court. One of my first cases involved John Russell, who was 15. All I knew at the beginning was that it was the height of the Philadelphia gang wars. Children were killing children in record numbers. John was charged with shooting a member of an opposing gang. The victim survived, but the DA sought to transfer my client to adult court.

I was able to get John released from detention, where he had languished for several months. I then visited John at the Russells' home in West Philadelphia. One of the ways I sought to show clients that they were about to receive a different kind of lawyering was by interviewing them in their homes. That way I also developed a sense of their families, I could rebut or confirm government claims about how my clients lived, and I did not have to rely on my imagination to put my client in context.

It turned out that John had been "drafted" into his gang. He was threatened with serious harm as the alternative. He was handed a gun and told to retaliate for a perceived offense committed by the victim against one of John's fellow gang members. John went out, shot the victim, turned himself into the police immediately, and led them to the weapon. He was badly beaten by his own gang for that infraction. I discovered that John was an A student who had – until his detention – never missed a day of school in his life. He was the only client I ever had with a perfect attendance record.

Today in Pennsylvania, because he used a gun, John Russell would automatically start in adult criminal court. In early 1976, however, I was able to work with juvenile probation and the DA's office, which soon recognized that public safety did not require transfer to adult court after all. Together, like a rescue crew responsible for righting a derailed train, we put John back on track. We moved him out of the neighborhood, to his grandmother's house. We enrolled him in a new school. We arranged with the Catholic Archdiocese of Philadelphia to provide after-school and evening supervision. John was adjudicated delinquent, but neither the courts nor the DA felt the need to use him as an example by transferring him to adult court. They saw that they could hold John accountable and enable him to turn his life around.

The Philadelphia deputy DA in charge of the juvenile division at the time was a remarkable man named Lew Mitrano. He looked a little like Telly Savalas, and he could be intimidating. But Mitrano had a sense that public safety could be furthered if errant youth – even those charged with serious offenses – were able to reform. He was not interested in retribution, and he was willing to agree to an outcome that was just, given John's history and the nature of the crime. The result was my first satisfying juvenile court "win," even though John pled guilty to a very serious charge.

Because of the Juvenile Justice Center's activities in the suburbs, we had several referrals from nearby Montgomery County. In one case, former foster parents of a 16-year-old white girl named Chris called us because the teen wanted to be with them rather than with her father. I interviewed the girl at her foster home. She puffed on a cigarette as we talked, explaining why her home life was wretched, and why she ran from it in the first place.

In those days, runaways were treated as delinquents. Their status offense, to the system, was like any other crime. Their incorrigibility was "criminal" if it was committed by a minor. No adult could be prosecuted for running away from home, or for truancy, or for incorrigibility. Until the mid-to-late 1970s, when federal law gave states incentives to change the label of status offenders from delinquent to something more benign (such as "dependent children" or "children in need of supervision"), girls like Chris were arrested and processed in the juvenile justice system.

Soon I went to the Montgomery County juvenile court in Norristown on Chris's behalf. The judge was very appreciative of the way I handled the case, because I negotiated a result that pleased our client and her father, and allayed the fears of the foster parents. However, a county social worker who was involved in the case chastised me for my role. "You let the girl manipulate you," she charged, adding that Chris was "very manipulative." I nodded as though I understood what she was taking about. It was the first time I had heard "manipulative" used since my days after college, when I ran a youth center. I had never liked the term. People try to get what they want, sometimes with the guile of a bargainer at a bazaar, sometimes with the bluntness of a drill sergeant. I was never troubled by the idea that clients might try to get their lawyer to do their bidding. It struck me that people often accused me of being manipulated (read "duped") when they disagreed with the outcome I was seeking or the choices the client was making.

The Montgomery County judge thought that I was much less wise and thoughtful the next time I appeared before him. Perhaps it was because I behaved like a zealous lawyer whose client faced serious prison time; maybe it was because

I was representing an African American Philadelphia youth. (Many officials in Philadelphia's suburbs wanted to send a message to Philadelphia teens that they were unwelcome in their counties.) Kerry Roberts was charged with armed robbery. His mother had come to see us, explaining that because Kerry had his older brother's identification on him when he was arrested, the police thought he was over 18. As a result of this mistaken identity, her son was in the Montgomery County jail awaiting trial as an adult.

One night I visited Kerry in the jail, a medieval, thick-stoned structure with clanging cell doors and small rooms in which lawyers could interview clients. Kerry was philosophical about his plight. "You make your bed you got to sleep in it," he shrugged. I was just out of law school, and had not yet developed a philosophy of life. I was impressed by Kerry's, but I decided to fight for him anyway. I produced his birth certificate, and Kerry's case was sent to juvenile court. There the DA promptly moved to transfer him right back to criminal court for trial as an adult.

Under Pennsylvania law, a juvenile court judge would decide, at a transfer hearing, whether Kerry would be tried in criminal court. The DA had to make out a *prima facie* case that Kerry committed robbery. The DA would then have to prove that Kerry was not amenable to treatment in the juvenile justice system. The transfer hearing was listed before the same judge who a month earlier, in Chris's case, thought I was a savvy attorney. When Kerry's case was called, my stock plummeted. I argued that I should have time to put on a case. I said that I had none of Kerry's records, and I asked for a delay so I could be properly prepared. I needed to learn how Kerry had previously responded to juvenile court supervision in order to argue that he was still amenable to treatment.

The judge was exasperated. He said, "Mr. Schwartz, we're all here for the same purpose." I didn't know much, but I was pretty sure that my role was supposed to be different from that of the DA or the judge. The judge was not in the mood to debate the point, but he said that I could have access to Kerry's Philadelphia records, and he scheduled the case for a few weeks later.

As in John Russell's case, I argued that public safety could be achieved through the juvenile justice system, where Kerry, now 17, could be placed until he was 21. Unfortunately, this time I had less evidence to support the argument. My review of Kerry's records did not find many hooks on which I could hang winning arguments. Unlike John, who had never been in trouble, Kerry had a prior offense. Several months earlier he had been adjudicated delinquent in Philadelphia for a robbery, but the judge had sent him home, without supervision, to await an opening at a treatment facility. He was arrested before the "bed" became available. My best argument was that the juvenile justice system had not yet had a chance to work with Kerry. Or we might have tried to mitigate Kerry's blameworthiness by pointing out that the system had sent him complicated, contradictory messages when it sent him away and home at the same time. Neither was likely to prevail. Pennsylvania's juvenile justice system at most could work with Kerry until his twenty-first birthday. (By comparison, the system could have held John for almost six years, had that been necessary.) In 1976 I did not know about adolescent development. Nor, until after Kerry's case was closed, did we hire a social worker who could help me develop an affirmative case for Kerry to remaing in juvenile court.

It did not take long for the judge to transfer Kerry's case to the adult system. Police testimony made out a *prima facie* case, and his Philadelphia probation officer testified about Kerry's failures when he was under the supervision of the Philadelphia system. The judge ruled against us, ordering Kerry to be tried as an adult.

I asked the judge to explain his decision, but he refused. This struck me as reversible error, since in 1966, in *Kent v. United States*, the United States Supreme Court said that a statement of reasons was required in transfer cases. We took an appeal, and I filed a brief with confident arguments.

It was my first oral argument in the Pennsylvania Superior Court, at a time when the seven members of the Court sat *en banc*. One or two of the judges had read my brief. One or two of them pretended to listen to my argument while the others joked with each other or went to the restroom. I felt like I was in the middle of a Hogarth sketch. Shortly before the date for argument, the juvenile court judge had filed an opinion (as required by appellate rules), explaining his decision, and the appellate judges seemed satisfied that such an opinion could satisfy the Supreme Court's requirements for a statement of reasons. I argued that the statement of reasons was supposed to be contemporaneous with the transfer decision, but the Superior Court disagreed. I flung around ambitious expressions, like "post hoc, propter hoc," but to no avail. A few months later the Court affirmed the transfer order. It was my first appellate loss.

The bulk of children's lawyering in this country is done in delinquency and dependency cases, like those of Donna, John, and Kerry. The delinquency and dependency systems are the "involuntary," or coercive systems that enter the lives of children and families. The juvenile or family court hears evidence on whether the state has a right to take over some aspect of the child's life from the parent. If there is enough evidence to support the petition, the court must decide what order of disposition to enter. The "disposition" in delinquency cases is like the sentence in adult criminal court. Most lawyers in delinquency cases tend to focus on guilt or innocence – should this child be adjudicated delinquent? Most lawyers in dependency cases tend to ignore the adjudication and focus on disposition – what should be done with this child? It is easy to fall into that pattern of practice, and in dependency cases we were very much like other lawyers who felt that the abuse or neglect was obvious.

In delinquency cases, although we paid heed to the adjudication, the reality in the mid-1970s was that if a witness appeared in court, the juvenile court judge was likely to adjudicate the child delinquent. This was often out of the best of motives. Many judges, like Father O'Neill, believed that they could save the children who were at the bar of the court. For that reason, I hated to appear before judges who wanted to be helpful. They felt that lawyers got in their way with motions, or challenges to evidence, and they would therefore be unable to help. Many judges blithely found proof beyond a reasonable doubt on the flimsiest of evidence. As one judge said to me, "Maybe the boy didn't commit this crime, but he probably hasn't been caught for other crimes he has committed."

There were exceptions. We always liked to appear before Judge Harvey Schmidt, who was one of several judges who ran their courtrooms by the book. He had a reputation as a judge who was good on the law. If prosecutors did not prove that children committed delinquent acts by proof beyond a reasonable doubt, Judge Schmidt would dismiss the petitions. In most court rooms, however, the battle would be fought over disposition.

Our attitude about delinquency dispositions was strongly influenced in 1975 by the work of Jerome Miller and the Camp Hill Project. Around the time that Jerry Miller arrived in Pennsylvania, the State Correctional Institution at Camp Hill had two wings, one for adults and one that housed over 400 juveniles. It was, for adults and juveniles, a prison.

A youthful Miller had won a national reputation when he ran the Massachusetts juvenile justice system in the early 1970s. He had then closed Massachusetts's reform schools – also called "training schools" – sending their residents to a network of group homes, foster homes, and in-home care, each having several levels of supervision. A Republican governor hired Miller in Massachusetts. A Democratic governor, Milton Shapp, brought him to Pennsylvania as a deputy secretary in the state's Department of Public Welfare, which had oversight of the Commonwealth's youth development centers.

While we were establishing Juvenile Law Center, Shapp's Attorney General, Robert Kane, ordered the closing of Camp Hill. Many of the juvenile court judges in the state were livid. They felt that they had not been consulted, and they saw the removal of one of their important dispositional options as a slap at their authority. Many of the judges also saw nothing wrong with using the Camp Hill prison for children. They were powerless, however, to stop the closure.

In the year or two it took to close the prison to kids, Miller ignored neither the judges nor public safety. He arranged for each of Camp Hill's residents to have a new disposition plan, to be approved by a judge after a hearing, that would promote youth development and public safety. No juvenile would be released unless it was done pursuant to a court order.

Miller created a non-profit corporation, the Center for Community Alternatives (CCA), for the purpose of developing new plans for Camp Hill's residents. By examining the profiles of Camp Hill's youth, Miller determined that only about 10 percent were there for violent offenses. Those would go to youth development centers, while the rest of the youth could be moved to less secure settings or returned to their communities. CCA entered into a contract with Juvenile Law Center to represent a number of the Camp Hill residents at re-redisposition hearings in courts around the state.

CCA's staff, in particular Tony DeMarco (who later would found the Children's Law Center of Massachusetts), knew of Juvenile Law Center in part from Judy Chomsky's work in representing several Camp Hill youth at legislative hearings. There had been a disturbance at Camp Hill, several residents were beaten, and we were the only office willing and available to represent the youth when a legislative committee investigated the disturbance.

Judy and I were doing a significant amount of Juvenile Law Center's delinquency work at this time. Marsha was handling delinquency cases, but she was also taking mental health and education cases that came our way, and she was developing an affirmative litigation practice. Phil was immersed in child welfare cases. Judy and I traveled to different Pennsylvania counties, appearing before hostile juvenile court judges to present new disposition plans developed by CCA staff. In each case we had to show that the plan would address public safety and the needs of the youth.

One reason the judges opposed Camp Hill's closing was that Philadelphia's juvenile homicide rate had reached all time highs in the early 1970s. Most of the homicides were tied to youth gangs. True, in Pennsylvania a child of any age charged with murder was treated as an adult who would be sentenced, not to the children's wing, but to the adult wing of Camp Hill. But with violence so rampant, it seemed an inopportune time to close a maximum security prison. Critics of the closure predicted that juvenile crime would skyrocket once kids knew that the maximum security facility would cease to be available.

The opposite happened. Camp Hill closed, and youth violence diminished dramatically. Within a couple of years, juvenile homicides had dropped by almost 80 percent. I often remarked facetiously that the closing of the prison led to a reduction in youth crime. That was not true, of course, but the closing of Camp Hill showed that prisons were not necessary for public safety, especially when they were used for trivial offenders.

Through DeMarco and CCA, we at Juvenile Law Center learned during our first year how to develop a sound disposition plan to present to the juvenile court. It is more than a little ironic that the initials "CCA" today stand for the Corrections Corporation of America, one of the largest for-profit prison businesses in the world.

One Juvenile Law Center case with CCA had a unique spin, offering us a chance for a rare, undiluted win. Judy and I went to Cumberland County, just west of Harrisburg, seeking the release of Barry Taylor, a 16-year-old with long, blonde hair, placed in Camp Hill by an upstate judge for auto theft. Barry was in the adult wing at Camp Hill. He had tried to escape from the juvenile side. His plans were not very secret, however, and when he went over the wall he landed in the welcoming arms of a group of state troopers. Over the next eight hours, Barry was arrested, transferred to adult court, waived his right to indictment, and pled guilty to the adult charge of felony escape.

There was a bit of confusion over his status – as I recall, the Western Pennsylvania judge who sent Barry to Camp Hill expected him to complete his juvenile "sentence" before he started his adult time. Judy and I knew that the juvenile sentence was the least of Barry's problems – if he was legally an adult, we could probably get the juvenile disposition vacated. Our goal, however, was to have the adult conviction reversed, since under Pennsylvania's Juvenile Act, Barry was entitled to three days advance written notice before a hearing could be held on the prosecutor's motion to transfer his case to criminal court. We filed a post-conviction petition in Cumberland County Court, and on the day of the hearing the judge had to reverse Barry's conviction. Even if he had been an expert in a juvenile court version of three-card monte, the prosecutor would not have been able to convince the court that three days notice had been given to a boy who was arrested, transferred, and convicted in a single day.

Given the facts, the case should have been easy. We should not have had to file so many motions and memoranda, or had to appear for a contested hearing. We learned, though, that if authorities are determined to maintain control over a youth, they would fight us every step of the way. The case was less about fairness and more about the assertion of power. At the end of the hearing, the judge reluctantly remanded Barry to juvenile court, but it should not have been so hard for us to get him there. It seems to me now that if we had not been so callow, and so obviously challenging an established order, the whole case might have been resolved with a phone call. As first-year lawyers, we had not yet earned the right to obtain quick results.

As CCA was winding down its work, it ran out of money. Unfortunately, it still owed Juvenile Law Center 2,000 dollars, which was an enormous amount to us. After all, we had virtually no other income during our first year. Tony DeMarco said that he could pay us with furniture from CCA's office. That June, I took a colleague, a couple of summer law students, and a U-Haul to Harrisburg. We returned to Philadelphia with a load of desks and chairs that Juvenile Law Center still uses.

In July, 1976, with our first federal grant, Judy, Marsha, Phil, and I could look forward to earning $7–8,000 during the next year. We were now earning a living as lawyers for children. We found an office, now that we could pay rent. We had our own phones, and a brand new Xerox copier. We were in business.

Notes

1 Lois D. Forer, "No One Will Lissen": How Our Legal System Brutalizes the Youthful Poor (John Day Co., 1970).
2 Lisa A. Richette, The Throwaway Children (Lippincott, 1969).
3 Joseph Goldstein et al., Beyond the Best Interests of the Child (Free Press, 1973).
4 W. Vaughan Stapleton & Lee E. Teitelbaum, In Defense of Youth: A Study of the Role of Counsel in American Juvenile Courts (Russell Sage Foundaton, 1972).

7 Specializing in juvenile defense: the D.C. Public Defender Service as a case study

Kristin Henning, Randy Hertz and Hannah McElhinny

The Public Defender Service (PDS) for the District of Columbia has an expansive, specialized juvenile unit for the provision of high-quality defense representation for children charged with delinquency offenses. First-year attorneys represent children under the supervision of three highly experienced felony trial lawyers assigned to the unit, and each juvenile PDS client has access to dedicated juvenile social workers, educational attorneys, civil legal services attorneys, and an immigration attorney. This specialized juvenile representation is supported by PDS investigations and appellate divisions.

A hypothetical scenario helps illustrate how PDS's juvenile unit works:

> On a typical day, an attorney from PDS's juvenile unit will be assigned to represent a child who has been arrested. Let's call him Joseph. Joseph's attorney will investigate the facts of Joseph's case, negotiate with the prosecutor, take the case to trial or get it diverted, dismissed, or resolved by means of a favorable plea offer, and, in the event of an adjudication, persuade the judge to give Joseph the most lenient sentence possible. But, at the start of the new case, her first task will be to introduce herself to her new client and explain that she works for him, for his expressed interests, and what he is entitled to expect from her. Joseph's attorney will then fight as hard as she can at an initial hearing for Joseph's release.
>
> At PDS, juvenile clients like Joseph can expect a lot of support. His public defender will have been well-trained in a two-month-long program that covered criminal and juvenile law as well as trial skills. She will participate in a juvenile trial practice group that meets two hours each week, as well as in trainings for the full trial division. And she will be closely supervised – meeting with her juvenile supervisor within a day of picking up Joseph's case to discuss the theory of the case and how to implement it and then meeting with her supervisor at least once a week thereafter to review her cases. She will also have her supervisor in the courtroom with her for all of her trials. She will be part of a class of attorneys who all came to juvenile court together, practicing in front of the same judges and working with the same probation officers and service provider. Her classmates will provide a significant source of support for

each other. They will even co-counsel the most serious cases that come in, so no individual attorney gets overwhelmed.

Joseph and his lawyer will have access to all the same resources that any adult PDS client with a criminal case would have. An investigator will be assigned to the case to find and interview witnesses, take photographs, view physical evidence and complete any other investigation the lawyer feels is necessary. If an expert is needed, either for an issue in the trial (eyewitness testimony or accident reconstruction) or for an issue affecting Joseph (his competency to waive his rights), the office will pay for such an expert without any reluctance although this is a delinquency case rather than a criminal one. Transcripts will be obtained if necessary.

In addition to a well-trained, well-supervised attorney and parity of resources, Joseph will have the benefit of PDS's team defense model. His attorney will decide, after meeting Joseph and interviewing him, whether to refer him to a special education attorney to help with the legal issues surrounding his school placement and education services, to a social worker for help accessing mental health and substance abuse programs, to a civil legal services attorney if he needs help with public benefits, child support or housing, or to an immigration attorney if he needs that kind of legal advice or assistance. If Joseph is detained at any point in his case, he will have access to PDS's Juvenile Services Program (JSP), which works inside the detention facilities for pre-trial and committed youth to ensure humane conditions of confinement and to represent them in disciplinary hearings and other types of administrative proceedings.

All of these professional team members are employed by PDS, and all are specialists who understand how their own practice areas interact with the juvenile justice system. The juvenile defender is the team leader, who decides which efforts are most supportive of Joseph's goals in his delinquency case. The team meets regularly to assess progress and chart a course, and appears in court to give reports to Joseph's judge. The whole team is guided by Joseph's expressed interests.

As Joseph's attorney enters the cellblock for their first meeting, she brings more than a law degree. She brings the promise of an entire agency committed to providing excellent holistic defense representation to Joseph.

This is the PDS juvenile unit of the present day. But it did not start out this way. It is useful to look back to see how the present approach emerged and why the office made the choices it did.

A look back: PDS before the juvenile defense specialty

In the 1970s and 1980s, PDS did not have a freestanding juvenile unit at all. New PDS lawyers were assigned to juvenile court for their first year of practice as essentially a training ground for learning the practices they would use throughout their career as defenders. Before picking up any cases, the new lawyer participated in an intensive, six-week training program that taught the information and skills they would need to represent juvenile clients in delinquency cases. Upon completing that training, the new lawyer would go to court once a week to pick up new cases and build up a caseload over time. As the cases came in, usually at a rate of about four or five a week, the new lawyer would prepare for trial and handle all of the tasks involved in representing their clients. During this time, they would receive intensive supervision from the training director and another senior lawyer to oversee the quality their work and ensure they were learning what they needed in order to become an outstanding lawyer.

The learning process went far beyond skills, of course. In the training program and thereafter, new PDS lawyers engaged with juvenile clients and their families and began to understand the myriad difficulties that indigent young people faced growing up in an urban environment. The lawyers learned about the educational challenges these young people faced in a school system that so often failed them; the psychological and emotional scars left by dealing with parents and other family members who suffered from substance abuse or other problems; and the seemingly insurmountable hurdles of governmental systems that discriminated against indigent black young men and women. As Professor Charles Ogletree wrote about his experiences as a new PDS lawyer in 1978:

> In our six-week orientation program, and throughout our tenure, PDS reminded defenders that most clients would be poor, uneducated, and from single-parent families, and that a family history of drug abuse would be common. We were taught to view the client as a victim – someone who had endured suffering and deprivation, and who would continue to suffer without our assistance. It was argued that there was a direct relationship between the client's social background and his present status. It was not enough to understand this connection in the abstract. We were encouraged to immerse ourselves in the reality of each client's life, to get to know him, his background, his family, and friends.[1]

The lawyers also came to understand that effective representation required the lawyer to deal with the client's school, family, and other problems because, in the event that the client was convicted at trial or took a guilty plea, avoiding incarceration depended on convincing the judge that the client would go to school regularly and stay out of trouble. So, it fell upon the lawyer to figure out solutions to years of abandonment or neglect of the client by the school system and possibly also the parent and other family members and a host of governmental social services agencies.

Unfortunately, the lawyers were often ill-prepared for this crucial dimension of juvenile court work. Although rigorously trained in trial skills that would serve them well in both juvenile and adult court, they often had only a very cursory preparation for these specialized, highly complex aspects of juvenile court practice. The feelings of dismay and frustration, often felt by the lawyers, are well captured by the following reminiscence of former PDS lawyer Randy Bellows, who began working at PDS in 1979 and wrote about his experiences in 1983:

> I disliked Juvenile Court. Adult clients were simple. Their needs were simple. They needed to get out of jail. That I understood. That I could help them achieve. My juvenile clients needed much, much more. They needed fathers and mothers who cared. They needed friends who would not lead them astray. They needed discipline and counseling and remedial reading and a thousand and one other things I could not give them. I was not trained to be a social worker, yet so much of Juvenile Court is social work.[2]

The fledgling defenders at PDS invariably managed to pull things together and come up with ways to deal with their juvenile clients' problems, at least to the extent necessary to handle the pending delinquency case successfully. Often the key was the assistance of PDS's unit of social workers and social service professionals – then known as the "Offender Rehabilitation Division" and now called the "Office of Rehabilitation and Development" (ORD) – which assisted the lawyers in identifying and arranging community-based social services of all sorts. In the course of doing so, ORD workers also helped the lawyers appreciate what holistic service to a client entails.

By the end of the year in juvenile court, a PDS lawyer had grown into an effective advocate, able to handle whatever challenges juvenile court was likely to throw at them or at least sufficiently savvy to know how to find whatever advice or assistance they needed from senior attorneys or from ORD. At the end of that year, the PDS lawyer moved on to adult court to handle misdemeanors and sometimes also felonies, and no longer took on new juvenile clients. Although the lawyer naturally continued working on their existing juvenile cases until their completion, the time in juvenile court was now effectively over.

The first glimmers of a juvenile defense specialty

In the 1970s and 1980s, PDS employed the then-prevailing model of a defender's office. PDS represented criminal defendants and alleged juvenile delinquents at the trial and appellate levels of a criminal or delinquency case, and its mental health division represented individuals in civil commitment proceedings. Although individual lawyers often went beyond these traditional conceptions by assisting clients in a wide range of matters – some of which grew out of their criminal or delinquency or mental health cases and others of which did not – the central focus was on individual representation in the pending court case.

The office began to break out of this model, however, in order to deal with the persistent, overwhelming inadequacies of the juvenile correctional facilities in the District of Columbia. In those years, youth who were prosecuted in delinquency cases in D.C. Superior Court Family Division's Juvenile Branch were detained pending trial and, in the event of conviction, "committed" (the euphemistic term for incarcerated) in a large facility in Washington D.C. known as the "Receiving

Home" (a medium-security residential facility in Laurel, Maryland, known as "Cedar Knoll") or a high-security residential facility, also in Laurel, known as "Oak Hill." The innocuous name of the first of these facilities and the bucolic names of the latter two were in sharp contrast with the appearance and conditions of these facilities. They were lock-down facilities, one of which (Oak Hill) was surrounded by barbed wire fences.

The conditions in these facilities first became the subject of judicial scrutiny in 1970, when lawyers for children confined at the Receiving Home challenged conditions at the facility in a motion for release. This litigation resulted in an order by D.C. Superior Court Judge Harold H. Greene in 1970,[3] declaring that the Receiving Home was not a suitable place of detention, and prohibiting use of that facility after October 13, 1972.[4] Yet, the facility remained in use. Thereafter, in 1976, the Family Division issued an order in the *Savoy* case, regulating the nature of procedures for disciplining children who were detained in D.C. juvenile facilities.[5]

In 1977, in response to allegations by four youth that they were seriously mistreated while at Cedar Knoll, D.C. Superior Court Judge Gladys Kessler – who was serving as the new referrals judge in the D.C. Superior Court Family Division's Juvenile Branch – initiated what she termed a "'special proceeding'" to "'inquire into the conditions surrounding the detention and incarceration of juveniles who come before it.'"[6] Judge Kessler ordered PDS to "'represent all juveniles detained and committed at Cedar Knoll' for purposes of the inquiry."[7] The court held six days of hearings, over the course of seven months (from September 1977 to April 1978). In 1978, the court issued an order mandating extensive reforms in the facility. The District of Columbia responded by filing a notice of appeal in the D.C. Court of Appeals and seeking a stay, which was granted. In 1981, following appellate briefing and argument (in which PDS continued to serve as counsel for youth confined at Cedar Knoll), the D.C. Court of Appeals vacated Judge Kessler's order, holding that:

> the trial court was without jurisdiction to grant the relief contained in its final order since the four juveniles originally before the court were no longer in custody at the Children's Center on August 7, 1978 [the date of Judge Kessler's order], and there was no class action complaint brought on behalf of all juveniles detained and committed at Cedar Knoll and Oak Hill.[8]

In the wake of the D.C. Court of Appeals' order, it was clear that the only hope for wide-scale relief for the children confined in D.C. detention and commitment facilities was a class action. PDS began conferring with the American Civil Liberties Union's National Prison Project and Georgetown University Law Center's Juvenile Justice Clinic about the possibility of bringing a class action suit. In the hope of resolving the matter short of litigation, PDS informed the agency in charge of the facilities – then called the Department of Human Services – that a class action was being contemplated, and suggested that the parties meet to discuss informal remedies. The agency was initially responsive, which led to repeated meetings over the course of the ensuing years to discuss reforms at the facilities. But the talks ultimately proved fruitless. On March 1, 1985, PDS and the National Prison Project filed a class action suit in D.C. Superior Court's Civil Division, challenging conditions in the juvenile detention and correctional facilities in use at that time, Cedar Knoll and Oak Hill. The 42-page complaint described Cedar Knoll as "an antiquated 'reform school' whose buildings have become unfit for habitation [and which 'are insufficiently heated and ventilated, … infested with vermin, and have gaping holes in walls and ceilings'], and whose programs are grossly limited and wholly inadequate"; and it described Oak Hill as a facility with "buildings [that] … are newer than those at Cedar Knoll and so … appear[ing] on the surface to be a better facility," but suffering from "services … [that] are as deplorably inadequate as those at Cedar Knoll."[9] The complaint also alleged that the plaintiffs – the class of "children who are or will be confined in juvenile detention facilities operated by the District of Columbia" – "live under conditions that are inhumane and that inflict needless suffering," and that they "are deprived of the educational, vocational, mental health, and other social services that they so desperately need and that defendants are obligated to provide."[10]

After extensive pre-trial discovery and briefing, the parties presented the court with a proposed settlement agreement. The court approved the agreement and issued a binding Consent Decree on July 24, 1986. As the D.C. Court of Appeals later recounted in one of the appeals in the case:

> The Consent Decree was based on three general principles. The first principle was "the right of children to be housed and provided services in the least restrictive setting consistent with the protection of the public, the youth's individual needs and with applicable court rules, statutory and constitutional provisions." The second principle was the right of a child not to be in secure confinement when capable of functioning effectively in a community based program. The third principle was that a child should remain in pre-trial detention for the shortest possible period and in no event to exceed 30 days or, in the case of a pre-trial shelter house placement, 45 days, but recognized that the presence of juveniles in pre-trial detention for longer periods as a result of court delays would require the District to provide additional detention slots.
>
> The Decree established a panel of three experts …, one named by the appellees, one selected by the appellants, and one chosen by the parties, to "determine the appropriate number of juveniles in need of secure confinement in the District and to develop a system for appropriate care, services, and placement of securely confined juveniles in YSA custody." The Decree also appointed a monitor to make findings and recommendations "concerning steps to be taken to achieve compliance."[11]

The construction of PDS's modern approach to juvenile defense

In the late 1990s, PDS began to consider what form of representation would work best for juvenile clients. So much of the child's liberty in a delinquency case depended on factors such as school performance and adjustment in the home, and the defense attorney needed support from specialists in those areas. The concept of team defense was born, and it revolutionized PDS's juvenile practice. PDS applied for grants to fill positions for educational attorneys, social workers, and a benefits specialist. As the success of this model became increasingly evident, PDS ultimately assumed responsibility for hiring full-time employees in these areas. Investment in the juvenile defender's training and support also grew to include more permanent juvenile defenders and dedicated juvenile supervisors, as well as ongoing trial practice training for juvenile defense.

This part of the story began with a wish list – a wish list that was conceived when the Office of Juvenile Justice and Delinquency Prevention (OJJDP) issued a Request for Proposals (RFP) for the Juvenile Justice Accountability Block Grant (JJABG). A team of PDS lawyers met with an ORD social worker who specialized in working with children. The team strategized about how to best serve the young people PDS was representing in juvenile court. The team realized that although case investigation and legal advocacy would always remain at the forefront of defending children, the office needed to enhance its efforts to address the social needs of its younger clients. PDS needed to think more creatively about accessing resources for youth and stop depending on government agencies to identify and obtain services for their clients. The office needed to improve its detention advocacy and disposition planning.

With these core principles in mind, PDS began to chart a new path and develop a blueprint for a team of advocates. PDS's JJABG proposal sought funding for two new juvenile social workers, two education attorneys and a civil legal services attorney who would help secure housing, public benefits, and other legal rights to improve juvenile clients' prospects for success within the juvenile justice system and upon discharge from that system.

Refusing to compromise their role as faithful advocates of their clients' expressed interests, PDS lawyers pledged to follow their juvenile clients' direction and agreed not to secure more services, create more obligations, or intrude more into the lives of their clients than the clients desired. Although juvenile court attorneys certainly would counsel clients on the benefits of collateral services and interventions, they would not presume to know what was "best" for their clients.

Social workers

The addition of social workers to the "Juvenile Unit" was a natural fit since PDS already had such a model. Lawyers relied heavily on the ORD, which had been created in 1964 (and then called the Offender Rehabilitation Project) to identify and develop rehabilitative services for PDS clients. Since the launch of the project, forensic social workers have worked with defenders to investigate and prepare psychosocial assessments, develop individualized treatment plans, write presentence reports, and refer clients to social and health services. These mitigation specialists have extensive knowledge of local rehabilitative programs, such as drug treatment, job training, education programs, and parenting classes, and are uniquely trained to work with a wide range of clients who have emotional, social, psychiatric, and substance abuse-related problems.

Like the trial division, ORD did not initially focus its attention on children. But in 1998, the one PDS social worker assigned to juvenile cases helped defenders think more broadly about the unique needs of children in the delinquency system. The first task was to clarify the nature and scope of the social worker's role within a defender office given concerns that the social worker's traditional obligation to protect the "best interests" of the child would conflict with the defender's ethical obligations to act in the child's expressed interest and protect the child's confidentiality. PDS ultimately structured the attorney-social worker relationship to make the social worker an *agent* of the child's lawyer and thus bound by confidentiality and the stated interests of the child.[12] The juvenile social worker began to accompany PDS lawyers to court, obtain resources, refer youth for services, co-author disposition letters, and advocate for youth in court.[13]

At first, ORD social workers were only available to defenders employed by PDS. Eventually PDS was able to extend ORD services to court-appointed defenders in D.C. who need assistance.[14] Today, PDS has three social workers who specialize in juvenile cases and the team is enhanced by a resource specialist who writes and updates a comprehensive directory of services available to its clients.[15]

Education advocates

PDS lawyers quickly realized that youth have needs that differ significantly from their adult clients. Most important, the defenders recognized that juvenile clients have unique educational needs. Although the nature of the "school to prison pipeline" was not as well understood back then as it is now, defenders in the 1990s recognized that there was a deep connection between school and the delinquency system. As school resource officers became increasingly common in schools, youth were more likely to be arrested for school fights, outbursts, and other normal adolescent behavior. Even when youth were not arrested at school, their school life had a significant impact on virtually every decision in the juvenile justice system. Judges in delinquency cases were reluctant to release youth from detention pending trial or to place youth on probation when they were truant from school or had a record of poor behavior and suspensions. When youth were released pending trial, judges often required them to attend school daily and carry an attendance card to document their compliance. Some judges who were concerned about the child's academic performance would also penalize youth who received poor grades. As to be expected, youth with significant educational challenges had difficulty complying with many of these standards and requirements upon release from detention or while on probation.

Fortunately, PDS was successful in its JJABG grant application and was able to use grant funds to hire a team of special education attorneys with expertise in advocating for youth under what is now the federal Individuals with Disabilities Education Improvement Act (IDEIA), which mandates special accommodations in public schools for children who cannot be adequately educated in a traditional classroom due to learning disabilities or other physical or intellectual challenges.[16] Education attorneys at PDS were essential in the team's effort to help youth improve their educational prospects and reintegrate into the community during and after a delinquency case. These attorneys began to collect student records, request evaluations, participate in IDEIA meetings at the youth's school, and advocate for new educational placements and compensatory services. These attorneys also assisted the defenders with disposition letters and treatment plans and accompanied defenders to court to advise the judge about the clients' educational developments. Today, PDS has three education attorneys who are part of the Civil Legal Services Team.

Here too, the team had to address complicated ethical issues. Because the child's education rights belong to the child's parents under federal law, education attorneys represent the parent and not the child. To avoid conflicts of interest and preserve client loyalty, juvenile defenders needed to secure the child's permission before seeking the assistance and appointment of an education attorney for the parents. The juvenile team developed a legal "retainer" form that made clear that education attorneys would only represent the parents to the extent that their educational objectives were consistent with the child's stated interest, and that the education attorney would withdraw from the parents' representation if the parents' interests began to diverge from the child's interests.

Civil legal services advocates

The Civil Legal Services Unit of PDS grew out of the agency's effort to build a holistic juvenile unit that would meet the comprehensive needs of children in the delinquency system. Defenders understood that children in the system not only needed assistance in education matters, but also in other civil proceedings – such as housing, public benefits, child support, abuse and neglect, and immigration proceedings. Each of these matters is deeply intertwined with the youth's success in the delinquency case.

The interplay between delinquency cases and other civil matters is profoundly demonstrated by federal law that permits state public housing authorities to evict entire families when one member of the family – including a child – is arrested for offenses involving drugs and other behavior that might affect the well-being of the housing complex.[17] When these cases arose, civil legal service attorneys at PDS worked with families to negotiate or litigate against housing authorities to prevent eviction.

Defense attorneys also began to attend their clients' neglect and other family court proceedings to advocate for the child's stated interest and, when appropriate, to advocate for services that would help extricate the child from the delinquency system. Each of these efforts was essential to help children succeed outside of the juvenile justice system.

Juvenile services program at detention facilities

The abysmal conditions and lack of quality programming in D.C.'s juvenile detention facilities made it essential that all children held in those places have direct access to legal assistance. In 1982, with the support of the D.C. City Council and the Superior Court, PDS initiated a Juvenile Services Program (JSP) to extend PDS's reach to all children detained in D.C. facilities.

Located in offices inside the facilities, with direct access to the residents, JSP is now staffed by a combination of three full-time attorneys and local law students. Disciplinary hearings and community status review hearings (similar to parole hearings) comprise the majority of JSP's work. JSP also works with detained youth to address complaints about staff or resident abuse, access to mental health and medical services, access to counsel and their families, and other conditions of confinement.

Leadership of the Juvenile Unit

PDS recognized that leadership was important to the long-term sustainability of the Juvenile Unit. To signal that the Juvenile Unit was as important as the Trial Division, PDS's director appointed a lead attorney for the Juvenile Unit and set their salary to be commensurate with that of other supervisors at PDS. The lead attorney is responsible for training, coordinating the team strategy, ensuring that the relationship between defenders and other advocates conforms to the rules of professional responsibility, supervising PDS attorneys in court, and representing PDS in court reform and legislative efforts.

Training for PDS and court-appointed juvenile attorneys

One of PDS's greatest assets is the defender's relatively small caseload. The downside is that PDS attorneys represent only a small number of youth in the system. As a result, PDS sought to raise the level of practice among the entire juvenile defense bar in the District of Columbia. By the 1990s, PDS had long been involved in training private court-appointed attorneys in the juvenile justice system. Shortly after the Juvenile Unit had been established, the Unit initiated two significant training programs: a three-day training for juvenile defenders on special education advocacy and a five-day training on litigation skills and substantive juvenile law.

Within the office, PDS established a Juvenile Trial Practice Group (TPG) that not only provided space for defenders to meet every week or two to discuss substantive juvenile law, conduct case rounds, and improve litigation skills, but also to meet with collateral advocates (special education attorneys, social workers, and civil legal services advocates). With so many players involved, the team had to clearly delineate responsibilities so as not to overwhelm the clients and waste time by duplicating efforts. To assist in this effort, the team leader created an organizational protocol that spelled out specific responsibilities for each team member and improved the initial client interview checklist so defenders could obtain information that would assist the entire team without making the client answer the same questions repeatedly.

Systemic reform

Although internal changes at PDS went a long way to improve the lives of children in juvenile court, defenders recognized that true success for youth would require long-term systemic reform. Since the agency's inception, PDS has engaged in criminal justice reform in the D.C. City Council, D.C. Superior Court, and the local Superior Court Rules Committees. Defenders in the newly formed Juvenile Unit were no different. The Unit's lead attorney led the Court's effort to draft and promulgate Attorney Practice Standards for Juvenile Defense and PINS attorneys, and served on various Family Court committees to improve the everyday practice and procedure of juvenile court. PDS's juvenile defenders also helped amend several important Superior Court Rules of Juvenile Procedure and served on the Family Court Training Committee to educate the community on national best practices in the juvenile justice system and to improve the work of all key stakeholders in D.C.'s juvenile court.

Appellate advocacy

Although PDS's Appellate Division was not officially incorporated into the Juvenile Unit, the team recognized the Appellate Division as an important part of the Unit's efforts to change the way youth were treated in juvenile court. Across the country, very few juvenile cases reach state appellate courts. Even today, attorneys often treat juvenile cases as social work and ignore critical legal issues. In addition, because many state defenders are overworked and underpaid, they have little time to focus on appeals, especially juvenile appeals. PDS's Appellate Division has resisted this paradigm by informally identifying one appellate defender to pay special attention to the legal questions unique to juvenile court and by expressly acknowledging that juvenile legal issues are just as important as other criminal legal issues.

Reflections on the Juvenile Unit and its evolution

Keys to success

Looking back, the period from 1997 to 2001 was a revolutionary time in PDS's thinking about how best to represent juvenile clients. The key to success in the late 1990s and the early 2000s was the buy-in from the office's director (JoAnn Wallace at the time) and all subsequent directors of the agency. The JJBAG award provided start-up money to launch the Juvenile Unit, but the long-term success of the Unit required the directors' commitment to raise money to fund it permanently. By collecting data to demonstrate the merits and success of the specialized juvenile unit, the director was able to convince Congress to incorporate juvenile social workers and special education attorneys into the office's annual budget.

The office also used the data it collected on juvenile court practice to consider what further improvements should be made. The data revealed a few obvious things: that having a few senior attorneys permanently in juvenile court increases institutional knowledge and provides continuity, and that horizontal representation is much better from the perspective of the juvenile client. The data also revealed a few more surprising things: that first-year lawyers can sometimes provide the best representation; that it can be very difficult to fill positions for more-experienced lawyers in juvenile court; and that horizontal representation presents a huge challenge, as juvenile cases tend to last much longer than adult ones. PDS has also examined the District's laws and practice with respect to trying children as adults – either as direct-filed cases or as judicial transfers – and determined that there is great need for improvement in how these cases are handled.

The future of high-quality juvenile defense

For a young person like our hypothetical client – Joseph – charged with a delinquency offense, PDS is providing the very best kind of representation. He will have a well-trained, well-supervised attorney in court with him, whose relatively low caseload allows for meticulous attention to the preparation of his defense. He will have access to investigators, experts, and transcripts for his case. He will have specialized legal representation at school disciplinary hearings and in the special education system. He will have a social worker to help him access the community supports he needs to address his mental and physical health. But there is still more work to do.

If Joseph ends up being incarcerated (or "committed") – if he is found to be involved in the delinquency offense and in need of services beyond what probation can provide – his case might stay open for years, until he turns 21 and ages out of the juvenile court system. His attorney might move on, either to a different practice level within PDS or to a different job, severing the continuity of representation that is ideal for children. With the pressure of the trial phase over, the case becomes mostly a matter of supervising and supporting a child with only the periodic and unpredictable need for legal assistance. This is when a juvenile defender office, designed to address a series of short-term emergencies, becomes an awkward fit for the needs of the client. There may be models other than single attorney representation that are better suited for youth in this position, such as post-commitment units staffed by attorneys and social workers who are better able to monitor a large number of such cases because they are not simultaneously coping with pre-trial demands.

If Joseph's charge had been more serious, such as an armed robbery charge, he would not have been a child in the eyes of the court. He would have been tried in adult criminal court, where the focus is on punishment rather than rehabilitation, and the reach of his defense team would have been greatly curtailed. Cases like this raise questions about how the defense should be approached: should the case be staffed according to who the client is, with a specialized juvenile defender and team trained in the needs of the adolescent client, or should the case be handled like a customary adult criminal case?[18] It seems clear that a child tried as an adult needs some specific support, and yet any effort to treat these children as a special group will carry some significant challenges. What of burnout for attorneys who will need to counsel impulsive, frightened kids on decisions with consequences that do not make any sense to a teenager's mind; who will need to form closer relationships with clients' families than in the typical criminal case; and who will appear before judges who have even less appreciation for adolescent development than judges in juvenile court?

Our legal system is moving in the right direction, with the help of career juvenile defenders who have worked on and written about the problem of treating adolescents like adults in the criminal courts, but progress is slow and injustice remains. PDS, as a model juvenile defender office, has an obligation to challenge itself to provide the best representation possible – not just the best representation that currently exists.

Notes

1 Charles J. Ogletree, Jr., *Beyond Justifications: Seeking Motivations to Sustain Public Defenders*, 106 HARV. L. REV. 1239, 1286 (1993) (footnotes omitted).

2 PHILIP B. HEYMANN & LANCE LIEBMAN, THE SOCIAL RESPONSIBILITIES OF LAWYERS: CASE STUDIES 69, 86–87 (Foundation Press, 1988).

3 *See generally* In re Savoy, 98 WASH. D. L. REP. 1397 (D.C. Super. Ct. 1970) (*Savoy I).*

4 In re Savoy, 98 WASH. D. L. REP. 1397, 1945 (D.C. Super. Ct. 1970) (*Savoy I*). *See also* In re W.L., 603 A.2d 839, 848 (D.C. 1991) (citing In re Savoy, 101 WASH. D. L. REP. 317, 321 (D.C. Super Ct. 1973) (*Savoy II*)) ("Two years after his withering exposé in *Savoy I* of conditions at the facility, former Chief Judge Greene, finding that little progress had been made, ordered that the Receiving Home be 'closed except that it may continue to be used as a temporary holding facility for [48 hours].'").

5 *See* In re Inquiry into Allegations of Misconduct against Juveniles etc., 430 A.2d 1087, n. 11 (D.C. 1981) (citing In re Savoy, No. J-4808–70 (D.C. Super. Ct., Jan. 12, 1973, Nov. 3, 1976) and stating that ["in two subsequent opinions, Chief Judge Greene followed through on problems surrounding the implementation of the original order and other allegations concerning care at the Receiving Home."]).

6 *Id.* at 1088–90.

7 *Id.* at 1089.

8 *Id.* at 1088.

9 Jerry M. v. District of Columbia, Civil Action No. 1519–85, Complaint (filed March 1, 1985), at 5–6.

10 *Id.* at 5–6.

11 District of Columbia v. Jerry M., 571 A.2d 178, 181 (D.C. 1990).

12 When social workers are agents of the attorney they are bound by the same confidentiality rules as the attorney. *See, e.g.*, ABA MODEL RULES OF PROF'L CONDUCT, Rule 1.6, https://www.americanbar.org/groups/professional_responsibility/publications/model_rules_of_professional_conduct/model_rules_of_professional_conduct_table_of_contents.html (last visited Sept. 17, 2017); DC BAR, Rule 1.6, 5.3, https://www.dcbar.org/bar-resources/legal-ethics/amended-rules/rule1-06.cfm (last visited Sept. 17, 2017); THE NATIONAL ASS'N OF SOCIAL WORKERS, *Code of Ethics*, 1.07(a), https://www.socialworkers.org/About/Ethics/Code-of-Ethics/Code-of-Ethics-English (last visited Sept. 19, 2017); ASS'N FOR PUBLIC DEFENSE, NAPD FORMAL ETHICS OPINION 14–1, http://www-old.publicdefenders.us/sites/default/files/ethics_opinion.pdf (last visited Sept. 17, 2017) (discussing social workers and their limits regarding reporting child or elder abuse without the express contemporaneous permission of the lawyer for whom they work). *See also* Maryann Zavez, *The Ethical and Moral*

Considerations Presented by Lawyer/Social Worker Interdisciplinary Collaborations, 5 Whittier J. Child & Fam. Advoc. 191, 207–209 (2005) (discussing intersection of mandatory reporting and confidentiality for social workers and lawyers in D.C. and stating that ["under Ethical Standard 1.07 … social workers are first admonished to respect their clients' privacy, and standards of confidentiality apply once private information is shared."]).

13 *See generally* Paula Galowitz, *Collaboration Between Lawyers and Social Workers: Re-examining the Nature and Potential of the Relationship*, 67 Fordham L. Rev. 2123 (1999) (examining the value of collaboration between lawyers and social workers to effectively serve clients).

14 In managing assignments for both PDS lawyers and outside defenders, ORD is highly attentive to potential conflicts of interest.

15 John D. Bess, *Directory of Youth and Family Services: Community and Confinement Access Guide 2014* (Dec. 2014), http://www.pdsdc.org/docs/default-source/default-document-library/juvenile-community-and-confinement-access-guide.pdf?sfvrsn=0 (last visited Sept. 17, 2017).

16 20 U.S.C. § 1400.

17 *See* 42 U.S.C.S. § 1437d; *see also* Kristin Henning, *Eroding Confidentiality in Delinquency Proceedings: Should Schools and Public Housing Authorities Be Notified?*, 79 N.Y. U.L. Rev. 520 (2004) (discussing impact on youth and their families when schools and public housing authorities are notified of criminal allegations and charges).

18 Some public defender offices, such as the Legal Aid Society, have units with attorneys dedicated to representing youth tried in adult court. *See* Chapter 9, "Raising the bar: improving the model of defense representation for adolescents prosecuted in adult courts," by Nancy Ginsburg.

8 The role of law school clinics in implementing the *Gault* decision

Wallace Mlyniec and Meghan Strong

Introduction

Prior to the Supreme Court's decision in *In re Gault*,[1] children's rights were hardly noticed in law schools or in society at large. If the legal needs of children were considered at all, they were discussed in terms of the responsibility owed to them by adults. Thus the needs of children in torts, contracts, marriage, or estates were considered as part of the substantive law regulating adult responsibility for the acts and welfare of children. When judges and legal academics considered the procedural needs of children, they discussed them not in terms of children's rights, but in terms of the duties of *guardians ad litem* or parents when bringing or defending legal claims.

The law was also concerned with crimes committed by children, but procedural rights were accorded only to children whose offenses brought them into adult courts as dictated by common law capacity doctrines. The special delinquency courts developed by the Progressives in the early 1900s accorded no particular procedural rights to children. Instead, the early juvenile courts were social welfare courts where children were treated informally by adults who decided what would be in their "best interest." Judges in these courts were not concerned with the rights of children because none existed. Judges and probation officers discussed instead the relative and competing rights of parents and the State (acting as *parens patriae*) to control the upbringing of children whose behavioral lapses – criminal and non-criminal alike – required intervention. Adhering to the emptiness of children's rights as a theoretical construct, law school faculty taught children's "rights" only as a minor facet of other common law obligations, parents' constitutional rights, and contractual theories.

Today it is hard to imagine a law school curriculum that does not consider, at least in some courses, the rights of children as a discrete academic inquiry. This development owes its existence to three completely different academic and social movements that began in the late 1960s and early 1970s. During this period, Earl Warren's Supreme Court jurisprudence constitutionalized criminal procedure, requiring the application of most of the Bill of Rights in state court criminal proceedings.[2] The application of due process to juvenile delinquency trials required by *In re Gault* must be understood within the context of this due process revolution.

During this same period, a great civil rights awakening generated interest in other rights-based movements related to the cultural upheavals of the time. The women's rights movement and the children's rights movement found their roots in the aspirations of those seeking to create racial equality. Civil rights lawyer Amelia Lewis, who represented Gerald Gault in Arizona, once commented that before this case, she never thought much about children's rights. But in the mid-1960s, she thought it was time to do so.[3] Because the existing law underpinned both the resistance to these movements and their growth, legal activists and scholars took note of the absence of serious academic inquiry into any of these legal and cultural upheavals. Spurred on by the political energy of the era, substantive law courses concerning the rights of various individuals and groups began to emerge as discrete courses within law school curricula.[4]

In the late 1960s and early 1970s, the academy's Socratic discourse about these legal, cultural, and social movements was joined by a third critical academic and social development called clinical legal education. Clinical education was modeled roughly on medical school training and financed by the legendary William Pincus, a program officer at the Ford Foundation and later Director of the Council on Legal Education for Professional Responsibility.[5] Relatively soon after their emergence, legal clinics devoted to representing marginalized Americans, including children, began to proliferate in law schools across America.[6] This combination of the criminal law revolution, the expansion of the rights movements, and the emergence of clinical education gave rise to the first juvenile justice clinics in the 1960s and 1970s. The convergence of the Supreme Court's children's rights jurisprudence, first hinted at in *Kent v. United States* and more fully expounded in *In re Gault*, with the other social, cultural, and pedagogical movements, has resulted in the development of clinical courses exploring issues related to juvenile justice in at least 55 law schools today.[7] These clinics specialize in the study of delinquency law, develop and advocate for changes in juvenile justice systems, and provide a cadre of student-lawyers to represent children accused of crimes.

This chapter will trace the development of juvenile justice clinics and describe how the efforts of law faculty and students have helped to shape the face of juvenile courts and implement the promises of *In re Gault*. Their efforts have been undertaken to fulfill *Gault*'s promise of zealous defense advocacy – an advocacy that is anchored in an understanding of the special needs of children and guided by the juveniles' "expressed interest" rather than their "best interest." Juvenile justice clinics were founded on these premises and continue the struggle to attain *Gault*'s lofty goal by creating a cadre of dedicated, competent, well-trained, and well-financed children's lawyers.

The criminal law revolution

Although we are celebrating the fiftieth anniversary of *In re Gault*, the case was not the first to extend Federal Constitution protections into state criminal proceedings. Indeed, it wasn't even the first case involving children wherein the Supreme Court discussed the concept of the due process of law. Between 1961 and 1974, the Court considered more than 100 cases[8] in which litigants requested the application of various Bill of Rights protections in their state criminal cases. Prior to the *Gault* case, the Supreme Court had imposed on state adult criminal trials: the right to counsel emanating from the Sixth Amendment;[9] search and seizure protections arising from the Fourth Amendment;[10] protection against self-incrimination and double jeopardy based on the Fifth Amendment;[11] the right to a speedy and public jury trial, the right to confront witnesses and to compel the attendance of witnesses arising from the Sixth Amendment;[12] bail and cruel and unusual punishment guarantees from the Eighth Amendment;[13] and procedural due process pursuant to the Fourteenth and Fifth Amendments.[14] On several occasions, the Court had even considered the validity of convictions of children in adult criminal proceedings.[15] Yet, prior to *Kent v. United States*,[16] the Court had never considered the constitutional ramifications of juvenile court proceedings. In *Kent*, a case involving the transfer of jurisdiction over a child accused of a serious crime from the juvenile delinquency court to adult criminal court, the Court explored the notion of constitutional due process for children, but ruled narrowly in the context of its supervisory authority over the courts of the District of Columbia and not by constitutional mandate. By the time the *Gault* case reached the Supreme Court, however, the Justices were prepared to look at state court delinquency proceedings within the context of U.S. constitutional protections.

It is hard to imagine that the Court would have plunged into the vagaries of the juvenile delinquency proceedings had not these other criminal law procedural guarantees preceded them. Between the creation of the first juvenile court in Illinois in 1899[17] and the *Kent* decision, the Supreme Court heard no cases involving the proceedings of this specialized court. Commentators, however, had for some time prior to *Kent* been lamenting the sorry state of juvenile delinquency courts and the punishments they doled out.[18] Even the Arizona Supreme Court had acknowledged as much in denying Gerald Gault's habeas corpus petition.[19] Although state juvenile proceedings had remained the province of the states and their own courts since their inception, the Warren Court was seldom deterred from intervening when state procedural rules clashed with Bill of Rights protections. When seen in the context of the criminal law revolution, a juvenile court with powers more drastic than that of the Star Chamber[20] but which provided children with the "worst of both worlds,"[21] was ripe for the Supreme Court's consideration. Moreover, Abe Fortas, the petitioner's lawyer in *Gideon v Wainwright*[22] which mandated that defendants be represented by counsel in adult criminal cases, was a Justice on the Supreme Court when the *Gault* case was decided. Justice Fortas wrote the opinion and was instrumental in convincing the other Justices to adopt a wide-ranging interpretation of the constitutional rights of children.[23] To Earl Warren, Fortas' opinion was the "Magna Carta of Juvenile Justice."[24]

The civil rights ferment

The late 1960s and early 1970s brought not only changes in criminal laws and procedures, but also dramatic changes in the culture of the United States. Spurred on by President John F. Kennedy's youthful enthusiasm and his exhortation that "the torch had been passed to a new generation,"[25] young men and woman of all races began to rebel against the conformity of the Eisenhower years and the obvious and intolerable racial discrimination of the Jim Crow era. All of the "rights movements" that emerged from this era owe their genesis to the African American civil rights movement. This is not the place to recite the entire history of the struggles and achievements of African Americans to throw off the shackles of racial oppression, anti-democratic institutions, lynching, and prison. Suffice it to say that beginning with the bus boycotts of 1955 and continuing until late in the 1970s, America witnessed many advances in civil rights for African Americans.

These victories came at a high cost, but the quest for self-determination and personal freedom spurred other marginalized communities to seek expanded freedoms for themselves. Cesar Chavez and Delores Huerta founded the first farm workers' union, the United Farm Workers Association,[26] and the Mexican American Legal Defense and Education Fund began protecting the civil rights of Mexican Americans in 1968. Between 1969 and 1973, Native Americans, led by Dennis Banks and Russell Means, began a series of occupations of Alcatraz prison, the Mayflower replica, Mount Rushmore, and Wounded Knee, signaling a new assertion of rights to former Native American lands.[27]

These political movements existed alongside the rising discontent with the Vietnam War. By 1965, protesters, many active in the civil rights movement,[28] began a concerted effort on campuses and in major cities to counter U.S. policies in Asia.[29] Their organizational strengths, combined with youthful idealism, led to protests against restrictions on student life as well. The numbers of students going to college had increased,[30] and parents who previously had not sent their children to college began to do so.[31] As a result, campuses teemed with men and women with the freedom to question any established norm that seemed counter to the concept of individual freedom. Students demanded expanded and equal rights, on campus and off, and were willing to assert them in the face of authority.

Other political and social movements also emerged. The role of women in society changed during World War II but reverted to pre-War roles during the prosperity of post-War America.[32] By the late 1960s, talented and well-educated women were demanding better pay and better positions at work, more equality within their domestic households, and more respect and equality within all aspects of American life. To further those goals, the National Organization for Women (NOW)[33] was founded in 1966, contributing to a series of legal victories.[34]

The Gay Rights Movement can also be traced to this era. The first major gay protest took place in 1969 at the Stonewall Inn in New York City when gay men protested police attempts to close down the bar.[35] Although slower to expand than others because of deep-seated antipathy towards gays and lesbians, the movement's current success can trace its roots to this same era.

Although one can trace the emergence of the movement to grant children constitutional rights and a legal identity separate from their parents to this era, its expansion was slower than the other rights movements because children had traditionally been seen to possess no independent agency. For centuries, they had been the property of their parents or came under the protection of the state pursuant to Anglo American law principles.[36] In addition, children's ages ranged from birth to majority, making it difficult to generalize about their rights. Early Supreme Court cases involving children had more to do with parents' rights in relation to the State than with children's rights in relation to the State or their parents.[37] Early legislation like child labor laws,[38] school attendance laws, and parental neglect laws were enacted to protect children rather than to give them bargaining power. Most organizations concerned with children prior to *In re Gault* asserted children's need for protection rather than their right to independence.

During the same period, the jurisprudence developed by Supreme Court Justice Abe Fortas began to change the way the law viewed children's legal autonomy. Although Justice Fortas is best known for his opinions in *Kent* and *Gault*, he also wrote the majority opinion in *Tinker v. Des Moines Independent Community School District* which gave children First Amendment rights.[39] Justice Fortas left the Supreme Court in 1970, but his children's rights and due process jurisprudence had struck a chord with the Court. Between 1970 and 1984, the Court decided *In re Winship*,[40] *McKeiver v. Pennsylvania*,[41] *Breed v. Jones*,[42] *Swisher v. Brady*,[43] and *Schall v. Martin*,[44] all of which analyzed the rights that a child had in juvenile delinquency proceedings independent of their parents. All of these decisions were based on the jurisprudence established by the Court in *In re Gault*. Moreover, the Supreme Court's interest in issues related to children spread beyond procedural issues in delinquency cases. It is clear, however, that none of these cases could have been brought without the landmark opinion in *In re Gault*. It is also reasonable to conclude that the Court's interest in children's rights might not have been furthered if it were not for the concurrent existence of the other rights movements of this era.

The clinical education movement[45]

Gault not only generated new laws, it generated scholarly opinion. In the five years following the *Gault* decision, at least 70 articles were published in more than 50 different law journals across the country describing and discussing the case in some way.[46] Most of these articles were published in an initial spike just after the decision was announced, with the bulk published in late 1967 and early 1968. The discussion quickly dropped off in the five years after *Gault*, ending with only one article published in 1972.

The people writing these articles were mostly law or political science professors, but several judges and practicing lawyers also contributed their thoughts on the case.[47] In particular, Norman Dorsen, counsel for the appellants in *Gault*, and his co-author Daniel A. Rezneck, published an article analyzing the Court's decision in December, 1967.[48] Also of note was the number of law student-written pieces on the topic, particularly in the months immediately following the decision. Of the works published, perhaps a third of them concerned recent state court decisions that were based on *Gault*. Most of the scholarship generated by *Gault* focused broadly on what the decision meant for juvenile courts, discussing the history of the courts before *Gault*, and what the application of due process rights post-*Gault* might require. Many articles focused on specific states, contemplating how *Gault* would be implemented in particular juvenile courts and how the state's code might need to be rewritten in order to accommodate *Gault*'s requirements.[49] Once some time had passed, these types of articles moved from speculation to more concrete examination of the earliest changes that were made.[50]

Another common theme in the early scholarship concerning *Gault* was the "identity crisis" of the juvenile courts.[51] Many authors noted that the juvenile courts had not lived up to expectations in the decades since their creation and that *Gault* had recognized these failings. Judge Orman W. Ketcham of the Juvenile Court of the District of Columbia saw the Court's decision as calling for "broad reconsideration of the basic premises of the juvenile court philosophy and the renovation of the entire system of children's courts in this country."[52] Scholars, judges, and lawyers alike saw *Gault* as a chance to resolve some of the more obvious problems in the juvenile court system. Judge William S. Fort, Circuit Court Judge of the Second Judicial District in Eugene, Oregon, and President of the National Council of Juvenile Court Judges described *Gault* as an opportunity to re-evaluate "the unfulfilled promise of the juvenile court."[53]

Although there was much discussion about how *Gault*'s holding would be applied, markedly absent from this scholarship was debate over what the holding of *Gault* was and what it meant. Everyone seemed to agree, for the most part, on what *Gault* did and did not hold.[54] This is not to say that the Court's holding escaped criticism. Of particular significance was the Court's refusal to characterize juvenile court proceedings as either criminal or civil.[55] This failure to classify along with the Court's failure to extend to juveniles accused of crime all the basic procedural guarantees accorded to adults were the primary criticisms that arose in the years following *Gault*. The Court seemed to have intentionally kept its holding in *Gault* relatively narrow where many felt it could – and perhaps should – have taken the opportunity to do more to reinvent the juvenile court system.

The new scholarship about juvenile courts did not directly address the role that law schools should play in advancing the *Gault* rulings. None suggested the development of clinical courses to provide lawyers for children in delinquency cases. The *Gault* decision, however, did provide an impetus for law schools to add courses on juvenile law to their curricula. Most of the early courses focused exclusively on delinquency law.[56] *Gault* also spurred the creation of legal organizations that focused exclusively on the legal rights of children.[57] As the scholarship and the new organizations were simultaneously developing, a new educational movement began to emerge in law schools. Students and some faculty members began to question the value of Christopher Columbus Langdell's casebook method of instruction that permeated legal education at the time.[58] They began to demand more practice-oriented courses and an educational experience that more clearly related to the intellectual ferment and freedom movements they were experiencing outside of law school. The Langdell method, however, eschewed legal practice as the basis for educating law students, and most law schools did not award academic credit for such practical training. Indeed, most law faculty looked down on clinical education, believing it warranted no place in academia.

Although law school legal dispensaries provided assistance to poor clients during the late 1890s and early 1900s, and a few American law schools awarded credit for practical work early in the twentieth century,[59] the integration of practice into the law school curriculum did not expand until the late 1960s.[60] Driven by the social upheaval that accompanied the civil rights and anti-Vietnam War movements,[61] the renewed dissatisfaction with the casebook method, and most importantly, the influx of money to law schools from the Ford Foundation and later the Council on Legal Education for Professional Responsibility (CLEPR), law schools began to establish clinical education programs throughout the late 1960s and the 1970s.[62] The CLEPR effort was led by William Pincus[63] who directed millions of dollars to law schools that were willing to create clinical courses established according to the model Pincus espoused.[64] Nonetheless, he and his money were met with some wariness by both courts and law schools. Law schools were reluctant to reintroduce law practice into the university-based academic law curriculum, while local courts worried about calendars being clogged by students and faculty complicating otherwise simple cases. Judges feared that social justice arguments of the 1960s and 1970s would intrude into every claim initiated by law student counsel.[65]

The clinical education movement was also advanced by the state bars and some courts that recognized that students might provide an inexpensive way to meet the new Supreme Court rulings requiring the appointment of counsel in all criminal and juvenile delinquency cases. Students could help the courts meet their constitutional obligations, but special practice rules had to be developed to avoid the unauthorized practice of law. The first state to implement a true student practice rule was Colorado in 1909 which enacted the rule to reflect the work of the Denver University College of Law's Legal Aid Dispensary. Despite the Denver rule, most other state and federal courts did not develop rules permitting students to engage in the limited practice of law until the 1970s and 1980s. Almost all of these later rules mandated that clinic students be supervised by a member of the bar.[66]

By 1968, one year after the *Gault* decision, at least 14 states had promulgated student practice rules.[67] The rest soon followed suit. The validity of these rules gained additional support when Supreme Court Justice William Brennan noted in his concurring opinion in *Argersinger v. Hamlin* that "law students can be expected to make a significant contribution, quantitatively and qualitatively, to the representation of the poor in many areas … ."[68] As CLEPR provided the flow of dollars, law schools began to search for faculty to staff their new clinical programs. Since traditional academic faculty members were unsuited for the rigors of clinical education and did not possess the skills needed to practice law, law schools looked to public interest lawyers to teach their students.[69] Many of the lawyers they found were the same lawyers who had been fighting to expand constitutional protections in state criminal cases and advocating, both in the streets and in the courts, for the expansion of the civil rights of all American citizens.[70] These lawyers thought they could increase their effectiveness, increase the number of clients they could serve, and expand their social and political agendas if they used supervised students to actually litigate cases. Although academic faculty members accused clinical teachers of diluting the essence of theoretical legal education and criticized clinical teachers for being anti-intellectual, clinical pedagogy survived those early attacks and came to permeate academic legal education. Today, every state has a student practice rule, every accredited law school has a clinical education program, and the American Bar Association has recently strengthened accreditation standards to reflect the significance of this movement.[71]

The creation of juvenile justice clinics

Although the stage seemed to be set for the creation of juvenile delinquency clinics shortly after the decision in *In re Gault*, it did not happen immediately. Criminal clinics, small claims clinics, landlord-tenant clinics, civil rights clinics, and general practice clinics all began to appear shortly after the *Gault* decision,[72] but the first juvenile delinquency clinics in U.S. law schools were not established until several years later. While perplexing at first, the reasons may now seem obvious. Prior to *In re Gault*, lawyers did not exist in most juvenile courts. As a result, there was no cadre of trained lawyers ready to move into law school clinics like there were in other legal disciplines. Once lawyers were required, there was a long debate after *Gault* about how attorneys for children were supposed to perform their lawyering role.[73] Legislatures were often slow to revise their statutes, so lawyers and judges alike were confused about how the new delinquency trials were supposed to be conducted.[74] Moreover, judges in the juvenile courts, even after *Gault*, were reluctant to abandon their *parens patriae* role.[75] If a lawyer was required to represent the child's best interest rather than the client's expressed interest, practicing in juvenile court did not really seem like the practice of law. Thus lawyers were deterred from the practice and clinicians were not anxious to use delinquency cases as teaching tools. Gender considerations may have also played a part. Children's needs had long been thought to be the province of women; but before the 1970s, few women attended American law schools.[76] The men graduating from law schools who were interested in criminal law wanted to engage in adult jury trials to further expand the Supreme Court's activist criminal procedure revolution. They did not want to go into juvenile court when the action was in the adult court.

Legal battles in the juvenile courts where lawyers did appear did not resemble criminal trials at first; they were hybrids where lawyers tried to act as lawyers and juvenile court judges tried to retain their formerly unquestioned authority to act in the best interest of children.[77] Public defender offices, where one would expect a radically different approach, offered little change. Prior to *Gault*, there were few organized public defender offices in the country and few of those had a special delinquency unit. Thus lawyers representing children in the delinquency courts had no role models and were learning as they went along. Moreover, public defender directors saw the stakes in juvenile court as low, and thus treated the juvenile court as a training ground for their new lawyers who would quickly move on to adult criminal cases.

This dearth of skilled lawyers resulted in no new clinical courses dedicated to delinquency practice in the years immediately following the *Gault* decision. As far as research can determine, the first clinic specifically designed for delinquency cases was a Family Law Clinic founded at the University of South Carolina in the Fall of 1969.[78] Students in the clinic prosecuted and defended children in the Richland County Family Court.[79] That clinic was directed by Assistant Professor Eldon Wedlock until 1971 and was offered until 1973.[80] A Juvenile Defense Clinic was offered in the Fall of 1972 by Assistant Professor Jon Thames. Additionally, teaching associates taught a Defense Clinic that represented juveniles between 1973 and 1976. By 1975, students were representing children and adults in a Criminal Defense Clinic while other students prosecuted juveniles and adults in a Prosecution Clinic.[81]

South Carolina's off and on status may qualify it as the first clinic to provide students to defend juveniles, but the first clinic to do so with any longevity was founded by Professor Peter S. Smith at the University of Maryland in 1972. It was the first clinical course at the University of Maryland and existed until 2014 when one of Professor Smith's successors retired.[82] In 1973, specialized juvenile clinics were also established at Georgetown University Law Center and at New York University School of Law, both of which continue to exist today.

Peter Smith[83] designed the Maryland clinic to provide representation to children in juvenile delinquency trials and appeals in state court, in law reform efforts, and in civil rights actions in federal court. Smith "had serious questions about the value of traditional legal education and noted frequently that no physician would be licensed to practice medicine without extensive clinical experience."[84] He chose to create a juvenile clinic for two reasons: "[h]e was aware that there was virtually no legal representation available to juveniles who could not pay to hire a lawyer; and he knew that the length of time for a typical juvenile case was short enough that a student would likely be able to start and finish a case [and possibly more than one case] in one semester. From a teaching perspective, that would give a student a rare and valuable opportunity to learn and then apply that knowledge. Professor Smith taught the clinic until he retired in the early 1990s."[85]

At Georgetown Law Center, Judith C. Areen was a young scholar specializing in issues related to children. At a time when Georgetown was expanding its emerging clinical program, Professor Areen approached local foundations to support a clinic to represent children. She obtained the funding and hired me, Wallace Mlyniec, to be its first litigation director. My background in delinquency law was substantial for the time, but still relatively sparse. I was a law student at Georgetown when *Gault* was decided and served as a volunteer in the District of Columbia Juvenile Court as it tried to determine how to comply with the procedural mandates created by the case. Prior to my appointment at the Georgetown clinic, I had been the reporter for a project comparing the American Bar Association Criminal Justice Standards to the District of Columbia criminal law and procedure.[86] As part of my duties, I had been representing alleged delinquent children in the District of Columbia Juvenile Court.

Areen and I began representing children primarily in delinquency and neglect cases, but also brought appeals to the District of Columbia Court of Appeals (the District's highest court). From time to time we also engaged in litigation on behalf of children in other kinds of legal cases and worked on legislative reform. After 1976, we slowly moved to representing only alleged delinquents because those cases provided the best vehicles for clinical teaching. The success and financial security of the program was soon enhanced by the strong support from Georgetown's successive deans and from the Clinic's association with Georgetown's E. Barrett Prettyman Program.[87]

The New York University (NYU) School of Law's juvenile clinic was founded by Martin Guggenheim, also in the 1973–74 academic year.[88] NYU's clinic grew out of efforts by the NYU-based Institute for Judicial Administration (IJA), a national project headed by Second Circuit Judge Irving Kaufman and supported through a partnership with the American Bar Association (ABA), to develop a multi-volume set of Juvenile Justice Standards.[89] Judge Kaufman, Chair of the IJA project, and its Executive Director, Lawrence Schultz, petitioned the dean of NYU's law school to open a juvenile justice clinic. In June 1973, NYU began looking for someone to create a juvenile delinquency clinic at the law school. At that time, Professor Guggenheim was a lawyer at the Juvenile Rights Division (JRD) of the New York Legal Aid office[90] who by then had handled more than 100 cases. Based on his experience, he was appointed to the faculty and immediately began litigating juvenile delinquency cases in the clinic.

The Maryland, NYU, and Georgetown clinics' early practice mirrored the ideals the Court had laid out in *Gault* and hewed closely to Pincus' theory of legal education. All were in-house clinics, taught and supervised by full-time faculty members,[91] where students received academic credit for their work. Every child facing a delinquency charge was assigned a student lawyer at arraignment who advocated for the child's rights and expressed wishes through all stages of the case. Students performed their tasks as zealously for their child clients as would a lawyer representing an adult client facing felony charges. Students were in court often, tried many cases, and fashioned the best possible dispositions for children within a limited range of options provided by the state. Because of the dearth of skilled lawyers in their various locales, each of the clinics became a major criminal defense office operating in the juvenile court while also providing the voices for reform of the juvenile system.

The work of the clinics began to affect the practice of law more broadly in Maryland, New York, and the District of Columbia, often to the displeasure of the prosecutors and judges. Guggenheim has noted that prior to the advent of delinquency clinics, the local "lawyers who were our adversaries weren't really up to our game. [The courts and prosecutors] had gotten used to having lazy lawyers and people who weren't going to read the statutes, investigate the facts, or file motions."[92] In the District of Columbia, the local prosecutor filed a Bar grievance against me for filing and litigating a motion to gain access to a complaining witness. As a result of the clinics' efforts, however, prosecutors' offices actually improved over time, and judges became more careful in their rulings as clinic students brought appeals of their rulings. Students and faculty members also testified and sometimes wrote drafts of legislation to improve the practice in juvenile courts.

Despite the good work being done by the few clinics that existed at the time, and despite the growth of adult criminal defense clinics in the 1970s, there was no similar increase in the number of specialized juvenile delinquency clinics. Our research, dependent on responses from individual law school clinicians, some CLEPR and ABA reports, some law journal articles, and conversations with long-time clinicians, reveals only four additional clinics specializing in delinquency defense being formed in that decade – at Vanderbilt Law School in 1974, at the University of Texas Law School in 1975,[93] at Tulane University Law School in 1979,[94] and at the now defunct Antioch Law School in Washington D.C. in 1973.[95] On the other hand, juvenile delinquency work was being performed in criminal clinics and general practice clinics at many other schools. In the CLEPR survey of clinical education for 1976–77, eighty schools reported that they had clinics doing at least some juvenile defense work.[96] Further research may illuminate what those schools were doing 50 years ago, but conversations with faculty members at several schools listed in the survey indicate that many were out-placement clinics and some were adult criminal clinics providing representation in some juvenile cases. The number may also reflect the idiosyncratic use of the word "clinic" in these self-reports.[97] The survey did not clearly distinguish between the various forms of educational experiences that law schools identified as clinic. Nonetheless, some schools, like Northwestern University Law School,[98] Washburn University Law School,[99] Seton Hall Law School,[100] and perhaps others, were providing representation in a significant number of delinquency cases and doing significant juvenile delinquency work as part of their general case-loads.

One can only speculate as to the reasons why separate juvenile delinquency clinics did not proliferate in the 1970s, but conversations with other clinicians provide some clues. Students and even some clinical faculty interested in criminal law and procedure often disparaged the juvenile clinics that did exist, calling them "kiddie clinics,"[101] and thus directed hard core future criminal defense lawyers and prosecutors away from them. David Katner, now the director at Tulane's juvenile clinic, recalls that the juvenile clinic there was disparaged by the criminal clinic students because the juvenile clinic students were trained by social workers as well as lawyers.[102] In addition, law schools were reluctant to invest in clinical education and looked to outside funding to cover the costs. Most of the early clinical courses were funded by outside money rather than by the schools themselves and money was not easy to find during the latter half of the 1970s.[103] Perhaps funders thought other areas of law such as landlord-tenant relations or domestic violence had a greater need, or they chose to fund clinics that protected the so-called "good kids," those entwined in the child welfare system rather than the delinquency system. Interestingly, the 1974 passage of the Child Abuse Prevention and Treatment Act[104] spurred soft money funding for the first child welfare clinic at the University of Michigan in 1974 and had a similar effect at other law schools as well. The power of the *Gault* decision, however, proved to be important even in the child welfare clinics.[105] Professor Donald Duquette, the founding director of the Michigan Child Advocacy Clinic, recently stated that "*Gault* influenced the [Michigan] clinic's work in that it contributed to a generalized heightened awareness of children as rights-holders."[106] Although there was an expanding number of legal organizations dedicated to children's rights, there were no national associations dedicated solely to juvenile defense.[107] There was also a turn against criminal and juvenile defenders and defendants in the 1980s as President Reagan's "war on crime" swept the nation in response to the explosion of drug-related violence.

Finally, other than in New York, there were still very few lawyers specializing in delinquency law and few of them were interested in an academic career in the late 1970s and 1980s. Public defenders still used juvenile court as a training ground for adult court practice, and due to the limited enrollments in most clinics, the few clinics that did exist had not yet trained a cadre of delinquency specialists who could also meet the increasingly difficult hiring standards that clinicians faced.

Juvenile delinquency clinics today

The 1980s and 1990s saw both growth and retraction of clinical education programs. Although some soft money was available,[108] CLEPR was gone and other foundations curtailed funding, suggesting it was time for law schools to fund the programs. Battles over the status of clinical faculty and the belief that the costs of clinical education were unsustainable saw many clinical programs collapse while others expanded. The American Bar Association's Directory of Pro Bono Children's Law Programs listed only 15 juvenile delinquency clinics in 1994.[109] The fourth edition, published in 1999, listed 18 clinics representing children in some capacity, with 3 representing children solely in delinquency cases.[110]

Perhaps the slow growth reflected the decreased rate of scholarship written about *In re Gault* after 1975. Although lawyers and professors continued to produce scholarly articles about the juvenile courts after 1975, the rate of publications about *In re Gault* specifically diminished. Between 1975 and 2000, fewer than 30 articles looking closely at *Gault* and its specific impact – as opposed to examining juvenile courts generally and citing *Gault* as one case among many – were published. During this era, there were a fairly even number of law professors and lawyers publishing their work, but judges no longer contributed to the conversation. As for the content of this wave of scholarship, there were three major themes: the ways *Gault* had not been applied to its full extent, the different models of representing children, and the movement away from the traditional rehabilitative philosophy of juvenile courts toward a growing punitive philosophy.

Despite early hopes that *Gault* would fix the juvenile courts, scholarship during this era seemed to agree that promise had still gone largely unfulfilled.[111] Though juvenile courts across the country had made substantive changes in response to *Gault*, rewriting their codes and adjusting the rights afforded to juveniles,[112] the juvenile courts were still rife with problems.[113] Juveniles were not always receiving the representation *Gault* promised them,[114] and studies showed that even when children were represented, their representation was often so incompetent they were likely to receive a more severe disposition than if they had been unrepresented.[115] Those writing about the impact of *Gault* complained juvenile courts were not implementing its mandate fully and offered suggestions for continued improvement and expansion of children's rights.[116]

The second major theme in these articles dealt with how children should be represented once they obtained counsel under *Gault*. Several authors offered arguments for and against the two major models. Some held that counsel should advocate for the child's best interest as viewed by the attorney, while others maintained that counsel should advocate for the child's best interest as expressed by the child.[117] Scholars made arguments for both models, often without coming to a resolution or making concrete suggestion for how to proceed.[118]

The final theme in this group of articles was seen mainly in the works published in the mid to late 1990s. Several articles spoke of growing desires to "get tough" on juvenile delinquents in response to a perceived rise in violent youth.[119] This attitude coincided with a growing emphasis on punitive ideals, rather than the rehabilitative ideals traditionally associated with juvenile courts.[120] Authors in the 1990s expressed concern over these two developments, viewing factors such as the broadening of statutes to allow for more transfers of juveniles to adult court as a warning sign of a larger problem.[121]

In general, the scholarship of the three decades following *Gault* echoed much of the same disappointment in the juvenile court system that the early scholarship had hoped would be resolved in *Gault*'s wake. Though the scholars believed *Gault was* certainly of great significance, they showed that *Gault* did not achieve everything people expected. This growing dissatisfaction with the implementation of *Gault* resulted in the establishment of more legal organizations dedicated to expanding the rights of children after 1999. Today the National Juvenile Defender Center (NJDC) advocates on behalf of counsel for children. Clinical education courses of all kinds have grown in number and have grown stronger within the legal academy. Our research has found juvenile delinquency clinics or multiple service clinics providing juvenile delinquency defense at 55 law schools today.[122] At least 30 of those clinic courses were created after 1995.

The children's rights foundation established in *Gault* has been the source of more than 20 additional Supreme Court cases and thousands of state and federal court cases that have strengthened *Gault's* foundational principles. Many of those cases are litigated by juvenile clinics every day. In addition, the due process jurisprudence of *Gault* propelled additional Supreme Court opinions granting children other rights during juvenile proceedings. Children may be found guilty only by proof beyond a reasonable doubt.[123] Due process applies at pre-trial detention decisions.[124] The prohibition on double jeopardy applies to delinquency cases.[125] Age must be considered when courts determine the validity of a child's decision to speak to the police.[126]

Although these cases have all been decided in the Supreme Court, lawyers for children have advanced the due process rights established in *Gault* in trial and appellate courts[127] and in legislatures in every state in America. Many of those lawyers are juvenile clinic directors and many of those cases have been litigated by clinic students and staff. Clinic faculty and staff work closely each day with private lawyers and public defenders on juvenile issues. Three of the National Juvenile Defender Center's regional affiliates – Mid-Atlantic, Northeast, and Southwest – are housed at law school clinical programs,[128] and clinical faculty are members of the other regions. The annual NJDC Juvenile Training Immersion Program (JTIP) Summer Academy is conducted in conjunction with the Georgetown Law Center's Juvenile Justice Clinic and several of the faculty of the Academy are clinical faculty members at other law schools. Many of the appellate briefs filed on behalf of children in courts of appeals throughout the country are either filed by clinical programs or have clinical programs signed on as amicus parties. The latest round of Supreme Court cases involving children, those concerning sentencing practices for children charged as adults, also bore the stamp of clinical programs. Bryan Stevenson, a clinical faculty member at NYU Law School, litigated the life without parole case *Miller v. Alabama*[129] in the Supreme Court, and other clinical faculty and programs contributed to amicus briefs in the juvenile death penalty case, *Roper v. Simmons*,[130] and in *Graham v. Florida*[131] and other life without parole cases.[132] These cases built on the work of psychologists and lawyers – many of whom were law school faculty – that showed the links between adolescent brain development and the impulsive acts of adolescents which lead to anti-social behavior.[133] In doing so, the arguments and the subsequent opinions reaffirmed what the *Gault* court and the founders of the juvenile court always knew intuitively: children are different, and the acts they commit as adolescents do not define their entire life.

The legacy of *Gault* and its relationship to law school clinical programs is enduring. The training that juvenile delinquency clinics provide prepares new lawyers for juvenile defense work. Telephone surveys with hiring attorneys and supervisors of some of the major juvenile advocacy groups in the United States attest to the power of this movement.[134] All the people interviewed stated that if they saw a juvenile justice clinic on a job applicant's resume, they were more likely to hire the applicant. These organizations get hundreds of applications for a single spot, and participation in a juvenile justice clinic shows the type of specific interest and dedication they are looking for in an applicant.[135] Some employers even place special trust in specific clinics – either because of a relationship with the clinic director or because of the clinic's superior training – and are especially likely to hire an applicant on the recommendation of that clinic's faculty.

Juvenile justice clinics provide students with a number of valuable experiences that make them better candidates to work in juvenile advocacy groups. Judith Sandalow of the Children's Law Center spoke of the emotional strain of working in this field.[136] Attorneys sometimes think they want to work with kids, but they burn out after just a few years because of the emotional toll it takes on them.[137] According to Sandalow, hiring from a pool of clinic alumni who already have experience working with children and who understand what this type of work requires means their new hires are less likely to burn out.[138]

Along similar lines, the experience of participating in a juvenile justice clinic is also valuable to employers because clinic students have already had to think about some of the more difficult problems that arise in representing youth and underprivileged clients in general.[139] They have already considered how the justice system is failing children and what it means to represent them.[140] They know about special techniques for interviewing children, are familiar with the effects of trauma and the importance of resilience, they have seen the disproportionate confinement of minority youth, and witnessed the school to prison pipeline first hand. The result is that clinic alumni are better able to contribute their views on the harder issues as soon as they are hired, are experienced problem-solvers, and are more committed to their cause, all of which are of the utmost importance in this challenging field of work.[141]

In addition to these less tangible advantages, juvenile advocacy groups also appreciate the lawyering skills clinic alumni possess. Clinic alumni are more prepared for the training new employees receive, already know how to interact with juvenile clients, understand the basics of taking witness statements and developing direct and cross examinations, and are more comfortable and confident in court than their counterparts who did not participate in a clinic.[142] Finally, clinic students have already applied their skills with a "human component;" they have real life experiences that simulations such as a moot court or trial advocacy course cannot fully replicate because the people affected are not real.[143] Although this early lead is not always sustained, the ability of clinic alumni to more effectively manage their work early on makes for a smoother transition from law school to law practice.[144]

In addition to the value juvenile advocacy groups place on clinic experience at the hiring level, some groups also work with juvenile justice clinics and their students as part of their regular advocacy work. The Campaign for the Fair Sentencing of Youth (CFSY), for example, often reaches out to clinics in a geographic area to join their fight for reform.[145] Once reforms have been achieved, CFSY also relies on clinics to represent those affected by the reforms after their staff have moved on to another geographic area.[146] Although not every juvenile advocacy group can work directly with juvenile justice clinics on a regular basis, organizers readily recognize the value of clinics and are eager to form even temporary relationships where appropriate. They view clinics as an additional resource to complete larger projects without overburdening their entire staff.[147]

If one views juvenile justice clinics as a source of person-power and a training ground for students who will go on to become juvenile advocates, then the growth of juvenile justice clinics in the wake of *In re Gault* has been an opportunity for juvenile advocacy groups to grow and expand the work they do. In fact, the organizations surveyed have done that, and they have increasingly turned to juvenile justice clinics for support as their efforts have grown.[148] Though these two phenomena – the growth of clinics and the growth of juvenile advocacy groups – have been a result of a myriad of factors, they have certainly contributed to each other in some measure as well.[149]

Conclusion

Given that *Gault* was decided almost 50 years ago, and the majority of juvenile delinquency clinics were established more than 20 years after the Supreme Court's opinion, one might be tempted to say the decision itself had little to do with the founding of most of these clinics. Only the few clinics that began soon after the *Gault* decision seem to have a direct link to the *Gault* case, and that connection arose by virtue of the intellectual preferences and choices of the faculty who developed the programs. Of course, there can be no doubt that those pioneers were influenced by the *Gault* decision. Each recognized the power of Justice Fortas' jurisprudence and they were among the first lawyers working in the field. They adapted their clinic practices to reflect the teachings of *Gault* and created a cadre of young lawyers who became juvenile defenders. Over time, those juvenile defenders matured and looked to clinical education as the next step in their careers and embraced the belief that the juvenile defense field and clinical education would improve with the addition of juvenile defense clinics to the law school curriculum. The work of the early clinics also helped spur the development of clinics in other aspects of children's rights such as child abuse and neglect, immigration, and school disciplinary and special education work. The work continues; and Justice Fortas' jurisprudence set forth in *In re Gault* and the sheer power of his rhetoric provide the foundation for all we do today.

Notes

1 387 U.S. 1 (1967).

2 Morton J. Horwitz, *The Warren Court and the Pursuit of Justice*, 50 WASH. & LEE L. REV. 5 (1993); Bernard Schwartz, *Chief Justice Warren and 1984*, 35 HASTINGS L.J. 975 (1984).

3 *Legal Heroes*, Produced by Professor Lawrence A. Dubin, interview with Amelia Lewis, University of Detroit Mercy Law School, 1988.

4 Professor Lawrence Schwartz taught a class in juvenile delinquency at Georgetown Law Center as early as 1968 and Professor Sanford Fox was teaching one at least by 1970 at Boston College Law School. *See also* Diane Geraghty, *The Role of Education in the Emerging Legal Specialty of Pediatric Law*, 26 LOY. U. CHI. L. J. 131, 131–32 (1995), discussing the emergence of early juvenile justice courses and clinics.

5 J. P. "Sandy" Ogilvy, *Celebrating CLEPR's 40th Anniversary: The Early Development of Clinical Legal Education and Legal Ethics Instruction in U.S. Law Schools*, 16 CLIN. L. REV. 1, 9–15 (2009).

6 Margaret Martin Barry et al., *Clinical Education for this Millennium: The Third Wave*, 7 CLIN. L. REV. 1, 6 (2000).

7 *See* Appendix A.

8 *See, e.g.*, Pointer v. Texas, 380 U.S. 400 (1965); Klopfer v. North Carolina, 386 U. S. 213 (1967); *see also* Morton J. Horwitz, *The Warren Court and the Pursuit of Justice*, 50 WASH. & LEE L. REV. 5, 9 (1993).

9 Gideon v. Wainwright, 372 U.S. 335 (1963).

10 Mapp v. Ohio, 367 U.S. 643 (1961).

11 Griffin v. California, 380 U.S. 609 (1965); Miranda v. Arizona 384 U.S. 436 (1966); Benton v. Maryland, 395 U.S. 784 (1969); Ashe v. Swenson, 397 U.S. 436 (1970).

12 Barker v. Wingo, 407 U.S. 514 (1972); Duncan v. Louisiana, 391 U.S. 145 (1968); Irvin v. Dowd, 366 U.S. 717 (1961); Washington v. Texas, 388 U.S. 14 (1967); United States v. Wade, 388 U.S. 218 (1967).

13 Trop v. Dulles, 356 U.S. 86 (1958); Kennedy v. Mendoza-Martinez, 372 U.S. 144 (1963).

14 Mason v. Brathwaite, 432 U.S. 98 (1977); Neil v. Biggers, 409 U.S. 188 (1972); Foster v. California, 394 U.S. 440 (1969); Simmons v. U.S. 390 U.S. 377 (1968); Stovall v. Denno, 388 U.S. 293 (1967).

15 Gallegos v. Colorado, 370 U.S. 49 (1962); Haley v. Ohio, 322 U.S. 596 (1948).

16 383 U.S. 541 (1966).

17 Illinois Juvenile Court Act 1899, Ill. Laws 131.

18 Nanette Dembitz, *Ferment and Experiment in New York: Juvenile Proceedings in the New Family Court*, 48 CORNELL L. Q. 499 (1963); Orman W. Ketcham, *Legal Renaissance in the Juvenile Court*, 60 NW. U. L. REV. 585 (1965); Chester James Antieau, *Constitutional Rights in Juvenile Court*, 46 CORNELL L. Q. 381 (1961); Daniel L. Skoler, *What You Should Know About Juvenile Courts and Young Lawyers*, 10 STUDENT LAW. J. 5 (1964); Charles W. Quick, *Constitutional Rights in the Juvenile Court*, 12 HOW. L. J. 76 (1966).

19 407 P.2d 760, 765 (1965).

20 "[T]he powers of the Star Chamber were a trifle in comparison with those of our juvenile courts and courts of domestic relations," Roscoe Pound, *The Challenge of the Juvenile Court*, 3 JUV. FAM. CT. J., No. 1, 18 (1952).

21 Kent v. United States, 383 U.S. 541, 556 (1966).

22 Gideon v. Wainwright, 372 U.S. 335 (1963).

23 David S. Tanenhaus & Eric C. Nystrom, *Pursuing Gault*, 17 NEV. L.J. 351 (2017).

24 Note from Earl Warren to Justice Fortas, cited in THE SUPREME COURT IN CONFERENCE (1940–1985): THE PRIVATE DISCUSSIONS BEHIND NEARLY 300 SUPREME COURT DECISIONS, ed. Del Dickson (Oxford University Press, 2001).

25 John F. Kennedy, Inaugural Speech, January 20, 1961. The full quote reads "Let the word go forth from this time and place, to friend and foe alike, that the torch has been passed to a new generation of Americans–born in this century, tempered by war, disciplined by a hard and bitter peace, proud of our ancient heritage–and unwilling to witness or permit the slow undoing of those human rights to which this nation has always been committed, and to which we are committed today at home and around the world."

26 United Farm Workers Union was born out of a merger between two workers' rights organizations: the National Farm Workers Association, created by Cesar Chavez and Dolores Huerta, and the Agricultural Workers Organizing Committee, created by Larry Itliong. *UFW History*, UNITED FARM WORKERS, http://www.ufw.org/_page.php?menu=research&inc=history/03.html (last visited May 31, 2016). Chavez and Huerta helped organize a series of strikes in California during the 1960s, of which the Delano Grape Strike was of particular note, which gained farm workers better pay and union recognition for the first time, among other benefits. *Id.*

27 Originally founded in 1968 to monitor and address police mistreatment of American Indians in tribal communities, the American Indian Movement (AIM) quickly grew to a national organization, focusing on issues like sovereignty, broken treaties, and the validity of tribal governments. Jeffrey Stotik, Thomas E. Shriver, & Sherry Cable, *Social Control and the Movement Outcome: The Case of AIM*, 27 SOC. FOCUS 53, 57 (1994). Dennis Banks and Russell Means led the AIM through the early 1970s, drawing inspiration from the black civil rights and antiwar movements. *Id.* at 56. Some of the key events during AIM's brief period of successful protest included the occupation of the abandoned federal prison on Alcatraz Island from 1969 to 1971, the occupation of the Bureau of Indian Affairs in 1972, and the occupation of Wounded Knee in 1973. *Id.* at 58–59.

28 On April 4, 1967, Martin Luther King, Jr., gave a speech entitled "Beyond Vietnam," speaking out against the Vietnam War and protesting that it drew funds and energy from domestic poverty programs and sent young black men to fight for liberties they had not received at home. Martin Luther King, Jr., Address at Riverside Church in New York, New York: Beyond Vietnam (Apr. 4, 1967). Muhammed Ali, who originally gained fame as a champion boxer, was vocal about his opposition to the Vietnam War and was initially convicted for evading the draft. Timothy L. Reed, *Peace Profile: Muhammed Ali*, 16 PEACE REV. 107, 108–110 (2004). Dick Gregory, comedian and civil rights activist, fasted from Thanksgiving Day 1967 to New Year's Day 1968 to protest the Vietnam War, for which he received widespread attention. Clovis E. Semmes, *Entrepreneur of Health: Dick Gregory, Black Consciousness, and the Human Potential Movement*, 16 J. AFR. AM. STUD. 537, 542 (2012).

29 As the number of active campus-based chapters of Students for a Democratic Society (SDS) at colleges grew, so did the number of student protests on campus. *Id.* at 202. SDS became increasingly radical and spread to cities, participating in a mass draft-card burning in New York City in 1967 and protests at the 1968 Democratic National Convention in Chicago that ended with hundreds injured and arrested. *Id.* at 215, 323–24.

30 College enrollment rose from 45.1 percent of high school graduates in 1960 to 53.3 percent in 1969. Thomas D. Snyder & Charlene M. Hoffman, *Digest of Education Statistics* 1999 at 215, DEPT. OF EDUC., NATIONAL CENTER FOR EDUCATION STATISTICS NCES (2000).

31 Prior to the first GI Bill, college was still mainly for the upper class, but after the war, the GI Bill prompted an initial flood of GIs who took advantage of their educational benefits for college. Karen Brodkin Sacks, *The GI Bill: Whites Only Need Apply, in* CRITICAL WHITE STUDIES 310, 310–11 (Richard Delgado & Jean Stefancic eds., Temple University Press, 1997). At the same time, the middle class expanded through the 1950s and 60s and increasingly sent its children to college. *Id.* at 311–12.

32 Although women mobilized to fill vacancies in the workforce during the War, they were often pushed out of higher-paying jobs in industry and science when men returned home. *Interview with Elain Tyler May in Tupperware! American Experience*, PBS, http://www.pbs.org/wgbh/americanexperience/features/interview/tupperware-may/ (last visited June 1, 2016). Though many women continued to work after the War, they were limited to lower-paid positions labeled as "women's work" or "pink collar," such as waitresses, teachers, and secretaries. *Id.*

33 The National Organization for Women was unofficially founded during the Third National Conference of Commissions on the Status of Women in June 1966 by Betty Friedan, Pauli Murray, and 15–20 other women. *Founding*, NAT'L ORGANIZATION FOR WOMEN, http://now.org/about/history/founding-2 (last visited June 1, 2016). It became an official organization at its first Organizing Conference in October, 1966, when it nominated a board of officers and created a Statement of Purpose calling for full participation of women in society and equal privileges and responsibilities for women and men. *Id.*

34 *E.g.*, Roe v. Wade, 410 U.S. 113 (1973) (permitting abortions in some pregnancies); Carey v. Population Serv. Int'l, 431 U.S. 678 (1977) (holding unconstitutional a NY statute which banned the distribution of contraceptives except by a licensed pharmacist and prohibited advertisement of contraceptives); Cannon v. University of Chicago 441 U.S. 677 (1979) (granting a female student the right to sue two universities who denied her admission to medical school because of her sex); Arizona Governing Comm. for Tax Deferred Annuity and Deferred Comp. Plans v. Norris, 463 U. S. 1073 (1983) (holding that an employer's practice of providing employees a choice of retirement benefits which all paid women less than men for the same contributions was unlawfully discriminatory).

35 Late on the evening of June 27, 1969, police raided the Stonewall Inn in New York, a bar known as a refuge for the gay community. Cynthia Cannon Poindexter,

Sociopolitical Antecedents to Stonewall: Analysis of the Origins of the Gay Rights, 42 Soc. Work 607, 607 (1997). During the raid, bar patrons fought back, causing a riot that lasted into the next three nights. *Id.* The Stonewall Riots are seen as a spark of the Gay Rights Movement. *Id.* at 611.

36 In addition to being the property of their parents, children were viewed as immature, incapable of looking after themselves, and unable to give legal consent. Stephen R. Arnott, *Autonomy, Standing, and Children's Rights*, 33 Wm. Mitchell L. Rev. 807, 812–13 (2007). Even when early children's rights and welfare reforms began, courts were reluctant to interfere in family affairs, limiting the government's role in protecting children.

37 *E.g.*, Prince v. Massachusetts, 321 U.S. 158 (1944); West Virginia Board of Education v Barnett, 391 U.S. 624 (1943); Meyer v Nebraska, 262 U.S. 390 (1923).

38 Fair Labor Standards Act of 1938, Pub. L. No. 75–718, ch. 676, 52 Stat. 1060.

39 393 U.S. 503 (1969) (permitting students to exercise a First Amendment right to wear black arm bands in school to protest the Vietnam War).

40 397 U.S. 358 (1970) (holding that when a juvenile is charged with a crime, the case against them must be proved beyond a reasonable doubt as a matter of due process).

41 403 U.S. 528 (1971) (holding that trial by jury in the juvenile court's adjudicative stage is not constitutionally required).

42 421 U.S. 519 (1975) (applying the protections of Double Jeopardy clause to juvenile proceedings and holding jeopardy attached at the adjudicatory hearing, thus requiring transfer hearings to be held before adjudicatory hearings).

43 438 U.S. 204 (1978) (finding that the State practice of filing exceptions to a master's proposals in a juvenile's case does not violate Double Jeopardy because the master's hearing and subsequent adjudication by a judge constitute a single proceeding, so the juvenile is not required to stand trial twice).

44 467 U.S. 253 (1984) (holding that a statute authorizing pre-trial detention of an accused juvenile delinquent based on a "serious risk" that the juvenile would commit a crime did not violate the Due Process Clause).

45 Much of the information in this section first appeared in Wallace J. Mlyniec & Haley D. Etchison, *Conceptualizing Student Practice for the 21st Century: Educational and Ethical Considerations in Modernizing the District of Columbia Student Practice Rules*, 28 Geo. J. Legal Ethics 207, 210–13 (2015).

46 *See, e.g.*, Martin A. Frey, *The Effect of the Gault Decision on the Iowa Juvenile Justice System*, 17 Drake L. Rev. 53 (1967); Orman W. Ketchum, *Guidelines from Gault: Revolutionary Requirements and Reappraisal*, 53 Va. L. Rev. 1700 (1967); B. J. George, Jr., *The Implications of Gault for Welfare Administration*, 2 Fam. L.Q. 182 (1968); Bradley C. Canon & Kenneth Kolson, *Rural Compliance with Gault: Kentucky, a Case Study*, 10 J. Fam. L. 300 (1971).

47 *E.g.*, Thomas A. Welch, Kent v. United States *and* In re Gault*: Two Decisions in Search of a Theory*, 19 Hastings L.J. 29 (1967) (written by a lawyer practicing in San Francisco); William S. Fort, *Gault – Adversity or Opportunity?* 51 Judicature 53 (1967) (written by a Circuit Court Judge of the Second Judicial District in Eugene, Oregon).

48 Norman Dorsen & Daniel A. Rezneck, *In re Gault and the Future of Juvenile Law*, Family L.Q., December 1967 at 1.

49 *E.g.*, Brian M. Bell & James Rode, Note, *In re Gault and the Colorado Children's Code*, 44 Denv. L.J. 644 (1967); Martin A. Frey, *The Effect of the Gault Decision on the Iowa Juvenile Justice System*, 17 Drake L. Rev. 53 (1967).

50 *E.g.*, Walter W. Reckless & Walter C. Reckless, *The Initial Impact of the Gault Decision in Ohio*, 18 Juv. Ct. Judges J. 121 (1968); Canon & Kolson, *supra* note 46.

51 *E.g.*, Aiden R. Gough, *Referees in California's Juvenile Courts: A Study in Sub-Judicial Adjudication*, 19 Hastings L.J. 3, 3 (1967).

52 Orman W. Ketcham, *Guidelines from Gault: Revolutionary Requirements and Reappraisal*, 53 VA. L. REV. 1700, 1700 (1967).
53 Fort, *supra* note 47, at 47 (quoting, without citing, Judge Ketcham, *see supra* note 52).
54 *E.g.*, Dorsen & Rezneck, *supra* note 48, at 2–8.
55 Fort, *supra* note 47, at 53–54.
56 Geraghty, *supra* note 4, at 131, 131–32.
57 Shabnam Naznin Ahmed, *The Breached Contract: What Society Owes Its Children for Minimizing Their Constitutional Rights*, 50 HOW. L. J. 841, 864 (2007).
58 Christopher Columbus Langdell was Dean of Harvard Law School from 1870 to 1895, during which time he is credited with having introduced the casebook method of teaching. ANTHONY KRONMAN, THE LOST LAWYER: FAILING IDEALS OF THE LEGAL PROFESSION 169–70 (rev. ed., Belknap Press, 1995). Before Langdell, much of legal education took place in law offices under the supervision of practicing lawyers. *Id.* Langdell believed the study of law needed to be more academic and scientific in order for law schools to become intellectually respectable. *Id.*
59 Thomas F. Geraghty, *Legal Clinics and the Better Trained Lawyer (Redux): A History of Clinical Education at Northwestern*, 100 NW. L. R. 230, 231 (2006).
60 Several law professors, most prominently Professor Jerome Frank of Yale argued in the 1930s that clinical education had a place in American law schools. Jerome Frank, *Why Not a Clinical Law School?*, 81 U. PA. L. REV. 907 (1933). The Langdell model, however, was so deeply entrenched that they did not alter the legal academy.
61 Barry et al., *supra* note 6, at 6 (2000).
62 *Id.; see also* J. P. "Sandy" Ogilvy, *Celebrating CLEPR's 40th Anniversary: The Early Development of Clinical Legal Education and Legal Ethics Instruction in U.S. Law Schools*, 16 CLIN. L. REV. 1, 9–15 (2009).
63 Elliot Milstein, Professor of Law, American University Washington College of Law, "Why the Clinical Section Award is Called the 'William Pincus Award,'" delivered January 2009 (on file with author).
64 Under Pincus, CLEPR would only grant funding to those clinical programs in which law students performed legal services for real clients for academic credit under the supervision of an attorney-supervisor hired by the law school. LESTER BRICKMAN, CLEPR AND CLINICAL EDUCATION: A REVIEW AND ANALYSIS, IN CLINICAL EDUCATION FOR THE LAW STUDENT: LEGAL EDUCATION IN A SERVICE SETTING 56, 61 (Meilen Press Inc., 1973). CLEPR also required all institutions to pay a share of the cost of the program that increased over time so that by the time the grant funds were spent, the institution would be funding most of the program, and the program could continue after the grant ended. *Id.*
65 Margaret Martin Barry et al., *Clinical Education for this Millennium: The Third Wave*, 7 CLIN. L. REV. 1, 13–14.
66 Mlyniec & Etchison, *supra* note 45, at 211.
67 Frank G. Avellone, *The State of State Student Practice: Proposals for Reforming Ohio's Legal Internship Rule*, 17 OHIO N.U. L. REV. 13, 13 n.1 (1990).
68 Argersinger v. Hamlin, 407 U.S. 25, 44 (1972) (Brennan, J., concurring).
69 This situation continues today. Between 2011 and 2015, 67 percent of those hired on a tenure-track at the top 26 ranked law schools held JD-PhD degrees. Twenty-one percent of entry-level professors hired on a tenure-track at all American law schools held both JD and PhD credentials. Lynn M. LoPucki, *Dawn of the Discipline-Based Law Faculty*, 65 J. LEGAL EDUC. 506 (2016). Few law professors, except those teaching in clinics, have extensive legal practice experience.
70 Stephen Wizner, *Beyond Skills Training*, 7 CLIN. L. REV. 327, 332 (2001); Minna J. Kotkin & Dean Hill Rivkin, *Clinical Legal Education at a Generational Crossroads: Reflections from Two Boomers*, 17 CLIN. L. REV. 197, 199 (2010); Praveen Kosuri,

Clinical Legal Education at a Generational Crossroads: S Marks the Spot, 17 Clin. L. Rev. 205, 206–07 (2010).

71 ABA Section of Legal Education and Admission to the Bar, ABA Standards and Rules of Procedure for Approval of Law Schools, 15–25.

72 Geraghty, *supra* note 56 (citing George S. Grossman, *Clinical Legal Education, History and Diagnosis*, 26 J. Legal Educ. 162, 172–73); *see also* Barry et al., *supra* note 6. *See supra* note 62.1.

73 *See supra* note 62.

74 *See supra* notes 49, 50.

75 Between 2000 and 2013, the National Juvenile Defender Center studied the operations of delinquency courts in 21 states. In many of those states judges still tried to retain their pre-Gault authority over the operation of the court. *State Assessments*, NJDC, *passim*, http://njdc.info/our-work/juvenile-indigent-defense-assessments (last visited June 15, 2016). *See also* Wallace J. Mlyniec, *In re Gault at 40: The Right to Counsel in Juvenile Court – A Promise Unfulfilled*, 44 Crim. L. Bull. 371 (2008).

76 Between 1947 and 1968, on average, women made up only 3.9 percent of first-year students at ABA-accredited law schools. A.B.A. Sec. of Legal Educ. and Admission to the Bar, *First Year and Total J.D. Enrollment by Gender (1947–2011)*, Statistics Archives, http://www.americanbar.org/content/dam/aba/administrative/legal_education_and_admissions_to_the_bar/statistics/jd_enrollment_1yr_total_gender.authcheckdam.pdf. For the class entering in 1968, however, that number jumped to 7.4 percent. *Id.* After that, the percentage of women in law schools grew rapidly through the 1970s. *Id.* By 1980, 36.1 percent of incoming first-years were women, a growth of 28.7 percent in just 12 years. *Id.*

77 This battle continues today. *See supra* note 75.

78 University of South Carolina Statistics for Juvenile & Family Law Clinics, 1969–1970, provided by Roy Stuckey, Webster Distinguished Professor Emeritus of Clinical Legal Education, University of South Carolina, via email, July 1, 2016.

79 Email exchange between Wallace Mlyniec and Larry Ritchie, Professor Law Roger Williams University Law School, June 8, 2016. Ritchie notes that the state had no student practice rule at that time, but had a statute dating back to colonial times that allowed a person to have a courtroom representative who was not a lawyer. The students began practicing under the authority of that statute. *See also* University of South Carolina Bulletin, August 25, 1971.

80 Email exchange between Wallace Mlyniec and Professor Stuckey, July 7, 2016.

81 University of South Carolina Bulletin, 1975.

82 Email from Professor Michael Millemann, Jacob A. France Professor of Public Interest Law at the University of Maryland Francis King Carey School of Law, August 4, 2016.

83 Prior to coming to Maryland, Professor Smith had spent his entire career providing legal services to minority and poor citizens, people with disabilities, and juveniles who did not have access to those services. Email from Mrs. Marjorie Smith to the author, dated June 5, 2016, on file with the author.

84 *Id.* He was also the first attorney of the Neighborhood Legal Services Program of Washington, which was the first civil appellate legal services program in the nation. Frederick N. Rasmussen, *Peter Smith Obituary*, Baltimore Sun (Mar. 13, 2015), http://www.baltimoresun.com/news/obituaries/bs-md-ob-peter-smith-20150313-story.html.

85 Email from Mrs. Marjorie Smith to the author, dated June 5, 2016, on file with the author.

86 Comparative Analysis of American Bar Association Standards for Criminal Justice with District of Columbia Law, Rules and Legal Practice (Wallace J. Mlyniec ed., District of Columbia Circuit Judicial Conference, Washington, D.C.1973).

87 The E. Barrett Prettyman Program was founded in 1960 by Professor A. Kenneth Pye to provide academic instruction and an LL.M. degree to lawyers seeking to become criminal defense attorneys or prosecutors. Wallace Mlyniec, *The Intersection of Three Visions – Ken Pye, Bill Pincus, and Bill Greenhalgh – and the Development of Clinical Teaching Fellowships*, 64 TENN. L. REV. 963, 968 (1997). The program continues today.

88 Telephone interview by Haley Etchison with Martin Guggenheim, Fiorello LaGuardia Professor of Clinical Law, New York University School of Law (Mar. 15, 2016). Most of the information about NYU comes from that interview.

89 *See, e.g.*, Barbara Danziger Flicker, *Standards for Juvenile Justice: A Summary and Analysis*, IJA-ABA JOINT COMM. ON JUVENILE JUSTICE STANDARDS (Ballinger Publishing, 1977); the Commission has published two volumes, the first in 1977, *supra*, and the second in 1982 to mark the completion of the project. Barbara Danziger Flicker, *Standards for Juvenile Justice: A Summary and Analysis*, IJA-ABA JOINT COMM. ON JUVENILE JUSTICE STANDARDS (2d ed., Ballinger Publishing, 1982). During that time, the Commission recommended the adoption of 23 volumes on the functioning of the juvenile justice system to the ABA House of Delegates, 20 of which were eventually approved. *Id.* at xii.

90 Legal Aid's JRD was a remarkable institution. Its founder, Charles Schinitsky, was committed to the principle that children deserved lawyers who advocated for their expressed interest rather than for the lawyer's assessment of what was in the child's best interest. He opened the office with three or four lawyers in 1962, five years before Gault was decided. By 1971, there were perhaps 35 or 40 lawyers, probably the largest contingent of juvenile defense lawyers anywhere in the world. Schinitsky's brand of advocacy was rare and well ahead of its time.

91 *See supra* note 64.

92 *See supra* note 87.

93 The Clinic was founded by Professor Michael Rosenthal who taught the seminar. Students were placed with defenders for case work. Email from Michael Churgin, the Raybourne Thompson Centennial Professor at the University of Texas Law School (Aug. 11, 2016).

94 Bradley Gator, Harvard JD, and Holly Ackerman, Howard MSW, were co-directors of the first Juvenile Clinic at Tulane. Email from David Katner, Professor of Clinical Law and Felix J. Dreyfous, Teaching Fellow at Tulane University Law School (Nov. 14, 2016).

95 Professor Barry Kowalski and Professor Lois Goodman were early directors of the Antioch Clinic.

96 SURVEY AND DIRECTORY OF CLINICAL EDUCATION, 1976–1977 (Council on Legal Education for Professional Responsibility, 1977).

97 In the early days of clinical education, most non-traditional courses with experiential components were lumped into the category of "clinic" whether or not they met the CLEPR definition. Thus, externships, practicums, service credits, and even Street Law courses were often considered clinics. The American Bar Association accreditation standards now provide distinct definitions of these terms. ABA STANDARDS AND RULES OF PROCEDURE FOR APPROVAL OF LAW SCHOOLS 2016–2017 f, Chapter 3, Program of Legal Education and Accompanying Interpretations, especially 304(b) and 305.

98 Email from Thomas Geraghty, James B. Haddad Professor Law, Northwestern University Pritzker Law School (June 3, 2016); *see also* Geraghty, *supra* note 59.

99 Email from James M. Concannon, Senator Robert J. Dole Distinguished Professor of Law, Washburn Law School (June 4, 2016).

100 Emails from Bernard Freamon, Professor of Law, Seton Hall University School of Law (Aug. 8, 2016).

101 Professor William Greenhalgh, long-time Georgetown Criminal Justice Clinic, Director of the Prettyman program, and early proponent of clinical education nationally was often heard to use the term. He may have also coined it.

102 Telephone interview by Haley Etchison with David Katner, Professor of Clinical Law, Felix J. Dreyfous Teaching Fellow in Juvenile Law, Director, Juvenile Law Clinic, Tulane University Law School (Mar. 15, 2016).

103 The Law Enforcement Assistance Administration of the Department of Justice funded some clinical programs in the 1970s after Ford Foundation funding ended. *See* Mlyniec, *supra* note 86; *see also* Harold R. Washington & Geraldine S. Hines, *"Call My Lawyer": Styling a Community Based Defender Program*, 8 BLACK L.J. 186, 193 (1983).

104 Pub. L. No. 93–247 88 Stat. 4 (1974).

105 The passage of the Child Abuse Prevention and Treatment Act, Pub. L. No. 93–247 88 Stat. 4 (1974) spurred soft money funding for the first child welfare clinic at the University of Michigan in 1974 and had a similar effect at other law schools.

106 Telephone interview by Haley Etchison with Don Duquette, Clinical Professor of Law, Founder, Child Advocacy Law Clinic, University of Michigan Law School (Mar. 16, 2016).

107 There were other organizations focusing on children like the Children's Defense Fund, the Youth Law Center, and various Legal Services Corporation backup centers but delinquency was not their focus.

108 As support for CLEPR from the Ford Foundation ended, the Department of Education began to fund clinical legal education programs, appropriating more than $87 million between 1978 and 1997. Barry et al., *supra* note 6, at 19 (2000).

109 American Bar Association, Section on Litigation Task Force on Children, A DIRECTORY OF PRO BONO CHILDREN'S LAW PROGRAMS, 2d ed. (1994).

110 American Bar Association, Section on Litigation Task Force on Children, A DIRECTORY OF PRO BONO CHILDREN'S LAW PROGRAMS, 4th ed. (1999).

111 Fort, *supra* note 47, at 53.

112 *E.g.*, Thomas E. Klinkel, *South Dakota Juvenile Procedures Ten Years After Gault: Still Unconstitutional?* 22 S.D. L. REV. 56 (1977); Robert J. Wiley, *The History of Juvenile Law Reform in Ohio Since Gault*, 12 OHIO N.U. L. REV. 469 (1985).

113 Paul Holland & Wallace J. Mlyniec, *Whatever Happened to the Right to Treatment? The Modern Quest for a Historical Promise*, 68 TEMPLE L.R. 1791 (1995); Gary B. Melton, *Taking Gault Seriously: Toward a New Juvenile Court*, 68 NEB. L. REV. 146, 149 (1989).

114 N. Lee Cooper et al., *Fulfilling the Promise of In re Gault: Advancing the Role of Lawyers for Children*, 33 WAKE FOREST L. REV. 651, 655 (1998).

115 Samuel M. Davis, *The Role of the Attorney in Child Advocacy*, 32 U. LOUISVILLE J. FAM. L. 817, 823 (1994).

116 Melton, *supra* note 113; Raymond Chao, *Mirandizing Kids: Not as Simple as A-B-C*, 21 WHITTIER L. REV. 521, 523 (2000).

117 Davis, *supra* note 115, at 826–27; *see also* Donald N. Bersoff, *Representation for Children in Custody Decisions: All That Glitters is Not Gault*, 15 J. FAM. L. 27, 31–34 (1976).

118 One major article about this issue was written by Professor Martin Guggenheim. He not only analyzed the different approaches to representing children but went so far as to argue that in a case where the child is too young to direct their own attorney, appointing counsel might actually create more problems than would exist without the child's lawyer. Martin Guggenheim, *The Right to be Represented but not Heard: Reflections on Legal Representation for Children*, 59 N.Y.U. L. REV. 76 (1984).

119 *E.g.*, Cooper et al., *supra* note 114, at 652.

120 *Id.*

121 Holly Beatty, Comment, *Is the Trend to Expand Juvenile Transfer Statutes Just an Easy Answer to a Complex Problem?* 26 U. Tol. L. Rev. 979, 979–80 (1995).
122 Appendix A lists the names of these law schools.
123 In re Winship, 397 U.S. 358 (1970).
124 Schall v. Martin, 467 U.S. 253 (1984).
125 Breed v. Jones, 421 U.S. 519 (1975).
126 J.D.B. v. North Carolina, 564 U.S. 261, 275 (2011).
127 David S. Tanenhaus & Eric C. Nystrom, *Pursuing Gault*, 17 Nev. L.J. 351 (2017).
128 The Mid-Atlantic Regional Center is at Georgetown Law Center, Northeast Regional Center is at Rutgers Law School, and the Southwest Regional Center is at the University of Houston Law School.
129 132 S.Ct. 2455 (2012).
130 543 U.S. 551 (2005).
131 560 U.S. 48 (2010).
132 Miller v. Alabama, 132 S.Ct. 2455 (2012); Montgomery v. Louisiana, 136 S.Ct. 718 (2016).
133 Many scholars and lawyers worked though the MacArthur Network to develop this research. Among the most prominent were Lawrence Steinberg, Temple University; Robert Schwartz, Juvenile Law Center; Elizabeth Scott, Columbia Law School; Jennifer Woolard, University of Florida and Georgetown University; Elizabeth Cauffman, University of California at Irvine; Sandra Graham, University of California, Los Angeles; Ed Mulvey, University of Pittsburgh; Franklin Zimring, Berkeley Law School; Jeffrey Fagan, Columbia School of Public Health and Law School; Thomas Grisso, University of Massachusetts Medical Center; Marie Banich, University of Colorado; Patti Lee, San Francisco Public Defender; Amy Holmes-Hehn, Oregon Prosecutor. MacArthur Network on Adolescent Development and Juvenile Justice. *See also* Laurence Steinberg & Elizabeth S. Scott, *Less Guilty by Reason of Adolescence: Developmental Immaturity, Diminished Responsibility, and the Juvenile Death Penalty*, 58 Am. Psychol. 1009 (2003); Jeffrey Arnett, *Reckless Behavior in Adolescence: A Developmental Perspective*, 12 Dev. Rev. 339 (1992).
134 Sarah Bryer, Director, National Juvenile Justice Network; James Dold, Advocacy Director, Campaign for the Fair Sentencing of Youth; Jennifer Morris, Director, Guardian ad Litem Program, Children's Law Center; Jee Park, Deputy District Defender, Orleans Public Defenders; Lisa Pilnik, Deputy Executive Director, Coalition for Juvenile Justice; Judith Sandalow, Executive Director, Children's Law Center.
135 Telephone interview by Meghan Strong with Lisa Pilnik, Deputy Executive Director, Coalition for Juvenile Justice (June 23, 2016).
136 Telephone interview by Meghan Strong with Judith Sandalow, Executive Director, Children's Law Center (June 23, 2016).
137 *Id.*
138 *Id.*
139 Telephone interview by Meghan Strong with Jee Park, Deputy District Defender, Orleans Public Defenders (June 27, 2016).
140 *Id.*
141 *Id.*
142 Email from Jennifer Morris, Director, Guardian ad Litem Program, Children's Law Center (June 23, 2016).
143 *Supra*, note 136.
144 *Id.*
145 Telephone interview by Meghan Strong with James Dold, Advocacy Director, Campaign for the Fair Sentencing of Youth (June 22, 2016).
146 *Id.*
147 Telephone interview by Meghan Strong with Sarah Bryer, Director, National Juvenile Justice Network (June 16, 2016).

148 *Id.*
149 *Id.*

Appendix A

Law schools with clinics providing juvenile delinquency defense as of March, 2016.

This list was compiled by researching clinic websites and speaking to clinical faculty.

1 American University Washington College of Law
2 Arizona State University Sandra Day O'Connor College of Law
3 Barry University Dwayne O. Andreas School of Law
4 Boston College Law School
5 Boston University School of Law
6 Brooklyn Law School
7 Campbell University Norman Adrian Wiggins School of Law
8 Columbia University Law School
9 Cornell Law School
10 Drake University Law School
11 Duquesne University School of Law
12 Elon University School of Law
13 Emory University School of Law
14 Florida Coastal School of Law
15 Harvard Law School
16 Hofstra University Maurice A. Deane School of Law
17 Howard University School of Law
18 Louisiana State University Paul M. Herbert Law Center
19 Loyola University Chicago School of Law
20 New York Law School
21 New York University School of Law
22 Northern Illinois University College of Law
23 Northwestern University Pritzker School of Law
24 Ohio State University Moritz College of Law
25 Rutgers Law School (Newark and Camden)
26 Seattle University School of Law
27 Seton Hall University School of Law
28 Southern Illinois University School of Law
29 Southern University Law Center
30 St. Louis University School of Law
31 Tulane Law School
32 University of California Berkeley Law School
33 University of California Los Angeles Law School
34 University of Alabama Little Rock William H. Bowen School of Law
35 University of Baltimore School of Law
36 University of Chicago Law School

37 University of Colorado Law School
38 University of Connecticut School of Law
39 University of Florida Levin College of Law
40 University of Maine School of Law
41 University of Michigan Law School
42 University of Minnesota Law School
43 University of Mississippi School of Law
44 University of Nevada, Las Vegas William S. Boyd School of Law
45 University of North Carolina Law School
46 University of San Francisco Law School
47 University of South Carolina School of Law
48 University of Texas School of Law
49 University of the District of Columbia David A. Clarke School of Law
50 University of Washington School of Law
51 Valparaiso University Law School
52 Washington University St. Louis Law School
53 Western Michigan University Cooley Law School
54 William & Mary Law School
55 Yale Law School

9 Raising the bar: improving the model of defense representation for adolescents prosecuted in adult courts

Nancy Ginsburg

Client narrative

Anthony[1] was 16 years old when he was arrested for starting a fire in his high school during the school day. He lit a piece of paper taped to a classroom door with his lighter. The incident was captured on videotape and he was charged with felony arson in adult criminal court and faced a sentence of 5–25 years in adult prison. In school, he received special education services to address symptoms of attention deficit hyperactivity disorder. Anthony was a well-liked student. Although he had a history of minor impulsive behavior, he was cooperative with counseling and his academic program.

Days after his initial arraignment, a lawyer, investigator, and social worker went to Anthony's school. They met with the principal, a few teachers, the school social worker, and a dean. The defense team observed the site of the incident and reviewed Anthony's academic and special education records with the school team. This discussion was the first in a series, during which it was agreed that Anthony would accept responsibility for his immature, impulsive behavior through community service at the school. School personnel agreed to advocate with defense counsel in an effort to convince the prosecution that a less serious charge was more appropriate and incarceration was unnecessary. The defense team social worker and the lawyer reviewed and synthesized the school records, mental health evaluations, interviewed school personnel and family members, and wrote a report for the prosecutor detailing Anthony's life history and amenability to rehabilitation.

After completion of the agreed upon community service, participation in increased counseling, and a written apology, the prosecutor agreed to dismiss the felony charges and consented to a guilty plea to a misdemeanor and Anthony's adjudication as a youthful offender. As a result, his case was sealed and he did not have a criminal record, allowing him to begin his adult life with a clean slate.

History of prosecuting adolescents in New York State

That Anthony was prosecuted as an adult at all is a product of New York's historically draconian laws. Until 2017, the state was one of only two in the country to set the age of majority for criminal prosecution at 16.[2] By definition, however, the adult criminal court system is not designed to meet the needs of teenagers. It lacks linkages to necessary support systems: foster care, education, and adolescent mental health, among others. Those who staff the adult courts, jails, and prisons are rarely trained to work with adolescents, and responses to normative adolescent behaviors in these settings can range from uninformed to abusive.[3]

New York State first designated 16- and 17-year-olds as adults for purposes of criminal prosecution in the late 1700s.[4] Despite the fact that almost every state set the age of adult criminal prosecution at 18, New York maintained that 16- and 17-year-olds were adults for purposes of criminal prosecution.[5] In 1978, New York enacted the Juvenile Offender Act, sending even younger children into adult criminal courts. The law created the category of Juvenile Offender – youth aged 13–15 who are charged with committing serious felonies.[6] These youth are incarcerated in juvenile facilities at all stages of the criminal proceeding[7] and face shorter periods of incarceration than adults, but significantly longer periods than children under age 16 charged as juvenile delinquents, who are prosecuted in family court and who do not receive criminal records.[8]

Juvenile Offenders, like 16- and 17-year-olds charged with violent felonies, face mandatory state sentences of incarceration unless the court makes a finding of a Youthful Offender adjudication, which replaces the criminal conviction.[9] Any youth who is convicted as a Juvenile Offender based on a crime committed between the ages of 13 and 15, or who is convicted of a crime committed between the ages of 16 and 18, may be eligible for consideration as a Youthful Offender under New York law.[10] In the interest of justice, the court may adjudicate a youth as a Youthful Offender in substitution for a criminal conviction, allowing for a reduced sentence and relieving the burden of a criminal conviction.

In 2005, the United States Supreme Court decided *Roper v. Simmons*,[11] in which it recognized research findings on adolescent brain development as a mitigating factor in sentencing. The Court determined that minors under the age of 18 bear a constitutionally different status for sentencing purposes.[12] The Court credited developmental science research to support its holding that "[a] lack of maturity and an underdeveloped sense of responsibility are found in youth more often than in adults and are more understandable among the young. These qualities often result in impetuous and ill-considered actions and decisions."[13] The Supreme Court has granted special dispensation for minors in *Roper* (disallowing the death penalty for offenders under the age of 18);[14] *Graham v. Florida* (prohibiting life without parole for non-homicide offenses for youth under the age of 18);[15] and *J.D.B. v. North Carolina* (holding that a child's age is a relevant factor to consider in determining whether a child is "in custody" for the purposes of *Miranda* warnings).[16] In *Miller v. Alabama*, the Supreme Court again held that "sentencing rule[s] permissible for adults may not be so for children,"[17] relying upon research showing that children are less capable of evaluating the possible outcomes of different courses of actions,[18] and "are more vulnerable … to negative influences and outside pressures, including from their family and peers; they have limited contro[l] over their own environment and lack the ability to extricate themselves from horrific, crime-producing settings."[19]

It is now well established that the adolescent brain does not fully develop until at least age 25.[20] Adolescence is defined by certain characteristics – susceptibility to peer influence, differential risk-benefit analyses, and impulsivity, among others – that profoundly affect executive functions such as judgment and decision-making. Age and developmental status are critical factors in evaluating a young person's degree of culpability and capacity for reform. In fact, society distinguishes adolescents from adults in virtually every area of the law except criminal law. Teens under the age of 18 are not allowed to enter into contracts, smoke, purchase alcohol, marry, drive without restrictions, or even legally get a tattoo.[21] With the exception of those sentenced to the longest periods of incarceration, all convicted youth will re-enter their communities at some point, many while still in their teens or twenties. Significantly, a growing body of research also establishes that the vast majority of adolescents cease involvement in criminal behavior as they enter adulthood without any systemic intervention.[22] This last point cannot be overemphasized. Almost all teenagers who engage in criminal activity age out of such behavior as they mature and become less impulsive.

Endorsing the legal and social science advances in the field of adolescent development and culpability, in April 2017, New York State enacted legislation to raise the minimum age for criminal prosecution of misdemeanors to 18. The law also creates an opportunity for certain felonies filed against 16- and 17-year-olds to be transferred to family court.[23]

Transforming the role of defense counsel representing adolescents in adult criminal court

Lawyers who represent teenagers charged with serious crimes bear responsibility for pushing the system – at all points along the continuum of a case – to provide age appropriate responses. It is for this reason that the Legal Aid Society of New York, the largest public defender office in the country, has provided specialized representation for teenagers prosecuted in the adult court system since 1996. The Adolescent Intervention and Diversion Project (AID) represents teenagers ages 13–18 charged in the adult court system with misdemeanors and felonies in New York City. The AID project grew out of a recognition that the fundamental developmental differences between adolescents and adults demanded a specialized approach to legal representation. AID is comprised of specially trained lawyers, social workers, and investigators who work as a team to provide legal representation as well as education, foster care, and mental health and policy advocacy.

The AID model relies on a multi-pronged approach consisting of individual, interdisciplinary case representation, city and state policy and legislative advocacy, and advocacy with administrative agencies. Legal Aid's role as the primary defender in New York City provides us with a unique ability to track trends and categories of need in the adolescent population across the city. A key to our success in case outcomes for young clients lies in the fact that courtroom advocacy is only one piece of our representational model.

It should be noted at the outset that we pursue traditional litigation routes for the cases that call for them. We begin fact investigation early in the life of a case: conducting crime scene investigations, interviewing witnesses, researching legal strategies, and hiring experts. We represent our clients in pre-trial hearings and at trial, where our clients are contesting the charges or we cannot negotiate a favorable case outcome. Early casework is a critical feature of representing youth in the adult courts, since multiple court appearances interfere with clients' school attendance and their parents' work schedules. Prompt investigations and case assessments can lead to meaningful discussions of the merits of each case with the assigned prosecutor at an early stage of the prosecution.

This approach facilitates early resolution of cases, including dismissal, which has significant benefits for clients and the efficient operation of the criminal justice system. However, even for cases we intend to actively litigate, we may concurrently pursue a mitigation or service plan route. The latter approach serves multiple functions: It creates a plan that can be presented to the court to support a bail application, it allows the client to demonstrate that they are amenable to treatment or services, it can stabilize family dynamics, and it creates a service plan that can be utilized in future plea negotiations.

In addition to developing all possible theories of a legal defense, the defense team begins to gather relevant information about the client's strengths and needs at the inception of the representation. This aids in the prompt referral for services and solutions the client and their family may have been seeking but could not obtain, such as substance abuse or mental health treatment, special education services, after school programming, or a more appropriate school setting.

Being a teenager is hard enough for those lucky enough to live with a loving family in a safe neighborhood and attend successful, nurturing schools. For many teens in the criminal court system, one or more of the elements of a healthy childhood are missing. The traditional analysis of an individual prosecuted for the commission of a crime looks to whether the crime was committed by the individual and the harm caused by the crime. This evaluation assumes that a person charged with a crime has control over most aspects of their life and has made one or a series of bad decisions leading to the crime. That rubric, however, rarely applies to teenagers who lack control over where they reside, with whom they live, and where they attend school, and who cannot access services without the aid and permission of an adult. The AID team urges decision-makers to take these factors into account at every stage of the criminal case.

A 14-year-old does not magically transform into an adult once charged with a serious crime. Thus, sanctions must be proportionate to both the crime and the youth's developmental status and be aimed at helping young people learn to function productively in their communities. This mandate includes providing access to age-appropriate, community-based, and custodial services with meaningful programming, staffed with adults trained in adolescent development and trauma. Sentences also need to reflect adolescents' general capacity to respond to rehabilitative services and to age out of antisocial behavior and should be related to the individual's state of mind, state of development, and maturity at the time of the crime. Finally, sanctions should never lose focus of the goal of rehabilitation.

One of the most significant effects of prosecuting youth under 18 years of age in adult courts is the exposure to the collateral consequences of criminal convictions. Aside from the significant direct effects of adult sentences and detention or imprisonment with adults, the collateral consequences of a criminal conviction can permanently remove an adolescent from the path to becoming a contributing member of society. A criminal conviction interferes with or bars an individual from access to many of the systems necessary to becoming a successful adult. Criminal convictions may create barriers to employment, college admission, and financial aid; lead to eviction and homelessness; and have significant immigration consequences.[24] Given the well-documented issue of disproportionate minority contact in the criminal justice system, it is important for us, collectively, to decrease the obstacles to success for minority youth.[25] Creating lifelong barriers for behavior that has been shown, for the most part, to be time-limited is an unjustifiably harsh and irreversible consequence.

Building a client narrative: the nuts and bolts of AID

In order to advocate effectively in the courtroom, defenders must truly understand their clients. It is critical to appreciate the circumstances that led the client to become involved in the crime. This information contributes to the assessment of the client's degree of culpability, his motivation to become involved in the offense, and whether his decision-making ability may have been compromised by developmental or mental health issues, a learning disability, or substance abuse. Some youth become involved in negative behaviors, for example, as a cry for attention, an attempt to flee family conflict, or to gain acceptance by their peers.

Assessing the case of a teenager prosecuted in the adult court system is akin to solving a puzzle with many pieces; defense attorneys must investigate and evaluate not only the crime charged but also the client's history, available family resources, educational history, mental health and substance abuse issues, and developmental history and status. The responsibility for representing these young people should lie with the most experienced lawyers in a defender office. However, this is not a job for an attorney alone; it requires building an interdisciplinary practice including attorneys, social workers, and investigators. In addition, and equally important, defenders must develop an expert pool of mental health professionals, educators, and service providers who understand the unique characteristics of adolescents and can place their lives, offenses, and rehabilitative potential in appropriate context.

The AID Project's specialized, inter-disciplinary defense teams begin by building a strong foundation of trust with their young clients. Nothing says more to a client than actually showing up. Learning his or her story and providing support underscores that the defender cares and will advocate for his or her expressed interests in areas that are important to him or her. Such relationship building is a necessary aspect of representing young people. It motivates youth to comply with court mandates and opens lines of communication between the defense team and the client. To that end, the experience of stepping into a client's shoes cannot be overstated. Members of the AID team go where the client goes: home, school, neighborhood, detention, and anywhere else the client may be. Any combination of the team may attend a particular meeting. If a client struggles in school, we meet with the school administration. To assess the stressors of living in a neighborhood, we visit the client's neighborhood. When a client is in treatment, we meet with the client's providers. Pounding the pavement is an important first step in building trust and establishing a successful relationship with the client and his or her family.

Consistent with national data, 20% of the AID project's youngest clients have been or presently are in foster care and half regularly use drugs and/or alcohol.[26] About half of our clients have a family member who is chemically addicted or dependent. A significant number of our clients have been exposed to sustained violence in their homes or neighborhoods, or both. Approximately two-thirds have known or undetected special education needs. Many do not attend school regularly because their school programs fail to meet their educational needs. Twenty-five percent have significant mental health needs, requiring medication and consistent counseling services. It is essential to obtain records from all systems with which each client has interacted in order to identify and begin to address these needs.

Field investigation, records review, and collaborative work with community providers contribute to the narrative the defense team presents to the court. A narrative might include a clients' history of hardship, mental health needs, running away from home to avoid abusive caretakers, substance abuse stemming from undiagnosed and untreated mental health problems, undiagnosed or inadequately addressed learning and emotional disorders, excessive school discipline, or truancy resulting from inappropriate or inadequate school placements or programming. Incorporating this information into an account of a client's life experience provides critical context as to how the client may have become involved in the behavior that led to the prosecution.

Development of the service plan

When consistent with defense strategy, team members also use this social information to develop a service plan aimed at stabilizing the youth and, if necessary and possible, his or her family. Care is taken to design individual plans that do not extend beyond what each client needs, in order to avoid net-widening. Some clients need little more than a curfew or a referral to an afterschool program. Others need intensive outpatient or residential treatment programs or foster care services. Some require therapeutic school settings, intensive academic remedial services, or special education services. This information also informs the defense team's presentation to the court when arguing for pre-trial release, alternatives to detention, and therapeutic services, and drives the conversation in court beyond the crimes charged towards a focus on the clients' histories and needs.

Re-framing the narrative in this way is critical because, setting aside the most egregious offenses where significant harm is caused and incarceration is the likely case outcome, New York permits a wide range of system responses to the majority of crimes charged against young people. Individualization and humanization can help persuade a court to pursue a less-onerous path at each stage of a criminal case.

Through pre-plea and pre-sentencing memoranda and in-court advocacy, the defense team presents educational and service plans to address clients' needs and highlight their strengths. Judges often require service plans for young clients who are charged with serious offenses or who appear to have significant and unaddressed social or emotional issues in order to avoid incarceration, and the AID-developed plans are often incorporated into the court's sentence in order to ensure accountability and provide a meaningful opportunity for rehabilitation. In fact, courts have come to rely on the AID project's ability to plan for its clients, which has resulted in better case outcomes, fewer incarcerated clients, and reduced recidivism. Judges will monitor a young person's compliance with a service plan for many months, sometimes far longer, to ensure that the client is on a stable path prior to considering a non-incarceratory setting.

Implementing and monitoring service plans

Many AID clients have not succeeded in structured settings, have histories of truancy, and have lacked stable living situations for some time prior to their arrest. These young people often present the greatest challenges to service providers. In order to help ensure the success of the intervention, the AID lawyer and the social worker stay in close contact with the provider after referring a client to a program. Service plans often require recalibration during the period of court involvement; maintaining ongoing communication allows such modifications to occur before a difficult situation becomes a crisis. Some clients require a higher level of care, some need less intensive services after demonstrating a period of compliance. Some clients are not developmentally ready for particular services, and sharing prior history with a service provider often results in a reconfigured, appropriate service menu for that young person. Occasionally, young people simply forget the motivation for compliance – further evidence of their immaturity – necessitating a meeting with the client and service provider to emphasize the stakes of non-compliance.

Service plans sometimes require modification when a particular intervention proves inappropriate or additional needs are identified. In those cases, AID staff will locate and arrange to place the client in a program that better meets their needs. It is critical for the defense team to provide judges with information about a client's participation in a program at all stages of a case to substantiate the need for these re-referrals with assurances that the next program referral can provide a different setting that may be more appropriate for the young person. This quick re-referral process minimizes or eliminates the use of incarceration after a program failure.

Avoiding collateral consequences

One way to avoid collateral consequences in New York, as well as the direct consequence of mandatory state prison sentences, is to convince the court to impose a "Youthful Offender" adjudication, which replaces a criminal conviction.[27] Most youth who are convicted of a crime between the ages of 13 and 18 may be eligible for consideration as a youthful offender under New York law.[28] This status allows for a reduced sentence and relieves the young person from the burden of a criminal conviction.[29] At the same time, youthful offender adjudications allow a court to ensure that a young person accepts responsibility for their behavior and complies with court mandates. Young people who are granted youthful offender status are afforded a critical opportunity to enter adulthood free of the lifelong collateral consequences of a criminal conviction.

The underpinnings of a youthful offender adjudication may involve a combination of legal basis and a client's social-emotional development. Many offenses involving adolescents are committed in groups and there is often a range of culpability within that group. Differential participation may form the basis of an argument that some youth should face less punitive sanctions than others. Mental illness, developmental delays, and drug and alcohol use also may mitigate a young person's culpability. Sometimes, mental health evaluations are provided to the court. Compliance with counseling and education or vocational training demonstrate amenability to treatment and a reduced likelihood to re-offend. Judges weigh considerations of public safety, potential for rehabilitation, and a youth's developmental capacity in determining whether to grant an application for youthful offender adjudication. The information provided by the AID team and the treatment plans contribute to high rates of youthful offender adjudications among our clients.

Post-sentencing advocacy

For those clients who are sentenced to periods of incarceration, attention is also paid to the settings. The AID lawyers and social workers periodically visit the facilities where our clients serve their sentences. School and mental health records collected during the pendency of the case are shared with the facility to inform service provision and aid, to the extent possible, continuity of education and treatment options.

Case outcomes

In its insistence on developmentally-appropriate responses to youth crime, the AID project has distinguished itself as a model of criminal representation for young people in the adult criminal courts. In 1998, the federal Office of Juvenile Justice and Delinquency Prevention highlighted the project as an innovative program providing high-quality defense to adolescents prosecuted in the adult court system.[30] Ten years later, in 2008, the New York City Criminal Justice

Coordinator's office conducted a citywide study of the cases of 13- to 15-year-olds, which established that the AID model of service delivery drastically improves outcomes for young people.[31] Youth represented by the AID project had a 53 percent conviction rate, in contrast with an 83 percent conviction rate for clients represented by other lawyers. Fully 31 percent of Legal Aid cases were dismissed or resulted in acquittal, while other lawyers achieved such results in only 13% of their cases. Lastly, only 40 percent of the AID clients were sentenced to a period of incarceration, as compared to 51 percent of the youth represented by other lawyers.[32]

Advocacy from outside the courtroom

Effective representation of young people often requires defenders to extend their advocacy beyond the traditional boundaries of the courtroom and to engage in problem-solving with other systems. Because our clients often have issues that require systems coordination, AID sometimes serves as the point for service referral and management.

Educational advocacy

Many youth prosecuted in the adult system read and perform math far below grade level. Approximately 50 percent of incarcerated students require special education services, compared to 11 percent of all students in New York City public schools.[33] The average age of admission to secure detention is 15. At that age, which normally corresponds with ninth or tenth grade, 90 percent of detained youth read below the seventh-grade level, 83 percent had math skills below the seventh-grade level, and 25 percent read below the fourth grade level.[34] Undiagnosed or unaddressed learning disabilities often lead to frustration and resultant behavioral challenges. These behaviors then become the primary presenting issue for educators, thereafter ensuring that the student will not obtain appropriate services to address their learning disability. Of the youth (aged 16–21) admitted to the city's jail system for adults, approximately 83 percent have previously been classified as requiring special education services.[35]

Schools all too often fail to provide effective interventions for at-risk youth. Instead, some schools criminalize behavioral problems and push youth into the criminal justice system, rather than providing ameliorative services that would prevent systemic involvement. Given the prominence of this "school-to-prison pipeline" in our criminal justice system, a young person's educational history is critically important to their legal representation.[36] (Although the school-to-prison pipeline narrative is often examined in the context of juvenile court cases, it is no less prevalent when teenagers are charged in adult court settings.) School also serves as a young person's social community, and a history of push-out or undiagnosed or unmet special education needs can lead to alienation and dysfunction. For these reasons, AID attorneys and social workers also provide essential educational advocacy to project clients.

The most prominent school-related problems confronting youth prosecuted as adults are unaddressed and unidentified disabilities, which contribute to school failure and place a child at risk of incarceration; a lack of residential placement options to address the special education needs of youth diagnosed with severe emotional and learning disabilities; significant barriers to re-enrollment upon release from incarceration; and a lack of appropriate educational placements for older teens with few course credits.[37] AID project staff tackle these issues first, by documenting a client's educational history and identifying any issues that require intervention. School records often contain critical information about a client's family and mental health history in addition to special education and academic histories.

AID social workers or lawyers next assess each client to determine whether they are on an appropriate educational track, examining both the availability of academic and vocational services and monitoring the youth's performance in school. The project's well-developed educational practice includes advocacy for special education services and appropriate school and program placements as well as representation in school suspension hearings.[38] Upon a client's discharge from pre-trial detention or longer-term incarceration, AID staff facilitate appropriate placements in the city's school system or in vocational training. The project also has fostered relationships with individuals throughout the school system who assist in finding appropriate programming and placement for its clients.

Meaningful attempts to divert youth from a criminal involvement should strive to increase academic engagement and build academic competence. More frequent use of suspension and expulsion without resort to remedial measures has been proven to increase the risk of school dropout.[39] In light of this, AID defense teams actively seek private day and residential school settings for clients who have fallen far behind academically. These schools have trained personnel to meet the needs of youth with significant learning disabilities and, often, young people make meaningful progress in these settings.

Systemic reform advocacy

A key factor in the AID project's success is its multi-pronged advocacy strategy. The AID model incorporates individualized interdisciplinary case representation, policy and legislative advocacy, and advocacy with administrative agencies. Because it is the primary public defender office in New York City, Legal Aid is uniquely positioned to track case trends and categories of need among particular client populations. This data informs AID's advocacy beyond the courtroom, addresses such issues as the school-to-prison pipeline, policing adolescents in their communities, gaps in the web of available social services for youth and their families and conditions of incarceration, and is critical in securing improved outcomes for court-involved youth. This work contributes to a more robust continuum of available services and interventions that reduce recidivism. Cultivating relationships and cooperative agreements with community providers and government agencies also is essential. As an example, we have nurtured productive collaborations with

New York City's child protective agency to facilitate the provision of preventive and residential services to court-involved youth.

Conversely, AID's experience in representing adolescents in court necessarily informs its policy reform. We often appear in court and in policy and legislative meetings and hearings in securing funding and services. These relationships are critical to our ability to advocate for our clients. For a number of years, we had a therapeutic social worker on the staff. We created this position because we found that our teenage clients were stabilizing after participation in community-based programs, but their families were still in crisis. Additionally, some clients did not have caretakers who were able to provide long-term support, and our young clients needed independent living skills to learn how to function on their own. Our social worker approached each family member to address their own needs as a first step in being able to care for others. She worked on issues such as time management and communication skills and referred family members to educational and job training services. She used role-play to teach family members to understand each other's feelings and respond appropriately to each other in a controlled environment, providing an experience they could draw upon to mediate future conflicts. Once many community-based agencies built this function into their own staffing, we discontinued this service internally.

Our individual casework drives our system advocacy in other ways. For example, we identified a pattern of depriving our clients of the right of re-entry to school and the award of credits for work completed while incarcerated, even for short periods of time. Commonly, credits were not transferred, course work and records were not transmitted, and, too often, schools simply refused to readmit returning students. Those students who spent periods of time unable to attend school languished without the structure that schools provide and that is often required by the courts and the probation department. As a result, these young people were at high risk of re-arrest, incarceration, and recidivism. We sought funding to create a re-entry transition team. A lawyer and social worker worked to facilitate re-enrollment after release from incarceration, collaborated with city agencies to ensure appropriate services were provided, and engaged in individual case advocacy to obtain appropriate special education and academic services and placements. Our staff also provided counseling and support to the young people and their family members, helping the transition to community school settings.

In order to systemically address the issue of educational transition, the Legal Aid Society partnered with Advocates for Children, an educational advocacy organization in New York City, and pro bono co-counsel Dewey Ballantine LLP, to file a class action lawsuit in the District Court for the Eastern District of New York on behalf of youth charged as juvenile delinquents (youth charged with offenses in the Family Court) and juvenile offenders who were denied timely enrollment and appropriate education upon return to New York City schools from detention centers and long-term incarceration.[40] Plaintiffs entered into a court-ordered consent decree with the New York City school district in 2011,[41] following a court-ordered settlement with the State, which guaranteed oversight, monitoring, and technical assistance, in 2008. The New York City school district agreed to a detailed set of obligations to make sure that all students returning from court ordered settings would be promptly enrolled in school upon their return to New York City community schools.[42] Compensatory relief was provided for school-aged students who were not allowed to return to school in a timely manner during the course of the lawsuit.[43] Monitoring of New York City's compliance is ongoing.

As part of a broad coalition of advocacy and legal groups, we also participated in the successful effort that led the City Council to pass the Student Safety Act, which provides for public reporting of data on suspensions and arrests in city schools.[44] The Act was signed into law in early 2011.[45] The transparency brought about by this law has led to an ongoing examination of discipline and police practices in our schools. Since the data has become publicly available, the numbers of suspensions and arrests in schools have decreased significantly.[46]

Finally, as a result of our educational advocacy, the AID project is widely respected for its expertise in the field of education and court-involved youth in New York City. The New York City school district and the City Council regularly consult with project leadership on policy issues related to service provision, programming, school discipline, and special education. New York City's one school district is comprised of 1,700 schools, making outreach and collaboration a sometimes complicated but rewarding process. Recently, for example, AID collaborated with the school system to train the counselors and teachers who work in the schools with incarcerated young people and to train school administrators and social service teams to assess young people's risks and serve as service referral resources to their students and their students' families before court involvement.

Ideally, all teenagers charged with committing crimes would be prosecuted in a court system specifically fashioned to recognize their developmental abilities, psychosocial maturity, trauma histories, and educational, mental health, and family challenges. Until such a system evolves, enhanced, specialized representation of teenagers prosecuted either as juveniles or adults can compel courts to consider these questions at every stage of criminal proceedings. Doing so would serve multiple goals in addition to the obvious aim of rehabilitation: guiding youth to accept responsibility for the harm caused by their actions; providing support systems to keep teenagers in school and help them reach the goals of graduation and college or work readiness; stabilizing families, many with unaddressed trauma histories; and ultimately reducing recidivism and making communities safer.

Justice for court-involved youth will only be achieved when the government, the judiciary, the defense bar, and the public acknowledge their adolescence and respond in an age appropriate manner. Adolescents are the sum of their experiences, are defined by mutability, and have the potential to become successful participants in their communities. They must, however, be given an opportunity to learn from their past wrongdoing and enter adulthood without a criminal record. Public defender offices play a critical and ongoing role in compelling systems that touch youth and their families to achieve this objective and, in doing so, stabilize and support our most vulnerable young people, while contributing to meaningful, long-term public safety.

Notes

1 The client's name and some details of the incident and case have been changed in order to protect the client's confidentiality.

2 In April, 2017, New York State passed legislation to raise the age of criminal responsibility to 18 for many offenses. North Carolina followed suit in June, 2017.

3 In 2015, the Legal Aid Society's Prisoners' Rights Project and co-counsel Ropes & Gray and Emery, Celli, Brinckerhoff & Abady joined by the United States Department of Justice entered into a settlement agreement with New York City to reform the widespread abuse of prisoners by correction staff on Rikers Island. Prior to the settlement, the office of the United States Attorney in the Southern District of New York issued a report based on their investigation of the treatment of adolescents on Rikers Island. *See* A Letter to Mayor de Blasio (Aug. 4, 2014), https://www.justice.gov/sites/default/files/usao-sdny/legacy/2015/03/25/SDNY%20Rikers%20Report.pdf (last visited Jan. 9, 2018). AID provided testimony to the New York City Council detailing the conditions experienced by adolescents incarcerated on Rikers Island. *See* Testimony, The Council of the City of New York Committee on Fire and Criminal Justice Services and Committee on Juvenile Justice (Oct. 18, 2014), http://www.legal-aid.org/media/189855/testimony_10.8.14.pdf. The settlement of Nunez v. City of New York, 11-CV-5845, included the elimination of solitary confinement for 16 and 17-year-olds, a new use of force policy providing clear directions and limiting certain categories of force, revamped staff training in conflict de-escalation, implementation of accountability measures, expansion of the use of video surveillance and body cameras, as well as new protocols and enhanced training for staff working with for adolescents.

4 *See* Ashley Cannon, Citizens Crime Comm'n of N.Y.C., Guide to Juvenile Justice in New York City 4–5 (Richard Aborn & John Bennett eds., 2010), http:// www.nycrimecommission.org/pdfs/GuideToJuvenileJusticeInNYC.pdf (last visited Jan. 9, 2018).

5 *Id.* at 19.

6 1978 N.Y. Laws ch. 481, § 27 (codified as amended at N.Y. Penal Law § 10) (McKinney, 2013)).

7 *See* N.Y. Exec. Law § 508 (McKinney, 2017) (Juvenile Offenders can be transferred to adult correctional facilities at age 16 with the permission of the sentencing court upon a showing that the youth is no longer benefitting from services provided in a juvenile facility. At age 18, youth can be transferred by administrative decision of the agency running the facility. All Juvenile Offenders are transferred to adult correctional facilities at age 21 if they are still in custody.).

8 *See* N.Y. Fam. Ct. Act § 353.3 (McKinney, 2017); Penal § 70.05 (McKinney, 2013).

9 *See* Penal § 60.10.

10 *See* N.Y. Crim. Proc. Law § 720.10(1)-(2) (McKinney, 2017).

11 543 U.S. 551 (2005).

12 *See id.* at 569, 578–79 (relying on such research in holding that "[t]he Eighth and Fourteenth Amendments forbid imposition of the death penalty on offenders who were under the age of 18 when their crimes were committed"); *see also* Eddings v. Oklahoma, 455 U.S. 104, 115 n.11 (1982) ("[A]dolescents, particularly in the early and middle teen years, are more vulnerable, more impulsive, and less self-disciplined than adults." (alteration in original) (quoting Franklin E. Zimring, *Confronting Youth Crime: Report of the Twentieth Century Fund Task Force on Sentencing Policy Toward Young Offenders* 7 (Holmes & Meier Publishers, 1978)) (internal quotation marks omitted)).

13 Roper, 543 U.S. at 569 (alteration in original) (quoting Johnson v. Texas, 509 U. S. 350, 367 (1993) (internal quotation marks omitted)).

14 *See id.* at 578–79.

15 560 U.S. 48 (2010).

16 131 S. Ct. 2394 (2011).

17 132 S. Ct. 2455 (2012).

18 *Id.* at 2470.

19 *Id.* at 2463 (alterations in original) (quoting Roper v. Simmons, 543 U.S. 551, 569 (2005)) (internal quotation marks omitted).

20 American Academy of Child & Adolescent Psychiatry, *Teen Brain: Behavior, Problem Solving, and Decision Making* (Sept. 2016), https://www.aacap.org/aacap/families_and_youth/facts_for_families/fff-guide/The-Teen-Brain-Behavior-Problem-Solving-and-Decision-Making-095.aspx (last visited Jan. 9, 2018).

21 *See* N.Y. C.P.L.R. 105(j) (McKinney, 2013) (defining "infant" as an individual under the age of 18); N.Y. DOM. REL. LAW § 2 (McKinney, 2013) ("A 'minor' or 'infant', as used in this chapter, is a person under the age of 18 years."); N.Y. GEN. OBLIG. LAW § 1–202 (McKinney, 2013). New York State restricts the rights of 18-year-olds in the following areas: alcohol possession and sale, *see* N.Y. ALCO. BEV. CONT. § 65c(1)-(2) (McKinney, 2013) (establishing minimum age at 21); contractual rights, *see* C.P.L.R. 105(j) (defining infancy); *see also* N.Y. U.C.C. LAW § 9–403(b)(4)(A) (McKinney, 2013) (establishing defense based on infancy); marriage, *see* DOM. REL. § 7; voting, *see* N.Y. ELEC. LAW § 5–102 (McKinney, 2013)); wills, *see* N.Y. EST. POWERS & TRUSTS LAW § 3–1.1 (McKinney, 2013); pawnbrokers, *see* N.Y. GEN. BUS. LAW § 47-a (McKinney, 2013) (prohibiting pawnbrokers from dealing with minors under age 18); gambling and lottery, *see* N.Y. GEN. MUN. LAW § 486 (McKinney, 2013) (restricting minors under age 18 from participating in licensed bingo games); *see also* N.Y. TAX LAW § 1610 (McKinney, 2013) (prohibiting sale of lottery tickets to minors under age 18); jury duty, *see* N.Y. JUD. LAW § 510 (McKinney, 2013); pornography, *see* N.Y. PENAL LAW § 235.21 (McKinney, 2013); tattoos, *see* PENAL LAW § 260.21(2); firearms sales, *see* PENAL LAW § 265.16 (crime to sell firearms to minors under age 19); cigarette possession and purchase, *see* N.Y. PUB. HEALTH LAW § 1399-cc(2) (McKinney, 2013); driving, *see* N.Y. VEH. & TRAF. LAW § 502(2) (McKinney, 2013).

22 LAURENCE STEINBERG ET AL., U.S. DEPT. OF JUSTICE, OFFICE OF JUVENILE JUSTICE AND DELINQUENCY PREVENTION, PSYCHOSOCIAL MATURITY AND DESISTANCE FROM CRIME IN A SAMPLE OF SERIOUS JUVENILE OFFENDERS (Mar. 2015), https://www.ojjdp.gov/pubs/248391.pdf.

23 RAISE THE AGE NY, http://raisetheageny.com/wp-content/uploads/2017/06/rta.billsummary.final_June-2017.pdf (last visited Sept. 10, 2017).

24 *See* LEGAL ACTION CTR., SETTING THE RECORD STRAIGHT: WHAT DEFENSE ATTORNEYS NEED TO KNOW ABOUT THE CIVIL CONSEQUENCES OF CLIENT CRIMINAL RECORDS 8–13 (2001), http://hirenetwork.org/sites/default/files/setting_the_record_straight.pdf (last visited Jan. 9, 2018); *see also* Collateral Consequences Criminal Charges (Nov. 25, 2013), http://www2.law.columbia.edu/fourcs (providing overview and detailed information on collateral consequences of criminal convictions in New York State) (last visited Jan. 9, 2018).

25 The Sentencing Project, *Racial Disparities in Youth Commitments and Arrests* (Apr. 1, 2016), http://www.sentencingproject.org/publications/racial-disparities-in-youth-commitments-and-arrests (last visited Jan. 9, 2018).

26 JULIAN D. FORD, NATIONAL CTR. FOR MENTAL HEALTH AND JUVENILE JUSTICE, TRAUMA AMONG YOUTH IN THE JUVENILE JUSTICE SYSTEM: CRITICAL ISSUES AND NEW DIRECTIONS (June 2007), https://www.ncmhjj.com/wp-content/uploads/2013/07/2007_Trauma-Among-Youth-in-the-Juvenile-Justice-System.pdf (last visited Jan. 9, 2018).

27 N.Y. PENAL LAW § 60.10.

28 N.Y. CRIM. PROC. LAW § 720.10(1)-(2).

29 *See id.* § 720.20(1). An adolescent is eligible only one time for Youthful Offender adjudication on a felony, *see id.* § 720.20(2), as long as there are no events barring such an adjudication as set forth by statute. *See id.* at § 720.10.

30 *See* PATRICIA PURITZ & WENDY WAN LONG SHANG, UNITED STATES DEP'T OF JUSTICE, OFFICE OF JUVENILE JUSTICE & DELINQUENCY PREVENTION, INNOVATIVE APPROACHES TO

Juvenile Indigent Defense (1998), https://www.ncjrs.gov/pdffiles/171151.pdf (last visited Jan. 9, 2018).

31 New York City Criminal Justice Coordinator's Office. Internal report. Case outcomes for the year 2008 were evaluated.

32 *Id.*

33 *See* Timothy Lisante & Christine Pahigian, NYC Students: Promising Practices in Educational Re-Entry 3 Tbl. 5 (2013), http://www.nyls.edu/documents/P4%20-%20Lisante%20PPT.pdf (last visited Jan. 9, 2018).

34 This data, which used to be published on the website of the Department of Juvenile Justice, which is now the Division of Youth and Family Justice, is no longer made publicly available.

35 *Id.*

36 New York City School-Justice Partnership Task Force Keeping Kids In and Out of Court (May 2013), http://www.nycourts.gov/ip/justiceforchildren/PDF/NYC-School-JusticeTaskForceReportAndRecommendations.pdf (last visited Jan. 9, 2018).

37 In New York City, there were approximately 138,000 students between the ages of 16 and 21 who are "overage and under-credited." *See* Office of Multiple Pathways to Graduation, N.Y.C. Dep't of Educ., Multiple Pathways Research and Development: Summary Findings and Strategic Solutions for Overage, Under-Credited Youth 9 (2006), http://schools.nyc.gov/NR/rdonlyres/B5EC6D1C-F88A-4610-8F0F-A14D63420115/0/FindingsofOMPG.pdf (last visited Jan. 9, 2018).

38 Because AID is assigned by the court to represent the youth in the criminal proceeding, that relationship continues in our education advocacy.

39 Katie Mosehauer et al., Washington Appleseed & Team Child, Reclaiming Students: The Educational and Economic Costs of Exclusionary Discipline in Washington State (2012), http://docs.wixstatic.com/ugd/4569ed_e44ccb42cf-f21777ea479f4125d347df.pdf (last visited Jan. 9, 2018).

40 *See* Second Amended Class Action Complaint, J.G. ex rel. F.B. v. Mills, No. 04-CV-5415, 2011 WL 239821 (E.D.N.Y. Jan. 24, 2011), 2005 WL 6004341. The action alleged that Juvenile Delinquents and Juvenile Offenders returning from detention or court-ordered placement were often turned away from school altogether or not placed in appropriate schools, grade level, classes, and services, in violation of their constitution due process rights, the Individuals with Disabilities Education Act, the Americans with Disabilities Act, the Rehabilitation Act, the New York State Constitution, and New York education law.

41 *See* J.G. ex rel. F.B. v. Mills, No. 04-CV-5415, 2010 WL 5621274, at *13 (E.D.N.Y. Dec. 28, 2010) (report and recommendation of magistrate judge), adopted by No. 04-CV-5415, 2011 WL 239821 (E.D.N.Y. Jan. 24, 2011).

42 *See id.* at 2, 13.

43 *See id.* at 2.

44 City Council, Local Law No. 6, (N.Y.C. 2011) (codified as amended at N.Y.C., N.Y. Admin. Code §§ 8–1101, -1102, -1103 (2011)).

45 *See id.; see also* The Student Safety Act, N.Y. Civ. Liberties Union, http://www.nyclu.org/schooltoprison/ssa (last visited Jan. 7, 2014); Noah Rosenberg, *City Will Require Police to Report on School Arrests*, N.Y. Times (Dec. 21, 2010) at A30.

46 New York Civil Liberties Union, Student Safety Act Reporting on Suspensions, 2015–2016 School Year, http://www.nyclu.org/files/SSA_Suspension_Fact-Sheet_2015–2016.pdf (last visited Sept. 10, 2017).

10 Building a national juvenile defense community: the National Juvenile Defender Center

Patricia Puritz

How do you begin to talk about the evolution of children's legal rights in America, not from a theoretical perspective, but from the vantage point of the lawyers, the champions, who actually try to enforce these rights every day and stand up for children in the justice system? Why is it so important to tell the children's stories, build a national juvenile defense community, and bring voice and cohesion to this group of lawyers in the first place? Because the old clichés ring true: we are stronger together, there is power in numbers, and fairness for children demands it. But community-building is a multifaceted endeavor that does not necessarily have a tidy or precise beginning. It leverages and builds on the work of so many others over time. So, the best place to start, then, is to thank those who came before us and gave us the inspiration and foundation upon which to build. We are grateful for their courage, their service, and their leadership, which we strived to emulate and honor as we moved toward new ground.

Hard-working parents like Paul and Marjorie Gault, chasing down a lawyer to ensure their young son Gerald could get legal assistance as he was being processed through an unfair and brutally harsh justice system. Or Amelia Lewis who took on that case, determined to bring visibility and fairness to the issues, resulting in the foundational *Gault* decision 50 years ago establishing a child's right to counsel and other critical due process protections.[1] Or you could talk about the amazing Abe Fortas and his brilliance as the architect of the indigent defense system as we know it today, arguing *Gideon*[2] before the United States Supreme Court and then deciding *Gault* while on that same court. You could go way back to the visionary Clara Shortridge Foltz, California's first woman attorney[3] who saw a clear and urgent need for the creation of a public defense system. Or even further back to the brave young women of Hull House in Chicago and the creation of the first juvenile court in America.[4] Do you focus on ground-breaking Supreme Court decisions or those who get up every day and fight as those laws continue to be ignored and undermined? Although there are indeed absolutely clear and defining moments along the way, the field of juvenile defense builds on the good work of so many before us in a slow and steady fashion. The work inches along and the setbacks are many, but over time a resilient group of juvenile defense professionals has emerged, and they will continue to have a strong voice and will drive practice and policy reforms moving forward.

The landscape inherited

The two decades between 1963 and 1983 were extremely turbulent times. The militarization of police departments was not an uncommon sight. Tanks, strong water hoses, batons, and dogs trained to be vicious were being used to fight back children who were peacefully demonstrating for their civil rights. Remember the Children's Crusade in 1963 in Birmingham, Alabama, a pivotal moment in the Civil Rights Movement when children courageously stepped up and engaged in nonviolent activism in order to desegregate their city.[5] It was a moment that changed history. A moment when President Kennedy knew he could no longer look away at the depths of the horrors inflicted on so many adults and children during the Civil Rights Movement, a moment when the whole world watched how shamefully we treated our children … and it was, as many have said, the birth of the Civil Rights Act,[6] led by children.

A few short months later, President Kennedy was dead, assassinated before our eyes, and unimaginable pain was inflicted on the nation. Then, to our horror, Martin Luther King, was assassinated. Then Bobby Kennedy, the Attorney General. And then the four little girls in the 16th Street Baptist Church in Birmingham, Alabama were killed by bombs planted in the church by white supremacists. The world was coming apart at the seams. We all knew it. Yet in the midst of these horrors and turbulence also arose some of the greatest legal decisions of our times, decisions like *Gideon, Kent,* and *Gault*[7] that changed forever the nature of criminal and juvenile justice in America or, at the least, gave indigent children and adults a fighting chance.

In 1974, juvenile justice professionals celebrated the promise of the newly enacted Juvenile Justice and Delinquency Prevention Act (JJDPA)[8] and then watched it become unduly and unfairly politicized in the succeeding decades over and over again. The JJDPA was the first and remains virtually the only comprehensive piece of federal juvenile justice legislation in the United States. In sum, the Act has three main components that, despite nearly 40 years of amendments, remain similar to their original conception. Essentially, those components include the establishment of: (1) institutions within the federal government that coordinate and administer federal juvenile justice efforts; (2) grant programs to assist the states; and, (3) core mandates that states must meet in order to be eligible to receive grant funds.[9]

In its original form, the JJDPA focused on prevention and early intervention with a special concentration on the rehabilitation of young people. The Congressional Statement of Findings noted that "understaffed, overcrowded juvenile courts, probation services, and correctional facilities are not able to provide individualized justice or effective help."[10] The driving philosophy behind the Act was one of rehabilitation rather than retribution, with a primary focus on the offender and secondary emphasis on the offense. Over time, however, the Act shifted its focus and became more intent on sanctions and youth accountability. This shift in philosophy, realized through legislative amendments, took the Office of Juvenile Justice and Delinquency Prevention (OJJDP),[11] the office created by the Act, in a more punitive and harsher direction.

As the 1980s drew to a close

In the late 1980s and early 1990s, new work emerged and was ignited, in part, by the promise of *Gault*. Over a ten-year period, the American Bar Association (ABA) promulgated, adopted, and released 23 volumes of comprehensive juvenile justice standards. *The Institute for Judicial Administration/American Bar Association Standards for Juvenile Justice (the IJA/ABA Standards)*[12] unleashed sweeping opportunities across the country to address and improve our nation's juvenile justice system. The Standards were fair and balanced, honoring due process and community safety. Scores of drafters, reviewers, and experts worked together over a decade to produce those seminal and foundational standards, standards that still carry great weight today.

Spurred on by the work of implementing the *IJA/ABA Standards*, the American Bar Association Juvenile Justice Center (ABA/JJC) became increasingly engaged in juvenile justice reform. In 1995, the ABA/JJC released a groundbreaking report entitled *A Call for Justice: An Assessment of Access to Counsel and Quality of Representation in Delinquency Proceedings*,[13] which triggered alarm across the nation. OJJDP had commissioned the report in response to the 1992 amendments to the JJDPA. It was the first time a report of this sort had been issued, and it was based on an intensive assessment of access to counsel and the quality of lawyering received by youth across ten diverse states over a three-year period. Although most professionals knew that state and local juvenile indigent defense systems were lacking, the extent of the problems as documented in *A Call for Justice* were stunning, and it was not just lawyers for children who were stunned. Judges, probation officers, detention and corrections officers, child advocates, and even prosecutors shared the defense community's sense of emergency and urgency. The ABA was surprised as well. *A Call for Justice* was a game-changer.

In 1993, when the OJJDP funded the ABA/JJC and its partners[14] to determine the status of juvenile defense services in the United States, to conduct an investigation and produce a report, and then to develop a training and technical assistance response, no one expected such compelling information to emerge. For three years, the ABA team diligently conducted an extensive literature review, a national survey, and on-site investigations of public defense systems, court-appointed systems, law school clinics, and related policies, statutes, rules, and regulations, in urban, suburban, and rural areas across ten states. When all the material from this comprehensive, multi-year, national effort was analyzed and synthesized, the collaborators felt a great weight and great responsibility to call upon and engage stakeholders across America to address the panoply of barriers related to access to counsel and fundamental fairness for children in the justice system. Stakeholders were called upon to devise strategies to build and enhance juvenile defense systems and to train and support the lawyers who defend children in juvenile court.

It was true then, and it remains true now, that despite the high stakes involved in today's juvenile court proceedings and the dedicated systems reform advocacy over the years, many children still fail to receive effective legal representation. In too many jurisdictions across this great country, children regularly appear in delinquency proceedings with no attorney at all.[15]

Overworked, underpaid public defenders struggle to provide their young clients with the skilled, vigorous advocacy that *Gault* demands. The rotation through juvenile court is typically very fast, and in most places there is little opportunity for a culture of excellence to take hold. Youth are quite often encouraged by probation officers or the court to waive their right to counsel and enter into uncounseled plea agreements, leaving the defender with little role to play. If defenders are not even appointed, and there is no one to properly advise the child on the probable *lifetime* collateral consequences that will attach to a juvenile court conviction, blindsiding that child down the road, then the role of juvenile defense counsel is misunderstood, and children are being left defenseless and legally exposed. Courts must adhere to the important role juvenile defense counsel play in a delinquency court proceeding and not conflate that role with that of a *Guardian ad Litem* appointed to represent a child's best interest in a child welfare proceeding.[16]

The core recommendations from *A Call for Justice* in 1995 challenged states and local jurisdictions to get involved. Although straightforward and unimaginative in some ways, the recommendations were considered trailblazing, drawing national attention to the plight of youth in the justice system and their inability to access counsel or obtain quality legal representation. The recommendations included:

A. *State and local jurisdictions should increase the resources available to support representation of juveniles in delinquency proceedings.*

1. Local jurisdictions should ensure that sufficient resources are available to increase the number of attorneys representing juveniles in delinquency proceedings and increase the availability of non-lawyers with special expertise to assist in case planning and representation.
2. Agencies responsible for funding defender programs should ensure that a fair and equitable share of available resources is allocated for juvenile representation.
3. Courts and others responsible for the allocation of defender funding should ensure that strategic decisions in juvenile cases are made on the basis of sound legal practice rather than funding incentives.

B. *State and local jurisdictions should improve the quality of representation of juveniles in delinquency proceedings.*

1. Attorneys representing minors in delinquency proceedings should receive comprehensive training.
2. Every attorney's caseload should be low enough to permit the attorney to provide quality representation to juveniles in delinquency proceedings.
3. The legal profession should elevate the status of attorneys providing representation in juvenile court.
4. Courts, bar associations, or agencies with authority to certify or appoint counsel should adopt minimum standards for representation in juvenile court.

C. *State and local jurisdictions should collect data on the representation of juveniles in delinquency proceedings.*

1. Local courts or bar associations should routinely collect data regarding representation of juveniles to identify systemic weaknesses and provide a baseline for improvement.
2. Jurisdictions should conduct local workload assessments in order to determine the appropriate caseload and staffing needs for each jurisdiction.
3. A statewide agency or organization should compare and publish local assessments.

Defenders cannot stand alone. The report made clear that defenders themselves could not solve these long-standing systemic problems and called for judges, state legislatures, state and local bar associations, public defender offices, law schools, Congress, citizens, and other justice system stakeholders to work together and engage in strategies to ensure that young people are treated fairly and that due process is honored. It is a travesty of justice that allows our most valuable and youngest assets to become our most vulnerable and unprotected defendants.

The report called for simultaneous action, by many different groups, to work toward the same end. It challenged Congress and state and local legislatures to address the critical need for the collection of data, a nearly absent commodity, and to conduct oversight hearings on access to counsel, quality of representation, adequacy of funding and training, adoption of standards of practice, and to ensure that caseloads are manageable. The report called upon state and local bar associations to become engaged in meaningful ways and to assist in the development of standards and guidelines. It urged law firms and members of the private bar to take on juvenile delinquency cases pro bono and help elevate the status of juvenile law. It urged law schools to develop new clinical programs and stimulate interest through increased academic offerings. It revealed a juvenile court culture entrenched in the past and one that too often does not honor the due process rights of children in any meaningful way. And most important, *A Call for Justice* squarely placed responsibility on the heads of public defender offices to stop treating juvenile court as a second-class defense practice and to ensure that juvenile defenders can practice holistic defense and have manageable caseloads, access to investigators, ongoing training, supervision, and support for specialization in juvenile defense.

The ABA and its partners continued to provide training and technical support around the country to enhance juvenile defense practices and policies and continued to develop methods to build the capacity of the juvenile defense bar. The ABA/JJA had the wind in its sails and was able to benefit from the release and momentum of the formidable *IJA/ABA Juvenile Justice Standards* over the previous decade. Because the *Standards* consisted of 23 multi-disciplinary volumes, engagement of all system actors in juvenile justice reform was required. It was an enormous undertaking, but Livingston Hall, as an early chair of the ABA Criminal Justice Section Council, quickly secured ABA approval and adoption of these comprehensive *Standards*. The *IJA/ABA Juvenile Justice Standards*, along with the recommendations in *A Call for Justice*, created the foundation and set in motion a series of activities, programs, assessments, trainings, symposia, and other national events that ultimately resulted in the creation, in 1998, and then the launching, in 2005, of the National Juvenile Defender Center (NJDC).[17]

Building a national juvenile defense community

Those who worked on *A Call for Justice* had the distinct privilege of meeting lawyers all over the country who were trying their best to represent children in juvenile courts under trying circumstances. We met lawyers who were told they could not file motions or who were forced to stand in on cases without even knowing the child's name, lawyers who could not get access to investigators because chief defenders would not permit it in juvenile cases, lawyers whose pay would be reduced if they went back to practice in juvenile court, and private lawyers trying to make a living in an industry with limited guidance on the special role of counsel in delinquency cases. But most of these lawyers did not know and had no means of communicating with each other. With great intention, the ABA and NJDC staff devised strategies to reach out and identify juvenile defenders in every state and the District of Columbia and to build the capacity, the independence, and the voice of the juvenile defense bar. Essential components of those community building strategies included those listed below.

The Juvenile Defender Leadership Summit

The first step was to gather everyone together. With the generous support of foundations and the federal government, the first annual Juvenile Defender Leadership Summit was launched in October 1997, in Chicago, Illinois. Assembling all the people we had worked with from across the country, the group met for three days of community-building, leadership development, and for the first time ever, collectively designed strategies to reform state juvenile indigent defense systems. The Summit has been held every year since, bringing together public defenders, court-appointed lawyers, law school clinic directors, juvenile offender services representatives, policy advocates, and others to examine the complex issues related to juvenile defense services and recommends strategies for improving these services. Topics related to juvenile defense are not a sidebar in the agenda – juvenile defense has finally become the agenda itself. The Summit was viewed as a turning point, a moment when a community was formed. When lawyers who were struggling alone met others like themselves from all over the country, it was electrifying. Hearing similar stories; discussing new strategies and ideas with one another; sharing resources, briefs, and motions; talking about detention and post-disposition with people who understood the legal implications at each end; and believing deeply in the need to create a specialized practice of juvenile defense helped these strangers bond quickly. The twenty-first anniversary Summit was held in October 2017 and was as electrifying as the first.

All professional organizations and agencies have conferences and meetings, but there is something strangely different and uniquely special about the Juvenile Defender Leadership Summit. Ask anyone who has attended a Summit and they will tell you. Yes, finding colleagues and comrades is critical. Yes, receiving cutting-edge training is imperative. Yes, having a safe place to discuss and hash out complex ethical and legal strategy is mandatory. But having juvenile defense and fundamental fairness for children be the *very first and the very last* thing on everyone's lips is unique and creates a stimulating and dynamic real-time environment. Juvenile defense is the primary focus and the lens through which all the work is done.

The Summit has become essential for juvenile defenders to recharge and reload.[18] The Summit as an enterprise has identified, promoted, created, developed, and spun off hundreds of new and innovative juvenile defender initiatives and continues to thrive as an incubator for success.

The regional juvenile defender centers

Another essential component of building the national juvenile defense community was ensuring participation and buy-in from across the nation. From the start, NJDC intended to be inclusive, bottom-up, and an organization whose existence would serve the juvenile defense community – not the other way around. To that end, it was essential that the juvenile defense community play a central and ongoing role in the mission and management of NJDC. Thus, the creation of the first six, and then quickly nine, regional juvenile defender centers emerged. The regional juvenile defender centers expanded the breadth and width of NJDC. The country was divided into regions, and each region set up a juvenile defender center in partnership with NJDC. The regional centers are governed by an advisory board made up of members from each state in their respective regions, ensuring national coverage and partnership reflecting the NJDC goals and objectives. The directors of the regional juvenile defender centers and the NJDC staff and board convene at least twice a year and meet monthly via teleconference to keep the work and momentum threaded together. NJDC leadership, staff, and the regional centers work in very close partnership on an ongoing basis to devise strategies to improve the nation's juvenile defense system and ensure due process for children.[19] NJDC's commitment to this somewhat cumbersome management model has not waned; if anything it has strengthened. The community is stronger together.

A core principle of both NJDC and the regional centers is that juvenile defense is a specialized practice anchored in juvenile-specific training and practice skills. Juvenile defense requires zealous advocacy that is individualized for each unique client, and lawyers must demonstrate proficiency in court rules and the law. NJDC and the regional centers help juvenile defenders provide representation that is individualized and developmentally appropriate. Juvenile defense is based on the clients' expressed interests and the belief that young clients must be meaningful participants in their defense. NJDC and the regional centers help juvenile defenders to counsel clients through the legal and extralegal processes, ensuring that all clients and their families are treated with dignity and respect and that there is decorum in the courtroom. NJDC and the regional centers work closely together to ensure that systemic barriers and deficiencies do not impair the juvenile defender's abilities to provide high-quality representation.

The articulation of shared values

A community needs a common language and a shared value system. It was no easy task for the NJDC staff, leadership, and the directors of the regional centers to work together to produce a shared mission and vision statement.[20] This mission and vision guides the collective work and keeps the community focused and from straying too far from the tasks at hand. NJDC revisits and tests this mission and vision and holds itself and the regional centers accountable to the principles articulated below.

The mission of NJDC is to *promote justice for all children by ensuring excellence in juvenile defense.* A strong juvenile defense delivery system is a vital mechanism for ensuring that all children in the justice system have ready and timely access to skilled, well-resourced, well-trained lawyers; are afforded full protection of their constitutional, statutory, and human rights; receive legal representation that is client centered, individualized, developmentally and age appropriate, and free of bias; and have opportunities to attain their potential and to become productive members of society. To achieve these goals, the juvenile defense bar must enhance its skill, capacity, and commitment to professionalism; cultivate leadership to promote accountability and bring about reform in the juvenile justice system; and build collaborations, partnerships, and community involvement to advance the juvenile defense delivery system.

NJDC's vision is to create a strong and fair juvenile defense delivery system in which the representation of children is specialized and resources and opportunities exist for juvenile defenders to fully exercise and enhance their legal, management, leadership, and advocacy skills; all children are treated with respect, dignity, and fairness; juvenile court personnel are knowledgeable, sensitive, and responsive to the needs of children; juvenile defenders have parity of resources, compensation, and opportunity for advancement with adult defenders and prosecutors; and excellence is routine.

The state-based juvenile defense assessments

Since 2000, NJDC has conducted a series of state-based assessments of juvenile indigent defense delivery systems. Unlike child welfare systems across the nation that have historically benefitted from hundreds of millions of Court Improvement Project dollars from the federal Department of Health and Human Services, the delinquency courts have no such comparable funding to help states understand and assess the functioning, effectiveness, and provision of legal services to youth in delinquency proceedings. Thus, undertaking this critical assessment work has become a cornerstone of the NJDC agenda – to document how juvenile defense systems *actually* operate, to understand how legal services are currently *delivered* to children, and to *support* the lawyers who represent children in the delinquency system.

After the regional juvenile defender centers were established, the directors called for a shift in strategy to continue and advance the assessment work begun in *A Call for Justice.* Although that national report was groundbreaking, the directors conveyed that it did not give them the bandwidth they needed at the state level, absent the required local data and information needed to engage and motivate local stakeholders. The group decided that the methodology used in *A Call for Justice* would no longer be viewed as a national tool but would be adapted for state use and local reform. Thereafter, for each state assessment, the ABA, and then later NJDC, sought the invitation of the state supreme court, a legislative commission, or a statewide indigent defense system director to completely and comprehensively evaluate a state's juvenile indigent defense system. Every state report sets forth recommendations and an action plan. This foundational work became the centerpiece of NJDC, and the organization made a commitment to conduct one statewide assessment in every state, and the District of Columbia, to ensure that key policy-makers and stakeholders have comprehensive information upon which to base decisions regarding their state juvenile defense systems. To date, more than half the states have been assessed with more assessments in progress.[21]

As additional state-based juvenile indigent defense assessments were conducted (consistent with the original methodology but customized for each state), clear themes and trends began to emerge across the country. Working assiduously to tease out and capture those themes and develop strategies to address them drove NJDC's national agenda forward. A dedicated commitment to working with state and local partners on these issues has been successful in a multitude of ways and has resulted in the development of new laws, new policies, new rules and regulations, new law school clinical programs, new specialized juvenile defender units, new juvenile defender collaborations, new initiatives and partnerships, and more. Assessments have helped to break down the juvenile defense system into the following component parts, allowing systemic reform efforts to proceed in a more targeted, organized manner, with more shading and nuance.

Timing and appointment of counsel: Understanding when and how a child actually gets an attorney is critical. Often counsel is appointed far too late in the process to make a meaningful difference in the case. Many children do not get an attorney until after the critical detention decision has already been made. Or, sometimes counsel is appointed simultaneously with the case being called, and the lawyer and child have never met, leaving no time for consultation.

Waiver of counsel: Alarmingly high percentages of children waive their right to juvenile defense counsel before they have even seen a lawyer to discuss the long- and short-term consequences of the waiver decision or the impact of a juvenile court adjudication. Waivers can happen at the initial hearing, or even earlier at the probation intake interview, with the result that the child ultimately ends up navigating the complex juvenile court process alone. Assessments reveal that there is both direct and indirect pressure on children to waive counsel by prosecutors, probation officers, judges, and sometimes parents.

Plea agreements: The vast majority of juvenile court cases are resolved by plea agreements, often at the initial hearing. Most plea agreements are entered into without previous, independent investigation or any pre-trial advocacy to test the strengths and weaknesses of the government's case. In this way, plea agreements foreclose legal advocacy. Often young people do not understand the terms of the plea agreement or sometimes the onerous conditions of release set them up to be uninformed and fail.

Caseloads: By any objective standard, many juvenile defenders' caseloads are too high. Some juvenile defenders reported caseloads as high as 500–1,000 per year. High caseloads impact every facet of a child's defense. There is evidence that, because defenders' caseloads are so high, waiver of counsel and swift guilty pleas, despite their final and long-term consequences, are being used as case reduction tools.

Inadequate resources: Juvenile defenders routinely operate without adequate resources. Many juvenile defenders do not even have access to the bare necessities to mount a vigorous defense – computers, office file cabinets, access to online legal research tools – let alone access to paralegals, investigators, social workers, and experts. Assessment investigators have too often seen juvenile defenders who do not even have client files.

Inadequate training and supervision: Many young people who cannot afford to hire an attorney are appointed contract attorneys or public defenders. Contract attorneys are usually solo practitioners and are often disconnected from trends and developments in juvenile law due to the nature of their general practice. Even in public defender offices, juvenile defenders often do not have access to specialized juvenile court trial advocacy. In most places across the country, meaningful juvenile defender training, supervision, and mentoring opportunities are extremely limited.

Inadequate oversight and monitoring: Juvenile indigent defense systems are extremely varied and *ad hoc*. Many states do not have juvenile-specific practice standards or guidelines, and some need to amend their juvenile court rules. The lack of uniformity in oversight and monitoring is dangerous and irresponsible.

Juvenile court culture: The culture in many juvenile courts reflects society's persistent ambivalence about what those courts should look like, that is, whether juvenile courts should copy the adult criminal justice model or should be a forum in which benevolent courts connect with wayward youth or something in-between. Fifty years after the decision, far too many juvenile courts across the nation still operate in a pre-*Gault* mode, as if the defense attorney is irrelevant and unnecessary. In some jurisdictions, lawyers complain that judges punish them and their clients when they engage in legal advocacy. Many other states still use juvenile court as a training ground, where inexperienced attorneys can hone their advocacy skills at the expense of indigent children or where seasoned lawyers have long since lost interest in keeping up with new research and tools.

Many juvenile defenders are unclear about their role and ethical obligations, so vigorous and thorough legal advocacy goes unmet.

Parity: There is an overall lack of fairness and equality in the juvenile indigent defense system. Often, public defender offices do not value juvenile defenders as highly as they do criminal defenders. Salary increases are attached to moving "up" from juvenile court into adult criminal court. Most offices have forced rotations so that juvenile defenders who chose to devote their careers to representing youth are forced to represent adults if they want access to promotions, raises, or support with law school debt if you work in public service. Outside of their offices, juvenile defenders often do not have pay parity with juvenile prosecutors, receiving starting salaries that are not on a par with their prosecutorial colleagues.

Lack of leadership: Leadership and advocacy is lacking on issues related to juvenile defense, and the juvenile defense bar lacks capacity. Juvenile defenders must be involved and included as stakeholders in all juvenile justice initiatives. Chief defenders are also central to the distribution of resources and to creating professional opportunities for juvenile defenders to advance. Chief judges of state and local courts are also crucial to any systemic reform process and can help ensure that juvenile defenders are engaged and have access to training and support.

The impact of these issues on the justice system is serious, and without a strong community of well-trained juvenile defense attorneys, the due process rights of children will continue to be routinely diminished. Such deprivations lead to actual harm. Tragic and lasting consequences result from botching children's representation, including the impact of demeaning and devaluing children and families during the juvenile court process. Specialized juvenile defense counsel is required to correct these systemic deficiencies.

Training and technical assistance

As the juvenile defense community grew and developed a better sense of its needs, and as new issues emerged, NJDC was ready to meet those needs through high-quality training and technical assistance on a broad range of subjects. NJDC's training and technical assistance is interactive, not didactic, and built from the ground up. Training can be in large or small groups, but what matters most is the dedicated focus on juvenile defense practice and improving juvenile defense systems. Training style and topics always vary and are based on actual, rather than perceived, needs. Often lawyers want input and assistance on cases, or they are seeking experts or other lawyers with whom to strategize. Whatever the training need, NJDC will fill it.

The drive toward excellence

Almost two decades after the publication of *A Call for Justice*, NJDC has developed compelling new products that have propelled the juvenile defense field forward,[22] incorporated the developmental science as best evidenced by the Supreme Court's elaborate juvenile jurisprudence since 2005,[23] inspired a renewed commitment to justice for children at the Department of Justice,[24] and changed overall the landscape of juvenile justice. NJDC along with the National Legal Aid and Defender Association led the way in releasing the *Ten Core Principles for Providing Quality Delinquency Representation Through Public Defense Delivery Systems* in 2004 which were reaffirmed and reprinted in 2008. In 2009, the foundational *Role of Juvenile Defense Counsel in Delinquency Court* was released, and in 2012, the highly acclaimed *National Juvenile Defense Standards* and the *Juvenile Training Immersion Program,* considered to be the gold standard in juvenile defense policy and practice, were both launched. These foundational documents and programs have elevated the national conversation about juvenile defense and provide practical guidance to the field. Also in 2012, NJDC was honored with national and international recognition as one of the recipients of the highly prestigious MacArthur Award for Creative and Effective Institutions.[25]

Solidifying reform and moving ahead

Although it is an open secret that countless children accused of crimes are still arrested, prosecuted, and convicted every year without ever seeing a lawyer, a robust juvenile defense community has nonetheless grown and matured and has become highly successful in collaborating, problem-solving, building infrastructure, and attracting new resources and talent to this area of work. There is no turning back. NJDC, the nine regional juvenile defender centers, and their partners will continue to lead the way on juvenile defense practice and policy reform into the future.

The way forward is clearly laid out in a 2016 report released by NJDC entitled *Defend Children: A Blueprint for Effective Juvenile Defender Service.*[26] This compelling national report presents a clear, current, and comprehensive assessment of today's juvenile defense system and sets forth definitive steps for removing barriers to fairness and improving access to counsel and quality of representation for children. The report acknowledges that although a great deal has been accomplished, the work is far from done.

The multi-year, special initiative that produced *Defend Children* was extensive, and the level of expert input and discourse on this dedicated topic was unrivaled. For several years, scores of juvenile defenders and dozens of other justice system experts participated in structured interviews, national surveys, focus groups, and working groups. An extensive literature review was completed, and specific improvements in practice and policy were identified. As part of this process, new and tested innovations were documented. Gaps in practice and policy were examined. All this intelligence was dissected and analyzed, and recommendations were carefully crafted. A massive amount of collective work and national dialogue contributed to the thinking and intent behind *Defend Children.*

This report reminds us of the ongoing challenges and problems facing juvenile defense systems. Without question "fair and reasonable treatment of children in the delinquency courts is virtually impossible without the availability of specialized and highly skilled counsel advocating for the expressed legal interests of the child client."[27] Many barriers to fairness remain in place, and far too many juvenile court practices and policies are not developmentally appropriate and not kind toward children.

Children face dual injustices in the system when both their civil rights and due process rights are violated. So many children are funneled into the juvenile court pipeline for what is arguably normative adolescent behavior in most instances. Children of color have historically been arrested, charged, convicted, and sentenced at higher rates than white youth, and that has not changed. *Defend Children* stated that in 2010, for example, black youth represented 17 percent of the youth population but 31 percent of all youth arrested. Latino youth experience similar arrest rates. In 2011, black youth were 269 percent more likely than white youth to be arrested for violating curfew laws and 250 percent more likely to be arrested for a property offense.

Despite the fact that children have the constitutional right to counsel, *Defend Children* unequivocally demonstrates that juvenile defense systems are often not constitutionally sound and lack the vital core elements of fair, decent, and humane practices toward children. The federal government and the Supreme Court have identified and called for the need for specially trained counsel in juvenile court at the state and local level, but the results and appropriations have not been forthcoming in most jurisdictions.[28] Future work needs to target state and local action in order to ensure that the right to counsel for children is fulfilled.

Defend Children calls for a comprehensive and system-wide approach to solving these problems and reaffirms, once again, that juvenile defenders cannot do this alone. The juvenile defense system is highly complex and intersects with many other systems. Children do not have the capacity to pay lawyers and should be presumed indigent for the purpose of appointment of counsel and throughout the duration of the court process. If the child wishes to opt out and hire counsel, they should be allowed to do so, but children cannot realistically be expected to bear the costs of counsel and the potential conflict this creates between parents, or guardians, and the child's due process.

Protecting and defending the legal rights of America's children should never be a partisan issue, yet initiatives related to children frequently turn on political, partisan ideologies, instead of science, law, and fact. Children have no political leverage in America since they don't vote or donate. Fifty years after the United States Supreme Court resolved that it is of *vital* importance for children to have access to qualified counsel, and 40 years after the introduction of the Juvenile Justice and Delinquency Prevention Act, the nation still fails to ensure equal justice under the law for children.

These *rights*, these constitutional determinations, are not optional privileges set aside for only some. They were intended for all children. In fact, the Chief Justice of the United States Supreme Court at the time, Earl Warren, memorably wrote in a 1967 memo to Justice Abe Fortas that he hailed the *Gault* decision as the "Magna Carta for juveniles."[29] And after more than two decades of studying these systems, it is clear that their failure can and does cause measurable and demonstrable short- and long-term harm to thousands of youth and families. It is just as clear, that when done right, these systems can and do promote better outcomes and provide essential supports to youth.[30] As Mary Ann Scali, executive director of NJDC said, "We must cultivate passionate leaders in juvenile defense, end the insidious racism that drives court practices and policy, and continue fighting to uphold children's rights, freedoms, and futures."[31]

Amen sister.

Notes

1 In re Gault, 387 U.S. 1 (1967).
2 Gideon v. Wainwright, 372 U.S. 335 (1963).
3 1 Notable American Women 641 (Edward T. James et al. eds., Belknap Press, 1971).
4 ABA Division for Public Education, Part I, The History of Juvenile Justice, https://www.americanbar.org/content/dam/aba/migrated/publiced/features/DYJpart1.authcheckdam.pdf (last visited Aug. 18, 2017).
5 Mighty Times: The Children's March (Southern Poverty Law Center, 2004).
6 *See* Civil Rights Act 1964, Pub. L. No. 88–352, 78 Stat. 241.
7 Gideon v. Wainwright, 372 U.S. 335 (1963); Kent v. U.S., 383 U.S. 541 (1966); In re Gault, 387 U.S. 1 (1967).
8 Juvenile Justice and Delinquency Prevention Act (JJDPA), Juvenile Justice and Delinquency Prevention as amended, Pub. L. No. 93-415 (1974).
9 Congressional Research Service Report to United States Congress (2012) (Mar. 2013), https://www.loc.gov/crsinfo/about/crs12_annrpt.pdf.
10 42 U.S.C. 5601(a)(4).
11 *Office of Juvenile Justice and Delinquency Prevention*, U.S. Dep't of Justice, https://www.ojjdp.gov/ (last visited Aug. 22, 2017).
12 *Juvenile Justice Standards Project*, Institute of Judicial Administration-American Bar Ass'n, https://www.americanbar.org/groups/criminal_justice/standards/JuvenileJusticeStandards.html (last visited Aug. 22, 2017).
13 American Bar Ass'n Juvenile Justice Ctr. et al., A Call for Justice: An Assessment of Access to Counsel and Quality of Representation in Delinquency Proceedings (1995), http://njdc.info/wp-content/uploads/2013/11/A-Call-for-Justice_An-Assessment-of-Access-to-Counsel-and-Quality-of-Representation-in-Delinquency-Proceedings.pdf [hereinafter *A Call for Justice*].
14 Partners included the Youth Law Center of San Francisco, California and the Juvenile Law Center of Philadelphia, Pennsylvania.
15 *See, e.g., A Call for Justice, supra* note 13; *see State Assessments,* The Nat'l Juvenile Defender Ctr. (NJDC), http://njdc.info/our-work/juvenile-indigent-defense-assessments/ (last visited Aug. 22, 2017); *see* The Nat'l Juvenile Defender Ctr. (NJDC), Defend Children: A Blueprint for Effective Juvenile Defender Service (Nov. 2016), http://njdc.info/wp-content/uploads/2016/11/Defend-Children-A-Blueprint-for-Effective-Juvenile-Defender-Services.pdf.
16 *See* The Nat'l Juvenile Defender Ctr. (NJDC), Role of Juvenile Defense Counsel in Delinquency Court (2009), http://njdc.info/wp-content/uploads/2013/11/NJDC-Role-of-Counsel.pdf.
17 *See* The Nat'l Juvenile Defender Ctr. (NJDC), NJDC.info (last visited Aug. 22, 2017).
18 *Id.*
19 *Id.*
20 *Id.* (*see* their Mission & Vision Statement at http://njdc.info/about-njdc/mission-vision-statement).
21 *Id.* (*see* the State Assessments at http://njdc.info/our-work/juvenile-indigent-defense-assessments).

22 Such products include: (1) *Ten Core Principles for Providing Quality Delinquency Representation through Public Defense Delivery Systems*: Adopted in partnership with the American Council of Chief Defenders in December 2004 and revised and reissued in July 2008, these *Core Principles* provide criteria by which a public defense delivery system may provide high-quality delinquency representation and fully implement the holding of *In re Gault*; (2) *Role of Juvenile Defense Counsel in Delinquency Court:* This policy paper reflects best practices and describes the specialized role of the juvenile defender and the importance of the juvenile defender's responsibility to advocate for the client's expressed interests; (3) *National Juvenile Defense Standards:* These standards strengthen and guide the ethical and professional performance of the juvenile defense attorney – the *Standards* set out a framework for representation that is anchored in the law, science, and professional codes of responsibility; (4) *Juvenile Training Immersion Program:* The Juvenile Training Immersion Program (JTIP) is a highly specialized, comprehensive, trial advocacy training program for juvenile defense attorneys. JTIP is delivered in three different ways: (i) Ongoing JTIP training, (ii) Certification JTIP training, and (iii) Summer Academy JTIP.

23 *See, e.g.*, Roper v. Simmons, 543 U.S. 551(2005); Graham v. Florida, 560 U.S. 48 (2010); J.D.B. v. North Carolina, 562 U.S. 1001 (2011); Miller v. Alabama, 567 U.S. 460; 132 S.Ct. 2455 (2012).

24 *See Civil Rights Division, Department of Justice Statement of Interest Supports Meaningful Right to Counsel in Juvenile Prosecutions*, U.S. DEP'T OF JUSTICE (Mar. 13, 2015), https://www.justice.gov/opa/pr/department-justice-statement-interest-supports-meaningful-right-counsel-juvenile-prosecutions.

25 NJDC, *supra* note 17.

26 THE NAT'L JUVENILE DEFENDER CTR. (NJDC), DEFEND CHILDREN: A BLUEPRINT FOR EFFECTIVE JUVENILE DEFENDER SERVICE (Nov. 2016), http://njdc.info/wp-content/uploads/2016/11/Defend-Children-A-Blueprint-for-Effective-Juvenile-Defender-Services.pdf.

27 *Id.*

28 *Id.*

29 Letter from Chief Justice Earl Warren to Justice Abe Fortas (Mar. 17, 1967) (on file as part of the Abe Fortas Papers (MS 858), Manuscripts and Archives, Yale University Archives, Box 36), http://drs.library.yale.edu/HLTransformer/HLTransServlet?stylename=yul.ead2002.xhtml.xsl&pid=mssa:ms.0858&query=Fortas&clear-stylesheet-cache=yes&hlon=yes&big=&adv=&filter=&hitPageStart=1&sortFields=&view=all#ref11 (last visited Aug. 22, 2017).

30 The MacArthur Foundation's Models for Change Juvenile Indigent Defense Action Network (JIDAN) has demonstrated that system reform can succeed. Launched in 2008, JIDAN engaged the leadership of eight states in targeted strategies to improve juvenile indigent defense policy and practice (California, Florida, Illinois, Louisiana, Massachusetts, New Jersey, Pennsylvania, and Washington). *See Pennsylvania*, MODELS FOR CHANGE, http://www.modelsforchange.net/about/States-for-change/Pennsylvania.html (last visited Sept. 5, 2017). In Pennsylvania, for example, significant improvements were made in aftercare services and supports, reducing disproportionate minority contact with the system, and the coordination of mental health and juvenile justice systems. *Id.*

31 *NJDC Releases New Report, Lays Out Roadmap to Fulfill Children's Rights in Court*, THE *GAULT* AT 50 BLOG, (Nov. 14, 2016), https://gaultat50.org/2016/11/14/hello-world.

Part III

Challenges and reform

11 Being David: the future of juvenile defense and the Goliath of youth injustice

Mary Ann Scali

Attending one of the many events marking the fiftieth anniversary of *In re Gault*, I ran into a highly respected juvenile justice partner and offered a Gault at 50 wristband. He recoiled and replied, "I hate *Gault*, it criminalizes children." To which I fervently responded, "*Gault* doesn't criminalize children, we criminalize children by outlawing normal youth behavior. *Gault* affirms children's constitutional protections and envisions a field of justice where children have access to effective lawyers protecting their interests and fighting for their rights to ensure they aren't arbitrarily criminalized." He replied, "But children don't have those lawyers and we still criminalize them." I agreed, "Yes, 50 years past *Gault we incarcerate children at the highest rate in the world and still don't afford them access to qualified juvenile defenders.* We all have a lot of work to do to ensure justice for children." He agreed, accepted the wristband, put it on, and walked away.

Although I was awestruck that someone I respect and have learned a great deal from over the years had such a fundamentally different view of *In re Gault*, it illuminated the path toward improving outcomes for children who face our system of justice. *Gault* is not simply a historic case granting children the right to counsel, it is a living foundational proclamation designed to safeguard justice and equity for all children.

Often a child's only advocate in the court system is their defense attorney – a constitutional right affirmed for youth in the 1967 United States Supreme Court decision, *In re Gault.*[1] Juvenile defenders are the Davids who cry for justice, equality, and a developmentally normed justice system, against the Goliath of injustices inflicted upon our youth.

But, as Representative Karen Bass of California noted at a June 22, 2017, House Judiciary subcommittee hearing, too often "[children] don't have legal representation."[2] She recalled witnessing young people in juvenile court meet their attorneys five minutes before walking into the courtroom, where their cases were then pled out, and youth "[went] on to be incarcerated."[3] Rep. Bass called the juvenile justice system nothing more than "state-sponsored child abuse."[4]

Research and data on the treatment and outcomes of youth who are prosecuted in juvenile court can lead a reasonable person to no other conclusion. Children are labeled as criminals, forced to bear humiliating degradation, and are exposed to trauma that, to most Americans, is simply unimaginable. And this system of injustice is too often levied against children who come from impoverished neighborhoods and children who are predominately black and brown.

As we look to the future, these brief but powerful words of a U.S. congresswoman should serve as a guidepost for where we next lead our work: toward a revolution of the juvenile justice system by first finding the strength to revolutionize ourselves, our courageous community of juvenile defenders.

The worst of both worlds

The United States stands alone in its establishment of laws and policies that criminalize youth. The world over, children and adolescents are able to test the boundaries of independence and identity development without facing arrest, shackling, strip searching, prosecution, and imprisonment. Here, though, children are arrested for behavior such as cursing in school, loitering in their communities, and disturbing the peace.

Nearly one million youth are arrested in this country each year.[5] Children are charged with behavior that is deemed disruptive in school more than 10,000 times a year.[6] This criminalization of youth is most profound in impoverished communities of color: racial and ethnic minority youth comprised 45 percent of the general youth population in 2015, yet they were almost 70 percent of the youth being held in residential facilities by juvenile courts.[7] Similarly, since the late 1980s, the number of youth living in poverty has averaged about 20 percent, yet estimates gauge that more than half of the youth in delinquency court live in poverty.[8]

The United States Supreme Court recognized more than 50 years ago that without due process, "the child receives the worst of both worlds: that he gets neither the protections accorded to adults nor the solicitous care and regenerative treatment postulated for children."[9] Every state struggles to fulfill its constitutional obligation to provide children with effective lawyers in juvenile court. But when the civil rights of children are violated because they are unequally prosecuted for normal youth behavior, access to a juvenile defender to push back against systemic injustice is crucial.

Recent efforts by the United States Department of Justice amplify the critical need for well-qualified juvenile defenders. In April 2012, the Department issued an investigative report concluding that the Juvenile Court of Memphis and Shelby County in Tennessee failed to provide constitutionally required due process to children of all races.[10] The report offered detailed evidence about how the court's administration of justice denied critical elements of due process and discriminated against black children.[11] In compelling the juvenile court to take action, the findings specifically note, "Vigorous advocacy by defense counsel ensures that the youth's voice is heard in the process and a fair, just and appropriate result is achieved."[12]

In March 2015, the Department delivered a Statement of Interest in *N.P. et al. v. The State of Georgia*, a case asserting that the public defense system in Georgia's Cordele Judicial Circuit was so underfunded and poorly staffed that low-income adults and youth accused of committing criminal acts were routinely denied their right to legal representation.[13] The Department took a strong stance on the right to counsel for youth and the need for procedural safeguards against an uninformed waiver of that right, and emphasized that children who face the loss of liberty must be zealously represented by skilled counsel at every stage of delinquency proceedings.[14] The statement made clear that "the unique qualities of youth demand special training, experience and skill for their advocates."[15] The Department's articulation of the specific qualities and expectations of juvenile defenders provides strong evidence to support the assertion that a lack of skilled counsel is constructive denial of counsel.[16]

The Department produced another investigatory report in July 2015 offering details of how the St. Louis Family Court in Missouri engages in conduct that violates the constitutional guarantees of due process and equal protection under the law.[17] Among the Department's findings were the denial of constitutionally adequate access to counsel in delinquency proceedings and the disproportionate placement of black youth in custody.[18]

Department actions taken in several school cases include additional instances of due process deprivations, focusing on the deprivation of access to counsel. On August 1, 2012, the Department released findings from its investigation of Meridian, Mississippi's public schools' practice of referring youth to law enforcement for minor school-based offenses.[19] The investigation revealed that children reported that they are not always appointed an attorney for detention or adjudication hearings, and that the public defender who is appointed pursuant to a contract with the Youth Court does not provide meaningful or effective representation.[20]

More than 70 percent of prosecutions in juvenile court are for non-violent, non-person offenses.[21] Children burdened with a juvenile court adjudication can lose access to their local school, higher education, professional licenses, military service, housing, and other future opportunities.[22] At each juncture of the court process, though we know adolescent behavior is consistent across race and ethnicity, youth of color are prosecuted more frequently and treated more harshly than their white peers.[23] Couple the prosecution of children for what is often typical teenage behavior with the disproportionate prosecution of youth of color and add the ongoing denial of access to effective lawyers, and we have a civil rights crisis that warps a child's view of fairness and justice[24] and must garner the attention of the current generation of activists.

Needed system reforms

In May 2017, the National Juvenile Defender Center (NJDC) released *Access Denied: A Snapshot of States' Failure to Protect Children's Right to Counsel*, a report exposing deep fractures in the constitutional protections affirmed for children in *Gault*.[25] States drive young people through the court system while refusing them the protection of a strong advocate at their side.[26] The report details how state laws and court rules curtail young people's access to representation in court, sharing the stories of youth like Micah, who was neither told of his right to an attorney nor asked if he wanted counsel present during his first court appearance, and Jonathan, who was denied counsel because he could not afford to pay the state's $275 fee for a public defender.[27]

Access Denied also emphasizes that children who are appointed lawyers might receive representation on paper only.[28] Overwhelming caseloads, the dismal budgets allocated to publicly funded defender offices and individuals and the infrequency of youth-specific training for defense counsel mean attorneys often cannot provide young people with the fierce advocacy their cases require, and that they, as children, deserve.

The vast majority of states delay appointing counsel until after considering the child's financial eligibility.[29] Those who argue against affording all children immediate access to a publicly funded lawyer cite a misuse of public dollars, but it is clear that children who are able to afford a high-quality private lawyer are few and far between in juvenile court, and they do not utilize public lawyers. One estimate indicates that nearly 80 percent of children in juvenile court come from families making less than $30,000 a year.[30]

Juvenile courts should not consider the income and assets of parents in deciding whether to honor a child's right to counsel. The financial review process causes significant barriers to children's access to a lawyer,[31] and the stigmatization of proving financial instability causes unnecessary shame in a process that is already filled with degrading and humiliating experiences.[32] Children should be automatically deemed eligible for a publicly funded juvenile defender by virtue of their status as children, regardless of financial circumstances.

Automatic appointment of counsel would also lead the way for youth to be represented by counsel at interrogation. As early as 1948, the U.S. Supreme Court made clear that in the interrogation room, the child "needs counsel and support if he is not to become the victim first of fear, then of panic."[33] Manipulation, coercion, and lying are standard practices during interrogation.[34] Common sense knowledge of youth, as well as significant empirical research on adolescent development, confirm that youth are more susceptible to coercion and false confessions.[35]

Young people must be appointed an attorney at interrogation to protect them from overt threats, use of force, false promises, and other tactics applied to extract statements from youth. In a study funded by the National Institute of Health, as many as one-third of the youth interviewed said they had falsely confessed to crimes as a result of methods used during their interrogation.[36] States should guarantee lawyers to children during interrogation to ensure they are not manipulated and compelled to make statements against their interests.

Children should not be charged fees to exercise their constitutionally guaranteed right to a lawyer. As explained in *Access Denied*, "the 'blessings of liberty' so eloquently outlined in the Constitution are not protected for all people" and that "[f]or some, liberty can only be accessed for a price."[37] The majority of states allow children to be charged some level of fee for receiving assistance from a defense attorney.[38] States charge application fees, processing fees, administrative fees, and reimbursement of costs for attorney fees. These fees can result in liens against wages, garnishment of tax dollars, and long-term financial harm to the child when seeking financial aid or other loans to support their future success.[39] Most critically, the assessment of fees can lead youth to decide to proceed without an attorney to avoid any potential financial obligations associated with accessing a lawyer, which can result in additional time in the system and incarceration.[40]

Youth waiver of their right to counsel has been a significant issue in at least half of the states NJDC has analyzed in our state-by-state reviews of access to and quality of juvenile defense.[41] In over half of the 22 states assessed thus far, we have observed children at all phases of court proceedings without a defense lawyer.[42] Youth are subtly and overtly persuaded to waive their right to counsel at every point in the court process, starting at interrogation when they are read the *Miranda* warnings and asked to waive a series of rights, including their right to counsel, before police can proceed with questioning. The juvenile court system structure makes it more convenient for children to waive their constitutional rights than to exercise them. Youth are often told they can go home, they can resolve the entire matter immediately, or that it is better for them if they proceed without a lawyer. The long-term consequences of a juvenile adjudication and record are rarely reviewed when a child has no lawyer.

Children must have a meaningful opportunity to consult with a qualified juvenile defender before they are ever asked if they would like to waive their right to counsel. Having a child navigate the court system without a lawyer is like having them drive on the highway at rush hour without ever having been behind the wheel. It is fast, confusing, and dangerous. And the rules of the road are far less complicated than the rules of juvenile court. In states where children are required to consult with an attorney, waiver of their right to counsel is rare because they learn about the potential outcomes of a juvenile court case and the role of the juvenile defender in asserting their rights and interests.[43]

Given the substantial harms to children placed in juvenile facilities, as well as the legal issues youth face post-disposition, children must have ongoing access to a lawyer until they are no longer involved with the court system. Few states provide youth with meaningful access to an attorney for matters after sentencing.[44] This means harmful conditions of confinement, abusive solitary confinement practices, hearings for release from facilities and problematic probation issues persist for youth who have no legal resources. In the few states where children have an explicit, comprehensive right to post-disposition advocacy, their juvenile defense attorney works with them to carve a path leading to the best possible outcomes. States must ensure early and continuous appointment of counsel until a child's case is closed and the child is no longer under any type of juvenile court or state supervision.

Our way forward

In light of systemic injustice, insufficient resources, and the codified denial of counsel, how can juvenile defenders respond – and improve – in the years ahead? The answer lies in seeking power where we know it exists: in our community, and in the communities we serve.

Working toward reconciliation

Implicit and explicit biases influence the experiences and judgment of every person in the juvenile justice system, from law enforcement officers' decisions to intervene and arrest, to prosecutors' decisions to charge, to judges' decisions to detain, adjudicate, and sentence. Juvenile defenders are no exception. Our own implicit biases can impact how we evaluate evidence, interact with our clients and their families and view the fairness of plea offers and sentences.[45] Although we work to protect our clients from a biased system, we must also acknowledge and address our own biases. We cannot assign blame while failing to remedy our own faults.

Our community also has work to do to diversify our ranks. Although a defender's passion, skill, and advocacy are their most important traits, we cannot lose sight of the importance of our clients seeing themselves in us. Racial and ethnic diversity is critical to building inspiration and innovation within the field. We need to partner with law schools and reform our own leadership decision-making to recruit, train, and promote defenders whose racial and ethnic diversity reflect the communities we serve.

Defending children's civil rights

The future of the juvenile defense community lies in the intersectionality of our roles as civil rights lawyers and juvenile defense lawyers. We must bridge our fight for children's dignity and freedom with the civil rights movement.

The juvenile justice system disproportionately impacts children who are already vulnerable. A report by the Sentencing Project found that one in three black males born today will be imprisoned at some point in their lives, compared with one in seventeen white males.[46] Children with disabilities or mental health issues and children who identify as LGBTQ+ are also overrepresented in the juvenile justice system.[47]

From the moment a young person makes contact with law enforcement or the court system, an attorney should be on the front lines defending their rights against unbridled bias and unbalanced power.

Empowering youth and families

Participatory defense is a community organizing model that engages people facing criminal charges and their families to impact the court system and fight against mass incarceration.

Based in San Jose, California, Silicon Valley De-Bug is a nationally recognized model for community-based justice work that uses storytelling and community organizing to amplify the voices of the people directly impacted by the criminal and juvenile justice systems.[48] In New Orleans, Louisiana, the Louisiana Center for Children's Rights involves youth in its campaigns to reform the justice system, and has worked successfully to raise the age to include 17-year-old youth in the juvenile justice system and to advance legislation to end juvenile life without parole.[49]

Although juvenile defenders are the voice of our clients in the courtroom, participatory defense efforts can amplify our clients' voices in the community, in the public consciousness and in the policy-making realm. Providing individual representation to clients will always be a juvenile defender's primary role, but by aligning ourselves with participatory defense efforts, we can empower our clients and their families and communities to impact the larger system.

Changing the narrative

Consider this: one of the only ways the word "juvenile" is used today is in the context of the court system. It has an immediate stigma, stripping young people of their childhood and aligning their identities with the court, with crime, and with wrongdoing.

Reforming the juvenile court system begins with challenging the very foundation on which it stands: the lexicon of its common vocabulary. More obvious words like "delinquent" are also stigmatizing for youth, but even seemingly less harmful words, such as "intake" and "processing," introduce – and more dangerously, normalize – the notion of institutionalization in young minds.

Language is power. And the language of the court dehumanizes the children we represent. Moving forward, NJDC pledges to work alongside the juvenile defender community to liberate ourselves from the vocabulary of an oppressive system, and instead, introduce empowering words in courtrooms and in our offices as tools to achieve freedom and to honor the dignity of children. In taking back the way we talk about children, their behavior. and their experiences, we will one day change the way they are treated.

Developing new partnerships

It is critical for the juvenile defender community to seek out new partners who, in their respective capacities, will join our efforts in leading the charge for young people's right to counsel. The potential for new partners is boundless: when children are involved in the court system, every aspect of their lives is impacted, from schools and neighborhoods to religious communities and employment opportunities. Each direct and collateral impact of a youth's court involvement implicates a community of people who have an interest in improving the juvenile justice system.

We also must actively seek partnerships with legal organizations that can advocate for our clients in ways we cannot. In 2017, the American Civil Liberties Union of Washington filed a lawsuit against the state's Office of Public Defense, claiming children do not receive quality legal representation.[50] The complaint noted stories of youth who pled guilty despite having strong cases for innocence, and of children who received unreasonably long sentences behind bars with no objection from their attorneys.[51] The ACLU's action prompted a wave of media coverage, drawing attention to the glaring lack of resources budgeted for children's defense.[52]

Being creative agitators

In 2016, Missouri State Public Defender Director Michael Barrett assigned a case to then-Governor Jay Nixon.[53] Barrett was frustrated with Missouri's chronically underfunded and under-resourced public defender system, and appointed Nixon under a statute allowing Barrett to appoint any member of the state bar in extraordinary circumstances. Nixon refused to accept the appointment and a court ultimately ruled in Nixon's favor.[54] But Barrett's creative move garnered national attention and shone a spotlight on Missouri's overworked public defenders, backlogs of cases, and violations of constitutional rights.

Our role as defenders is to zealously defend our clients within the juvenile justice system. But we must also agitate against the system's manifest injustices. Creative agitation, like what happened in Missouri, can disrupt the inexorable forward movement of a system so much larger and more powerful than our clients.

Pursuing systemic reform

Juvenile defenders must become increasingly involved in efforts to change the laws and rules that are most detrimental to our clients. Defenders are best situated to expose the shortcomings of the defense system, the overreach of the justice system, and the impact these have on our clients, their families, and our communities. We need to make our voices and our clients' voices heard at policy-makers' tables.

We must demand oversight and accountability for ourselves and every actor in the juvenile justice system, and push for evidence-based reforms to elevate the strengths of youth and eliminate policies that feed our youth to a system breeding mass incarceration. With data, collaboration, creativity, and a commitment to building strong juvenile defense systems in every state, we will fulfill the constitutional right to legal counsel for every youth who faces arrest, prosecution, and incarceration.

Besting Goliath

David felled Goliath not by equaling Goliath's size and strength, but by optimizing the seemingly paltry tools in his possession. Being David means honing the skills and capacities of the juvenile defense community and juvenile defense systems. Juvenile defenders are uniquely situated as the harbinger of youth voice, strength, and empowerment. Defenders seek to liberate the child from the system rather than to propel them further into its bars, chains, and mazes of demands.

Being David means employing new strategies that grow the work, the expertise, and the participants in our efforts. It is time to look outside the courtroom and into our communities and neighborhoods to strengthen and empower defense of children. The communities that lose the most children to the justice system have the most to offer in defense of their children.

Ending the state-sanctioned abuse of children through delinquency courts cannot be done without juvenile defenders. And elevating juvenile defense is not only the work of the juvenile defense community; it requires persistent, intentional efforts by everyone committed to ending the injustices our youth face in the legal system.

Conclusion

Although inscribed on the American conscience, the phrase "innocent until proven guilty" is wearied and worn from neglect. The scales of justice tilt toward the prosecution and away from the accused. Children in the juvenile justice system – children who are mostly poor and nonwhite – rarely receive the benefit of the doubt, the benefit of a childhood in which mistakes are made and then learned from and remedied.

Over the past five decades, the legal community has witnessed the birth of the juvenile defender in tandem with the proliferation of laws and policies outlawing adolescence. The successes and tragedies of the juvenile defense community have aligned to bring light to the fact that we violate our children's civil rights when we disproportionately arrest and incarcerate them, and we violate their due process rights when we then deny them access to effective lawyers.

This arbitrary injustice must issue a loud and echoing call to action to everyone concerned about the future of our nation, our communities, and each of our children. For in the immortal words of Dr. Martin Luther King, Jr., "injustice anywhere is a threat to justice everywhere."[55] And where that injustice is chained around the arms and legs of our children, we must stand together and sound the alarm.

To be a juvenile defender is to be David, facing a Goliath system determined to ensnare our young clients. As we hone our skills, share our stories, and liberate our children, we must turn toward our communities and our youth to help us gather the stones of justice and work together to topple the injustices looming over children in schools, in neighborhoods, and in communities in every state.

Until we live in a nation where children are treated as children, the juvenile defense community must continue to strengthen its capacity and skills to protect the civil and due process rights of youth.

Notes

1 387 U.S. 1, 34–35 (1967).

2 *Juvenile Justice Reform in the Modern Era: Hearing before the Subcomm. on Crime, Terrorism, Homeland Security, and Investigations*, 115th Cong. (2017), https://judiciary.house.gov/hearing/juvenile-justice-reform-modern-era (statement of Rep. Karen Bass, Member, H. Comm. on Crime, Terrorism, Homeland Security, and Investigations).

3 *Id.*

4 *Id.*

5 Office of Juvenile Justice and Delinquency Prevention, U.S. Dep't of Justice, *Statistical Briefing Book: Law Enforcement and Juvenile Crime*, http://www.ojjdp.gov/ojstatbb/crime/qa05101.asp?qaDate=2015 (reporting that in 2015, law enforcement agencies made 921,600 arrests of people under 18) (last visited Aug. 22, 2017); *Arrest*

Data Analysis Tool, BUREAU OF JUSTICE STATISTICS, OFFICE OF JUSTICE PROGRAMS, https://www.bjs.gov/index.cfm?ty=datool&surl=/arrests/index.cfm (reporting that in 2012, law enforcement agencies made 1,320,043 arrests of people under 18) (last visited Aug, 22, 2017).

6 Amanda Ripley, *How America Outlawed Adolescence*, THE ATLANTIC (Nov. 2016), https://www.theatlantic.com/magazine/archive/2016/11/how-america-outlawed-adolescence/501149.

7 *Statistical Briefing Book: Juveniles in Corrections*, OFFICE OF JUVENILE JUSTICE AND DELINQUENCY PREVENTION, U.S. DEP'T OF JUSTICE, http://www.ojjdp.gov/ojstatbb/corrections/qa08208.asp?qaDate=2015 (last visited Aug. 22, 2017).

8 *Statistical Briefing Book: Juvenile Population Characteristics*, OFFICE OF JUVENILE JUSTICE AND DELINQUENCY PREVENTION, U.S. DEP'T OF JUSTICE, http://www.ojjdp.gov/ojstatbb/population/qa01401.asp?qaDate=2015 (showing the general rates of youth poverty); Tamar R. Birckhead, *Delinquent by Reason of Poverty*, 38 WASH. U. J. L. & POL'Y 53, 58–59 (2012), http://openscholarship.wustl.edu/law_journal_law_policy/vol38/iss1/4 (noting that of the families with children in the juvenile delinquency system, nearly 60 percent "were either on public assistance or had annual incomes of less than twenty thousand dollars" and an additional 20 percent of families "had incomes of less than thirty thousand dollars").

9 Kent v. United States, 383 U.S. 541, 556 (1966) (internal citations omitted).

10 U.S. DEP'T OF JUSTICE, CIVIL RIGHTS DIV., INVESTIGATION OF THE SHELBY COUNTY JUVENILE COURT, SHELBY COUNTY, TENNESSEE (2012), https://www.justice.gov/sites/default/files/crt/legacy/2012/04/26/shelbycountyjuv_findingsrpt_4–26-12.pdf.

11 *Id.* at 1–4 (finding that the Juvenile Court of Memphis and Shelby County had failed to provide adequate notice of delinquency matters, failed to protect children from self-incrimination during probation conferences, failed to hold timely probable cause hearings for children arrested and detained without a warrant, and failed to provide adequate due process protection before transferring children to adult court, and additionally finding that black children were disproportionately represented at almost every stage of the delinquency system).

12 *Id.* at 47.

13 U.S. DEP'T OF JUSTICE, Statement of Interest for N.P. et al. v. Georgia, No. 2014-CV-241025 (Ga. Super. Ct. 2014).

14 *Id.* at 7–15.

15 *Id.* at 11.

16 *Id.* at 11–15.

17 U.S. DEP'T OF JUSTICE, CIVIL RIGHTS DIV., INVESTIGATION OF THE ST. LOUIS FAMILY COURT, ST. LOUIS, MISSOURI (2015).

18 *Id.* at 2–4.

19 U.S. DEP'T OF JUSTICE, CIVIL RIGHTS DIV., INVESTIGATION OF LAUDERDALE COUNTY YOUTH COURTS, MERIDIAN POLICE DEPARTMENT, AND MISSISSIPPI DIVISION OF YOUTH SERVICES (2012).

20 *Id.* at 6.

21 *Easy Access to Juvenile Court Statistics: 1985–2014*, OFFICE OF JUVENILE JUSTICE AND DELINQUENCY PREVENTION, U.S. DEP'T OF JUSTICE, https://www.ojjdp.gov/ojstatbb/ezajcs/asp/display.asp (last visited Aug. 22, 2017); SARAH HOCKENBERRY & CHARLES PUZZANCHERA, NAT'L CTR. FOR JUVENILE JUSTICE, JUVENILE COURT STATISTICS 2013 at 7 (2015).

22 *See, e.g.*, ABA Committee on Legal Aid & Indigent Defendants, Report to the House of Delegates 102A (2010).

23 Kristin N. Henning, *Criminalizing Normal Adolescent Behavior in Communities of Color: The Role of Prosecutors in Juvenile Justice Reform*, 98 CORNELL L. REV. 383, 412 (2013).

24 *See* Tamar R. Birckhead, *Toward a Theory of Procedural Justice for Juveniles*, 57 BUFF. L. REV. 1447, 1476–83 (2009).

25 *Access Denied: A National Snapshot of States' Failure to Protect Children's Right to Counsel*, NAT'L JUVENILE DEFENDER CTR. (2017), http://njdc.info/wp-content/uploads/2017/05/Snapshot-Final_single-4.pdf [hereinafter *Access Denied*].
26 *See generally id.*
27 *Id.* at 21, 25.
28 *Id.* at 6, 18–19, 32–35.
29 *Id.* at 10.
30 *See* sources cited *supra* note 8.
31 NAT'L JUVENILE DETENTION CENTER, *Access Denied, supra* note 25, at 10–13.
32 Children face mug shots, fingerprinting, line-ups, DNA swabs, urine samples, strip searches, open showers, and shackles, just to name a few indignities, when they are processed into the court system.
33 In re Gault, 387 U.S. 1, 46 (1967); Haley v. Ohio, 332 U.S. 596, 599 (1948) ("That which would leave a man cold and unimpressed [during an interrogation] can overawe and overwhelm a lad in his early teens.").
34 *See, e.g.*, Laura Nirider et al., *Gerald Gault, Meet Brendan Dassey: Preventing Juvenile False and Coerced Confessions in the 21st Century*, THE CHAMPION 30–33 (2017).
35 Thomas Grisso et al., *Juveniles' Competence to Stand Trial: A Comparison of Adolescents' and Adults' Capacities as Trial Defendants*, 27 LAW & HUM. BEHAV. 333 (2003) (finding that youth's tendencies to be more compliant with authorities may increase their vulnerability to police coercion); *see also* J.D.B. v. North Carolina, 564 U.S. 261, 269 (2011) (noting that the inherent coercion of custodial interrogation "is all the more troubling – and … all the more acute – when the subject … is a juvenile"); Joshua A. Tepfer et al., *Arresting Development: Convictions of Innocent Youth*, 62 RUTGERS L. REV. 887 (2010) (exploring the reasons that youth are particularly vulnerable to false confessions).
36 Lindsay C. Malloy et al., *Interrogations, Confessions, and Guilty Pleas among Serious Adolescent Offenders*, 38 LAW & HUM. BEHAV. 181 (2014).
37 NAT'L JUVENILE DETENTION CENTER, *Access Denied, supra* note 25, at 22.
38 *Id.* (finding that 36 states allow children to be charged attorney's fees).
39 *Id.* (noting that fees and costs for representation can lead to direct consequences, such as liens, as well as worse outcomes where counsel is waived as a result of these fees and costs).
40 *Id.*
41 *See generally State Assessments*, NAT'L JUVENILE DEFENDER CTR., http://njdc.info/our-work/juvenile-indigent-defense-assessments (last visited Apr. 11, 2017).
42 Of the 22 states assessed, NJDC observed excessive waiver of counsel in 13. *See* NAT'L JUVENILE DEFENDER CTR. & CENTRAL JUVENILE DEFENDER CTR., MISSOURI: JUSTICE RATIONED: AN ASSESSMENT OF ACCESS TO COUNSEL AND QUALITY OF REPRESENTATION IN JUVENILE DELINQUENCY COURT (2013); NAT'L JUVENILE DEFENDER CTR. & COLO. JUVENILE DEFENDER COALITION, COLORADO: AN ASSESSMENT OF ACCESS TO COUNSEL AND QUALITY OF REPRESENTATION IN JUVENILE DELINQUENCY PROCEEDINGS (2012); NEBRASKA: JUVENILE LEGAL DEFENSE: A REPORT ON ACCESS TO COUNSEL AND QUALITY OF REPRESENTATION FOR CHILDREN IN NEBRASKA (2009); NAT'L JUVENILE DEFENDER CTR., FLORIDA: AN ASSESSMENT OF ACCESS TO COUNSEL & QUALITY OF REPRESENTATION IN DELINQUENCY PROCEEDINGS (2006); NAT'L JUVENILE DEFENDER CTR. & CENTRAL JUVENILE DEFENDER CTR., INDIANA: AN ASSESSMENT OF ACCESS TO COUNSEL AND QUALITY OF REPRESENTATION IN DELINQUENCY PROCEEDINGS (2006); AM. BAR ASS'N & MID-ATLANTIC JUVENILE DEFENDER CTR., MARYLAND: AN ASSESSMENT OF ACCESS TO COUNSEL AND QUALITY OF REPRESENTATION IN JUVENILE DELINQUENCY PROCEEDINGS (2003); AM. BAR ASS'N ET AL., OHIO: JUSTICE CUT SHORT: AN ASSESSMENT OF ACCESS TO COUNSEL AND QUALITY OF REPRESENTATION IN DELINQUENCY PROCEEDINGS IN OHIO (2003); AM. BAR ASS'N & JUVENILE LAW CTR., PENNSYLVANIA: AN ASSESSMENT OF ACCESS TO COUNSEL AND QUALITY OF REPRESENTATION IN DELINQUENCY PROCEEDINGS (2003); AM. BAR ASS'N, NAT'L JUVENILE

Defender Center, & Northwest Juvenile Defender Ctr., Washington: An Assessment of Access to Counsel and Quality of Representation in Juvenile Offender Matters (2003); Am. Bar Ass'n & Mid-Atlantic Juvenile Defender Ctr., Virginia: An Assessment of Access to Counsel and Quality of Representation in Delinquency Proceedings (2002); Am. Bar Ass'n et al., Kentucky: Advancing Justice: An Assessment of Access to Counsel and Quality of Representation in Delinquency Proceedings (2002); Am. Bar Ass'n & Southern Ctr. for Human Rights, Georgia: An Assessment of Access to Counsel and Quality of Representation in Delinquency Proceedings (2001); Am. Bar Ass'n et al., The Children Left Behind: An Assessment of Access to Counsel and Quality of Representation in Delinquency Proceedings in Louisiana (2001).

43 Nat'l Juvenile Detention Center, *Access Denied, supra* note 25, at 27.

44 *Id.* at 31–35.

45 Kristin Henning, *Race, Paternalism, and the Right to Counsel*, 54 Am. Crim. L. Rev. 649, 656–60 (2017).

46 Marc Mauer, *Addressing Racial Disparities in Incarceration*, 91 Prison J. 87S, 88S (Supp. 2011).

47 *See, e.g.*, Bianca D. M. Wilson et al., *Disproportionality and Disparities among Sexual Minority Youth in Custody*, 46 J. Youth Adolescence 1547 (2017).

48 Silicon Valley De-Bug, https://www.siliconvalleydebug.org (last visited July 24, 2017).

49 Louisiana Ctr. for Children's' Rights, http://www.laccr.org (last visited July 24, 2017).

50 Davidson v. State, No. 17–2-01968–34 (Sup. Ct. Wash. Apr. 3, 2017), https://www.aclu-wa.org/docs/complaint-davison-v-state-washington.

51 *Id.*

52 *See, e.g.*, Gene Johnson, *ACLU: Washington Note Ensuring Kids Get Adequate Legal Help*, U.S. News (Apr. 3, 2017), https://www.usnews.com/news/best-states/washington/articles/2017–04-03/aclu-washington-not-ensuring-kids-get-adequate-legal-help.

53 Elise Schmelzer, *Missouri Public Defender, Fed Up with Meager Funding, Appoints Governor to Defend Assault Suspect*, Washington Post (Aug. 4, 2016), https://www.washingtonpost.com/news/morning-mix/wp/2016/08/04/mo-public-defender-blames-governor-for-huge-caseload-problem-appoints-him-to-defend-assault-suspect/?utm_term=.8245844e6268.

54 Celeste Bott, *Court Rules Public Defender Can't Appoint Missouri Governor as a Defense Attorney*, St. Louis Post-Dispatch (Aug. 25, 2016), http://www.stltoday.com/news/local/govt-and-politics/court-rules-public-defender-can-t-appoint-missouri-governor-as/article_c59059f8-98c8-50fe-9068-12a9b092b7f3.html.

55 Martin Luther King, Jr., Letter from a Birmingham Jail at 2 (Apr. 16, 1963), http://okra.stanford.edu/transcription/document_images/undecided/630416–019.pdf.

12 Pride and prejudice: juvenile defenders for racial justice 50 years after *Gault*

Kristin Henning and Erin Keith

> Imagine that you are a teenager, accused of shoplifting. The policeman who arrested you, the prosecutor seeking to convict you, the judge deciding your fate, and the public defender assigned to represent you are white. You are the only person of color in the courtroom. You wonder if your attorney knows how scared you are – despite your tough exterior – or if she assumes you "know the drill" because of where you live. You wonder if she can understand why you would run from police although you are innocent, and whether she will even try to explain this to the judge. You wonder if she can relate to you – if she protested when police killed Michael Brown and Tamir Rice – or if her first time "taking to the streets" with outrage was after the 2017 presidential inauguration. As hateful political rhetoric streams daily on the news, you wonder whether your defender will truly fight for you – resisting classism, paternalism, and pervasive stereotypes. While you can tell your attorney takes *pride* in defending children, you wonder how she feels about confronting *prejudices*, including her own.

A half-century has passed since the United States Supreme Court affirmed children's right to counsel in the seminal case *In re Gault*. As we reflect on the great strides we have made as a juvenile defense community, we recognize that there is still much work to do. Fifty years after *Gault*, the overcriminalization of youth of color continues to be one of the greatest challenges facing the juvenile system. For example, in 2014, whites comprised 70 percent of youth ages 10–17 in the United States, but only 35 percent of detained youth, 41 percent of adjudicated youth, and 33 percent of youth waived into the adult system.[1] Conversely, black youth were vastly overrepresented, comprising just 16 percent of all minors ages 10–17 nationally, but accounting for 42 percent of all detained youth, 37 percent of all adjudicated youth, and 53 percent of youth waived into the adult system.[2]

In our current socio-political climate, there are few issues more pressing than the fight for racial equity in the juvenile and criminal justice systems. Yet, there are also few issues more difficult for frontline defenders to take on. Racial justice advocacy requires awareness, courage, creativity, legal strategy, social support, and persistence in the face of overwhelming caseloads and incredible resistance. Courageous defenders must be willing to face indignation and maybe even retaliation from judges, prosecutors, and other stakeholders who yearn for an era of colorblindness or who do not wish to have their perspectives and decisions probed for implicit bias. Nevertheless, zealous youth advocates must overcome these obstacles, place themselves in the shoes of the youth they serve, and embrace their role as both juvenile defenders *and* champions for racial justice.

The first section of this chapter challenges juvenile defenders to confront their own prejudices by taking a hard look at the role they play in perpetuating racial disparities within the system. The second section urges defenders to be "color brave,"[3] raising race at every stage of the juvenile case and developing positive narratives to replace the stereotypically negative images of children of color and their families. The third section empowers defenders to advocate for legislative, policy, and practice reforms that will eliminate the disparate treatment of youth of color in juvenile courts across our nation. Ultimately, this chapter is a call to action – a reminder that as juvenile defenders in contemporary America, it is our duty to fight for a system free of prejudice and racial bias – a system that recognizes all children as children.

It's not just them, it's us: confronting our own bias and paternalism

It is jarring to contemplate racial bias among defenders. Given the defenders' career-long opposition to systemic oppression and state coercion, we expect defenders to be among the least likely to harbor racial biases of any kind. Yet, even when individuals stand firmly against racism and are ideologically opposed to *explicit* bias, they may have *implicit* biases that effect their perspectives, behaviors, and decisions.[4] Defenders are no exception.

While client-directed advocacy protects the child's autonomy to make case-related decisions consistent with the child's own cultural, racial, and ethnic views, paternalism allows attorneys to make decisions based on their preconceived notions and stereotypes about a client's race and class.[5] When defenders rely on their own perceptions of what is "best" for their clients of color and ignore their ethical mandate to honor youths' expressed interests, they often relegate their clients to the role of victims who need saving from their parents and communities. Effective juvenile defenders must be willing to confront and dismantle their own cognitive predispositions while simultaneously fighting systemic racism in the courtroom.

Acknowledging implicit racial bias

There is little dispute that defenders with heavy caseloads and limited resources make decisions and recommendations in fast-paced contexts, with incomplete information, under intense time pressure and emotional stress. Research shows that stereotypes and assumptions flourish when a task is complex, a decision is difficult, or time is scarce.[6] Thus, the very nature of the contemporary criminal justice system may cause defenders to rely on cognitive shortcuts and biases.[7] Exacerbating the problem, defenders may be susceptible to a phenomenon known as "bias blind spot" – the belief that others are biased, but they are not, because of their otherwise progressive or socially conscious views.[8] Confidence in one's own egalitarianism may prevent defenders from recognizing their own bias and leave them more vulnerable to its effects.

Juvenile defenders are not alone in this vulnerability. Implicit racial bias has been well documented among various systemic actors including judges, trial attorneys, police officers, and probation officers.[9] For example, in one study of the perceptions of childhood innocence, researchers showed police officers a series of photographs of white, black, and Latino children purportedly engaged in a misdemeanor or felony offense and asked them to estimate the age of each child.[10] While officers overestimated the age of adolescent black felony suspects by almost five years, they underestimated the age of adolescent white felony suspects by one year.[11] Moreover, the older an officer thought a child was, the more culpable the officer perceived the child to be in the suspected criminal conduct.[12] Further nuancing their study, researchers asked officers to take a "dehumanizing" implicit association test to determine the extent to which the officers associated black people with apes. This study found that the more readily participants implicitly associated blacks with apes, the higher their culpability ratings were for both black misdemeanor and black felony suspects.[13]

While less investigation has been done on how implicit racial bias affects defense counsel specifically, existing research reflects that defenders are not immune from the racial biases plaguing other stakeholders. In one study using the Implicit Association Test (IAT) with three groups (capital habeas lawyers, capital trial lawyers, and first year law students), researchers measured the response time in which participants were able to associate a racial group with either a positive or negative evaluation.[14] All three groups were able to react more quickly when white was paired with good and black was paired with bad, than when black was paired with good and white was paired with bad.[15] Those who scored higher in pairing white with good than black with good were deemed to have an "automatic preference" for white, even though this preference may not be conscious.[16] These findings of white preference among capital defense and habeas lawyers were consistent with IAT findings across the larger population.[17]

In another empirical study, researchers found that defenders were more willing to accept plea offers that included more severe sentences for black clients than for white clients.[18] Although defenders in the study did not appear to harbor explicit bias in presuming that blacks were more likely to be guilty than whites, the pleas they felt they could obtain for minority clients contained longer sentences and were more likely to include some jail time.[19] Because the study protocol indicated that defenders were not basing their recommendations on fears that jurors would react less favorably to black defendants at trial, the results suggest that the defenders' own personal biases inflated the plea recommendations they would make and deem appropriate for a black client.[20] In accepting higher sentences for black clients, defenders acting on cognitive short cuts and implicit racial biases may choose not to investigate mitigating evidence because they inflate or overestimate the strength of the government's case, discredit the client's version, or discount the value of defense evidence.[21]

The existence of automatic or implicit preferences does not mean that every individual will act on those preferences or that defense attorneys, in particular, will treat their black clients differently from white clients.[22] It may be that defenders' positive interactions with their clients make them somewhat more willing to acknowledge their prejudices and resist stereotypes in favor of facts.[23] However, because research confirms that all stakeholders are impacted by implicit racial biases, defenders must be empowered with techniques, office-wide support, and resources to overcome these biases.

Understanding race-based paternalism

Until recently, few defenders specialized in delinquency cases. In fact, in many jurisdictions, juvenile cases are still the training ground for newly-hired public defenders, or a place of refuge or punishment for defenders who burn out in adult court.[24] Defenders frequently rotate through a juvenile court assignment with minimal, if any, specialized training on adolescent development or critical skills like youth counseling.[25] Unlike most adult representation, defense advocacy in juvenile cases is further complicated by challenges inherent in any attorney-child relationship, including the power imbalances that naturally exist between children and adults and the unique interplay between advocacy and rehabilitation in juvenile-criminal cases. In virtually every context – family, school, and recreation – adults establish rules and make critical decisions for children. Yet, juvenile court is one of the few contexts in which children are granted a voice – even if not control – in critical decisions that affect them. Principles of due process and fundamental fairness afford children the right to counsel and the opportunity to assert or waive other important constitutional rights. Unfortunately, lawyers who subconsciously buy into paternalistic norms, and believe that children of color need protection from purportedly degenerate parents and communities, may disavow these legal and ethical mandates.

Racially-motived paternalism is not new. The ethos of paternalism for children in state care or supervision has long been colored by societal views on race and class. In the early twentieth century, black leaders worked hard to challenge the myth that black children were delinquent because their mothers were immoral and incompetent.[26] Today, children of color often find themselves in both the child welfare and delinquency systems[27] – first, as "dependent" victims of the state's presumption that their parents are neglectful, and second, as alleged delinquents in a system that is predisposed to criminalize normal adolescent behavior among children of color.

Although we expect juvenile defenders to protect children from the state's coercive and punitive intervention, advocates who see their minority clients as victims of their parents and communities no longer feel compelled to shield them from the state's intrusion. Differences between lawyers and their child clients persist not only across race and class,[28] but also across age, education, legal knowledge, communication skills, access to financial power, and the youth's general dependence on adults for advice. Each of these gaps creates an opportunity for paternalistic advocates to consciously or subconsciously dominate the relationship and render children powerless to resist. Paternalism is particularly vulnerable to implicit racial bias. The more ambiguous the standard of care, the more susceptible it is to manipulation by the lawyer's subjective biases and presumptions. For example, the combination of implicit racial bias and paternalism may cause well-meaning defenders to ignore their clients' expressed wishes and advocate for out-of-home residential placements instead of exploring community-based resources, such as churches, recreation centers, and structured afterschool activities.

More perniciously, lawyers who are committed to getting "help" for their clients may even reject legal strategies that, if successful, would result in dismissal of the child's case and secure the child's release from the juvenile justice system altogether. These lawyers may ignore Fourth and Fifth Amendment violations by the police, neglect to investigate the government's allegations, fail to litigate winnable cases through trial, or sabotage the trial by not objecting to evidence. Paternalistic lawyers may also deprive youth of the very basic choice of whether to plead guilty or challenge allegations by withholding critical information about affirmative defenses, convincing the child their case is hopeless, or manipulating options to suggest that a plea is the only viable alternative. At disposition, lawyers may outright deny a child's preference by advocating for placement in direct contravention of the client's stated goals or manipulate the child's stated objectives by extolling the benefits of out-of-home care without advising them of the harms and consequences of residential placement and incarceration. Even worse, paternalistic advocates who buy into racial stereotypes may attempt to "save" the child by referring the child to the dependency system as a "way out" of delinquency proceedings. These advocates fail to recognize the child welfare system as another form of coercive state intervention that wreaks havoc on families and perpetuates harmful stereotypes about parents and their children of color. In these ways, paternalism and bias interfere with the attorney's ethical mandate to advocate for the child's stated interest and stand guard in the space between the child and state.

Strategies to combat racial biases and paternalism

> We've done some training about how to deal with racial bias when it's coming from judges, prosecutors, and police, and how to litigate racial disparities and implicit bias. But then we said … wait! We need to look at ourselves too! And what we discovered when we started our office-wide racial justice circles is that staff wanted more.
>
> (Gina Pruski, Wisconsin State Public Defender's Office)[29]

Defenders must take affirmative steps to educate themselves and their colleagues about implicit bias and ameliorate it within their own practice. Educating defenders about the existence of implicit racial bias and encouraging candid conversations about racial stereotypes is an important first step. Outraged by the prevalence of racial disparities across their state, advocates in the Wisconsin State Public Defender's Office (WISPD) decided to take a closer look at the link between implicit racial bias among system stakeholders – including public defenders – and the overcriminalization of minorities in their area. Partnering with the YWCA in Madison, Wisconsin, WISPD trained 20 staff members – both attorneys and non-attorneys – as facilitators for a racial justice initiative for public defenders.

Rather than clicking through a traditional PowerPoint presentation during each session, WISPD encouraged its defenders to have real conversations about race and criminal justice through office-wide "racial justice discussion circles." Defenders in these circles were encouraged to take the Implicit Association Test, and share their results with the group, becoming familiar with terms like implicit bias and paternalism in the process. Each week the groups asked and answered real questions such as: "What keeps you from talking about your own biases in mixed company?" and "What do you think people of color want *you* to do about race?" Through role-play exercises, defenders also used realistic scenarios to practice culturally competent client counseling and interaction and avoid microaggressions that might weaken the attorney-client relationship. Since the discussion-circles were expanded across the state in 2012, WISPD has trained over 550 attorneys, and inspired many other advocates from across the country to implement similar programs in their offices. Although implicit bias training is not a magic wand that will eradicate systemic racial disparities overnight, it lays an important foundation. Training equips attorneys with the confidence and the vocabulary to discuss subconscious racial prejudices and empowers them with concrete tools to confront their biases.

Interactive racial justice workshops provide defenders with an opportunity to practice corrective techniques such as counter-stereotypic imaging and individuation.[30] Although defenders have frequent, and often positive, contact with their clients, initial attorney-client contacts in the juvenile justice system typically follow allegations of criminal activity that subconsciously confirm stereotypes about children of color. Counter-stereotypic imaging requires defenders to visualize their black clients in positive scenarios, completely disconnected from the juvenile justice system, such as in a college classroom or interviewing for a job.[31] Defenders may also seek additional opportunities to engage with commonly stereotyped client populations outside of the courtroom, through community service or extra-curricular activities. Individuation requires defenders to obtain more specific information about each client and the facts of each case before making any judgments about the child, the child's family, or the advantages and disadvantages of a plea versus trial.[32] Attorneys who interact with their young clients in the client's own space and who gain insight from the youth and their parents, siblings, teachers, coaches, and mentors will better understand and appreciate the child's case in a culturally relevant context.

Defender offices might offer periodic case rounds in which attorneys must justify their actions, beliefs, and feelings about their clients and their client's cases to other attorneys who can help them guard against inappropriate mental shortcuts and biases that distort decision-making.[33] Case rounds would increase the complexity of the attorney's analysis, require the attorney to respond to their colleagues' objections, and generate a wider range of disparate and even conflicting view points in the office.[34] This type of accountability would help defenders recognize their own biases, re-evaluate their initial impressions and opinions about each case, and ultimately improve their client's outcomes.

In jurisdictions where there is no defender office, state-wide continuing legal education requirements should mandate implicit racial bias training for all attorneys, and state resources should be set aside for these trainings. When funding is not forthcoming, private and court-appointed defenders may partner with local bar associations to lobby for increased funding and support for indigent defense reform or partner with non-profit organizations to access free racial justice training.

Finally, defenders may also shift their office culture by adopting an office-wide mission statement that expressly encourages cultural competency. The statement should require all attorneys to resist paternalism, confront biases that undermine effective representation, and be intentional about incorporating racial justice arguments into the attorney's advocacy. In 2011, a group of chief and assistant public defenders from across North Carolina founded the North Carolina Public Defender Committee on Racial Equity (NC PDCORE) to fight against racial disparities.[35] This excerpt from NC PDCORE's mission statement[36] is an excellent example of an explicit commitment to racial justice:

> The mission of NC PDCORE is to reduce and ultimately eliminate racial disparity in the criminal justice system through education, collaboration, and litigation. The objectives of NC PDCORE are: initiating an ongoing dialogue within the defender community regarding race and justice; facilitating alliances and collaborations with criminal justice stakeholders and organizations within our districts on issues of race and justice; ensuring that addressing racial inequities is a priority within our offices and within the defender community and Indigent Defense Services (IDS); encouraging our defenders to offer culturally competent services by working harder to understand our clients' backgrounds, communities and lives; encouraging defenders to recognize and litigate issues of race more often; and collecting and tracking data and anecdotal evidence to assist in our objectives.

The change must start with juvenile defenders and their willingness to point the finger at themselves – to explore the ways that well-meaning advocates subconsciously contribute to the overcriminalization of minority youth through implicit racial bias and paternalism. As defenders become more attentive to their own racial biases, they will become more adept at recognizing and challenging racial injustice in individual cases and spearheading systemic reform.

The defender's duty: raising race in individual cases

> If we truly believe in equal rights and equal opportunity in America, I think we have to have real conversations about this issue [race] … We cannot afford to be colorblind, we have to be color brave … I'm asking you to show courage. I'm asking you to be bold … I'm asking you not to be colorblind, but to be color brave, so that every child knows that their future matters, and that their dreams are possible.
>
> (Mellody Hobson, President, Ariel Investments)[37]

As a juvenile defender in today's America, there are few obligations more important than "raising race" in a client's juvenile case. Racial justice advocacy requires tenacity and boldness. It requires defenders to be courageous – to inform stakeholders that racial bias exists and undermines the fairness of our legal system. It requires advocates to be "color brave" – unashamed and unafraid to make racial justice arguments on behalf of children of color.

Raising race not only leads to better case outcomes, but it may also improve client satisfaction and enhance the client's confidence in their lawyer's loyalty and commitment. Few empirical studies have looked at the relationship between racial attitudes among service providers and their clients' perceptions of service delivery, but in one study of mental health case managers and their clients, researchers found that clients whose case managers scored higher on a Racial Oppression Sensitivity Scale felt better about the services they received and had less difficulty receiving services than clients whose case managers were less sensitive to racial oppression issues.[38] Although research is needed on the link between client satisfaction and lawyers' sensitivity to racial justice in criminal representation, it is fair to assume that clients want lawyers who are willing and able to interpret facts, evaluate their cases, and tell their stories within the racial realities of contemporary society.[39] Further, criminal justice scholars like Jonathan Rapping and Robin Walker Sterling contend that criminal defense attorneys are uniquely positioned to fight racial injustice in the juvenile and criminal justice systems.[40] As defenders learn more about implicit racial bias and the way it operates, they will be increasingly more sensitive to its pernicious impact at every phase of a client's case.

In the criminal system, defenders should be vigilant in educating the court on the impact of implicit racial bias through motions practice, *voir dire*, expert testimony, narrative reconstruction, jury instructions, and sentencing advocacy.[41] In the juvenile system, defenders may also raise racial justice arguments at the pre-trial detention phase, challenge the prosecutors' decisions to transfer a disproportionate number of youth of color to the adult criminal court, encourage judges to evaluate police-youth encounters based on what we know about race and adolescent development, and begin to alter harmful narratives about children of color and their families at the disposition phase. Raising race is a critical component of providing holistic, effective, client-centered advocacy to youth of color.

Although disproportionate minority contact begins at arrest, it is exacerbated at every stage thereafter. At the outset, defenders should urge prosecutors to serve as gatekeepers of the juvenile system – offering diversion programs in lieu of formal processing, resisting court referrals for normal adolescent behavior, and avoiding the criminalization of children of color for conduct that would not typically be prosecuted in white communities. Defenders may remind prosecutors of disparities in school-based referrals for offenses like fistfights and disorderly contact that impact youth of color at far greater rates than their white counterparts and challenge prosecutors to more fairly exercise their discretion.[42]

Racial disparities are particularly significant at the pre-trial detention phase of the cases when judges and prosecutors are concerned that a child will not return to court or will pose a danger to themself or the community. The pre-trial detention decision is one of the most important decisions in a juvenile case because it predicts, more than any other factor, whether a child will be pulled further into the juvenile system and eventually land in the adult criminal system. Unfortunately, research suggests that racial bias among prosecutors and probation officers may impact their recommendations regarding pre-trial release, as black youth are often perceived to be more mature and dangerous than their white counterparts.[43] In pre-trial release arguments, defenders may incorporate statistical evidence of racial disparities in the local jurisdiction and urge the judge to consider alternatives to detention that are culturally appropriate for the client.[44] A motion to reduce detention should thoroughly introduce the court to alternate narratives about the child and their parents and highlight the parents' capacity to support and supervise the child at home. Defenders should also become familiar with any pre-trial risk assessment instrument used in the local jurisdiction and identify factors that will perpetuate racially disparate outcomes. Defenders might systemically, or in case-by-case pleadings, challenge the validity of risk assessment instruments that use racially-coded factors such as past incarceration of family members, parental absence from court hearings, unemployment, and even prior arrests for uncharged allegations. These arguments may be useful at both pre-trial detention hearings and subsequent disposition proceedings.

In pre-trial motions alleging Fourth and Fifth Amendment violations, defenders should encourage judges to consider the unique interplay between race and adolescence in evaluating an officer's purported justification for an encounter with or interrogation of a youth. Defenders may argue that racial profiling is a violation of the Equal Protection Clause when police explicitly rely on race or fail to articulate a legitimate reason to stop an accused youth. Additionally, Fourth Amendment pleadings and expert testimony should help judges understand how implicit bias compromises the officer's recollection of facts and interpretation of a suspect's behavior.[45] Defenders should also encourage judges to revisit long-held inferences about flight, nervousness, and furtive gestures in a typical police-youth exchange. For example, in cross examination and oral argument, defenders might consider how heightened media attention to police-involved shootings of black males undermines traditional inferences of consciousness of guilt when a child runs from the police or acts nervously. Police violence against black youth has permeated the news with stories of multiple unarmed young black males killed by police officers during causeless stops.[46] In this context, fear of the police, which manifests in the form of nervousness, furtive gestures, or flight, is an arguably rational response by any black child who is approached by the police.

Fortunately, defenders have been successful in convincing several federal and state courts to acknowledge that innocent minorities sometimes flee from the scene of a crime for entirely innocent reasons, including a desire to avoid unwarranted harassment by the police, fear of being apprehended for a crime they did not commit, and fear of physical injury, or even death, at the hands of an officer.[47] For example, in a 2016 case, *Commonwealth v. Warren,* the Supreme Court of Massachusetts held that police had no reasonable articulable suspicion to stop a black man, Jimmy Warren, given the vagueness of the suspect description, the lapse of time between the reported burglary and the stop of Warren, and Warren's distance from the location of the reported crime at the time he was stopped.[48] Of note, the author of the opinion was Justice Geraldine Hines, a former director of the Roxbury Defenders' Committee who also litigated civil rights claims of police misconduct throughout her distinguished career.[49] In declining to treat Warren's purported "flight" from the police as a meaningfully contributing factor in the officers' suspicion, the court held that:

> where the suspect is a black male stopped by the police on the streets of Boston, the analysis of flight as a factor in the reasonable suspicion calculus cannot be divorced from the findings in a recent Boston Police Department report documenting a pattern of racial profiling of black males in the city of Boston.[50]

Justice Hines further noted that a black male's flight "might just as easily be motivated by the desire to avoid the recurring indignity of being racially profiled as by the desire to hide criminal activity."[51]

Defenders may also raise race to challenge the validity of seizures based on a client's presence in a high crime area or purported association with a known criminal. Because most inner-city communities are over-policed, it is not unusual for youth of color to associate with someone, including a family member, who has been arrested, adjudicated, or convicted. Typical innocuous teenage behavior, such as being on one's own street with a group of friends or neighbors, should not justify police harassment and arbitrary stops and frisks. Similarly, in both the Fourth and Fifth Amendment contexts, defenders should help judges better evaluate the onset and validity of seizures and custody and the voluntariness of a child's consent to search or answer questions in light of the fears caused by police-on-black violence as discussed above.

At the plea stage of a juvenile case, defenders should track the plea offers extended to all clients and hold prosecutors accountable for making similar plea offers across race and class. Of course, defenders must be attentive to the impact of their own implicit racial biases and be careful not to acquiesce to worse pleas for children of color.[52]

At trial, defenders should be particularly attentive to the frailties of eyewitness identification and introduce research and expert testimony on cross-racial identifications when the victim and perpetrator are of different races.[53] In *State v. Henderson*, the Supreme Court of New Jersey held that an instruction on the unreliability of cross-racial identification should be given "whenever cross-racial identification is in issue."[54] This ruling aligns with research that shows that people are less able to recognize faces of a different race than their own due to a phenomenon known as "own-race bias."[55] Defenders may educate the judge about the inherent problems of cross-racial identification by filing a motion to appoint an expert that incorporates a summary of the research and the expert's proffered testimony regarding the scientific evidence of misidentification and cross-racial identification. Even if the judge does not grant the motion, simply reading it will educate the judge and potentially influence their rulings on the motion to suppress identification or the reliability of the identification at trial.

In opening statements and other oral arguments, defenders should use narratives that resist racial stereotypes and instead highlight other important demographics about the child, such as "loving son or daughter," "devoted caretaker for younger siblings," or "hard working student."[56] Defenders might also consider incorporating ideas about fairness and equality within the defense theory of the case.[57] When a witness has expressed racial bias or demonstrated racial animus through past actions or statements, defenders may raise this explicitly, for example, by showing that the witness's prejudice motivated them to falsely accuse the client. Defenders might also object to any arguments made by the prosecutor that rely on and encourage racial biases. Recognizing that improper prosecutorial statements may impermissibly interfere with a client's right to a fair trial,[58] local jurisdictions may have favorable case law that limits what prosecutors may say.

At the sentencing or disposition phase, defenders may use disposition letters to highlight statistics that document national and state-wide racial disparities in sentencing. These letters may also help contextualize the actions of youth of color as "normal" adolescent behavior. Specifically, defenders may draw upon developmental research to demonstrate that youth of all races and classes exhibit the same features of normal adolescent behavior and to challenge assertions that children of color cannot be rehabilitated unless they are removed from the community.[59] As noted above, research shows that youth of color are often viewed as older, more dangerous, and more culpable than their white peers, due to implicit racial bias.[60] While some youth of color appear more mature than they actually are, because of traumatic life experiences and forced self-reliance, this does not mean they are more developmentally advanced or more "responsible" for their behavior than white adolescents of the same age. Defenders may help judges during disposition to understand that system-involved youth of color are still children who can learn and rebound from their mistakes.

Defenders may also oppose recommendations for out-of-home placements by educating the juvenile court on the impact of implicit racial bias on the probation officer's assessment of the child's conduct and home environment. In one empirical study of probation officers' sentencing recommendations, researchers found that even after controlling for the severity of the youth's current and prior criminal behavior, juvenile probation officers were more likely to attribute crime to "internal" factors in black youth compared to "external" or environmental factors for white youth.[61] External factors included dysfunctional families, drug and alcohol use, difficulties at school, and evidence of delinquent peers.[62] Internal or personality factors included lack of remorse, lack of cooperation with the probation officer, and failure to take the proceedings seriously.[63] Probation officers consistently portrayed black youth with more negative personality traits than white youth for the same or similar behavior in probation reports.[64] Probation staff were also more likely to view black youth as more responsible for their criminal behavior and more likely to reoffend than white youth, leading to more severe penalties for black youth, including confinement.[65] Providing this information in a disposition letter can help defenders bolster their arguments that a probation officer's proposed disposition plan is overly punitive or unreasonably harsh and fails to meet the rehabilitative needs of the child.

Finally, when opposing a disposition recommendation, defenders may also suggest culturally appropriate alternatives with programs and services that are attentive to the client's rehabilitative and cultural needs. For example, members of a black sorority or fraternity might mentor a black youth and provide positive support and strong examples for the child, even after the case is closed. Defenders may also identify culturally competent community supports for tutoring and General Education Development (GED) classes through churches and local community centers to prevent court involvement for youth who are primarily in need of academic help.

This section provides just a few tools defenders can use to improve their representation of the racially diverse clients they serve. There are many other strategies to imagine. Confronting racial injustice in these ways may reduce feelings of helplessness and revive veteran defenders' waning sense of outrage about discrimination in the delinquency system.

Leading the change: defenders as systemic reformers

In addition to self-reflection, internal reform, and individual case advocacy, effective defender offices must also engage in systemic reform. Defenders who participate in legislative advocacy, data collection, and coalition building have countless opportunities to exercise their power as change agents, boosting their morale and restoring their resolve to withstand overwhelming caseloads. Through the additional measures outlined in this section, attorneys can transcend their role as effective defenders in the courtroom to become dynamic systemic reformers and innovators in the communities they serve.

Legislative advocacy

While most lawmakers are removed from the day-to-day workings of the juvenile court, defenders have a unique, first-hand opportunity to observe the ways statutes disparately impact youth of color. For this reason, defenders can be a tremendous asset in the legislative process. Public defender offices may assign one or more staff attorneys or legislative specialists to track juvenile legislation, testify before state lawmakers about proposed bills, and educate other defenders about the effects of new laws on juvenile clients. For example, the Public Defender Service for the District of Columbia has a full-time legislative counsel assigned for this purpose. The attorney in this role serves as a liaison between local legislators and defenders engaged in direct representation.

Even if office or government protocols prevent employees from lobbying for or against legislation, defenders may provide educational information to legislators. Recently, defenders in the District of Columbia met with individual city council members and testified before the full council in favor of legislation that would significantly curtail detention of youth who commit status offenses and that would prevent the pre-trial detention of youth who were believed to be a danger to themselves, but not to others or to property. Defenders have also used legislative advocacy to highlight racially-based prosecution caused by unconstitutionally vague loitering, vagrancy, and disorderly conduct statutes. Testifying before state and local lawmakers about ways that existing statutes perpetuate the over-criminalization of minority youth is an important strategy in racial justice reform.

Additionally, defenders might encourage their legislators to adopt "racial impact" statutes. These statutes require lawmakers to consider the likely racial impact of any newly proposed legislative action by evaluating relevant data and seeking input from stakeholders. Racial impact statements allow legislators to modify bills that would worsen racial disparities before they are voted into law. Several states, including Iowa, Connecticut, and Oregon, have passed versions of this legislation.[66]

Data collection

Data collection can be a powerful tool in the fight for racial justice in the juvenile system. Juvenile defenders can submit Freedom of Information Act (FOIA) requests for government records that may demonstrate a pattern of racially biased policing or racially motivated misconduct. Requests might include data on school-based referrals to the court system, police stops in a particular neighborhood, or prosecutorial charging decisions. When government agencies resist or delay FOIA requests or fail to track relevant data, defenders may track statistics on their own using in-office databases and hand-written forms. For example, in state-wide offices, defenders might record the race and county of every youth convicted of shoplifting, and those receiving diversion for shoplifting, to establish evidence of racially motivated selective prosecution. They might also track the race of youth being referred to juvenile courts for school-based offenses, to show evidence of inconsistent treatment.

By monitoring arrests, charges, and alleged offense locations, defenders can identify patterns of discrimination and develop a more coordinated office-wide strategy to attack racial disparities.[67] For example, once data has been collected, defenders may file state and federal equal protection claims to challenge one or more charging or transfer decisions. Even if such claims are not likely to succeed, given the Supreme Court's persistent reluctance to do little more than verbally denounce racial bias in criminal cases,[68] defenders may use these challenges to raise awareness among prosecutors and judges and create skepticism about the validity of charges alleged at a recurring location. Defenders can also share data with policy organizations, legislative committees, think tanks, and non-profit organizations that are well equipped to analyze raw data, calculate accurate statistics, and use the findings in their advocacy.

Join local policy coalitions and committees

Finally, whenever possible defenders should serve on policy committees or commissions that promote open dialogue about challenges facing the juvenile system.

The defenders' close interaction with youth, their families, and their communities provide juvenile defenders with a unique opportunity to identify problems that other stakeholders overlook. Defenders who serve on court reform committees or agency review teams may push for changes in court rules, agency policy, or standard practices and procedures. In the District of Columbia, defenders serve on a variety of internal coalitions and rules committees that work collaboratively to resolve systemic deficiencies. Work on one such committee led to the implementation of an administrative order creating a rebuttable presumption that children should be unshackled during all court proceedings.[69] In other states, defenders have joined committees that focus on topics such as the sealing of juvenile records and task forces that are expressly committed to addressing the overcriminalization of minorities. Public Defenders for Racial Justice in California is one such example. Comprised of public and private defenders, the grassroots organization is dedicated to raising racial justice arguments and litigating disparities throughout the courts.[70] If a defender's jurisdiction does not have a policy coalition, the chief defender or line staff should consider creating a committee in collaboration with other stakeholders to address systemic concerns.

There are also nationwide coalitions and initiatives that can assist defenders with their reform efforts. The Annie E. Casey Foundation's Juvenile Detentions Alternatives Initiative (JDAI) began two decades ago as "a pilot project to reduce reliance on local confinement of court-involved youth."[71] Today, JDAI publishes practice kits, hosts annual conferences, and funds local and state level model sites to teach others how to spearhead detention reform efforts and implement detention alternatives in their jurisdiction. JDAI techniques have been used successfully in over 300 counties within 40 different states to reduce pre-trial and post-disposition detention. JDAI sites in participating jurisdictions have "reduced their average daily population in detention by 44% since launching their JDAI efforts."[72] Additionally, sites following JDAI techniques "have reduced the number of youth of color in detention by 40%."[73] Defenders should consider joining organizations that advance alternatives to detention and seek out resources, such as JDAI trainings, on detention reduction strategies in their jurisdiction.

Conclusion

The campaign for racial justice is not the first call for radical reform of juvenile practice and jurisprudence. We can be inspired by the successes achieved during the due process revolution, the fight for evidence-based practices, and the incorporation of adolescent development into various aspects of the law. Although 50 years have passed since *Gault* was decided, there is still much work to do to ensure that the juvenile system is in fact a *justice* system. Today, line defenders and local courts once again have an opportunity – a duty – to shift law and practice to account for what we know about race and paternalism.

In order to fully advocate for juvenile clients, it is imperative that defenders confront their own subconscious prejudices, attack racial injustice at every stage of their clients' cases, and participate in systemic reform efforts to prevent the overcriminalization of minority youth. Using the strategies outlined in this chapter, defenders can go above and beyond traditional courtroom advocacy to become the policymakers and change agents that youth of color need and deserve. Juvenile defenders are their clients' voices; if they do not speak out against racial injustice in the delinquency system, children of color will continue to be disadvantaged and overrepresented in U.S. courts and detention centers. Defenders must take pride in their work as youth advocates and their work to eradicate prejudice in the juvenile system. By answering this chapter's charge, juvenile defenders will continue to advance *Gault's* legacy and provide zealous racial justice advocacy for accused children over the next 50 years.

Notes

1 *Easy Access to Juvenile Populations: 1990–2015*, Off. Juv. Just. & Delinq. Prevention, https://www.ojjdp.gov/ojstatbb/ezapop (last visited Aug. 24, 2017); *Easy Access to Juvenile Statistics:* 2013, Off. Juv. Just. & Delinq. Prevention, http://www.ojjdp.gov/ojstatbb/ezajcs/asp/selection.asp (last visited July 28, 2017).

2 *Id.*

3 *See* Mellody Hobson, *Color Blind or Color Brave?* TED (Mar. 2014), https://www.ted.com/talks/mellody_hobson_color_blind_or_color_brave#t-825953.

4 *See* Vanessa Edkins, *Defense Attorney Plea Recommendations and Client Race: Does Zealous Representation Apply Equally to All?*, 35 Law & Hum. Behav. 413, 415 (2011).

5 Kristin Henning, *Loyalty, Paternalism, and Rights: Client Counseling Theory and the Right to Counsel in Delinquency Cases*, 81 Notre Dame L. Rev. 245, 260–63, 288–89 (2005).

6 *See* Theodore Eisenberg & Sheri Lynn Johnson, *Implicit Racial Attitudes of Death Penalty Lawyers*, 53 DePaul L. Rev. 1539, 1555 (2004).

7 L. Song Richardson & Phillip Atiba Goff, *Implicit Racial Bias in Public Defender Triage*, 122 Yale L.J. 2626, 2631 (2013) (noting that biases thrive in situations where individuals are cognitively depleted, anxious, distracted, and forced to make decisions with imperfect information).

8 Emily Pronin, *Perception and Misperception of Bias in Human Judgment*, 11 Trends Cognitive Sci. 37, 37–39 (2007).

9 *See, e.g.*, Kristin Henning, *Criminalizing Normal Adolescent Behavior in Communities of Color: The Role of Prosecutors in Juvenile Justice Reform*, 98 Cornell L. Rev. 383, 418 (2013).

10 *See generally*, Phillip Atiba Goff et al., *The Essence of Innocence: Consequences of Dehumanizing Black Children*, 106 J. of Personality and Soc. Psychol. 526 (2014).

11 *Id.* at 534–535 (noting that police officers overestimated black youth's ages with an average age error of 4.59).

12 *Id.* at 540.

13 *Id.* at 527.

14 Eisenberg & Johnson, *supra* note 6, at 1542–53.

15 *Id.* at 1545.

16 *Id.* at 1552 (noting that black subjects had an automatic preference for black faces or names, but that preference was weaker than white subjects' automatic preference for white).

17 *Id.*

18 Edkins, *supra* note 4, at 419.

19 *Id.* at 419–420.

20 *Id.* at 422.

21 Richardson & Goff, *supra* note 7, at 2636–37.

22 *See* Eisenberg & Johnson, *supra* note 6, at 1542; Edkins, *supra* note 4, at 415.

23 Jonathan Rapping, *Implicitly Unjust: How Defenders Can Affect Systemic Racist Assumptions*, 16 N.Y.U. J. LEGIS. & PUB. POL'Y 999, 1034 (2013); Edkins, *supra* note 4, at 423. *See id.* at 1022–23; *see also* Robin W. Sterling, *Raising Race*, THE CHAMPION (2011), https://www.nacdl.org/champion.aspx?id=16236 (last visited Sept. 8, 2017).

24 *See, e.g.*, ABA JUVENILE JUSTICE CTR. ET AL., A CALL FOR JUSTICE: AN ASSESSMENT OF ACCESS TO COUNSEL AND QUALITY OF REPRESENTATION IN DELINQUENCY PROCEEDINGS 43 (1995) (results of national survey showing 55 percent of juvenile defenders stay less than 24 months in juvenile court); Leonard P. Edwards, *A Comprehensive Approach to the Representation of Children: The Child Advocacy Coordinating Council*, 27 FAM. L.Q. 417, 419 (1993); Katayoon Majd & Patricia Puritz, *The Cost of Justice: How Low-Income Youth Continue to Pay the Price of Failing Indigent Defense Systems*, 16 GEO. J. ON POVERTY L. & POL'Y 543, 557–58 (2009).

25 ABA JUVENILE JUSTICE CTR. ET AL., *supra* note 24, at 11.

26 Cheryl N. Butler, *Blackness as Delinquency*, 90 WASH. U. L. REV. 1335, 1388–89 (2013); GEOFF K. WARD, BLACK CHILD SAVERS: RACIAL DEMOCRACY & JUVENILE JUSTICE (University of Chicago Press, 2012).

27 Jane Marie Marshall & Wendy Haight, *Understanding Racial Disproportionality Affecting African American Youth Who Cross Over From The Child Welfare to the Juvenile Justice System: Communication, Power, Race and Social Class*, 42 CHILDREN AND YOUTH SERVICES REVIEW 82 (2014) (Study "examin[ing] reasons for racial disproportionality affecting African American youth who cross over from child welfare to juvenile justice system involvement from the perspectives of professionals who work within these systems."); Models for Change, *Is There a Link between Child Welfare and Disproportionate Minority Contact in Juvenile Justice?* (2011), http://www.modelsforchange.net/publications/317 ("Even if African-American and White youths in [Illinois] child welfare were at equal risk of arrest, the child welfare system would still account for a disproportionate number of African-American youths in the juvenile justice system.").

28 *See* Annette R. Appell, *Representing Children Representing What?: Critical Reflections on Lawyering for Children*, 39 COLUM. HUM. RTS. L. REV. 573, 608–09 (2008) [hereinafter *Representing Children Representing*]; Edkins, *supra* note 4, at 415 (citing the United States Department of Labor in 2009 to show the vast majority of attorneys in the United States – 88 percent – are Caucasian).

29 Interview, Sept. 28, 2016.

30 Patricia G. Devine et al., *Long-Term Reduction in Implicit Racial Bias: A Prejudice Habit-Breaking Intervention*, 48 J EXP. SOC. PSYCHOL. 1267 (2012).

31 *Id.* at 1270–1271.

32 ZIVA KUNDA & STEVEN J. SPENCER, AMERICAN PSYCHOLOGICAL ASSOCIATION, PSYCHOLOGICAL BULLETIN, WHEN DO STEREOTYPES COME TO MIND AND WHEN DO THEY COLOR JUDGMENT? A GOAL-BASED THEORETICAL FRAMEWORK FOR STEREOTYPE ACTIVATION AND APPLICATION 522–44, 523 (2003), http://www.arts.uwaterloo.ca/~pthagard/ziva/psychbul2003.pdf (last visited Sept. 8, 2017) (research has shown that even ten minutes of interacting with a member of a stereotyped group can be enough to stop stereotype activation).

33 Matthew I. Fraidin, *Decision-Making in Dependency Court: Heuristics, Cognitive Bias and Accountability*, 60 CLEV. ST. L. REV. 913, 953 (2013).

34 *Id.* at 954.

35 CAITLIN FINNIGAN, THE NORTH CAROLINA PUBLIC DEFENDER COMMITTEE ON RACIAL EQUITY (NC PDCORE), THE FOUNDING OF THE COMMITTEE, ITS MISSION AND ITS WORK SINCE 2011 (Apr. 2015), http://ncids.com/pd-core/wp-content/uploads/2013/06/The-North-Carolina-Public-Defender-Committee-on-Racial-Equity-NC-PDCOR

E-The-Founding-of-the-Committee-its-Mission-and-its-Work-Since-2011.pdf (last visited Sept. 8, 2017).

36 *Id.* at 23–24.

37 Ben Lillie, Be Color Brave, Not Color Blind: Mellody Hobson Speaks at TED2014, TED Blog (Mar. 20, 2014, 1:13 P.M.), http://blog.ted.com/be-color-brave-not-color-blind-mellody-hobson-at-ted2014.

38 Sharron M. Singleton-Bowie, *The Effect of Mental Health Practitioners' Racial Sensitivity on African Americans' Perceptions of Services*, 19 Soc. Work Res. 238, 241 (1995).

39 Carolyn Copps Hartley & Carrie J. Pertrucci, *Practicing Culturally Competent Therapeutic Jurisprudence: A Collaboration Between Social Work & the Law*, 14 Wash. U. J. L. & Pol'y 133, 169 (2004).

40 Rapping, *supra* note 23, at 1016–19; Robin Walker Sterling, *Defense Attorney Resistance*, 99 Iowa L. Rev. 2245, 2251 (2014).

41 *See id.* at 1022–23; *see also* Sterling, *supra* note 23.

42 Henning, *supra* note 9, at 411 ("The increase in referrals from schools to juvenile courts has disproportionately affected youth of color. For example, in Florida, Black students were 2.5 times as likely as White students to be arrested and referred to the state's Department of Juvenile Justice in the 2007–08 academic year. In Colorado, black students were more than twice as likely as white students to be referred to law enforcement, while Latino students were 50% more likely than white students to be referred. In Philadelphia, a black student was three-and-a-half times more likely to be taken into police custody than a white student, and a Latino student was 60% more likely to be taken into police custody than a white student.").

43 Elizabeth Scott & Laurence Steinberg, *Blaming Youth*, 81 Tex. L. Rev. 799, 809–10 (2003); *see also* George S. Bridges & Sara Steen, *Racial Disparities in Official Assessments of Juvenile Offenders: Attributional Stereotypes as Mediating Mechanisms*, 63 Am. Soc. Rev. 554, 561, 563–64 (1998).

44 Annie E. Casey Foundation, *Juvenile Detention Alternative Initiative*, http://www.aecf.org/work/juvenile-justice/jdai (last visited July 27, 2017) (provides helpful data on pre-trial and post-trial detention and racial disparities that defenders can utilize in their motions and oral arguments).

45 Kristin Henning, *The Reasonable Black Child: Race, Adolescence and the Fourth Amendment*, 67 Amer. U. L. Rev. (forthcoming 2018).

46 *See, e.g.*, Scott Calvert, *Baltimore Prosecutors Say Freddie Gray Arrest Was Illegal Before Finding Knife*, Wall Street Journal (May 19, 2015, 6:54 P.M.), https://www.wsj.com/articles/baltimore-prosecutors-say-freddie-gray-arrest-was-illegal-before-finding-knife-1432076045; *see also Unarmed Teen Michael Brown Killed By Ferguson Police*, The St. Louis American (Aug. 10, 2014), http://www.stlamerican.com/news/local_news/update-unarmed-teen-michael-brown-killed-by-ferguson-police/article_1160a5ba-2050-11e4-aa5c-001a4bcf887a.html (last visited Sept. 8, 2017).

47 *See, e.g.*, Illinois v.Wardlow, 528 U.S. 119, 132 (2000); In re T.L., 729 A.2d 334, 341–42 (D.C. 1999) (finding flight not sufficient for reasonable articulable suspicion when respondent and his companions "rapidly retreated" into the house when the police approached).

48 Commonwealth. v. Warren, 58 N.E.3d 333 (Mass. 2016).

49 Associate Justice Geraldine S. Hines, Massachusetts Court System, http://www.mass.gov/courts/court-info/appealscourt/appeals-court-justices/justice-geraldine-s-hines.html (last visited Aug. 3, 2017).

50 Warren, 58 N.E.3d at 342.

51 *Id.*

52 Edkins, *supra* note 4, at 422–23.

53 *See, e.g.*, Gary Wells & Elizabeth Olson, *Eyewitness Testimony*, 54 Ann. Rev. Psychol. 277 (2003) (a review of variables that affect eyewitness identifications).

54 State v. Henderson, 27 A.3d 872, 922 (N.J. 2011).

55 *See* Elizabeth Loftus, Eyewitness Testimony § 4.9 (1997 & Supp.1999); *see generally* Christian A. Meissner & John C. Brigham, *Thirty Years of Investigating The Own-Race Bias in Memory for Faces: A Meta-Analytic Review*, 7 Psychol. Pub. Pol'y & L. 3 (2001).

56 Rapping, *supra* note 23, at 1037–38.

57 *Id.*

58 *See* Andrade v. United States, 88 A.3d 134 (D.C. 2014).

59 *See, e.g.*, Rebecca Epstein et al., Girlhood Interrupted: The Erasure of Black Girls' Childhood (2017), http://www.law.georgetown.edu/academics/centers-institutes/poverty-inequality/upload/girlhood-interrupted.pdf (last visited Sept. 8, 2017); He Len Chung et al., *The Transition to Adulthood for Adolescents in the Juvenile Justice System: A Developmental Perspective*, On Your Own Without a Net: The Transition To Adulthood For Vulnerable Populations 68, 77–78 (D. Wayne Osgood et al. eds., 2005).

60 *Id.* at 2.

61 George S. Bridges & Sara Steen, *Racial Disparities in Official Assessments of Juvenile Offenders: Attributional Stereotypes as Mediating Mechanisms*, 63 Am. Soc. Rev. 554, 561, 563–64 (1998).

62 *Id.* at 559.

63 *Id.*

64 *Id.* at 561, 567 (based on a study of 233 narrative reports written by probation officers for judges in anticipation of a youth's disposition after a crime).

65 *Id.* at 561, 563–64, 567.

66 Nicole D. Porter, *Racial Impact Statements*, The Sentencing Project (Dec. 1, 2014), http://www.sentencingproject.org/publications/racial-impact-statements.

67 Henning, *supra* note 9, at 430.

68 *See, e.g.*, Whren v. United States, 517 U.S. 806, 818–19 (1996) (upholding police officers' use of minor traffic violations as a pretext to stop drivers for suspected drug involvement); United States v. Armstrong, 517 U.S. 456, 460–62 (1996) (holding defendant not entitled to discovery in selective prosecution case unless defendant shows that others similarly situated were not prosecuted).

69 Superior Court of the District of Columbia: Administrative Order 16–09, D.C. Courts (May 31, 2016), http://www.dccourts.gov/internet/documents/16-09-Individual-Determinations-for-the-Use-of-Restraints-on-Respondents-Supersedes-15-07.pdf (last visited Sept. 8, 2017).

70 Public Defenders for Racial Justice, Facebook, https://www.facebook.com/publicdefendersforsocialchange (last visited July 27, 2017).

71 The Annie E. Casey Foundation, Juvenile Detention Alternatives Initiative, http://www.aecf.org/work/juvenile-justice/jdai (last visited July 27, 2017).

72 *Id.*

73 *Id.*

13 Gerald Gault meet Brendan Dassey: preventing juvenile false and coerced confessions in the twenty-first century[1]

Laura Nirider, Megan Crane and Steven Drizin

In 1964, 15-year-old Gerald Gault was taken into custody by the Sheriff of Gila County, a rural jurisdiction about 80 miles east of Phoenix, after a neighbor accused him of making prank telephone calls of the "irritatingly offensive, adolescent, sex variety."[2] Over the course of the following week, Gerald appeared twice in the chambers of a juvenile court judge, accompanied by his mother, older brother, and two probation officers. Though the hearings were not transcribed, later testimony indicated that the judge questioned Gerald on both occasions about whether he had in fact made the calls. Gerald's mother recalled that he had told the judge only that he dialed his neighbor's phone number and handed the phone to his friend Ronald; one probation officer recalled that he had admitted making the lewd calls and later recanted; and the judge himself recalled that Gerald had admitted making some of the lewd statements – but only the less "serious" ones.[3] Based on these statements, Gerald was taken from his parents and held in detention. It is not known whether his uncorroborated, uncounseled confession – or, if there was more than one, which version – was true or false. In many respects, it didn't matter; the authorities believed that Gerald had done something wrong and were free to act accordingly.

Two and a half years later, in 1967, the United States Supreme Court ordered Gerald's release in an opinion that was nothing less than a reckoning for the nation's juvenile court system. Blinded by "neither sentiment nor folklore,"[4] Justice Abe Fortas, writing for the Court, laid bare the gulf between juvenile court's rhetoric – characterized by speeches about "kindly"[5] judges, informality, and the therapeutic treatment and rehabilitation of youthful offenders – and its reality. Juvenile courts, according to the Justice, too often operated as "kangaroo courts"[6] prone to inaccurate fact-finding, unchecked abuses of discretion, and arbitrary punishments. His prescription was a healthy dose of due process, including most prominently the right to counsel. To Justice Fortas, only a child aided by a lawyer's "guiding hand"[7] could both "ascertain … a defense and prepare and submit it."[8]

Gault revolutionized juvenile court process by not only requiring counsel for kids, but also granting them other basic ingredients of due process: the right to notice of the charges, the rights to confrontation and cross-examination, and the right against self-incrimination. Perhaps for these reasons, Chief Justice Earl

Warren, upon receiving a draft of the *Gault* opinion, sent his colleague Justice Fortas a personal note: "I join your magnificent opinion in the above case. It will be known as the Magna Carta for juveniles."[9]

In 2017, which was the fiftieth anniversary of *In re Gault*, the opinion's discussion of the right to counsel was rightfully feted across the country. But tucked among the decision's later pages is an equally important discussion: one concerning a child's right against compelled self-incrimination. This fifty-year-old discussion still resonates today precisely because the problem it describes still exists: the problem of unreliable confessions from juveniles. These are the pages we wish to celebrate in this essay.

"Authoritative opinion has cast formidable doubt upon the reliability and trustworthiness of 'confessions' by children,"[10] decreed Justice Fortas, wrapping the word *confession* in ever-so-slightly acerbic quotation marks to underscore just how formidable the Court's doubts were. In an era when DNA testing was not known or thought of, and when the notion of a false confession was hard to imagine and even harder to prove, the Court pointed out that a child subject to police interrogation might admit "whatever he thought was expected so that he could get out of the immediate situation."[11] And Justice Fortas turned his searching gaze on pressure-filled interrogation techniques, finding that false confessions could occur "wherever the innocent person is placed in such a situation that the untrue acknowledgment of guilt is at the time the more promising of two alternatives between which he is obliged to choose."[12] These words inspired the undersigned authors to create and develop the Center on Wrongful Convictions of Youth nearly ten years ago – the first and only organization dedicated in large part to representing children who falsely confessed to crimes they never committed.

Gault's bold words should have resounded as a clarion call for interrogation reform – but the need for such a Center persists to this day. Perhaps no more widely recognized proof exists than the uncounseled, uncorroborated confession of our client: 16-year-old, mentally limited Brendan Dassey, whose videotaped confession to murder was publicized in the 2015 Netflix Global docuseries *Making a Murderer*. Brendan was interrogated alone on video camera by Wisconsin police in 2005 until he gave a confession to the rape and murder of a young woman named Teresa Halbach. Watched by audiences worldwide, the series has generated a worldwide groundswell of support for Brendan because many believe him to be innocent and his confession to be false.

Viewers watched as police used a series of misguided techniques to elicit a confession: they told the impressionable Brendan that everything would be okay as long as he told them what they already believed he had done; they fed him crucial, non-public details about the murder, like the fact that Halbach had been shot in the head; and they falsely led him to believe that he would be returned to school in time to finish a project – even after he confessed to rape and murder. The series serves as a vivid reminder that the concerns articulated in Gerald's case haven't gone away. Even in the new millennium, a child subject to uncounseled interrogation might agree to "whatever he thought was expected" in order to go back home – or, in Brendan's case, back to school. And by putting a heartbreaking face on the problem of juvenile false confessions, the series has reminded us of the fierce urgency of the task at hand: working to reform juvenile interrogation techniques before more Brendan Dasseys end up behind bars.

To be sure, the legal terrain has not gone completely unchanged since the era of Gerald Gault. After decades of dormancy, the high Court revivified *Gault*'s concern about the unreliability of juvenile confessions in 2011's *J.D.B. v. North Carolina*. There, the Court noted that empirical studies undertaken in the era of DNA-proven exonerations have shown that the problem of false confessions is indeed "all the more acute"[13] when the subject of custodial interrogation is a juvenile. Building on a decade of reinvigorated juvenile jurisprudence, the Court explained that juveniles are vulnerable during interrogation precisely because they "are more vulnerable or susceptible to … outside pressures"[14] and "often lack the experience, perspective, and judgment to recognize and avoid choices that could be detrimental to them."[15]

Recognition of the problem has spread beyond the courts, too. Although many police interrogation training firms have been loath to alter their techniques, some law enforcement agencies have agreed on the need for reform, including the International Association of Chiefs of Police. In 2012, that Association issued a juvenile interrogation manual specifically geared at preventing false confessions that recommended, among other things, the use of different and more child-sensitive interrogation techniques. Hearkening back to *Gault*'s warning that children might admit to anything if they think they will get to go home, the Association cautioned officers to avoid "even … indirect promises of leniency"[16] that imply that confession will result in help or that silence will result in negative consequences. Similarly, it warned against using deception with children, including the use of false evidence during interrogation, and insisted that officers refrain from disclosing crime-scene facts during the interrogation. To be sure, this manual binds not a single officer, but it stands as a reform-minded template for departmental interrogation policies around the country.

Many state legislatures have also taken basic steps to improve the conditions surrounding juvenile interrogation. Indeed, Brendan's case is emblematic of one of the most significant reforms that has swept the nation in the past ten years: the videotaping of interrogations. To date, about 20 states have adopted rules requiring the recording of interrogations from start to finish. This reform has been crucial, shining a spotlight into the hitherto secret confines of the interrogation room, but it does not directly alter interrogation techniques themselves. And reforms beyond videotaping have been scattershot. A few states have adopted simplified juvenile *Miranda* warnings, while a few others, including Illinois in 2016, have mandated counsel in the interrogation room for children under the age of 15 in highly limited circumstances. These reforms are unquestionably important, giving heft to important Fifth and Sixth Amendment protections for juveniles – but again, they leave untouched interrogation techniques themselves.

The bottom line? After decades of recognition that juvenile interrogation techniques must be fixed, the time is finally right to reform them. In the wake of

Making a Murderer, front-line defenders and others concerned with making interrogations less coercive and more reliable have an unprecedented opportunity to pursue change. More than ever before, a global outcry about juvenile interrogation techniques is incentivizing judges, politicians, and law enforcement officers to change the way interrogation works in order to ensure the reliability of confessions. And the best places to start are the very tactics used on Brendan Dassey, including false promises of leniency, lies about the evidence, and fact-feeding. That toxic bundle of techniques is used around the country – not just in Wisconsin – and each has long been identified as a risk factor for false confession, especially when used on juveniles. Those techniques should have been discarded in the days of *In re Gault*. It is time to rid ourselves of them now.

False promises of leniency

> If you did some things … it's OK. As long as you can be honest with us, it's OK. If you lie about it that's gonna be problems.
>
> (Interrogation of Brendan Dassey, Wisconsin, 2006)[17]

> All everyone's waiting for today is for you to admit to what you did so that we can start the process of getting you some help.
>
> (Interrogation of Nga Truong, Massachusetts, 2008)[18]

> You need to start thinking about what you are going to do for yourself because I know you got a couple of kids out there and I'd hate to see the kids miss their daddy for a long time because you didn't want to talk about what's going on.
>
> (Interrogation of Anthony Polk, Iowa, 2008)[19]

Any defender who has had a case involving a recorded interrogation will recognize these refrains or variants thereon. Taught to officers during interrogation trainings that are offered to police departments nationwide, such statements are dangled in front of suspects to provide them a reason to confess. The use of such ploys is, too often, standard practice, and for good reason. It should be obvious that confession is a profoundly self-damaging act, the likes of which few rational persons would do. In a legal system characterized by public stigma, lengthy sentences, and harsh prison conditions, most people would rationally conclude that the physical costs of confessing to a serious crime outweigh the benefits of a relieved mind. To convince someone to confess who is not already predisposed to do so, therefore, officers are regularly trained to obfuscate the harm, to trick a suspect into believing that his or her self-interest actually lies with confession, not with silence. In this sense, the task of interrogation is to make the irrational choice – confessing – seem rational.

That said, courts often look askance at direct promises of leniency, like "if you confess, you will go home." Such obvious lies are too much for many courts to stomach in light of a Fifth Amendment that insists that any self-incrimination must be done voluntarily after a suspect freely weighs the costs and benefits of confessing. The Seventh Circuit put a fine point on this in *U.S. v. Villalpando*:

> The reason we treat a false promise differently than other somewhat deceptive police tactics (such as cajoling and duplicity) is that a false promise has the unique potential to make a decision to speak irrational and the resulting confession unreliable.[20]

In reaching this conclusion, the court recognized that "[p]olice conduct that influences a rational person who is innocent to view a false confession as more beneficial than being honest is necessarily coercive, because of the way it realigns a suspect's incentives during interrogation."[21]

Against this legal landscape, officers are trained to dance around the issue: to suggest leniency without ever saying it outright, using language that clearly telegraphs the message without crossing the line. Many interrogators, thus, tell suspects that if they confess, the prosecutor will "understand" and "work with" them; that everything will be "all right"; that the suspect will receive "help," such as counseling; and that the suspect's future will remain bright. Some interrogators even explicitly say "I can't promise you anything," only to follow, a sentence or two later, with an assurance that everything will be okay if the suspect confesses. While common sense tells us that these types of statements communicate leniency as clearly as a direct promise – particularly to the ears and mind of a child – such common sense has yet to take hold in some courtrooms. Indeed, trial courts are often blinded by the content of a confession and thus bend over backward to find the confession voluntary, resulting in a jurisprudence that purports to prohibit "if you confess, you will go home" but may tolerate "if you cooperate, everything will be okay."

But should this repackaging – in which the thinnest of veils are drawn over unmistakable promises of leniency – insulate such interrogation tactics from judicial scrutiny? The answer is a clear no. In a White Paper summarizing the position of its membership, the American Psychological Association (APA) identified even *implied* promises of leniency as risk factors for false confession and warned that interrogation tactics that imply leniency "may well lead innocent people who feel trapped to confess."[22]

This is particularly true when the person being interrogated is a juvenile. When asked, children who falsely confessed to crimes that they did not commit frequently offer the same explanation: I confessed because I thought I would go home. The consistency of this refrain is remarkable, and it demonstrates that children hear these promises loud and clear. And the United States Supreme Court has acknowledged the reasons for this clear pattern: children are indeed more susceptible to the pressures of interrogation precisely because their still-developing brains render them ill-equipped to weigh long-term costs and benefits – which, in turn, makes them easy marks for interrogation tactics that distort the consequences of confessing. In short, it simply takes a lot less to realign the interrogation room incentives for a juvenile than for an adult – even when the juvenile is factually innocent. It is up to defenders to point this reality out.

Practice tips:

- Challenge courts' tolerance of implied promises of leniency in motions to suppress.
- Rely on the scientific foundation provided by the American Psychological Association's White Paper on false confessions.
- Cite cases, including *Dassey, Truong, and Polk.*

Lies about evidence

> They pointed you out. They gave me your name! They gave me your last name. I had your first name. "Who's this? Do you recognize anybody in this picture?" "Yeah, that's Trevon Yates."
>
> (Falsehood during Interrogation of Trevon Yates, Illinois, 2013)[23]

> [We need to figure out] why you feel like you want to touch a three-year-old little girl. Okay? Cause it did happen. She explained it perfectly.
>
> (Falsehood during Interrogation of Elias V., California, 2013)[24]

> There's an item that you touched, all right, that left some [DNA] particles on it that did some damage to somebody … . The evidence shows you were there. The evidence shows it. I can't lie about the evidence.
>
> (Falsehood during Interrogation of Robert Davis, Virginia, 2003)[25]

Lies about the evidence – known in the false confession literature as "false evidence ploys" – are prohibited in the United Kingdom and most other European countries. But courts across the United States have blessed police lies about the evidence, even when the person being interrogated is a child – albeit in a series of outdated opinions that are ripe for refreshing. In 1969, in *Frazier v. Cupp*, the United States Supreme Court affirmed the legality of deceptive interrogation tactics.[26] The *Cupp* court held that a police falsehood about the evidence will not render a confession involuntary on its own; instead, the use of such a tactic is just one factor to consider in the totality of the circumstances. Lower courts read *Cupp* as a virtual green light for police deception and now regularly sign off on a wide range of police lies, from generalized assertions like "we already know what you did" to highly specific claims like "we found your fingerprints on the gun" and even lies about whether police are permitted to lie.

But the reality is that lies about the evidence are another risk factor for false and unreliable confessions. In its White Paper, the APA noted that "[a]t times, American police will overcome a suspect's denials by presenting supposedly incontrovertible evidence of his or her guilt … even if that evidence does not exist."[27] Outrageously, it noted, such a tactic is even recommended in some police training manuals. But the APA warned that "outright lies can put innocents at risk to confess by leading them to feel trapped by the inevitability of the evidence against them."[28] Indeed, an evidentiary lie often tips the scales by convincing a suspect that the odds are so stacked against him or her that nothing can be done but mitigate the damage by admitting guilt. In other words, lies about the evidence can help make the irrational choice to confess look rational.

Some courts have placed limits on police deception during interrogation; courts in both Florida and New Jersey, for instance, have drawn the line at actually manufacturing fake evidence.[29] And the Seventh Circuit Court of Appeals has taken a different tack by prohibiting lies about specialized forms of medical evidence that a suspect is not able to contradict.[30] But such limits are incomplete guards against false confessions. For this reason, the APA recommends a complete ban on police lies about the evidence but, in the alternative, proposes criterion for case-by-case evaluation, including

> the extent that a suspect is vulnerable (*e.g.*, by virtue of his or her youth, naiveté, intellectual deficiency, or acute emotional state) and . . . the extent that the alleged evidence is presented as incontrovertible, sufficient as a basis for prosecution, and impossible to overcome.[31]

Indeed, as the APA recognizes, youthful suspects are particularly ill-equipped to push back against false assertions by authority figures. Many juveniles do not have the basic knowledge or life experience to question or suspect that the police are allowed to lie, nor do many have the maturity or confidence to challenge a lying officer. More likely, the juvenile will simply throw up his or her hands, admit defeat in the face of apparently inculpatory evidence that he or she cannot challenge or explain, and yield to the demand for a confession – whether guilty or not.

Pursuant to the APA's recommendation, defense attorneys should advocate for significant limits on police deception, particularly when the subject of interrogation is a juvenile. This has already been successful in some courts. For example, in a 2015 California Court of Appeals case, an appellate court found a 13-year-old boy's confession to be involuntary, noting among other reasons that "[t]he use of deceptive techniques is significantly more indicative of involuntariness where, as here, the subject is a 13-year-old adolescent."[32] It is high time for other courts to catch up – and it is up to front-line defense attorneys to make sure that they do.

Practice tips:

- Argue for a ban – or at least a limit – on false evidence ploys with juvenile suspects.
- Cite the many juvenile false confession cases that involved lies about the evidence; use resources like the National Registry of Exonerations to find such cases.
- Cite the APA White Paper.
- Cite cases like *In re Elias V.* and *Aleman v. Village of Hanover Park.*
- Cite the developmental and social science proving both that children are especially vulnerable to deception and psychological manipulation, and that they are ill-equipped to confront such lies from authority figures.
- Remember that the United States Supreme Court has recognized in cases like *Haley v. Ohio* that tactics which may leave an adult criminal suspect "cold and

unimpressed" may "overwhelm and overawe" a youthful suspect. In other words, tactics which may not render an adult's confession involuntary may require suppression of a juvenile confession.

Contamination

> We are really going out on a limb here with you. Would it make you feel better if we told you exactly who was with you?
>
> (Interrogation of Robert Davis, Virginia, 2003)[33]

> I know Kenzell wasn't up at the door because there was only two people. Okay, so the only two people that did the robbery was you and Devan, right?
>
> (Interrogation of Trevon Yates, Illinois, 2013)[34]

> I'm just gonna come out and ask you. Who shot her in the head?
>
> (Interrogation of Brendan Dassey, Wisconsin, 2006)[35]

Perhaps no problem in the sordid realm of false confessions is more pernicious than the problem of contamination. As a California court noted, police too often disclose specific facts regarding the crime during the interrogation process, thus enabling the suspect to adopt those facts and weave them together into a detailed narrative of guilt – even if they are innocent – that virtually seals their fate because of its plausibility. Indeed, Brendan Dassey's case provides a disturbing example of the power of a contaminated confession. Brendan's videotaped interrogation shows the officers feeding him nonpublic information about the crime when he was unable to produce it, including the whereabouts of the victim's personal effects, the disabling of the victim's car, and – most crucially – the method by which the victim was murdered ("I'm just going to come out and ask you. Who shot her in the head?"). At closing argument, however, prosecutors suggested that Brendan's confession should be believed precisely because he gave accurate information about these nonpublic details – while glossing over the reality that his "knowledge" of those facts was based on contamination. Like the overwhelming majority of other false confessors who take their cases to trial, Brendan was convicted and sentenced to life in prison based on a confession that ended up including accurate-sounding details but that still misled the jury about his guilt.

Even law enforcement interrogation trainers recognize the danger of contaminating a confession. In its training manual, John E. Reid & Associates emphatically warn officers against intentionally or inadvertently providing suspects with key facts of the crime. Interrogators are instructed that when reviewing a confession that appears to be corroborated, "the investigator should be certain that the details were not somehow revealed to the suspect through the questioning process, news media, or the viewing of crime scene photographs."[36] The manual stresses that "[i]t is highly important … that the investigator let the confessor supply the details of the occurrence, and to this end, the investigator should avoid or at least minimize the use of leading questions."[37]

Despite these warnings, fact-feeding still occurs too often – but because some defenders are not trained to think of fact-feeding as cognizable during a traditional motion to suppress, many are left unsure how to combat it. But the trick to challenging contamination in a motion to suppress is to cast fact-feeding – appropriately, we believe – as part of an interrogator's arsenal of coercion and manipulation. Indeed, many defenders who have argued that contamination or fact-feeding is itself a form of coercion have succeeded. The notion that contamination was constitutionally problematic was first introduced in the *Miranda* decision itself, where the Court spoke critically of police tactics that cause a suspect to "merely confirm[ ] the preconceived story the police seek to have him describe."[38] Since then, many lower courts have followed suit. In 2014, for instance, a federal court suppressed an 18-year-old's confession where the police "asked him the same questions over and over until he finally assented and adopted the details that the officers posited."[39] Similarly, courts have suppressed confessions in cases where "there is not a single inculpatory fact in defendant's confession that was not suggested to him"[40]; where "the majority of [suspect's] final confession was comprised of details that [suspect] had adopted from the officers' suggestions"[41]; and where the confession "contains little information that was not first provided or suggested by the interrogating officers."[42] Clearly, it is possible – and indeed wise – to argue that contamination itself is, in essence, coercive.

Practice tips:

- Litigate contamination as a form of police coercion that violates constitutional guarantees of due process.
- Persuade more judges to apply heightened scrutiny to juvenile confessions, like in *Elias V.*
- Cite cases like *In re Elias V., U.S. v. Preston*, and *State v. Rettenberger*.

In short, the time is ripe for wholesale reform of the ways in which our police interrogate our youth. Although piecemeal progress is being made in law enforcement-driven reforms and a few state legislatures, the most effective vehicle for change can be made by front-line defense attorneys who can bring to life not only *Gault*'s call for zealous advocacy but also its concern for the unreliability of youthful confessions. Now, more than ever, those concerned about the reliability of children's confessions should act to break through the legal fictions that can insulate such confessions from rigorous scrutiny – drawing on the time-honored lessons of *In re Gault* to insist that after 50 years, our system can no longer tolerate interrogation tactics that imperil children. With dedication, creativity, and perseverance, the wise words of *Gault* can finally be turned from a rhetorical mandate into legal reality.

Notes

1 This chapter originally appeared in the April 2017 issue of THE CHAMPION [(c) 2017, National Association of Criminal Defense Lawyers]. Reprinted with permission.

2 In re Gault, 387 U.S. 1, 4 (1967).

3 *Id.* at 7.
4 *Id.* at 21.
5 *Id.* at 27.
6 *Id.* at 28.
7 *Id.* at 36.
8 *Id.* at 37.
9 Letter from Chief Justice Earl Warren to Justice Abe Fortas (March 17, 1967) (on file in Abe Fortas Papers (MS858), Manuscripts and Archives, Yale University Archives, Box 124).
10 Gault at 52.
11 *Id.*
12 Gault, 387 U.S. at 45.
13 J.D.B. v. North Carolina, 564 U.S. 261, 269 (2011).
14 *Id.* at 262.
15 *Id.*
16 International Association of Chiefs of Police, Reducing Risks: An Executive's Guide to Effective Juvenile Interview and Interrogation (2012), http://www.theiacp.org/Portals/0/pdfs/ReducingRisksAnExecutiveGuidetoEffectiveJuvenileInterviewandInterrogation.pdf (last visited Jan. 2, 2018).
17 Interrogation video on file with the authors.
18 *Id.*
19 State v. Polk, 812 N.W.2d 670, 672 (Iowa 2012).
20 U.S. v. Villalpando, 588 F.3d 1124, 1128 (7th Cir. 2009) (internal citation omitted).
21 *Id.*
22 Saul M. Kassin et al., Police-Induced Confessions: Risk Factors and Recommendations (2010), http://web.williams.edu/Psychology/Faculty/Kassin/files/White%20Paper%20-%20LHB%20(2010).pdf (last visited Jan. 2, 2018).
23 Interrogation video on file with the authors.
24 *Id.*
25 *Id.*
26 349 U.S. 731 (1969).
27 Kassin et al., *supra* note 22.
28 *Id.*
29 State v. Patton, 362 N.J. Super. 16 (N.J. 1993); State v. Cayward, 552 So. 2d 921 (Fla. 1989).
30 662 F.3d 897, 906 (7th Cir. 2011).
31 Kassin et al., *supra* note 22.
32 In re Elias V., 237 Cal. App. 4th 568, 586, 587, 591, 593–95 (1st Dist. June 9, 2015).
33 Interrogation video on file with the authors.
34 *Id.*
35 *Id.*
36 Fred Ebrau et al., Criminal Interrogations and Confessions 305 (5th ed., Jones & Bartlett Learning, 2013).
37 *Id.* at 315.
38 Miranda v. Arizona, 384 U.S. 436, 455 (1996).
39 U.S. v. Preston, 751 F. 3d 1008, 1023–24 (2014).
40 People v. Thomas, 8 N.E. 3d 308, 316 (N.Y. 2014).
41 In re J.F., 987 A.2d 1168 (D.C. 2010).
42 State v. Rettenberger, 984 P.2d 20 1009, 1020 ¶ 40 (Utah 1999).

14 No more "desert Devil's Island": the right to counsel for incarcerated children

Laura Cohen and Sandra Simkins

Gerald Gault's sentence of up to six years at the Arizona State Industrial School for Boys for making a lewd phone call is the creation story of the modern juvenile justice system. The disconnect between Gerald's low-level prank and his lengthy incarceration spurred the United States Supreme Court to mandate due process protections and, specifically, the right to counsel for all children charged with delinquency. Writing for the majority, Justice Abe Fortas stressed the essentiality of legal representation to ensure procedural fairness and as a safeguard against systemic abuse:

> The juvenile needs the assistance of counsel to cope with problems of law, to make skilled inquiry into the facts, to insist upon regularity of the proceedings, and to ascertain whether he has a defense and to prepare and submit it. The child requires the guiding hand of counsel at every step in the proceedings against him … . We hold now that it is … essential for the determination of delinquency, *carrying with it the awesome prospect of incarceration* in a state institution until the juvenile reaches the age of 21.[1]

Despite this ringing endorsement of the right to counsel for children, the opinion fails to flesh out the meaning of "every step of the proceedings" because the record of the case, such as it was, stopped at the juvenile courthouse door. Had the Court known what Gerald would encounter at Fort Grant, later termed a "desert Devil's Island," it may well have deemed the length of any period of juvenile incarceration a "critical stage of the proceedings," requiring the "guiding hand" of counsel for as long as young people remain in state custody.[2]

Fort Grant: the "desert Devil's Island"

The history of the Industrial School reflects that of similar "training schools" across the country. The facility, which opened in 1912, was located at Fort Grant, a geographically isolated former military post four hours from Phoenix on largely unpaved roads. Because the school's leadership positions were plums of political patronage, early superintendents were unqualified and inexperienced, and the facility was rocked by numerous scandals. The lack of any judicial or state oversight exacerbated the situation, creating a "brutal institution" in which children were forced to work in "physically demanding jobs under inhumane conditions" and regularly were beaten, shot, and held in isolation for lengthy periods of time.[3] Investigations of the school conducted in the years just before and just after Gerald Gault arrived there revealed appalling conditions of confinement; in 1972, the Fort Grant Centennial Committee dubbed the Industrial School a "desert Devil's Island."[4]

The facility's horrific conditions made national news in 1952, when two recently-released teenagers sought out Charles C. Bernstein, the then-Chief Judge of the Maricopa County Juvenile Court, in Phoenix. The boys told "hair-raising" stories about their experiences at Fort Grant, including tales of "whippings, blackjackings, and assorted cruelties that were hard to believe."[5] Like many juvenile court judges, Bernstein knew little about the remote facility to which he sent children, but he set his incredulity aside and launched an investigation. This led to an FBI probe and, in turn, the 1953 firing of the then-superintendent and the hiring of Steve Vukcevich, a well-connected local Democrat, who retained his position for the next 20 years.[6]

Vukcevich improved Fort Grant's physical plant and fired the worst-offending correctional staff members.[7] But he clung to the institution's corporal punishment practices and imposed "paramilitary-style" discipline on the youth incarcerated there. Sanctions for misbehavior included razor-strap whippings – or "swats," solitary confinement, food deprivation, and monetary fines.[8] Five years after Vukcevich's appointment, a report by the National Probation and Parole Association (NPPA) condemned these and other institutional policies and practices and made numerous recommendations for reform. These included eliminating the use of corporal punishment, hiring social workers and psychologists,[9] expanding the educational staff to include more certified teachers, and an overall increase in staffing and concomitant relaxation of militaristic movement and other controls, among others.[10]

In 1964, when Gerald Gault arrived at Fort Grant, the Board of Directors of State Institutions for Juveniles released a "Progress Report" on the facility's efforts to comply with the NPPA's recommendations. Although the report, essentially a self-assessment, documented some areas of improvement, the overall picture remained bleak. The Progress Report recommended no expansion of Fort Grant until staffing levels and programming complied with its recommendations, but the average daily population had mushroomed, from 62 boys in 1952–53 to 352 in 1961–62, and the administration had opened several new housing units to accommodate the influx.[11] Although a change in policy mandated that the superintendent approve any disciplinary sanctions "to ensure consistency," the authors of the 1964 report acknowledged that razor strap beatings and the use of isolation continued.[12] Flouting the 1958 report's recommended ratios of 1 social worker for every 30 boys and 1 staff psychologist for every 150, in 1964 the facility employed only 2 social workers for its 392 residents and no psychologists.[13] Youth received no counseling, no case conferences, no psychological testing except IQ and aptitude tests, and no pre-release re-entry services.[14] Family visits were permitted only one time per month, and militaristic population management techniques had decreased but had not been eliminated.[15]

Despite the 1964 report's positive spin, hints of Fort Grant's ongoing troubles seeped through. Regarding the training, morale, and attitudes of staff, it noted:

> A weakness was noted among staff relationships in terms of an inability to identify their scope of function and authority … . As a retraining school for delinquent boys, the Industrial School *has failed to meet the criterion of a treatment oriented institution* and, in concrete terms, it remains doubtful that such qualification can be attained in the immediate future as long as certain social conditions remain unchanged.[16]

This state of affairs festered from June 1964, when Gerald began his purportedly rehabilitative sentence, until the facility finally was converted to an adult prison in 1973. Gault later said that, rather than "retraining" him, Fort Grant taught him "how to be angry, to be mean," and that he spent the next 30 years trying to overcome this legacy.[17]

Sadly, not much changed during that time. In 1986, eight young people committed to the Arizona Department of Juvenile Corrections filed a civil rights class action, alleging excessive force, lengthy solitary confinement, inadequate medical and mental health treatment, and educational deprivations, among other abuses.[18] Even today, Arizona's incarcerated children still are held in solitary confinement, denied essential mental health treatment and subjected to high rates of institutional violence.[19]

Dangerous conditions of confinement persist today

Arizona reflects the situation in the rest of the country, which continues to lock up its most vulnerable youth in antiquated, dangerous, ineffective, and expensive facilities. A 2011 report of the Annie E. Casey Foundation revealed the magnitude of the problem:

> America's heavy reliance on juvenile incarceration is a failed strategy for addressing youth crime … . Correctional confinement exposes incarcerated youth to widespread maltreatment; results in alarming levels of recidivism; incarcerates children who do not pose significant threats to public safety; ignores the emergence of treatment models that produce better outcomes; wastes money with *costs that often exceed $100,000 per young person per year* … .[20]

YouthFirst, an organization dedicated to eliminating juvenile incarceration, offers a graphic description of these facilities: Youth prisons embody facility features common to adult prisons, including large bed capacity (over 30 beds); correctional staff whose main role is to count and cuff youth; locked rooms, cells, or units; razor wire fences; and practices similar to those used in adult prisons, including use of chemical restraints such as pepper spray; mechanical restraints such as leg irons, handcuffs, wrap restraints; hogtying; use of isolation and solitary confinement; and documented instances of physical and sexual violence, physical and verbal abuse, and neglect such as underfeeding, removal of sanitary napkins, and toiletry items.[21]

Even superficially humane facilities, furthermore, inflict substantial harm:

> Removing a young person from his or her family, community, and support networks is traumatic and interrupts normal positive development. Recent research indicates that the vast majority of children who are in trouble with the law will grow out of their misbehavior if they are allowed to transition normally into adulthood. A growing body of research also reveals that community-based support systems are more successful in setting children on the right path and in reducing recidivism – at a fraction of the cost of incarceration.[22]

And so, 50 years after the Supreme Court issued its "Magna Carta for juveniles,"[23] the yawning gap between the "rehabilitative" ideals of juvenile court and the dangerous reality of juvenile prisons remains. Even as the juvenile justice system casts judgment on young people and insists on accountability for lawbreaking behavior, it refuses to demand similar accountability from dangerous, failing juvenile prisons. These abuses persist, furthermore, because youth rarely have access to lawyers after they leave the courtroom. As a result, they continue to be denied the care, treatment, and pathways to productive adulthood that are the asserted ends of their incarceration.

Characteristics of confined youth

America's infatuation with incarceration begins with our children. In 2015, 921,000 youth were arrested,[24] and 57,190 – roughly the population of Greenland – were confined in long-term residential facilities.[25] The U.S. rate of juvenile arrests for violent crimes is only slightly higher than that of most other Western nations, but our juvenile incarceration rate is exponentially greater.[26] More than half of youth in custody are confined due to offenses involving drugs, property, public order violations, and violations of probation, rather than violent crimes.[27]

The gross racial and ethnic disparities that define juvenile incarceration are nothing short of immoral. Black youth are 5.3 times more likely to be detained than Caucasian youth; Native Americans, 3.5 times as likely; and Latinos, twice as likely.[28] These disparities are not attributable to differential crime rates; to the contrary, youth of color are treated more harshly than white youth at every decision-making point along the continuum of system involvement, even when they are charged with similar offenses and have similar prior histories.[29]

Our country's most vulnerable children are also those most likely to be behind bars. Most youth in custody are poor, and many have prior histories in the child welfare system.[30] At least 75 percent have experienced prior "traumatic victimization" and 50 percent have post-traumatic stress disorder (PTSD). Further, "[y]outh in secure juvenile justice settings are at particularly high risk for histories of complex trauma, including poly-victimization, abuse and family violence, and losses that compromise core attachments with caregivers."[31] According to the National Center for Mental Health and Juvenile Justice, approximately 70 percent of young people in the juvenile justice system suffer from mental illness, with 27 percent of these deemed severe and 60 percent having co-occurring substance abuse.[32]

Even those young people without mental health needs are profoundly affected by the fact of adolescence. Normative adolescent maturation continues well into one's twenties, and developmental immaturity significantly affects young people's judgment and decision-making.[33] As a result, young people in custody are less able to understand or exercise their legal rights than adults and more likely to acquiesce to institutional authority figures.[34]

Despite these profound disparities and unmet treatment needs, in 2016 only six states required bi-annual judicial review hearings for incarcerated youth and roughly a dozen jurisdictions routinely continue attorney appointments throughout the length of custodial terms.[35] Even those states in which young people receive extraordinarily long juvenile sentences fail to provide for such accountability and oversight.[36] Yet, post-dispositional review and advocacy are essential to achieving the rehabilitative goals of juvenile court, for without ongoing monitoring and timely intervention, incarcerated youth are unlikely to receive the treatment, care, and services that are the very justification for their commitment to state custody.

Constitutional grounds for post-dispositional right to counsel

Do children have a constitutional right to post-dispositional representation? Although *Gault* locates the right to counsel in adjudicatory hearings in the due process clause, subsequent federal appellate court decisions have extended Sixth Amendment rights to youth in interrogations, waiver proceedings, and direct appeals.[37] As early as 1969, in fact, the Seventh Circuit held that "*Gault* must be construed as incorporating in juvenile court procedures, which may lead to deprivation of liberty, all of the constitutional safeguards of the Fifth and Sixth Amendments to the Constitution of the United States which apply, by operation of the Fourteenth Amendment, in criminal proceedings."[38] It is true that courts have been reluctant to extend a post-sentencing right to counsel to adult inmates, except in direct appeals,[39] in parole revocation proceedings,[40] and in limited situations when they are illiterate or otherwise unable to access the courts.[41] But the developmental immaturity and unique vulnerabilities of adolescents in custody, coupled with the rehabilitative purpose and indeterminate sentencing schemes that characterize most juvenile codes, demand continuous legal representation for incarcerated young people. The constitutional grounds for asserting that right may vary, however, depending on the legal context of the representation. A young person's right to counsel at a parole revocation hearing, for example, may be rooted in different reasoning from his or her right to be represented in a motion for early release from custody.

The Sixth Amendment

The Sixth Amendment guarantees to all criminal defendants the right to "[a]ssistance of counsel for his defense."[42] In *U.S. v. Cronic*,[43] the Supreme Court made clear that "[l]awyers in criminal cases 'are necessities, not luxuries.' Their presence is essential because they are the means through which the other rights of the person on trial are secured."[44] Consistent with this observation, the Court has extended the Sixth Amendment guarantee to all "critical stages" of a criminal case:

> It is central to that principle that in addition to counsel's presence at trial, the accused is guaranteed that he need not stand alone against the State *at any stage of the prosecution, formal or informal, in court or out, where counsel's absence might derogate from the accused's right to a fair trial.*[45]

The Ninth Circuit subsequently fleshed out the meaning of "critical stage."

> First, if failure to pursue strategies or remedies results in a loss of significant rights, then Sixth Amendment protections attach. Second, where skilled counsel would be useful in helping the accused understand the legal confrontation, we find that a critical stage exists. Third, the right to counsel applies if the proceeding tests the merits of the accused's case.[46]

Thus, the Supreme Court also has found competency evaluations,[47] guilty pleas and sentencing proceedings,[48] preliminary hearings,[49] post-indictment interrogations,[50] and any trial that poses a possibility of incarceration to be "critical stages," giving rise to the right to counsel.[51] Each of these decision-making points has a corollary in juvenile court, with a concomitant guarantee of legal representation.

Although the Supreme Court has not yet held any post-sentencing decision to be a "critical stage," the nature of juvenile court dispositions compels Sixth Amendment protections.[52] Because most juvenile commitments are indeterminate and grounded in rehabilitative principles, the actual length of a young person's incarceration is not fixed at the time of sentencing. Instead, projected release dates fluctuate throughout the course of a commitment term according to the youth's behavior, progress in school and treatment programs, and post-release plans. The actual length of a juvenile sentence, then, is not determined at the dispositional hearing but re-calculated repeatedly throughout the commitment term. Since sentencing is a critical phase, so, too, is the entire course of an indeterminate juvenile disposition.

Due Process

The Supreme Court also has used the Due Process clause to extend the right to counsel, albeit conditionally, to adults in contexts other than those traditionally deemed to be "critical stages" of criminal proceedings but which nonetheless implicate a liberty interest, such as probation or parole revocations. In *Gagnon v. Scarpelli,*[53] for example, the Court recognized that "the unskilled or uneducated probationer or parolee may well have difficulty in presenting his version of a disputed set of facts where the presentation requires the examining or cross-examining of witnesses or the offering or dissecting of complex documentary evidence."[54] Fundamental fairness – "the touchstone of due process" – thus requires provision of counsel if the probationer or parolee requests representation on the basis of a

> timely and colorable claim (i) that he has not committed the alleged violation of the conditions upon which he is at liberty; or (ii) that, even if the violation is a matter of public record or is uncontested, there are substantial reasons which justified or mitigated the violation and make revocation inappropriate, and that the reasons are complex or otherwise difficult to develop or present [*pro se*].[55]

This reasoning applies with equal force to virtually every incarcerated adolescent. Their developmental immaturity, cognitive limitations, mental health status, and special education needs render most youth in custody incapable of representing themselves or other youth effectively in revocation hearings or any other judicial or quasi-judicial proceeding.[56] Similar considerations apply in other post-dispositional contexts, too, such as hearings to determine parole eligibility.

The First Amendment

The First Amendment guarantee of access to courts offers another strong constitutional foundation for a right to post-dispositional representation that would permit youth to challenge unlawful conditions of confinement. As early as 1941, the Court struck down a Michigan regulation requiring inmates to seek approval from prison officials before they could file habeas petitions on the ground that the rule impeded judicial access.[57] In subsequent decisions, the Court held that "meaningful access" to the courts required the provision of free transcripts to indigent inmates pursuing appeals[58] and waiver of court fees for those seeking appellate or habeas relief.[59] Regulations prohibiting "jailhouse lawyers" from providing writ-writing and other legal assistance to their fellow inmates were struck down on similar grounds.[60] And, in *Bounds v. Smith,*[61] the Court held that the "fundamental constitutional right of access to the courts requires prison authorities to assist inmates in the preparation and filing of meaningful legal papers by providing prisoners with adequate law libraries or *adequate assistance from persons trained in the law*."[62] *Bounds* also made clear that the existence of a law library was insufficient for illiterate inmates and that specialized prisoner legal services officers, pro bono attorneys, or law students might be necessary to ensure that all inmates had adequate access to the courts.[63]

Almost 20 years later, Lewis v. Casey sharply curtailed the *Bounds* ruling by imposing an "actual injury" requirement on court access claims.[64] In order to prevail, adult inmates now must prove that inadequate legal resources or assistance caused "actual prejudice with respect to contemplated or existing litigation, such as the inability to meet a filing deadline or to present a claim."[65] The Court further limited the right of legal access to challenges to criminal convictions and civil rights violations.[66] In short, *Lewis* makes it impossible for many inmates, even those whose convictions are illegal or who have suffered significant civil rights violations, to pursue judicial remedies. If, as is likely, the inmates lack adequate assistance to assert their legal claims, they may fail to comply with statutes of limitations, filing rules, and other requirements and, so, waive the right to challenge their convictions or conditions of confinement. At that point, although they have incurred "actual" injury, their only recourse is a lawsuit asserting a First Amendment violation, which may lead to injunctive relief or an award of monetary damages but not correct the illegalities they originally sought to challenge.

The *Lewis* strictures are even more limiting for young people than they are for adults. The prevalence of intellectual disabilities and mental illness among incarcerated youth, coupled with their developmental immaturity, significantly impedes their ability to understand and assert their legal rights. Similarly, a "jailhouse lawyer" system provides no meaningful assistance in juvenile facilities, where inmate paralegals also are adolescents. Thus, although they routinely suffer substantial injuries (and, so, would satisfy the demands of *Lewis*), youth in custody are denied meaningful access to the courts. As a result, they remain incarcerated unlawfully or longer than necessary, and unconstitutional conditions of confinement go unchecked.

How, then, can young people assert their right of judicial access in the wake of *Lewis*? A possible answer lies in *John L. v. Adams*,[67] which was decided after *Bounds* but before *Lewis*. There, the Sixth Circuit made clear that "meaningful access" depends on the abilities and limitations of those who seek it, and that neither a law library nor a cadre of "jailhouse lawyers" provides adequate access for incarcerated youth:

> The remedy for a constitutional deficiency in access could not be the same for juveniles as it is for adult prisoners … . "[W]ithout assistance, the students could not make effective use of legal materials. Furthermore, the students' ages, their lack of experience with the criminal system, and their relatively short confinement means that there cannot be a system of writ writers for students who need them."[68]

John L., then, recognized that the developmental and experiential differences which distinguish adolescents from adults compel more robust protections, specifically the provision of lawyers to youth who wish to assert their legal rights. But does the case remain good law in the wake of *Lewis*?

Marsha Levick and Neha Desai have argued convincingly that it does. In the sentencing and custodial interrogation contexts, the Supreme Court's recognition of the unique vulnerabilities associated with developmental immaturity has given rise to a specialized jurisprudence of youth.[69] If the Eighth, Fifth, and Sixth

Amendments require differential interpretation and application when adolescents are involved, so, too, must the right of access to the courts. In fact, even *Lewis* acknowledged that heightened protections, including counsel, may be necessary for inmates who are illiterate, do not speak English, or otherwise cannot obtain meaningful access through law libraries or jailhouse lawyers alone.[70]

National juvenile justice standards

For nearly four decades, national juvenile justice standards and legal scholars have embraced this robust interpretation and agree that children must be afforded counsel at every stage of the delinquency process, from pre-petition to post-disposition.[71] In 1980, the Institute of Judicial Administration and the American Bar Association's *Juvenile Justice Standards* outlined the post-dispositional responsibilities of juvenile defenders:

> If the client has been found to be within the juvenile court's jurisdiction, the lawyer should maintain contact with both the client and the agency or institution involved in the disposition plan in order to ensure that the client's rights are respected and, where necessary, to counsel the client and the client's family concerning the dispositional plan.[72]

The lawyer who represents a client during initial juvenile court proceedings should ordinarily be prepared to represent the client with respect to proceedings to review or modify adjudicative or dispositional orders made during earlier hearings or to pursue any affirmative remedies that may be available to the client under local juvenile court law.[73]

During the 1990s, several reports highlighted the fundamentality of post-dispositional representation. In 1995, the American Bar Association Juvenile Justice Center released *A Call for Justice: An Assessment of Access to Counsel and Quality Representation in Delinquency Proceedings*. The forerunner to dozens of individual state assessments, the report found that over 40 percent of juvenile defenders closed their files at the conclusion of the dispositional hearing and that fewer than a quarter monitored implementation of their clients' treatment plans.[74] The report further concluded that "The failure to maintain representation during the entire period of juvenile court jurisdiction is a serious problem. It means that attorneys do not monitor their clients' progress in programs or institutional placements or assure that the services ordered by courts are actually provided and that conditions in programs and institutions are lawful."[75] Two years later, the National Association of Counsel for Children reached a similar conclusion.[76]

The following decade brought even more urgent calls for post-dispositional access to counsel. In 2005, the Council of Chief Defenders and the National Juvenile Defender Center released the *Ten Core Principles for Providing Quality Indigent Defense Representation through Indigent Defense Delivery Systems*, which require juvenile defense attorneys to "provide[] independent post-conviction monitoring of each child's treatment, placement or program to ensure that rehabilitative needs are met" and to "interven[e] and advoca[te] before the appropriate authority" when necessary.[77] The National Council of Juvenile and Family Court Judges soon followed suit with the *Juvenile Delinquency Guidelines*, which exhort juvenile court judges to "ensure that effective post-disposition review is provided to each delinquent youth as long as the youth is involved in any component of the juvenile justice system."[78] So important is legal representation to the post-disposition review process that the *Guidelines* urge not only the continuing appointment of counsel but also that "the same counsel" should appear at every hearing for the child.[79]

The *Guidelines'* emphasis on mandatory review hearings is essential, as such hearings compel the provision of post-dispositional representation and hold prison officials accountable to the court. During these hearings, the court evaluates the young person's adjustment to and treatment within the custodial setting. The judge can determine whether the child is receiving the services ordered during disposition, such as anger management or trauma counseling or speech therapy; assess the effectiveness of various programs; and make adjustments to the disposition, if necessary. Review hearings also provide an opportunity to promote and eliminate obstacles to successful re-entry and work as an important safeguard against institutional abuse. Finally, compulsory review hearings compel continuing legal representation for youth. In jurisdictions where hearings are not routinely held, children in custody rarely have access to counsel.

Finally, in 2012, the National Juvenile Defender Center released the *National Juvenile Defense Standards*, which also require post-dispositional representation and further define the obligations of attorneys at this stage by detailing the wide range of legal issues faced by youth once they leave the courtroom.[80] In each of these contexts, the "guiding hand of counsel" is essential to protect the well-being and due process rights of system-involved youth.[81]

What can lawyers do?

A host of legal problems confront children in custody, although without representation most youth cannot and do not assert their legal rights. To address this problem in New Jersey, the Rutgers Law School Criminal and Youth Justice Clinic and Children's Justice Clinic launched a post-dispositional representation project in 2009 that to date has provided legal representation to nearly 600 young clients. The project's work encompasses many of the legal issues that might arise in any post-dispositional practice.

Combat abuse

Among the most compelling reasons for post-dispositional access to counsel is the prevention of further trauma to and abuse of confined youth. Clients of the Rutgers clinics have suffered lost eyesight, fractured jaws,[82] fractured orbital bones, and lost teeth while in custody. In several instances, the young people were restrained in handcuffs and on the ground when these injuries occurred. In another, well-publicized incident, a detained Pennsylvania boy died after guards pinned him down in a lengthy four-point restraint.[83]

Unfortunately, these types of injuries are all too common within the nation's juvenile facilities, which often cultivate a systemic culture of "rampant and extreme" violence and abuse.[84] The U.S. Department of Justice has conducted numerous investigations of juvenile facilities around the country and found unconstitutional levels of violence in many.[85] A 2010 national survey by the Office of Juvenile Justice and Delinquency Prevention found that 38 percent of all youth who are confined fear being attacked and 22 percent of youth fear being attacked by staff.[86] The number is higher (42 percent) for youth who are in secure facilities.[87] Similarly, the Annie E. Casey Foundation's *No Place for Kids* report[88] found conclusive evidence of system-wide mistreatment in 42 of the 50 states.[89]

In addition to physical violence, sexual abuse within juvenile prisons is pervasive. A 2010 Department of Justice study on sexual victimization in juvenile corrections facilities included self-reports from more than 26,000 youth, nearly 12 percent of whom had been sexually abused at least once in the previous year.[90] In some facilities, as many as 30 percent of confined youth reported sexual abuse.[91] Because a high percentage of girls in the juvenile justice system have been sexually assaulted prior to their confinement and suffer from PTSD, the subsequent re-traumatization of institutional abuse has profoundly harmful, often life-long consequences.[92]

Access to counsel for these young people is critically important because most juvenile justice systems are deliberately opaque. In 2007, the *Texas Observer* reported that youth incarcerated in Texas Youth Commission facilities had submitted 750 complaints of sexual misconduct by administrators and employees over the previous seven years.[93] Reporters described the cover-up that allowed this pervasive victimization to continue:

> Even when the kids did file complaints, they knew it wouldn't do them much good. Staff covered for each other, grievance processes were sabotaged, and evidence was frequently destroyed. Officials in Austin ignored what they heard, and in the very rare instances when staff were fired and their cases referred to local prosecutors those prosecutors usually refused to act. Not one employee of the Texas Youth Committee during that six-year period was sent to prison for raping the children in his or her care.[94]

This culture of complicit secrecy, however, is difficult to sustain when incarcerated youth have legal representation. When lawyers visit facilities regularly, maintain frequent telephone and written communication with their clients, and obtain and review institutional records, abuses quickly come to light and behavioral patterns emerge. In addition, the presence of attorneys in the facilities has a chilling effect on the types of behavior that run rampant behind closed doors.

When incidents of physical or sexual violence do occur, attorneys can take a number of steps to protect individual clients and achieve systemic change. These include, among others, advocating for essential medical and mental health treatment for injuries or trauma sustained during the incident; guiding the client through the institutional grievance process, which is a necessary predicate (and, for unrepresented youth, often an insurmountable barrier) to seeking judicial remedies under federal and state law;[95] seeking a change in housing unit or facility to protect the client from further abuse or retaliation; reporting the incident to the appropriate state oversight or investigative authorities; in the case of sexual abuse or inappropriate sexual contact or conduct, assisting the client to submit a complaint pursuant to the Prison Rape Elimination Act;[96] filing notices of claim to protect the client's ability to pursue civil legal remedies; and either representing or referring the client for representation in civil litigation pursuant to 42 U.S.C. § 1983 or relevant state law.

Combating solitary confinement

The United Nations has declared solitary confinement, usually defined as isolation in a small cell, with little to no human contact, education, recreation, or programming for 22–24 hours per day, to be torture.[97] The reasons for this are clear. Even adults held in isolation for short periods of time engage in self-mutilation, suffer emotional breakdowns, and experience overall deterioration of mental and physical health, increased aggression and rage, PTSD and depression.[98] Because adolescents still are developing mentally, emotionally, and physically, the use of isolation in juvenile facilities is even more damaging.[99] Solitary confinement further harms youth by exacerbating pre-existing mental illness, increasing suicide rates, denying access to education and rehabilitative programming, and stunting development due to lack of exercise and stimulation.[100] Indeed, the American Academy of Child and Adolescent Psychiatry opposes the use of isolation for youth, stating that "the potential psychiatric consequences of prolonged solitary confinement are well recognized and include depression, anxiety and psychosis. Due to their developmental vulnerability, juvenile offenders are at particular risk of such adverse reactions."[101]

Recognizing these dangers, a number of states have taken steps to reduce or eliminate solitary confinement in juvenile facilities.[102] Nevertheless, youth in many states spend days, weeks, and months in isolation.[103] Its use often is masked by euphemistic statutory or regulatory language. For example, Troy D., a mentally ill 16-year-old client of the Rutgers clinic, was isolated for over 6½ months, yet the term "isolation" never appeared in the facilities' records. Instead, he at different times was described as being in "segregation," "pre-hearing room restriction," "medical custody," "protective custody," "behavior modification unit," and "close watch." Regardless of the terminology, however, the result was identical: he was confined to a 7 x 7 foot cell for 22–24 hours a day, without school, programming, and, frequently, exercise; visits from mental health staff; or contact with any human being other than correctional officers.[104]

Troy's abuse came to light only because he had an attorney who visited him in the facility, reviewed his records, and took a number of steps on his behalf. These included a successful motion for modification of sentence, which led to Troy's transfer to a psychiatric hospital, and the filing of a federal civil rights suit, which ultimately led to a substantial monetary settlement and compensatory education services. And, because it was the first time in recent memory that the State of New Jersey was forced to compensate a juvenile inmate, the settlement spurred legislation banning the use of punitive isolation in juvenile prisons. Then-Governor Chris Christie, not generally considered a champion of civil rights for the incarcerated, signed the bill into law in August 2015.[105]

Reduce lengths of stay

Longer periods of incarceration do nothing to reduce recidivism and may well lead to higher rates of re-offending.[106] Lengthy custodial terms also are enormously expensive[107] and subject young people to harmful separations from their families and more difficult transitions back to the community, with potentially lifelong negative ramifications. For these reasons, legal advocacy for incarcerated youth often involves efforts on several fronts to reduce lengths of stay.

Early release and parole

As noted above, most juvenile dispositions are indeterminate, with the authority to determine how long a child remains in custody vested in the juvenile court, the placement agency, or, in a few states, the State Parole Board.[108] Decisions to release young people before the end of their placement terms generally are determined by the youth's institutional behavioral and programming history, statements of remorse and regret for their crimes, and outside support systems and post-release plans.[109] Lawyers for incarcerated youth help their clients gather the necessary documents, formulate their own presentations to the decision-maker, develop and implement release plans, and prepare for parole hearings.[110] In addition, if early release is denied, the attorney can pursue any available administrative or judicial appellate remedies.

Probation, parole, and aftercare revocation hearings

Many youth in juvenile prisons are there as a result of violations of probation, parole, or "aftercare" supervision.[111] Extensive and complicated release conditions are difficult to follow and frequently lead to release revocation hearings. Zealous legal representation at these hearings can change the trajectory of a young person's life. Often, the charged violations are "technical" in nature, such as failure to attend school, disobeying curfew, violating home rules, or failure to report to the probation or parole officer. An effective advocate puts the violations in context, presents alternatives to incarceration to the fact-finder, and engages in persuasive advocacy. As a result, young people are released sooner, with better outcomes for themselves and their communities.

Modifications of dispositional orders

A detailed dispositional order is a powerful tool for post-dispositional juvenile defenders. Well-crafted orders set forth the reasons for the commitment; specify the educational, medical, mental health, and rehabilitative services the youth should receive while in custody; and, if possible, direct the placement agency to provide those services.[112] Lawyers for incarcerated youth monitor the agency's compliance with these orders and, if necessary, seek judicial enforcement or modification. As discussed above, a child's positive disciplinary record and successful completion of the court-ordered programming can serve as grounds for a motion for early release from custody, while an agency's ongoing failure to provide those services might give rise to a modification of the disposition or transfer to a more appropriate setting. In one Rutgers case, the 18-year-old client had a lifelong history of mental illness but had received no meaningful treatment during her four years in custody, despite a dispositional order recommending intensive counseling. As a result, she incurred numerous disciplinary violations, spent over one year in various forms of isolation, and was the victim of multiple assaults by correctional staff. Because clinic students visited the client frequently and closely monitored her status, they were able to write a compelling and ultimately successful motion to modify the disposition from incarceration to probation and placement in a residential treatment facility. The client stabilized and transitioned to "independent living" long before expiration of her custodial term.

Changes in classification or housing assignment

Apart from cases involving solitary confinement or administrative segregation, courts are reluctant to interfere with institutional classification or housing assignment decisions. Nevertheless, when an incarcerated youth is placed in an inappropriate setting or is assigned an unduly restrictive security classification, his or her lawyer can provide support and advocacy on numerous fronts: helping the client prepare and submit an institutional grievance, which is often the sole means of challenging such decisions; assisting the client in pursuing any available administrative appeals; engaging in informal discussions with agency personnel; and, in some cases, pursuing judicial remedies.[113]

Disciplinary hearings

Like classification decisions, institutional disciplinary violations can lead to substantial changes in the length and conditions of confinement for youth. Nevertheless, although young people do have certain procedural protections in disciplinary hearings, these do not include the right to counsel. In *Wolff v. McDonnell*,[114] which challenged disciplinary procedures in adult prisons, the United States Supreme Court balanced the correctional considerations implicated in disciplinary decisions against the need to protect inmates from irrational or retaliatory decision-making. The Court determined that, at least in cases involving "major" discipline (e.g., the threat of loss of good time credits or imposition of segregation), due process requires written notice of charges at least 24 hours before a disciplinary hearing, a fair hearing, and a written decision by the fact-finder. The Court also identified several qualified procedural protections: the right to present both witnesses and documentary evidence when not "unduly hazardous to institutional safety or correctional goals," and, when the inmate is "illiterate" or the case involves "complex" issues, the right to representation by another inmate or a staff member.[115]

Setting aside the question of whether the *Wolff* procedures are adequate for adult inmates, incarcerated young people do not have the cognitive capacity, the reading and analytical skills, or the experience necessary to represent themselves effectively – or, for that matter, other youth – in disciplinary hearings. Similarly, "representation" by agency staff members is fraught with potential conflicts. For these reasons, youth in custody need lawyers to help them prepare for disciplinary hearings, even if the lawyers cannot participate. Lawyers can help their clients identify witnesses or relevant documents; obtain those documents and ensure the witnesses' appearance at the hearing; draft witness examinations, cross-examinations, the client's statement, and legal arguments; navigate the administrative appeal process after an adverse decision; and, when possible and practicable, challenge the hearing officer's decision in court.

Access to education

Incarcerated children enjoy the same educational rights as their non-incarcerated peers, regardless of whether they are in general or special education.[116] Under federal law, furthermore, children who have been classified for special education are entitled to additional protections, including an Individualized Education Plan (IEP), even if they are placed in a secure facility.[117] Despite these robust protections, and although approximately one-third of incarcerated youth are in need of special education, juvenile correctional agencies often fail to develop effective IEPs, implement those that are in place, or even follow bedrock laws governing the number of instructional hours children must receive or the content of that instruction.[118] These failings have profoundly negative consequences. For example, children with special needs who do not receive essential educational and therapeutic services are more likely than their peers to engage in disruptive behavior and, as a result, to receive disciplinary charges, be placed in solitary confinement, and suffer additional educational disruptions.[119]

When incarcerated youth have lawyers, however, they can vigorously assert their educational rights. Attorneys request IEP meetings, in which they advocate for the development of an educational plan that meets the educational needs of their clients; monitor compliance with the IEPs; pursue due process administrative and, ultimately, judicial remedies should the IEP fall short or the agency not follow it; and, for clients with certain disabilities, utilize the Americans with Disabilities Act to obtain necessary accommodations. As a result of such advocacy, the Rutgers clinic secured a Braille computer and adaptive sports equipment for a blind incarcerated 17-year-old client, succeeded in changing the facility's disciplinary practices to take into account his disability, and ensured that the facility correctional and educational staff were adequately trained in helping him navigate the facility and its classrooms. In order to compel placement agencies to afford every child in their care a high-quality and appropriate education, lawyers monitor their clients' progress in school, seek out educational testing for those who are struggling, ensure that clients in high school receive the necessary number and type of credits to graduate, and advocate for access to college or vocational courses for clients who have completed secondary school.

Mental health and medical treatment

Juvenile court judges often commit young people to state custody because previous attempts to engage them in psychological or psychiatric treatment have failed. Mental health services in many juvenile corrections facilities, however, are either woefully inadequate or non-existent. Without access to an attorney, youth in custody fall victim to these shortcomings and do not receive the treatment that is the raison d'être of their incarceration. Post-disposition representation ensures that what the court intended actually occurs. Attorneys engage in informal advocacy with the correctional agency or mental health service provider to obtain necessary treatment, help the client navigate the institutional grievance process for that purpose, or, if circumstances at the facility inhibit or prevent access to the treatment, advocate for release and to obtain appropriate services in the community. Similar efforts ensure access to essential medical care.

Family engagement

Like juvenile prisons in many states, those in New Jersey are located in rural regions that are not serviced by public transportation and are far from the urban areas in which their wards reside. Families of these young people frequently are poor and lack the means to visit their children regularly. As a result, many Rutgers clients do not have any visitors throughout the entirety of what are often multi-year commitments.

A 2013 Vera Institute of Justice study examined the effects of family visitation on incarcerated juveniles.[120] The researchers concluded that youth who see their families performed better, academically and behaviorally, while in custody.[121] Another study evaluated the correlation between depressive symptoms and the number of visitors incarcerated youth received and concluded that "[the] positive effects of visitation on depressive symptoms were linear, such that the more parental visits a youth received, the stronger the rate of decline in depressive symptoms over the course of the first two months of incarceration."[122] On the other hand, broken connections with family impede young people's successful return to their communities.

Some placement agencies also raise insurmountable barriers to visitation, such as requiring visitors to provide social security numbers (impossible for undocumented immigrants) or prohibiting visits by anyone with a felony record. Attorneys for incarcerated youth can advocate for transportation assistance, waivers of onerous visitation prohibitions or policy changes, and creative use of technology like videoconferencing to facilitate communication when in-person visits are not possible.

Limit collateral consequences

Despite the allegedly rehabilitative purposes of juvenile court intervention, numerous collateral consequences attach to delinquency adjudications. Traditional confidentiality protections, intended to permit children to learn from their mistakes and grow into productive adulthood unencumbered by their juvenile court involvement, eroded throughout the 1990s and early 2000s, giving rise to widespread information sharing and stigmatization of young people.[123] Youth who have been adjudicated or even merely arrested are suspended or expelled from their schools via expansive "zero tolerance" policies covering incidents that occur both on and off school grounds.[124] Others who attempt to return to school following a period of incarceration confront insurmountable obstacles, including the refusal of many schools to accept credits earned in correctional facilities; local policies shunting previously-incarcerated youth to "alternative" school settings and evening programs intended for adults; and other exclusionary practices.[125] Even those who successfully complete high school confront new barriers when they attempt to attend college. For example, the Common Application requires students to provide information about delinquency adjudications.[126] Many system-involved youth cannot obtain employment, due to the public availability of juvenile records and also to the failure of correctional agencies to afford them vocational training.[127]

Children with delinquency adjudications and their families routinely are excluded or evicted from public housing, leaving many homeless when they are released from custody.[128] Immigrant youth face possible deportation as a result of the actions that gave rise to their adjudications, even if they have never visited their country of origin and have no family members there.[129] In many states, adjudications of delinquency for certain offenses lead to loss of driving privileges, which in turn can adversely affect young people's ability to maintain employment or attend school.[130]

Given these wide-ranging and destructive consequences, it is essential for young people to pursue every available means of preventing disclosure of their juvenile records. Remedies are creatures of state law and generally take two forms: sealing, in which the records are shielded from public view but still maintained by the relevant agency; and the more protective expungement, which historically meant actual destruction of records but today may also connote a process similar to sealing. Sealing or expungement of juvenile records is possible in most states, but the breadth and availability of these protections varies widely. Young people often do not know that these processes exist and lack the knowledge and skills necessary to pursue them. Here, too, they need the "guiding hand of counsel" to ensure that, if eligible, they are accorded the benefit of these confidentiality protections.

Sex offender registration

Among the most draconian consequences of juvenile adjudications is the application of sex offender registration and notification laws to youth. Young people in 38 states are compelled to register, and some of these also are subject to community notification requirements.[131] Those on the registry suffer social stigmatization, ostracizing, and depression. They are

> [S]hot at, beaten, even murdered; many are repeatedly threatened with violence. Some young people have to post signs stating "sex offender lives here" in the windows of their homes; others have to carry drivers' licenses with "sex offender" printed on them in bright orange capital letters. [They] are sometimes denied access to education because residency restriction laws prevent them from being in or near a school … . [They] despair of ever finding employment, even while they are burdened with mandatory fees that can reach into the hundreds of dollars on an annual basis … . [They] often cannot find housing that meets residency restriction rules, meaning that they and their families … often experience periods of homelessness. Families of youth offenders also confront enormous obstacles in living together … because registrants are prohibited from living with other children. Finally, the impacts of being a youth offender subject to registration are multi-generational … . The children of youth sex offenders often cannot be dropped off at school by their parent. They may be banned by law from hosting a birthday party involving other children at their home; and they are often harassed and ridiculed by their peers for their parents' long-past transgressions.[132]

Clients of the Rutgers clinics have experienced many of these ordeals. An 18-year-old was legally prohibited from returning to his family's federally-subsidized apartment following his release. Another was forced to leave the apartment he shared with his wife and infant son after the police circulated flyers containing his photo, name, address, and offense throughout the apartment complex, leading neighbors to demand his eviction. A third lost his dream job when his ankle monitor malfunctioned, alerting his employer to his past history. All of these young men became homeless for no rational reasons and continued to spiral downward.

Post-dispositional advocacy can ameliorate, if not prevent, the profound harms associated with juvenile sex offender registration.[133] In some states, lawyers can help young people challenge their registration "tier" assignments, which govern the levels of restriction and public notification to which they are subjected. At least 20 states, furthermore, either terminate juvenile registration when the youth reaches a certain age or permit juvenile registrants to petition the court for removal.[134] Legal representation is essential in these proceedings.

Re-entry

Upon release, youth often face numerous challenges, including the barriers to housing, school enrollment, employment, and parole compliance discussed earlier in this chapter. Effective post-dispositional advocacy continues throughout this transitional period to help clients overcome hurdles that can seem insurmountable if tackled alone.

Conclusion

Fifty years after *In re Gault*, a large gap exists between the "rehabilitative" ideals of juvenile court and the reality experienced by youth once they leave the courtroom. Incarcerated youth face numerous and complex post-disposition legal challenges, which they are unable to successfully navigate without an attorney. The combination of dangerous facilities, the vulnerabilities of adolescence, and the demographics of confined youth is further exacerbated by the lack of access to post-dispositional counsel. The time is ripe to fulfill the promise of *Gault*, guarantee access to counsel for all young people in custody, and ensure that no more children like Gerald Gault are exiled to a "desert Devil's Island."

Notes

1 In re Gault, 387 U.S. 1, 36–37 (1967) (emphasis added).
2 *Id.* (quoting Powell v. Alabama, 287 U.S. 45, 69 (1932)).
3 Mona Lynch, Sunbelt Justice: Arizona and The Transformation of American Punishment 29 (Stanford Law Books, 2010) [hereinafter *Sunbelt Justice*].
4 *Id.*at 29.
5 *Reasonable Punishment?,* Time Magazine (Mar. 10, 1952).
6 Lynch, Sunbelt Justice, *supra* note 3, at 29.
7 *Id.*
8 *Id.*
9 Nat'l Parole & Probation Ass'n, Correctional Services in Arizona (1958).
10 *Id.*
11 Bd. of Dirs. of State Insts. for Juveniles, Ariz. State Indus. Sch., Fort Grant, & Good Shepherd School of Girls, Phoenix, Ariz. Progress Report (1964).
12 *Id.*
13 *Id.*
14 *Id.*
15 *Id.*
16 *Id.* (emphasis added).
17 Peter Cahill & Lisa Pferdeort, In the Matter of gerald gault 51 Years Later, https://www.nawj.org/uploads/pdf/conferences/CLE/Gerald%20Gault%20NAWJ%20%2051%20Years%20Materials.pdf. (last visited Dec. 22, 2017).
18 *See* Sixth Amended Complaint, Johnson v. Upchurch, No. CIV-86–195, TUC-RMB (D. Ariz. April 9, 1990).
19 *See* Amy Silverman, *Warrior Dad: A Father's Journey into Arizona's Flawed Juvenile Justice System*, Phoenix New Times (June 7, 2017), http://www.phoenixnewtimes.com/news/son-threatened-donald-trump-could-warrior-dad-save-boy-from-adjc-9392931 (last visited Dec. 22, 2017).
20 Richard A. Mendel, the Maltreatment of Youth in United States Juvenile Correction Facilities, An Update 2 (2015), https://www.ncmhjj.com/wp-content/uploads/2015/07/aecf-maltreatmentyouthuscorrections-2015.pdf (last visited Dec. 22, 2017). In 2016, the United States had at least 80 youth prisons in use that are over 100 years old.

21 Youth First Initiative, http://www.youthfirstinitiative.org/thefacts/# (last visited Sept. 10, 2017).

22 W. Hayward burns Institute, Stemming the Rising Tide: Racial and Ethnic Disparities in youth incarceration and strategies for Change 2 (2016), http://www.burnsinstitute.org/wp-content/uploads/2016/05/Stemming-the-Rising-Tide_FINAL.pdf (last visited Dec. 22, 2017).

23 Letter from Chief Justice Earl Warren to Justice Abe Fortas (Mar. 17, 1967) (on file as part of the Abe Fortas Papers (MS 858), Manuscripts and Archives, Yale University Archives, Box 36), http://drs.library.yale.edu/HLTransformer/HLTransServlet?stylename=yul.ead2002.xhtml.xsl&pid=mssa:ms.0858&query=Fortas&clear-stylesheet-cache=yes&hlon=yes&big=&adv=&filter=&hitPageStart=1&sortFields=&view=all#ref11 (last visited Aug. 22, 2017).

24 Charles Puzzanchera, Office of Juvenile Justice and Delinquency Prevention, Juvenile Arrests 2015 (2015), https://www.ojjdp.gov/ojstatbb/crime/qa05101.asp (last visited Dec. 22, 2017).

25 Sarah Hockenberry et al., Office of Juvenile Justice and Delinquency Prevention, Juvenile Residential Facility Census 2012: Selected Findings (Mar. 2015), http://www.ojjdp.gov/pubs/247207.pdf (last visited Dec. 22, 2017).

26 Melissa Sickmund, Nat'l Ctr. for Juvenile Justice, Juvenile Residential Facility Census, 2012: Special Findings (2015), http://www.ncjj.org/pdf/247207.pdf (last visited Dec. 22, 2017).

27 National Center for Juvenile Justice, *Easy Access to the Census of Juveniles in Residential Placement* (2013), http://www.ojjdp.gov/ojstatbb/ezacjrp/ (last visited Sept. 12, 2017).

28 *Id.; see, e.g.*, Robin Walker Sterling, *Fundamental Unfairness: In re Gault and the Road Not Taken*, 72 Md. L. Rev. 607, 661 (2013); Kristin Henning, *Criminalizing Normal Adolescent Behavior in Communities of Color: The Role of Prosecutors in Juvenile Justice Reform,* 98 Cornell L. Rev. 383, 383–461 (2013).

29 *See Racial Inequality in Youth Sentencing*, The Campaign for the Fair Sentencing of Youth, http://fairsentencingofyouth.org/the-issue/advocacy-resource-bank/racial-inequality-in-youth-sentencing (last visited Sept. 10, 2017).

30 The federal Office of Juvenile Justice and Delinquency Prevention cites both poverty and child welfare involvement as leading risk factors for delinquency. *See* Michael Shader, Office of Juvenile Justice and Delinquency Prevention, Risk Factors for Delinquency: An Overview 4 (Jan. 2004), https://www.ncjrs.gov/pdffiles1/ojjdp/frd030127.pdf (last visited Dec. 22, 2017).

31 Jessica Feierman & Lauren Fine, trauma and resilience: a new look at legal advocacy for children in the juvenile justice and child welfare systems 4 (Juvenile Law Center, 2014) (internal citations omitted), http://jlc.org/resources/publications/trauma-and-resilience (last visited Dec. 22, 2017).

32 Jennie L. Shufelt & Joseph J. Cocozza, Nat'l Ctr. for Mental Health and Juvenile Justice, Research and Program Brief, Youth With Mental Health Disorders in the Juvenile Justice System: Results from a Multi-State Prevalence Survey 2, 4 (2006), http://www.ncmhjj.com/wp-content/uploads/2015/02/2006_Youth_with_Mental_Health_Disorders_in_the_Juvenile_Justice_System.pdf. In New Jersey, for example, children prosecuted in juvenile court can receive a sentence of up to 20 years. *See* N.J.S.A. § 2A:4A–44(d).

33 *See, e.g.*, Elizabeth Scott & Thomas Grisso, *The Evolution of Adolescence: A Developmental Perspective on Juvenile Justice Reform,* 88 J. Crim. L. & Criminology 137 (1997); Dustin Albert & Laurence Steinberg, *Judgment and Decision-Making in Adolescence*, 21 Journal of Research on Adolescence 211 (2011); Laurence Steinberg & Elizabeth Scott, *Less Guilty by Reason of Adolescence,* 58 Am. Psychol. 1009 (2003); *see also* Marsha Levick & Neha Desai, *Still Waiting: The Elusive Quest to Ensure Juveniles a Constitutional Right to Counsel at All Stages of the Juvenile Court Process,* 60 Rutgers L. Rev. 175, 191–92 (2007); Laura Cohen, *Freedom's Road:*

Youth, Parole, and the Promise of Graham v. Florida and Miller v. Alabama, 35 CARDOZO L. REV. 1031, 1043–48 (2014).

34 Thomas Grisso et al., *Juveniles' Competence to Stand Trial: A Comparison of Adolescents' and Adults' Capacities as Trial Defendants*, 27 LAW & HUM. BEHAVIOR 333 (2003); Thomas Grisso, *Juvenile's Capacities to Waive Miranda Rights: An Empirical Analysis*, 68 CAL. L. REV. 1134, 1152 (1980) (only 20.9 percent of juveniles, compared with 42.3 percent of adults, understood all four *Miranda* warnings; similarly, 55.3 percent of juveniles, compared with 23.1 percent of adults, did not comprehend any of the warnings); *see* Levick & Desai, *supra* note 33, at 192–93.

35 NAT'L JUVENILE DEFENDER CTR., ACCESS DENIED: A NATIONAL SNAPSHOT OF STATE'S FAILURE TO PROTECT CHILDREN'S RIGHT TO COUNSEL (May 2017).

36 In New Jersey, for example, juvenile courts can impose sentences of up to 20 years, yet the Juvenile Code mandates neither regular review hearings nor ongoing Public Defender representation. *See* N.J.S.A. 2A:4A-20 *et seq.*

37 *See, e.g.*, Murray v. Earle, 334 F. App'x 602 (5th Cir. 2009) (unpublished opinion applying Sixth Amendment analysis to juvenile case); Machacek v. Hofbauer, 213 F.3d 947 (6th Cir. 2000) (applying Sixth Amendment analysis to juvenile interrogation); Deshawn E. by Charlotte E. v. Safir, 156 F.3d 340, 349 (2d Cir. 1998) (assuming that Sixth Amendment protections apply in delinquency proceedings); Bills by Bills v. Homer Consol. Sch. Dist. No. 33-C, 959 F. Supp. 507, 514 (N.D. Ill. 1997) (impliedly acknowledging Sixth Amendment application to juvenile proceedings); United States v. Myers, 66 F.3d 1364, 1370 (4th Cir. 1995) (applying Sixth Amendment protections to waiver proceedings); John L. v. Adams, 969 F.2d 228, 237 (6th Cir. 1992) ("[T]here is an independent constitutional right to counsel for juvenile appeals that is grounded in the Sixth Amendment's right to counsel."); United States v. M.I.M., 932 F.2d 1016, 1018 (1st Cir. 1991) (juvenile right to counsel on first direct appeal located in Sixth Amendment).

38 Reed v. Duter, 416 F.2d 744, 749 (7th Cir. 1969).

39 *See* Evitts v. Lucey, 469 U.S. 387 (1985); Douglas v. California, 372 U.S. 353 (1963).

40 Gagnon v. Scarpelli, 411 U.S. 778 (1973).

41 Bounds v. Smith, 430 U.S. 817 (1977).

42 U.S. CONST. amend. VI.

43 United States v. Cronic, 466 U.S. 648 (1984).

44 *Id.* at. 653–54 (internal citations omitted).

45 U.S. v. Wade, 388 U.S. 218, 226 (1967) (emphasis added). *Cf.* United States v. Ash, 413 U.S. 300 (1973) (no right to counsel at photographic arrays).

46 Menefield v. Borg, 881 F.2d 696, 698–99 (9th Cir. 1989).

47 Estelle v. Smith, 451 U.S. 454 (1981).

48 Mempa v. Rhay, 389 U.S. 128 (1967).

49 White v. Maryland, 373 U.S. 59 (1963) (when defendant entered guilty plea at preliminary hearing, the hearing was a "critical stage"); Coleman v. Alabama, 399 U.S. 1 (1970).

50 Massiah v. United States, 377 U.S. 201 (1964); Miranda v. Arizona, 384 U.S. 436 (1966) (held that the right to counsel attaches in pre-indictment custodial interrogations as well).

51 Argersinger v. Hamlin, 407 U.S. 25 (1972).

52 *See* Levick & Desai, *supra* note 33, at 188–90.

53 Gagnon v. Scarpelli, 411 U.S. 771 (1973); *cf.* Morrissey v. Brewer, 408 U.S. 471 (1972) (holding that Due Process clause applies to parole revocation hearings but not reaching the question of the right to counsel).

54 411 U.S. 771, at 787 (1973).

55 *Id.* at 790.

56 Some states have created a statutory right to counsel in parole and probation revocation matters. *See, e.g.*, D.C. SUP. CT. JUV. R. 32(h)(3); McKinney's Family Court Act,

N.Y Fam. Ct. Act § 360.3(4)(1983); Juvenile Justice Act of 1977, Wash Rev. Code Ann § 13.40.210(4)(a)(2014). If the case involves an administrative rather than judicial hearing, however, representation generally is not provided to indigent youth. *See, e.g.*, N.J.S.A. § 30:4–123.63 (1995).

57 Ex parte Hull, 312 U.S. 546 (1941).

58 *See* Griffin v. Illinois, 351 U.S. 12, 20 (1956).

59 *See* Burns v. Ohio, 360 U.S. 252, 257 (1959); Smith v. Bennett, 365 U.S. 708 (1961).

60 *See* Johnson v. Avery, 393 U.S. 483 (1969) (assistance with writs and appeals); Wolff v. McDonnell, 418 U.S. 539, 577–80 (1974) (civil rights actions).

61 Bounds v. Smith, 430 U.S. 817 (1977).

62 *Id.* at 828 (emphasis added).

63 *Id.* at 823 (citing Johnson v. Avery, 393 U.S. 483, 502 (1969)).

64 Lewis v. Casey, 518 U.S. 343 (1996).

65 *Id.* at 348.

66 *Id.* at 355.

67 John L. v. Adams, 969 F.2d 228 (6th Cir. 1992).

68 *Id.*, (internal citation omitted). The *John L.* injunction remains in place today, and states within the Sixth Circuit have failed to provide for access to counsel for incarcerated youth.

69 *See* Haley v. Ohio, 332 U.S. 596 (1948); Roper v. Simmons, 543 U.S. 551 (2005); Graham v. Florida, 560 U.S. 48 (2010); J.D.B. v. North Carolina, 131 S. Ct. 2394, 2403 (2011); Miller v. Alabama, 132 S. Ct. 2455, 2468 (2012).

70 Lewis v. Casey, 518 U.S. at 387. This is in keeping with a long line of pre-*Lewis* federal appellate cases that afforded counsel to disadvantaged or disabled inmates on the ground that legal materials alone were insufficient to assure meaningful access to the courts. *See, e.g.*, Ward v. Kort, 762 F.2d 856, 858 (10th Cir.1985) (psychiatric patients); Cruz v. Hauck, 627 F.2d 710, 721 n.21 (5th Cir. 1980) (non-English speaking or illiterate inmates); Hadix v. Johnson, 694 F.Supp. 259, 288 (E.D. Mich. 1988) (illiterate and segregated prisoners); United States ex rel. Para–Prof'l Law Clinic v. Kane, 656 F. Supp. 1099, 1105 (E.D.Pa.) (illiterate and segregated inmates), *aff'd without opinion*, 835 F.2d 285 (3d Cir.1987), *cert. denied*, 485 U.S. 993 (1988); Smith v. Bounds, 610 F.Supp. 597 (E.D. N.C. 1985) (illiterate and segregated inmates), *subsequent order entered*, 657 F.Supp. 1322 (E.D.N.C.1986), *aff'd*, 813 F.2d 1299 (4th Cir.1987), *aff'd on reh'g*, 841 F.2d 77 (4th Cir.) (*en banc*), *cert. denied*, 488 U.S. 869 (1988). None of these cases has been overruled or explicitly rejected post-*Lewis*.

71 *See, e.g.*, Nat'l Juvenile Defender Cent. & Nat'l Legal Aid & Defender Ass'n, Ten Core Principles for Providing Quality Delinquency Representation Through Public Defense Delivery Systems (2d ed., 2008), http://njdc.info/wp-content/uploads/2013/11/10-Core-Principles.pdf; Nat'l Juvenile Defender Ctr., National Juvenile Defense Standards (2012), http://njdc.info/wp-content/uploads/2013/09/NationalJuvenileDefenseStandards2013.pdf; National Council of Juvenile and Family Court Judges, *Juvenile Delinquency Guidelines: Improving Court Practice in Juvenile Delinquency Cases* 25 (Mar. 1, 2005), https://www.ncjfcj.org/resource-library/publications/juvenile-delinquency-guidelines-improving-court-practice-juvenile (last visited Sept. 15, 2017) [hereinafter *Improving Court*]; American Bar Ass'n, IJA-ABA Juvenile Justice Standards, Standards Relating to Counsel for Private Parties 10.1 https://www.americanbar.org/content/dam/aba/publications/criminal_justice_standards/JJ/JJ_Standards_Counsel_for_Private_Parties.authcheckdam.pdf (last visited Sept. 15, 2017) [hereinafter Private Parties]; Laura Cohen, *Extend the Guiding Hand: Incarcerated Youth, Law School Clinics, and Expanding Access to Counsel*, 17 U. Pa. J. L. & Soc. Change 401 (2014); Sue Burrell, *Contracts for Appointed Counsel in Juvenile Delinquency Cases: Defining Expectations*, 16 U.C. Davis J. Juv. L. & Pol'y 313 (2012); Marsha Levick & Neha Desai, *Still Waiting: The Elusive Quest to Ensure Juveniles a Constitutional Right to Counsel at All Stages of*

the Juvenile Court Process, 60 Rutgers L. Rev. 175 (2007); Katayoon Majd & Patricia Puritz, *The Cost of Justice: How Low-Income Youth Continue to Pay the Price of Failing Indigent Defense Systems*, 16 Geo. J. on Poverty L. & Policy 543 (2009). National standards are discussed in greater detail in Part IV, *infra*.

72 American Bar Ass'n, Private Parties, *supra* note 71, at § 10.1 (a).

73 *Id.* at § 10.2.

74 ABA Juvenile Justice Ctr., a call for justice: An Assessment of Access to Counsel and Quality Representation in delinquency proceedings 26 (1995), http://njdc.info/wp-content/uploads/2013/11/A-Call-for-Justice_An-Assessment-of-Access-to-Counsel-and-Quality-of-Representation-in-Delinquency-Proceedings.pdf (last visited Dec. 22, 2017).

75 *Id.* at 55.

76 National Ass'n of Counsel for Children, Policy Agenda (1997), www.naccchildlaw.org/policy/policy_agenda.html (last visited Sept. 10, 2017).

77 Nat'l Juvenile Defender Ctr. & Nat'l Legal Aid & Defender Ass'n, Ten Core Principles for Providing Quality Indigent Defense Representation through Indigent Defense Delivery Systems, Principle 8 (July 2008), https://www.americanbar.org/content/dam/aba/images/youth_at_risk/SUPP2-ROC-10Core.pdf.

78 *Improving Court, supra* note 71, at 177.

79 *Id.* at 181.

80 Nat'l Juvenile Defender Ctr., Nat'l Juvenile Def. standards §§ 7.1–7.7 (2013), http://njdc.info/wp-content/uploads/2013/09/NationalJuvenileDefenseStandards2013.pdf [hereinafter Standards].

81 In Powell v. Alabama, the United States Supreme Court stated that "[a defendant] requires the guiding hand of counsel at every step in the proceedings against him." 287 U.S. 45, 68–69 (1932).

82 In New Jersey, O.S. was attacked in his cell, leaving him with a broken jaw. In order to "keep him safe" he was placed in solitary confinement for weeks. *See* Sandra Simkins et al., *The Harmful Use of Isolation in Juvenile Facilities: The Need for Post-Disposition Representation*, 38 Wash. U. J.L. & Pol'y 241, 272–75 (2012).

83 Jacqueline Soteropoulos & Mark Fazlollah, *At Youth Facility, Restraints Turn Fatal*, Philadelphia Inquirer (Apr. 24, 2015), http://www.philly.com/mld/inquirer/n...l/11471894.htm.

84 Nell Bernstein, Burning Down the House: The End of Juvenile Prison 82 (The New Press, 2014).

85 *Id.*, at 83.

86 Andrea J. Sedlak & Karla S. McPherson, Juvenile Justice Bulletin: U.S. Dep't of Justice, Conditions of Confinement: Findings From the Survey of Youth in Residential Placement 7 Tbl. 5 (May 2012), https://www.ncjrs.gov/pdffiles1/ojjdp/227729.pdf (last visited Dec. 22, 2017).

87 *Id.*

88 Richard A. Mendel, no place for kids: The Case for Reducing Juvenile Incarceration (2011), http://www.aecf.org/m/resourcedoc/aecf-NoPlaceForKidsFullReport-2011.pdf (last visited Dec. 22, 2017).

89 *Id.* at 5, 7, Figure 2.

90 *Id.*

91 *Id.*

92 Sandra Simkins & Sarah Katz, *Criminalizing Abused Girls*, 8 Violence Against Women 1474 (2002).

93 Nate Blakeslee, *Hidden in Plain Sight: How Did Alleged Abuse at a Youth Facility in West Texas Evade Detection for So Long?*, Texas Observer (Feb. 23, 2007, 12:00 PM), http://www.texasobserver.org/hidden-in-plain-sight. Abuse included staff performing oral sex on youth, watching youth masturbate, talking to youth about sex toys, and touching them inappropriately.

94 David Kaiser & Lovisa Stannow, *The Crisis of Juvenile Prison Rape: A New Report*, The New York Review of Books (Jan. 10, 2007), http://www.nybooks.com/daily/2010/01/07/the-crisis-of-juvenile-prison-rape-a-new-report (last visited Sept. 16, 2017).

95 Pursuant to the Prison Litigation Reform Act, 42 U.S.C. § 1997e *et seq.*, all inmates, even those who are minors, must exhaust administrative remedies before seeking relief in the federal courts. Many states have similar exhaustion requirements.

96 The Prison Rape Elimination Act, 42 U.S.C. § 15601(2003) (PREA) is intended to prevent, deter, and collect data on sexual assault and abuse in juvenile and adult correctional facilities. Among other provisions, PREA requires that every federal, state, and local correctional facility create and make available to inmates mechanisms for internal and external reporting of such incidents.

97 Manfred Nowak, Special Rapporteur of the Human Rights Council, *Torture and Other Cruel, Inhuman or Degrading Treatment or Punishment in Accordance with General Assembly Resolution 62/148, transmitted by Note of the Secretary General* 18, 23, U.N. Doc. A/63/175 (July 28, 2008).

98 *See, e.g,* Stuart Grassian, *Psychiatric Effects of Solitary Confinement*, 22 Wash. U. J. L. & Pol'y 325 (2006).

99 *See* American Civil Liberties Union & Human Rights Watch, Growing Up Locked Down: Youth in Solitary Confinement in Jails and Prisons Across the United States (2012), https://www.hrw.org/sites/default/files/reports/us1012ForUpload.pdf (last visited Dec. 22, 2017).

100 American Civil Liberties Union, Advocacy Toolkit: Ending the Solitary Confinement of Youth in Juvenile Detention and Correctional Facilities (June 2014), http://njdc.info/wp-content/uploads/2014/10/ACLU-Advocacy-Toolkit- Ending-the-Solitary-Confinement-of-Youth-in-Juvenile-Detention-and-Correctional-Facilities.pdf.

101 Bernstein, *supra* note 84, at 131.

102 *See* Lowenstein Sandler, *51 – Jurisdiction Survey of Juvenile Solitary Confinement Rules in Juvenile Justice System* 2 (July 2016), https://www.lowenstein.com/files/upload/51-Jurisdiction%20Survey%20of%20Juvenile%20Solitary%20Confinement%20Rules.PDF (finding that 29 states ban punitive isolation for periods of longer than 4 hours per day; 15 states permit punitive isolation for periods of between 6 hours and *90 days*; and 7 states place no limits on the use of punitive isolation).

103 American Civil Liberties Union & Human Rights Watch, *supra* note 99.

104 *See* Troy D. and O'Neill S. v. Mickens et al., 806 F.Supp.2d 758 (2011).

105 *See* N.J. P.L.2015, c.89, § 5 (2015).

106 Justice Policy Institute, Sticker Shock: Calculating the Full Price Tag for Youth Incarceration (2014), http://www.justicepolicy.org/uploads/justicepolicy/documents/sticker_shock_final_v2.pdf.

107 *Id.* (average annual cost of juvenile incarceration is $400 per day or $150,000 per child).

108 *See* Children and Family Justice Center, Northwestern Pritzker School of Law, Rehabilitative Release of Youth from Illinois Prisons, Removing Bureaucratic Barriers to Your Reentry Success 3 (2016), http://www.law.northwestern.edu/legalclinic/cfjc/documents/Rehabilitative%20Release%20Report%20with%20Appendix.pdf (last visited Dec. 22, 2017).

109 An increasing number of jurisdictions also utilize a Risk Assessment Instrument to guide these decisions.

110 In most states, counsel is not permitted to attend these hearings.

111 Easy Access to the Census of Juveniles in Residential Placement (2013), Office of Juvenile Justice and Delinquency Prevention, http://www.ojjdp.gov/ojstatbb/ezacjrp/ (showing at least 14 percent of youth in residential placements are there for technical violations) (last visited Dec.22, 2017).

112 Some state juvenile codes do not authorize the court to enter such orders against the commitment agency, but even in those jurisdictions the court can strongly recommend the provision of specific services.

113 As in the adult correctional context, the institutional grievance process is the primary means for incarcerated young people to challenge most of the decisions and policies that govern their lives while in custody. Grievances also are the necessary first step in exhausting administrative remedies.

114 Wolff v. McDonnell, 418 U.S. 539 (1974).

115 *Id.*

116 *See* U.S. DEP'T OF EDUCATION & U.S. DEP'T OF JUSTICE, FIVE PRINCIPLES FOR PROVIDING HIGH-QUALITY EDUCATION IN JUVENILE JUSTICE SECURE CARE SETTINGS (2014), http://www2.ed.gov/policy/gen/guid/correctional-education/guiding-principles.pdf.

117 *See* LETTER FROM U.S. DEP'T OF EDUCATION TO CORR. & EDUC. ADM'RS (Dec. 5, 2014), https://www2.ed.gov/policy/gen/guid/correctional-education/csso-state-attorneys-general-letter.pdf. (hereinafter DEAR COLLEAGUE LETTER) (last visited Dec. 27, 2017). These educational rights are codified in the Individuals with Disabilities Education Act (IDEA), P.L. No. 94–102 (1990); § 504 of the Americans with Disabilities Act of 1990, P.L. § 101–336 (1990); and the implementing regulations and state codifications of these acts.

118 DEAR COLLEAGUE LETTER, *supra* note 22. Across U.S. jurisdictions, the percentage of incarcerated youth classified for special education ranges from 9 percent to 78 percent. *Id.*

119 *Id.; see* United States Department of Justice Statement of Interest, G. F. v. Contra Costa Cnty., No. 13-CV-03667-MEJ, 2015 WL 4606078 (N.D. Cal. July 30, 2015).

120 SANDRA VILLALOBOS AGUDELO, THE IMPACT OF FAMILY VISITATION ON INCARCERATED YOUTH'S BEHAVIOR AND SCHOOL PERFORMANCE, VERA INSTITUTE OF JUSTICE (April 2013), http://www.vera.org/sites/default/files/resources/downloads/impact-of-family-visitation-on-incarcerated-youth-brief.pdf (last visited Dec. 22, 2017).

121 *Id.*

122 Kathryn C. Monahan et al., *The Effects of Visitation on Incarcerated Juvenile Offenders: How Contact with the Outside Impacts Adjustments on the Inside,* 35 LAW & HUM. BEHAV. 143 (2011).

123 *See* Riya Saha Shah, Esq. & Jean Strout, Esq., Juvenile Law Center, *Future Interrupted: The Collateral Damage Caused by Proliferation of Juvenile Records* (2016), http://jlc.org/resources/publications/future-interrupted-collateral-damage-caused-proliferation-juvenile-records (last visited Dec. 22, 2017); Ashley Nellis, *Addressing the Collateral Consequences of Convictions for Youth Offenders,* THE CHAMPION 20, 22 (July/Aug. 2011).

124 Nellis, *supra* note 98, at 22.

125 *Id.*

126 *See* The Common Application, *Adjudicated Delinquent*, https://appsupport.commonapp.org/link/portal/33011/33013/Article/778/Adjudicated-delinquency (last visited Sept. 15, 2017).

127 *Id.* at 23.

128 *See* Housing Opportunity Program Extension Act 1996 (National Affordable Housing Act), Pub. L. Nos. 104–120 § 9(a)(2) (1996).

129 *See* 8 U.S.C. § 1182(a) *et seq.*

130 For more detailed information on these and other consequences, *see, e.g.,* MODELS FOR CHANGE, *New Jersey Collateral Consequences Checklist* (2015), http://www.modelsforchange.net/publications/807.

131 Human Rights Watch, R*aised on the Registry: the Irreparable Harm of Placing Children on Sex Offender Registries in the U.S.* 2 (Mar. 1, 2013), https://www.hrw.org/report/2013/05/01/raised-registry/irreparable-harm-placing-children-sex-offender-registries-us.

132 *Id.* at 5.

133 *Id.* at 2.

134 Center for Sex Offender Management, *The Effective Management of Juvenile Sex Offenders in the Community: A Training Curriculum,* http://csom.org/train/juvenile/1/1_1.htm (last visited Aug. 2, 2017).

15 *Gault* at 50: what juvenile defenders can do to dismantle the youth prison model

Liz Ryan and Carmen Daugherty

Youth First Initiative

A failed model from the start: origins of the youth prison model

The United States Supreme Court recognized in *In re Gault* that the hastiness of a judicial system can easily lead to the ultimate denial of liberty for youth – incarceration. The mandate for juvenile defenders is clear after *Gault*, but what is less clear is the role of defenders in dismantling the very system in which many of their clients end up. *In re Gault* was decided nearly 150 years after the establishment of the youth prison model – a model predicated, yet never fully realized, on the idea of rehabilitation over punishment. In 2017, the failed model still exists in every part of the country. Nearly 50,000 youth are placed out of home each day in facilities that are extensions of the unfilled promises of *Gault*. As Jerry Miller, the former Massachusetts Department of Youth Services Commissioner, once wrote, "Reformers come and reformers go. State institutions carry on. Nothing in their history suggests that they can sustain reform, no matter what money, staff and programs are pumped into them."[1]

Established nearly 200 years ago, the first youth prison in the United States and throughout the world was the New York House of Refuge, opening on January 1, 1825.[2] This youth prison could house up to 1,000 children.[3] By the end of the nineteenth century, every state in the United States had a youth prison or a "reformatory", as they were called at that time,[4] and this institution has become a signature feature of the juvenile justice system.

In his book *The Child Savers*, Dr. Anthony Platt details the concepts and principles underpinning the youth prison model from old reports dating from the late 1800s and early 1900s. Notably, one of the early principles stated that these facilities should be "guarded sanctuaries, combining love and guidance with firmness and restraint."[5] Essentially these facilities were designed to provide a caring environment for youth, away from the influences of the adult criminal justice system, and to give youth constructive supports to achieve their own rehabilitation, including education. Additionally, the creation of the youth prison model grew out of a desire to keep youth out of adult gaols and prisons and a hope that placement in youth prisons could reform their characters.[6]

According to experts, "[t]he desire to reform certain youth took precedence over a duty to determine guilt or even suspicion of delinquent behavior. As a consequence, youth frequently entered into institutions without having been convicted or even charged with an offense."[7] Thus, early youth prisons housed children who may not have been delinquent, but because these youth were deemed a problem to their communities, they were housed there.

Reform schools, designed to be better than Houses of Refuge, came later. In 1886, the Lyman School for Boys in Massachusetts was founded. But in reality, reform schools were no better than Houses of Refuge. Both were large, custodial, and repressive.[8]

Then, in 1899, Chicago established the first juvenile court, and within 25 years all states anchored the youth prison concept in law. The first juvenile courts were founded on the ancient legal doctrine of *parens patriae* (the state as parent), which declared the right and responsibility of the state to substitute its own control over children for that of natural parents when the latter appeared unable or unwilling to meet their responsibilities or when the child posed a problem for the community.[9] Thus, the juvenile court "provided the legal foundation for placing many more, like Gerald Gault, in training schools and other juvenile institutions (an operation previously executed on a more *ad hoc* basis) while skirting due-process protections."[10]

The new juvenile court, despite its noble intentions, did not change the fundamental nature of youth prisons. Jerry Miller states that "the practice was entrenched fifty years before the creation of juvenile courts,"[11] and "from the outset they [juvenile courts] failed to change the pattern of confining juveniles in unspeakable institutions."[12] In fact, admission rates increased so that "rather than diverting youth from adult facilities, the data suggest that the net was simply widened resulting in more youth being institutionalized than ever."[13]

From its inception, segregation permeated these institutions, with black activists calling the system "Jim Crow Juvenile Justice."[14] Geoff Ward chronicles the experience of African American youth during this time, underscoring the systemic racism embedded in juvenile justice from the creation of the first youth prisons through the establishment of juvenile courts. At the time, these institutions were viewed more positively than adult prisons, and those known as the Black Child Savers advocated to place African American youth in these facilities as an alternative to adult gaols and prisons. Ward states that "[b]lack youths were extensively committed to adult rather than juvenile institutions in most regions with significant black populations."[15]

A decade into the juvenile court movement, nearly three-quarters of committed black male youth were confined in adult prisons, jails, or workhouses, compared to one-third of all committed white male youth.[16] "In the South, black youths subject to incarceration were almost always confined in adult institutions until the black child-saving movement began to make substantial inroads in the provision of rehabilitative services for black youths around the 1920's."[17] When the Black Child Savers were able to get black youth into these facilities, they were placed in separate and even worse parts of the prison.[18]

Harmful, inequitable, and punitive: key features of the youth prison model

The model initiated in the early 1800s is largely still in place and has been an abysmal failure from the start. The Jim Crow juvenile justice system that the Black Child Savers advocated against also remains.

Today, youth prisons are filled with black and brown youth. According to the latest data from the United States Department of Justice's Office of Juvenile Justice and Delinquency Prevention (OJJDP), youth of color are significantly more likely to be incarcerated than white youth, comprising nearly 70 percent of incarcerated youth in the juvenile justice system. In 2015, black youth were 5.3 times more likely, Native American youth were 3.3 times more likely, and Latino youth were 1.65 times more likely to be incarcerated than white youth.[19]

So what started as an alternative has become a feeder system to, and shares many of the features of, disparate adult prisons.

Size

Youth prisons embody facility features common to adult prisons, including large bed capacity. Most youth confined to secure care in the juvenile justice system are in facilities of between 50 and 200 beds according to the Sentencing Project's latest report on juvenile justice.[20] And, at least 34 of the nation's largest facilities in operation today can house more than 200 youth, 19 of which have a design capacity of more than 300, 400, or even 500 beds.

Longtime youth justice expert Paul DeMuro says that "[i]t's critical that the facility director know every kid by name."[21] If the facility director cannot do that, the facility is too large. DeMuro believes that thirty youth should be the *maximum* number held in any one facility.[22] Other experts agree. Annie E. Casey Foundation President, Patrick McCarthy, speaking at the Juvenile Detention Alternatives Initiative (JDAI) convening in September, 2015, highlighted that if youth are in secure care, the facilities should house no more than 30 beds.

Research from the Bureau of Justice Statistics (BJS) documenting the rates of sexual victimization of incarcerated youth in the juvenile justice system shows that youth facilities holding 25 or more youth report much higher rates of sexual misconduct by staff members.[23] Concerns about the safety of youth in large facilities are underscored by allegations of sexual victimization of youth in juvenile facilities that have more than doubled in the last decade.[24]

Other systems that share similar goals can offer guidance for the design of youth prisons. For example, research on the public educational system, which also has the goal of improving communities through the care of children, shows that size matters. The projected average K-12 class size in the United States is now 15 as a result of research showing that smaller is better for kids.[25]

Rehabilitative focus

Youth prisons were designed to serve as an alternative to adult prisons by having a more rehabilitative focus. Yet these prisons have failed to rehabilitate youth even when the rehabilitative purpose of the juvenile facility is mandated and defined in a state's statute.

For example, in Connecticut, the Department of Children and Families (DCF) states that the mission of Connecticut's youth prison, the Connecticut Juvenile Training School (CJTS), "is to provide a safe, secure and therapeutic environment while providing opportunity for growth and success."[26] Yet this mission statement, which promotes a rehabilitative approach, is not consistent with the report[27] and videotapes[28] released by the Office of the Child Advocate in 2015 documenting youth being brutalized by staff.

The report found, among other problems, "532 cases of physical restraint and 134 cases of mechanical restraint over a twelve-month period."[29] There were 225 incidents of seclusion lasting four hours or longer and 100 lasting eight hours or longer – and those incidents included children who were in mental health crisis or threatening to hurt themselves. Between June 2014 and February 2015, there were at least two dozen cases of children in the facilities trying to kill or hurt themselves.[30]

Physical features

In many states, youth prisons, like adult prisons, are geographically isolated and far from family and community. This stems from the reform school era, when youth were placed in the countryside and housed in cottages, which were supposed to be homelike.[31] Yet this has resulted in youth being sent far from home, making contact with their families difficult and inconsistent.

Youth prisons also imitate adult prisons in the physical features and staffing of the facility. Most youth prisons use wire fencing around the perimeter and sometimes around specific buildings. Such facilities are constructed of concrete or brick that look similar to adult prisons and are staffed by correctional officers with no background in youth development or rehabilitation. Locks are everywhere – on cell doors; in hallways, corridors, and wings of the facility; at the public entrance and exit; and at the sallyport where youth enter. The cells are sealed with steel doors, sometimes with steel beds and a small opening for food or wet cells with a toilet and sink. Communal bathrooms and showers are visible by guards with no privacy, and during visitation, glass separates youth from their families and loved ones. Like adult prisons, youth prisons offer residents costly phone calls and video conferencing instead of in-person contact.

Clothing and food in youth prisons are similar to adult prisons. Youth wear jumpsuits and under garments that are sometimes washed in the general laundry and not returned to the original owner. They eat food that is carb loaded and greasy and have limited access to fresh fruit and vegetables. On occasion, the institutions fail to meet the youths' basic food needs, fail to account for youths' dietary restrictions, and almost never allow youth to have culturally relevant and religious holiday foods.

Violence and abuse in the youth prison model

However well intentioned it may have been, the youth prison model has had a long sordid history of abuse. As Allen, a formerly incarcerated youth from Cleveland, Ohio, states, "I'd rather die than be locked up. It's hard. I think probably for me starting so young on it it ain't right. It ain't for me. It ain't for nobody."[32]

Culture of violence and victimization

Violence and victimization persist in youth prisons. Incarcerated youth often experience dangerous conditions, such as physical and chemical restraints, sexual and physical abuse, and solitary confinement, and have a high risk of suicide. Abuse in these facilities has spread to more states, according to research by the Annie E. Casey Foundation in *Maltreatment in U.S. Juvenile Correctional Facilities*.[33]

The closed nature of these facilities makes young people vulnerable to sexual and physical abuse. As a recent Bureau of Justice Statistics survey found, one in ten youth in youth prisons have been sexually victimized.[34] According to the BJS report, rates of sexual victimization of incarcerated youth in the juvenile justice system have doubled over the last decade from 19 per 1,000 youths in 2005 to 47 per 1,000 in 2012.[35] The survey also found that youth identifying as lesbian, gay, or bisexual experienced youth-on-youth sexual assault ten times more frequently than heterosexual youth.[36]

These findings are confirmed by surveys of incarcerated youth themselves. The Survey of Youth in Residential Placement (SYRP), which was the first-ever nationally representative survey of youth in correctional care, shows that "fear of violence and staff maltreatment remain widespread in America's youth corrections facilities."[37] According to the SYRP, a majority of youth experienced some kind of victimization while in custody, such as theft, robbery, physical assault, or sexual assault. Youth victimization increased when staff used methods to physically control youth such as handcuffs, chains, pepper spray, restraint chairs, or strip searches. And according to the survey, the longer youth were incarcerated, the more likely those youth were to experience higher rates of violence.[38]

Solitary confinement

If the above-referenced government sanctioned responses to youth are not shocking enough, youth prisons use solitary confinement as a way to control many types of youth behavior. Correctional staff cannot escape the atrocity of "solitary confinement" by referring to it as "protective custody," "administrative segregation," "seclusion," "isolation," or "room confinement." Youth cannot avoid the harms of solitary confinement by calling it "the hole" or "the box," among other terms. According to the Juvenile Offenders and Victims 2014 report,[39] one in five facilities where youth are confined in the juvenile justice system reported locking youth in some type of isolation, with the youth prisons (referred to in this study as "training schools") as the most likely to lock a youth alone in some type of seclusion for four or more hours.

Youth incarcerated in the juvenile justice system confirm this report. Incarcerated youth (35 percent) surveyed under the SYRP reported being isolated – locked up alone or confined to their room with no contact with other residents. The majority of youth who were isolated (87 percent) said they were confined for longer than two hours, and more than half (55 percent) said they were alone for longer than 24 hours. More than half of the youth isolated for longer than two hours said they had not met with a counselor since arriving at the facility.[40]

There are so many dehumanizing and degrading practices in youth prisons, but with no national data collected on these kinds of practices, we do not have a complete snapshot. From press reports and accounts from incarcerated youth themselves, we are aware of inhumane practices that in some instances have become a routine part of youth prison operations.[41]

Lack of staff accountability

Despite rampant reports and evidence of abuse, correctional officers are rarely prosecuted for their inappropriate behavior in the juvenile or criminal justice systems. For example, experts report that prosecutions of correctional guards for sexual victimization are "extremely rare."[42]

Even after a death of a child in custody, staff are rarely held accountable. After the death of Gynnya McMillen in a juvenile detention center in Kentucky in 2016, no corrections staff have been prosecuted. Seventeen-year-old Gynnya died in her cell from a rare genetic disorder which caused an irregular heartbeat while a guard watched without providing any assistance.[43] The agency head and several staff were fired, but to date, no staff have been charged in relation to her death.[44] Correctional staff operating with impunity for their inappropriate, degrading, or illegal actions deter youth from reporting victimization by staff or other youth. This wall of silence furthers the violence and victimization inside youth prisons.

Expense

Despite such harsh treatment and poor outcomes, states devote the largest share of their juvenile justice resources to youth prisons, with an estimated annual cost of over $5 billion per year. According to the Justice Policy Institute, in *Sticker Shock: Calculating the Full Price Tag of Youth Incarceration*, 33 U.S. states and jurisdictions spend $100,000 or more annually to incarcerate a young person, and continue to generate outcomes that result in even greater costs.[45]

These costs are staggering, especially in comparison to the investments in education where the average annual per pupil cost of K-12 public education is substantially lower.[46] Communities are not safer as youth in prison experience high recidivism rates and incarceration in the juvenile justice system that substantially increases the likelihood that youth will be incarcerated in the adult criminal justice system.

Youth prisons are the most expensive option in the juvenile justice system and consistently produce the worst outcomes.

Lack of family engagement

Youth are often placed in youth prisons far from their families, with limited access and visits. Families are often not included in the treatment plans for youth. Yet families are paying for at least some of the daily cost of confinement according to the National Center on Juvenile Justice.[47] A study from the Juvenile Law Center, *Debtors' Prison for Kids? The High Cost of Fines and Fees in the Juvenile Justice System*,[48] finds that every state permits juvenile courts to impose system costs on youth and their families, and the impact is felt most by youth of color and youth in poverty. A *Washington Post* article exposed this heinous practice.[49]

At its core the youth prison model is institutional, not homelike, and attempts to replace a youth's family with a placement devoid of positive, caring relationships. In her seminal book on the youth prison, *Burning Down the House*, Nell Bernstein captures this, stating,

> [w]hen I interviewed wards of the current system … I asked them what they thought might improve their lives and prospects. The great majority offered the very same answer: trusting relationships with adults who saw them as human beings. However, many children longed for this, few had experienced it, despite the countless cycles of "reform" over the intervening years.[50]

Evolution of reform

In nearly every juvenile or criminal justice reform effort across the country, attorneys play a critical role in achieving change and holding systems accountable. Since their inception, youth prisons have been the subject of abuse, scandal, litigation, and reform, and in the last 50 years, juvenile defenders have actively engaged in efforts to close these facilities. Through litigation, legislative changes, and coalition building, lawyers have been there.

Litigation

The Fifth and Fourteenth Amendments to the U.S. Constitution prohibit depriving a person of life, liberty, or property without due process of law, and due process protections govern the standards for conditions of confinement for youth in juvenile facilities.[51] From the start, advocates have fought to reform youth prisons, with a major focus on improving conditions of confinement. Chief among the legal strategies was the 1971 case, *Morales v. Thurman,* a suit against the Texas Youth Council challenging conditions of confinement on behalf of 11 youth confined in Texas facilities.[52] Legal scholars characterize *Morales* as "the leading case in youth prison conditions."[53]

Since 1970, more than 50 lawsuits have been filed to challenge conditions of confinement for youth in youth prisons and other facilities.[54] Legal organizations such as the Juvenile Law Center, Prison Law Office, American Civil Liberties Union's (ACLU's) National Prison Project, and the Youth Law Center were founded with support from private foundations, and later with federal support, and successfully engaged in litigation to improve the conditions in facilities where youth were held.[55]

Litigation can help elevate awareness of the issue and pressure state officials to stop the worst abuses. However, it can also "reinforce reliance on an institutional model"[56] as policy-makers may use litigation as a justification for increasing staffing and funding to the institution itself. Fortunately, in a number of states, lawsuits so burdened the juvenile justice systems that change was inevitable. Litigation, in conjunction with other strategies deployed through a comprehensive campaign, is a powerful tool to set the stage for closing youth prisons. As Kim Brooks Tandy, the founder and Executive Director of the Children's Law Center, writes, "Bringing lawsuits against officials at a youth correctional facility can take years of work to force needed changes, but sometimes is necessary."[57]

Case example: Ohio

In 2004, the Children's Law Center, Youth Law Center, and private counsel filed a suit against the Ohio Department of Youth Services (DYS) over conditions of confinement at the Scioto youth facility, including solitary confinement, physical and sexual abuse of youth, and inadequate medical treatment. In 2007, the litigation, *S.H. v. Stickrath*, extended to cover all facilities in the Ohio DYS.[58] In 2015, the litigation ended with the signing of an order by Federal Judge Algenon Marbley. Five of the Ohio facilities closed, and the number of youth in the remaining three facilities has decreased from 1800 to 470.[59]

Even with this successful litigation, Tandy says that "litigation has its limits"[60] and is not a "panacea."[61] Agency heads must do more than what the law requires, including a focus on improved outcomes for youth in their care. Tandy concludes that "[p]erhaps the new 'fourth wave' of juvenile justice reforms will work to reduce youth incarceration and continue to close harmful and ineffective correctional facilities, improve recidivism rates and improve overall youth life outcomes."[62]

Legislation

Legislative advocacy also is vital to the reform movement. Thus, lawyers must have a wide range of knowledge and skill to not only identify needed statutory and regulatory change to benefit their clients, but also to influence the legislative process.

Case example: California

> Abundant federal money was made available to support the construction of new facilities for youth and, not surprisingly, they closely resembled adult prisons.
>
> (Sue Burrell, juvenile justice expert)

In the 1980s, the youth prisons in the California Youth Authority (CYA) were abysmal institutions that utilized pepper spray and solitary confinement, placed children in cages, and failed to protect children from physical abuse and suicide. In light of these abuses, attorneys encouraged key legislators to hold hearings to document the abuse and to sponsor legislation. Litigation helped to keep the issue in the public spotlight while legislative negotiations occurred. Longtime juvenile justice expert Sue Burrell says that "[c]ivil rights litigation filed by the nonprofit Prison Law Office and extensive media reports kept the parade of institutional abuses in the public eye, making it impossible to turn away from the failures of the existing system."[63] In addition, "Abundant federal money was made available to support the construction of new facilities for youth and, not surprisingly, they closely resembled adult prisons."[64]

Ultimately, California advocates were successful at obtaining the passage of major pieces of legislation to prohibit youth with low level offenses from being committed to state youth prisons and "realigning" substantial resources to the counties to serve them locally, as well as allowing parole services to be handled locally.[65] Altogether these efforts achieved huge reductions in the incarcerated youth population – from more than 10,000 youth incarcerated in state youth prisons in 1996 to 659 in 2013 – and resulted in the closure of eight youth prisons.[66]

Coalitions

> Coalitions are like political positions: every once in awhile they're not only expedient, they're also good."
>
> (Petey2, DailyKos)

Coalition building is the "primary mechanism through which disempowered parties can develop their power base and thereby better defend their interests."[67] In order for coalitions to be effective, each member must contribute their unique experience and expertise to the effort, whether that's legislative drafting, community organizing, public speaking, or direct action – coalitions that draw on each member's strengths and diversity will often achieve their goals. According to one political blogger, "Coalitions are like political positions: every once in awhile they're not only expedient, they're also good."[68]

Often, the attorneys involved in campaigns to close youth prisons hail from organizations with name recognition and impressive reputations. In recent juvenile justice movements, such names as the Southern Poverty Law Center and the American Civil Liberties Union have joined coalitions giving campaigns the legal power often necessary for reform. However, the legal tactic is only one piece of work, not the goal, and those attorneys who recognize the contributions of each member of the coalition work more effectively.

Case example: District of Columbia

In Washington, D.C., local public defenders reached out to national organizations, including the Youth Law Center and Justice Policy Institute, for assistance with influencing the newly formed Mayor's Blue Ribbon Commission on Youth Safety and Juvenile Justice Reform. That commission was tasked with examining the strengths and weaknesses of the juvenile justice system and focusing on changes at Oak Hill, the local youth prison, several years after the pivotal 1985 lawsuit documenting abuses at the facility.[69] Vincent Schiraldi, the former director of the District of Columbia Department of Youth Rehabilitation Services, later wrote of Oak Hill:

> Beatings of children in custody were commonplace, inmates stuffed clothing around the toilets to keep out rats and cockroaches, young people were locked up for so long they often defecated or urinated in their cells. Youth who came in clean tested positive for marijuana after 30 days of confinement, suggesting it was easier to score drugs in my facility than on the streets of the District of Columbia.[70]

The Youth Law Center, Justice Policy Institute, and community members started serving as watchdogs at commission meetings. They decided to organize a formal coalition, the Justice for DC Youth Coalition, which called for the closure of Oak Hill. The commission's recommendations issued two years later included a call to close Oak Hill, keep most court-involved youth in the community, and invest in community-based alternatives to incarceration. For the small number of youth who may pose a real risk to public safety, the report recommended building a small, homelike facility.

Surprisingly, the mayor ignored his own commission's recommendations and introduced legislation to prosecute more youth in adult criminal court. Over the subsequent two years, Justice for DC Youth organized demonstrations and events in the community, engaged community members, participated in legislative hearings, and was ultimately successful, with the support of juvenile defenders, in its legislative efforts to close Oak Hill, replace it with a smaller, more rehabilitative facility, and expand community-based programs.[71] These efforts resulted in reducing the youth population from 250 in 2005 to 35 in 2016 and closing Oak Hill in 2009.[72]

Campaigns: when it all comes together

Campaigns to dismantle the youth prison model have one thing in common: change comes when those most affected are part of the reform movement. In the last 20 years, juvenile defenders have worked with formerly incarcerated youth, families of incarcerated youth, youth advocates, and community members together to take reforms a step further – beyond improving conditions of confinement to closing youth prisons. Juvenile defense attorneys played crucial roles in successful campaigns to shut down notorious youth prisons in several states, including Louisiana, New York, Mississippi, Texas, D.C., and California.[73]

Case example: Louisiana

> Seeing all of those parents and others out there in the rain, demanding change for their children, made me realize how committed they were to this cause. I guess my fate was sealed to help them be heard – every time I saw a "redshirt" in the capitol I was reminded of that coffin and I haven't looked back since.
>
> (State Senator Donald Cravins)[74]

The Tallulah youth prison was the creation of former colleagues of then-governor Edwin Edwards. It was established in 1994 under a no-bid contract, becoming the largest employer and taxpayer in Tallulah, Louisiana.[75] It was a profit-making venture with the owners earning more than $8 million. Describing the profit motive, advocates contend that "the idea from the beginning was to keep wages as low as possible (guards were paid $5.77 an hour), minimize services, and maximize the number of children locked up."[76]

Almost as soon as the facility opened, reports about abuse of children, lack of food and clothing, and grotesque conditions reached lawyers at the Juvenile Justice Project of Louisiana (JJPL). In 1998, they filed a class action lawsuit against the state on behalf of children locked up at the Tallulah facility. Later in the same year, the United States Department of Justice filed a lawsuit against the facility. By 2000, settlement agreements were in place, and JJPL became a monitor.[77]

Parents of youth at Tallulah were in touch with JJPL's attorneys and staff, including Gina Womack, who brought families together first as a support group and then as an advocacy effort that became Families and Friends of Louisiana's Incarcerated Children (FFLIC).

Heinous conditions persisted, and advocates recognized that litigation would not be enough, "[a]t best, the litigation was an imperfect means to deterring further harm while gaining access to inside facts and records necessary for another kind of advocacy."[78] Families organized continuous direct actions to keep the issue in the spotlight. Through this collaboration of the attorneys at JJPL and the families at FFLIC, the Close Tallulah Now campaign succeeded in closing Tallulah, enacting legislation to reduce youth incarceration, and reinvesting the savings into prevention, early intervention, alternative sanctions, and other reforms. The last child was removed from Tallulah in 2004, and Louisiana's youth incarceration population dropped from 2,000 to 350.[79]

Case example: Milwaukee, Wisconsin

> Lincoln Hills represents a failed model that just can't be fixed.
>
> (Jeff Roman, Youth Justice Milwaukee)

Lincoln Hills, located in Irma, Wisconsin, is one of the largest youth prisons in the country, with capacity for more than 550 youth. Copper Lake, a girl's facility, is also on the same campus. In December, 2015, federal and state officials were reported to have raided both facilities after a year-long investigation, and in February, 2016, the Federal Bureau of Investigation took over the investigation with the

United States Department of Justice's Civil Rights Division considering its own investigation.[80]

Press reports of these investigations by the United States Department of Justice and Wisconsin state agencies reference sexual abuse of youth, use of pepper spray, strangulation, and suffocation of youth; intimidation of youth to discourage reporting; and tampering with state and county documents concerning youth institutions. Former Wisconsin Department of Corrections Director Ed Wall reported in 2016 that the correctional staff at the facility had shredded complaints from youth about conditions at the facility.[81] *The Milwaukee Journal Sentinel* has done extensive investigative reporting on the facility and catalogued all of the articles in a special section on its website.[82] According to Jeff Roman, a local activist, "Lincoln Hills represents a failed model that just can't be fixed."[83]

In 2016, Youth Justice Milwaukee (YJM), a broad-based coalition of families, advocates, service providers, and attorneys formed after allegations came to light. In early 2017, the American Civil Liberties Union of Wisconsin partnered with Juvenile Law Center to file suit against the Wisconsin Department of Corrections for alleged abuse and treatment that it says violates the children's Eighth Amendment right to be free from cruel abuse and treatment. Per the lawsuit, at any given time, 15–20 percent of kids are being held in solitary confinement in 7-by-10-foot cells, for 22 or 23 hours of the day – in which they're often placed after non-violent infractions like disrespecting staff.[84] In June 2017, Western District Judge Peterson found that the use of solitary confinement, pepper spray, and restraints at two juvenile facilities in Wisconsin violate youth's constitutional rights under the Fourteenth Amendment.[85] Just one month later, the state agreed to severely limit its use of solitary confinement and chemical restraints.[86]

Conclusion

Breaking Down the Walls, a recent report from Youth First Initiative, highlights lessons learned from successful campaigns to close youth prisons in six states over the last 10–15 years.[87] Lessons include:

- Take the long view;
- Let youth and families lead;
- Be explicit about racial injustice;
- Embrace diversity and plan for conflict;
- Statewide reform needs local stakeholders;
- Harness the power of public opinion and the media.

These lessons learned can help inform the work as we confront the challenges ahead and encourage other attorneys to get involved. For instance, youth incarceration has been cut in half in the last decade. However, no state has fully rejected the youth prison model, and states continue to rely on these costly, inhumane, and outdated institutions.

Jim Crow juvenile justice remains. Like the early efforts by Black Child Savers in the 1920 to remove youth from adult gaols and prisons and to access juvenile institutions, black youth have not benefitted from the decarceration efforts equally. The disparities have widened. Racial and ethnic disparities have increased according to new analysis, *Racial Disparities in Youth Commitments and Arrests*, by The Sentencing Project. "Between 2003 and 2013, the racial gap between black and white youth in secure commitment increased by 15%."[88] The report concludes that "[t]hese trends suggest that the successful reforms that have led to fewer overall arrests and fewer commitments have not been shared equally among all youth and, in fact, are benefiting white youth the most."[89]

In *Last One Over the Wall*, Jerry Miller sums up the effort to close Massachusetts' youth prisons. He writes,

> [w]henever I thought we'd made progress, something happened – a beating, a kid in an isolation cell, an offhand remark by a superintendent or cottage supervisor that told me what I envisioned would never be allowed. Reformers come and reformers go. State institutions carry on. Nothing in their history suggests that they can sustain reform, no matter what money, staff and programs are pumped into them. The same crises that have plagued them for 150 years intrude today. Though the casts may change, the players go on producing failure.[90]

Dynamic campaigns consist of strategies that draw upon the various expertise of coalition members and lawyers who serve various roles at different times. A system bereft of constitutional protections should not exist and, at the very least, requires juvenile defenders to make the constitutional arguments against placing youth in such harmful facilities. Due process does not stop at the courtroom doors. The lessons learned through the decades provide hope for this reform to continue and protect the nearly 50,000 youth confined and separated from their communities each day.

Notes

1 Jerome G. Miller, Last One Over the Wall: the Massachusetts Experiment in Closing Reform Schools 18 (Ohio State University Press, 1998).
2 Nell Bernstein, Burning Down the House: The End of Juvenile Prison 39 (New Press, 2014).
3 *Id.* at 41.
4 *Id.* at 45.
5 Anthony M. Platt, The Child Savers: The Invention of Delinquency 54 (Rutgers University Press, 2009).
6 *Official Proceedings of the Annual Meeting in 1901 of the National Conference on Social Welfare*, Nat'l Conference on Social Welfare Proceedings, http://quod.lib.umich.edu/n/ncosw/ACH8650.1901.001?rgn=main;view=fulltext (last visited Mar. 7, 2017).
7 Ashley Nellis, A Return to Justice: Rethinking Our Approach to Juveniles in the System 9 (Rowman & Littlefield Publishers, 2015).
8 *Id.* at 7 (discussing the mistreatment and confinement conditions of juveniles).

9 *Juvenile Justice: History and Philosophy – The Origins of the Juvenile Court*, http://law.jrank.org/pages/1489/Juvenile-Justice-History-Philosophy-origins-juvenile-court.html#ixzz4a5TJicGi (last visited Mar. 1, 2017).
10 Bernstein, *supra* note 2, at 47.
11 Miller, *supra* note 1, at 5.
12 *Id.* at 7.
13 Nellis, *supra* note 7, at 16.
14 Geoff K. Ward, The Black Child-Savers: Racial Democracy & Juvenile Justice 1 (The University of Chicago Press, 2012).
15 *Id.* at 90.
16 *Id.* at 90–91.
17 *Id.*
18 *Id.* at 54.
19 *Easy Access to the Census of Juveniles in Residential Placement: 1997–2015*, Office of Juvenile Justice and Delinquency Prevention (June 1, 2017), https://www.ojjdp.gov/ojstatbb/ezacjrp (last visited Jan.5, 2018).
20 The Sentencing Project, Declines in Youth Commitments and Facilities in the 21st Century, http://www.sentencingproject.org/wp-content/uploads/2016/02/Youth-Commitments-and-Facilities.pdf (last visited Mar. 1, 2017).
21 Richard A. Mendel, The Missouri Model: Reinventing the Practice of Rehabilitating Youthful Offenders 15, http://www.aecf.org/m/resourcedoc/aecf-MissouriModelFullreport-2010.pdf (last visited Mar. 1, 2017).
22 *Id.*
23 U.S. Dep't of Justice, Prison Rape Elimination Act of 2003, PREA Data Collection Activities (June 2016), https://www.bjs.gov/content/pub/pdf/pdca16.pdf.
24 Allen J. Beck & Ramona R. Rantala, U.S. Dep't of Justice, Office of Justice Programs, Bureau of Justice Statistics, Sexual Victimization Reported by Juvenile Correctional Authorities, 2007–12 (Jan. 2016), https://www.bjs.gov/content/pub/pdf/svrjca0712.pdf.
25 Nat'l Ctr. for Educ. Statistics, Tbl. 68, https://nces.ed.gov/programs/digest/d10/tables/dt10_068.asp (last visited Aug. 18, 2017).
26 *Connecticut Juvenile Training School*, State of Connecticut (May 19, 2017), http://www.ct.gov/dcf/cwp/view.asp?a=4606&Q=539022#About (last visited May 19, 2017).
27 State of Connecticut, Office of the Child Advocate, Investigative Facility Report, Connecticut Juvenile Training School and Pueblo Unit (July 22, 2015), http://www.ct.gov/oca/lib/oca/oca_investigative_cjts_pueblo_report_july_22_2015.pdf.
28 Jacqueline Rabe Thomas, *State Watchdog Releases Videos of 'Dangerous' Restraints, Seclusions in Juvenile Jails*, The Ct.Mirror (Sept. 15, 2015), http://ctmirror.org/2015/09/15/state-watchdog-releases-videos-of-dangerous-restraints-seclusions-in-juvenile-jails.
29 Elizabeth Regan, *Juvenile Justice Advocates Call for Closure of DCF's Locked Facilities* (Aug. 12, 2015), http://www.ctnewsjunkie.com/archives/entry/juvenile_justice_advocates_call_for_closure_of_dcfs_locked_facilities.
30 *Id.*
31 Platt & Chávez-García, *supra* note 4, at 65.
32 Liz Ryan, *Kids Are in Youth Prisons*, https://medium.com/@LizRyanYJ/kids-are-in-youth-prisons-6d7d733ed03e.
33 Richard A. Mendel, Maltreatment in U.S. Juvenile Correctional Facilities An Update, http://www.aecf.org/m/resourcedoc/aecf-maltreatmentyouthuscorrections-2015.pdf (last visited Aug. 22, 2017).
34 Allen J. Beck et al, U.S. Dep't of Justice, Sexual Victimization in Juvenile Facilities Reported by Youth (2012), https://www.bjs.gov/content/pub/pdf/svjfry12.pdf (last visited Aug. 22, 2017).

35 *Id.*
36 *Id.*
37 Annie E. Casey Foundation, Maltreatment of Youth in U.S. Juvenile Corrections Facilities: An Update 7 (2015), https://www.ncmhjj.com/wp-content/uploads/2015/07/aecf-maltreatmentyouthuscorrections-2015.pdf.
38 Andrea J. Sedlak, Survey of Youth in Residential Placement: Conditions of Confinement 30–31 (2016), https://syrp.org/images/SYRP_CofC_RPT_final.pdf.
39 *Juvenile Offenders and Victims: 2014 National Report*, Nat'l Ctr. for Juvenile Justice (Feb. 16, 2015), http://www.ncjj.org/nr2014/index.html.
40 Sedlak, *supra* note 38 at 49.
41 *See, e.g.*, Erica L. Green, *Juveniles in Maryland's Justice System Are Routinely Strip-Searched and Shackled*, The Baltimore Sun (Mar. 13, 2016), http://www.baltimoresun.com/news/maryland/investigations/bs-md-strip-and-shackle-20160129-story.html; Jim DeFede, *Snacks for Attacks, Part 2: Detention Center Beatings Leave Kids Feeling Unsafe*, CBS Miami (Oct. 7, 2015), http://miami.cbslocal.com/2015/10/07/snacks-for-attacks-part-2-detention-center-beatings-leave-kids-feeling-unsafe; Antonia Noori Farzan, *Potentially Life-Threatening Conditions in Juvenile Detention Center, Public Defender Says*, Broward Palm Beach Times (July 18, 2016), http://www.browardpalmbeach.com/news/potentially-life-threatening-conditions-in-juvenile-detention-center-public-defender-says-7920191.
42 Joaquin Sapien, *Guards May Be Responsible for Half of Prison Sexual Assaults,* ProPublica (Jan. 23, 2014), https://www.propublica.org/article/guards-may-be-responsible-for-half-of-prison-sexual-assaults.
43 Graham Kates, *Lawsuit: Juvenile Detention Staffer Watched as Ky. Girl Took "Last Gasps"*, CBS News (Sept. 6, 2016), http://www.cbsnews.com/news/gynnya-mcmillen-lawsuit-juvenile-detention-staffer-watched-as-kentucky-girl-died.
44 Graham Kates, *Kentucky Officials Fired in Investigation of Gynnya McMillian's Death*, CBS News (Feb. 9, 2016), http://www.cbsnews.com/news/kentucky-officials-fired-in-investigation-of-gynnya-mcmillens-death.
45 Justice Policy Institute, Sticker Shock: Calculating the Full Price Tag for Youth Incarceration, http://www.justicepolicy.org/uploads/justicepolicy/documents/sticker_shock_final_v2.pdf (last visited Aug. 22, 2017).
46 *Annual Survey of School System Finances*, U.S. Census Bureau, https://www.census.gov/govs/school (last visited Aug. 20, 2017).
47 Linda A. Szymanski, Nat'l Ctr. for Juvenile Justice, Can Parents Ever be Obligated for the Support of Their Institutionalized Delinquent Children? (Apr. 2011), http://www.ncjj.org/pdf/Snapshots/2011/vol16_no4_Can%20Parents%20Ever%20Be%20Obligated%20for%20the%20Support%20of%20Their%20Institutionalized.pdf.
48 *Debtors' Prison for Kids, The High Cost of Fines and Fees in the Juvenile Justice System*, Juvenile Law Ctr., http://debtorsprison.jlc.org/#!/map (last visited Aug. 22, 2017).
49 Eli Hager, *Your Child's Been Sent to Jail: And Then Comes the Bill*, The Washington Post, https://www.washingtonpost.com/national/your-childs-been-sent-to-jail-and-then-comes-the-bill/2017/03/02/e2816c90-f949-11e6-9845-576c69081518_story.html?postshare=2751488506927437&tid=ss_tw&utm_term=.945c5cd21251 (last visited Aug. 22, 2017).
50 Bernstein, *supra* note 2, at 42.
51 Gary H. v. Hegstrom, 831 F.2d 1430, 1432 (9th Cir. 1987); Jones v. Blanas, 393 F.3d 918, 931 (9th Cir. 2004); Youngberg v. Romeo, 457 U.S. 307 (1982); Bell v. Wolfish, 441 U.S. 520 (1979).
52 Morales v. Thurman, 59 F.R.D. 157 (E.D. Tex. 1972).
53 Nellis, *supra* note 7, at 23.
54 Mendel, *supra* note 33.
55 Patrick McCarthy et al, U.S. Dep't of Justice, National Institute of Justice, The Future of Youth Justice: A Community-Based Alternative to the Youth Prison

MODEL (2016), https://www.ncjrs.gov/pdffiles1/nij/250142.pdf (last visited Jan. 5, 2018).

56 *Reforming Juvenile Justice: A Developmental Approach*, NAT'L RESEARCH COUNCIL 257 (2013), https://doi.org/10.17226/14685 (last visited Jan. 5, 2018).

57 Tandy, *supra* note 57.

58 S.H. v Stickrath, No. 2:04-CV-1206 (S.D. Ohio Apr. 14, 2010).

59 Kim Brooks Tandy, *Litigation is an Important Tool in Youth Justice Reform*, JUVENILE JUSTICE INFORMATION EXCHANGE (Mar. 9, 2016), http://jjie.org/2016/03/09/analysis-litigation-is-important-tool-in-youth-corrections-reform.

60 *Id.*

61 *Id.*

62 *Id.*

63 Sue Burrell, *The Legislature's Role in Juvenile Justice Reform: A California Example*, NAT'L COUNCIL ON CRIME AND DELINQUENCY NCCD BLOG (Apr. 7, 2014), http://www.nccdglobal.org/blog/the-legislature-s-role-in-juvenile-justice-reform-a-california-example.

64 *Id.*

65 *Id.*

66 YOUTH FIRST INITIATIVE, BREAKING DOWN THE WALLS, http://www.youthfirstinitiative.org/wp-content/uploads/2017/04/Breaking-Down-the-Walls.pdf (last visited Aug. 22, 2017) [hereinafter *The Walls*].

67 *Coalition Building*, CONFLICT RESEARCH CONSORTIUM, http://www.colorado.edu/conflict/peace/problem/coalition.htm (last visited Aug. 20, 2017).

68 Petey2, *How about a Right/Left Alliance over Trade?* (Aug. 17, 2017), https://www.dailykos.com/blog/Petey2.

69 NOTORIOUS TO NOTABLE: THE CRUCIAL ROLE OF THE PHILANTHROPIC COMMUNITY IN TRANSFORMING THE JUVENILE JUSTICE SYSTEM IN WASHINGTON, D.C., https://giving.files.wordpress.com/2011/11/notorious-to-notable-final.pdf (last visited Aug. 22, 2017).

70 Vincent Schiraldi, *What Mass Incarceration Looks Like for Juveniles*, N.Y. TIMES (November 10, 2015), https://www.nytimes.com/2015/11/11/opinion/what-mass-incarceration-looks-like-for-juveniles.html.

71 *Id.*

72 Youth First Initiative, *The Walls, supra* note 66.

73 *Id.*

74 *No Turning Back*, BUILDING BLOCKS FOR YOUTH INITIATIVE 71 (Oct. 2005) http://docplayer.net/95413-No-turning-back-promising-approaches-to-reducing-racial-and-ethnic-disparities-affecting-youth-of-color-in-the-justice-system.html [hereinafter *No Turning Back*].

75 *Id.* at 69–70.

76 *Id.* at 70.

77 Youth First Initiative, *supra* note 66.

78 *No Turning Back, supra* note 74 at 71.

79 Youth First Initiative, *supra* note 66.

80 Liz Ryan, *Youth Prisons Are under Scrutiny*, MEDIUM (Nov. 15, 2016), https://medium.com/@LizRyanYJ/youth-prisons-are-under-scrutiny-e4c3c6a8155b.

81 *Id.*

82 *PolitiFact: Is Unabomber's Confinement Less Strict than for Lincoln Hills Youth?*, MILWAUKEE JOURNAL SENTINEL (Aug. 18, 2017) http://www.jsonline.com/topic/192113c8-25da-46f2-aacf-7e65176ae64f/lincoln-hills-school.

83 Patrick Marley, *Group Calls for Closing Youth Prisons*, MILWAUKEE JOURNAL SENTINEL (Oct. 27, 2916), http://www.jsonline.com/story/news/politics/2016/10/27/group-calls-closing-youth-prisons/92837670.

84 3:17-cv-00047 (W.D. of Wis. Jan. 23, 2017), https://aclu-wi.org/sites/default/files/issue/pdf/20170123JJvLitscherComplaintefiled.pdf.

85 3:17-cv-00047-jdp (W.D. of Wis. June 23, 2017), https://www.courthousenews.com/wp-content/uploads/2017/06/WisJuvie.pdf.

86 3:17-cv-00047-jdp (W.D. of Wis. July 10, 2017), https://localtvwiti.files.wordpress.com/2017/07/lincoln-hills-copper-lake-order.pdf.

87 Youth First Initiative, *supra* note 66.

88 Joshua Rovner, *Racial Disparities in Youth Commitments and Arrests*, The Sentencing Project (Apr. 1, 2016), http://www.sentencingproject.org/publications/racial-disparities-in-youth-commitments-and-arrests.

89 *Id.*

90 Miller, *supra* note 1, at 18.

16 Busting the "juvenile super-predator" myth

Laura Cohen and Jane Spinak

At the end of the last century, the United States launched an all-out war against the unlikeliest of enemies: its children. From the late 1980s through the 1990s, a frenzied, media-fueled fear of escalating youth crime gripped the country. Pointing to what later proved to be a momentary blip in juvenile crime rates, Princeton political scientist John DiIulio and others warned of a "coming Armageddon" of "juvenile super-predators" who were "subhuman," "amoral," and "feral."[1] The press latched onto this unfounded prophecy with glee, unleashing a torrent of retributive rhetoric targeting the "urban" (i.e. black and brown) children whom DiIulio vilified. In response, state and federal lawmakers vied to out-do each other in cracking down on juvenile crime, often to their own political benefit. They were joined by prosecutors eager to prove their chops. This witch hunt fundamentally altered the way in which the United States viewed and responded to children who had broken the law for more than a generation, with little change until the Supreme Court began to reconsider how children are different from adults and should be treated differently.[2] At the time, however, children as young as 10, 11, or 12 were blamed for the perceived tide of violence, normative adolescent behavior was criminalized – helping to fuel the crisis of mass incarceration with which the country still struggles today – and the unconscionable racial disparities already embedded in the criminal and juvenile justices systems intensified. The core rehabilitative purpose of the juvenile court was replaced by a retributive purpose, with catastrophic and lifelong consequences for tens of thousands of children.

Around the country, advocates worked vigorously to fend off these draconian measures. Coalitions formed at the national, state, and local levels, utilizing a variety of organizing, communications, and political strategies. Juvenile defenders and defender organizations had unique and invaluable insights, client narratives, and data to contribute to the resistance movement, but confronted significant political, fiscal, and ethical barriers when they sought to become involved. This chapter considers the obligation of defender offices to advocate for their clients both within and outside of the courtroom and looks back on the efforts of one organization to do so during the late 1990s blitzkrieg: the Legal Aid Society's Juvenile Rights Division (JRD), New York City's principal defender for children charged with delinquency.[3] We, the authors, who were at the time JRD's Director of Training and Attorney-in-Charge, were deeply involved in the organization's fight to protect our clients from the fallout of the super-predator myth. The lessons of those battles continue to resonate in the ongoing quest for a rational, unbiased, and compassionate youth justice system.

The gathering storm

The punitive turn towards criminalizing the juvenile justice system that began in the late 1970s accelerated during the 1980s.[4] The two-decade-long legislative assault on America's children found its most terrifying narrative on April 19, 1989, when New York City was rocked by the news that an investment banker in her late-twenties had been viciously raped, beaten, and left for dead in Central Park. The victim was an avid runner, and the attack occurred when she was out for her evening jog on one of the park's main thoroughfares. She was dragged or chased into the bushes, stabbed repeatedly, tossed into a small ravine, and covered with dirt. When discovered four hours later, she was in a coma, suffering from hypothermia, and had lost most of her body fluids. Neither the police nor the medical team who initially treated her expected her to survive.

The attack on the runner was not the only one to occur in the park that night. The warm spring weather had lured many people into its leafy reaches, and the pathways and lawns were crowded with runners, bikers, and pedestrians enjoying the evening. At around 9:00 p.m., a group of approximately 30 teenagers converged at the northeast corner, at the edge of Harlem, and went into the park together. All were youth of color. As they roamed across the park, some members of the group assaulted two other joggers, while others robbed a homeless man before they all scattered.

Word of the marauding reached the police, who quickly took a number of boys from the neighborhood into custody. Five of these youths, four black and one Latino, were placed in separate interrogation rooms, denied access to their parents, and questioned for between 14 and 30 hours. The boys ranged in age from 14–16; video footage of the interrogations shows the faces of children who had only recently reached puberty. All eventually made statements to the police. Although these statements contradicted each other, the boys quickly recanted their "confessions," and no physical evidence linked them to the crime, the five were charged with attempted murder, rape, and other violent felonies. Because under New York law they would be prosecuted as adults, the triumphant police immediately announced their names to the press. The boys were forced to participate in a "perp walk" as they were transported from the local precinct to the courthouse downtown. Headlines raged against the five, and their images dominated the news for months afterwards.

The media portrayed the boys in demonic terms. They were dubbed a "wolf pack" that was "wilding" and "doing the wild thing" in the park that night.[5] New York City Mayor Ed Koch called them "monsters," and real estate developer (and media hound) Donald Trump took out a full-page ad demanding their execution, even though they had not yet been tried or convicted.[6] They became a symbol of out-of-control youth violence, fueling the public's fear and lawmakers' punitive fury. Ultimately, all five boys were exonerated, but not before they were convicted and incarcerated for many years. The damage had been done.

The repercussions of this coverage reached far beyond the Central Park case itself. Its racial undercurrents tapped into and played on white America's biased perceptions and irrational fears of black youth, animalizing and dehumanizing not just these five boys but all youth of color. This in turn allowed the public and, by extension, policy and lawmakers, to view youth of color as the other, increasing the emotional distance between the white majority and the "monsters" from whom politicians promised to provide protection. In short, it tilled the soil in which DiIulio's dire "super-predator" warning took root six years later.[7]

What of that warning, with its terrifying allusion to animals who eat their own? The theory was simple: a sharp increase in juvenile crime during the late 1980s, coupled with an anticipated rise in the youth population during the following decades, would lead to an unprecedented adolescent "crime bomb." Based on DiIulio's and U.C.L.A. Professor James Q. Wilson's faulty interpretation of crime statistics and demographic data, these future perpetrators would not only be "fatherless, Godless, and jobless" but also "radically impulsive, brutally remorseless youngsters, including ever more teenage boys, who murder, assault, rob, burglarize, deal deadly drugs, join gun-toting gangs, and create serious [linked] disorders."[8] Northeastern University Professor James A. Fox went one step further by overtly racializing a similar prediction. In a 1996 report to the United States Department of Justice, Fox claimed, "Our nation faces a future juvenile violence problem that may make today's epidemic pale in comparison."[9] He alleged that a projected increase in the population of black teenagers would lead to soaring rates of violence. Adolescents, particularly those in

> urban areas, are plagued with idleness and even hopelessness. A growing number of teens and preteens see few feasible or attractive alternatives to violence, drug use, and gang membership. For them, the American Dream is a nightmare: There may be little to live for and to strive for, but plenty to die for and even to kill for.[10]

A spate of high-profile school shootings followed in the wake of the super-predator panic and seemed to confirm the theory. On October 1, 1997, a 16-year-old boy bludgeoned his mother to death in their Pearl, Mississippi home and then went to his high school, where he killed two students and injured seven others. Three months later, on December 1, 1997, a 14-year-old boy opened fire on a student prayer group in his school in Kentucky, killing three and wounding five. On March 24, 1998, two boys, ages 11 and 13, killed four fellow students and a teacher at their middle school in Jonesboro, Arkansas and wounded ten others. A mere eight weeks later, on May 20, 1998, a 15-year-old boy in Springfield, Oregon murdered both of his parents. The next morning, he went to school, where he killed 2 fellow students and wounded 23 others. Within the year, on April 20, 1999, 12 students and one teacher were killed by two boys, ages 17 and 18, at Columbine High School in Littleton, Colorado. The boys then killed themselves.

While all of the school shooters were white, the media response to these incidents was as sensationalistic as the coverage of the Central Park jogger case. *Time* magazine's April 6, 1998 cover, for example, carried a photo of one of the Jonesboro shooters as a toddler, holding a full-size rifle and smiling broadly.[11] One year later, *Time's* cover bore similarly smiling photos of the Columbine shooters with a blazing headline: "The Monsters Next Door."[12] The wilding city animals had been joined by the monsters next door in an onslaught on society's safety.

The ascendance of the cable news industry amplified the seismic shocks of the super-predator threat. Although Ted Turner launched CNN in 1980, it was not until the early 1990s that the network began its reign as a leading U.S. news outlet. Fox News and MSNBC began operations in 1996, giving birth to both the cable ratings wars and the 24-hour news cycle. DiIulio's vitriol and the school shootings fed into the industry's seemingly insatiable thirst for sensationalism, and the stories were examined from every possible angle for weeks on end. The coverage portrayed a tsunami of crime was about to overtake the nation, where schools were no longer safe and gun-toting teenagers were to blame.

These portrayals, of course, were wild distortions of the truth. The tragic shootings, although horrific, were aberrational, and children remain safer in school than almost any other environment. Correspondingly, juvenile crime rates began to plummet in the mid-1990s and today are at their lowest point in nearly 40 years.[13] The super-predator myth was based on an overly-simplistic misinterpretation of crime statistics and demographic data that was incorrect from its inception. Despite DiIulio's subsequent disavowal of the theory, the apocalyptic rhetoric he and Fox promulgated continues to drive U.S. public opinion two decades later,[14] in the face of still-declining crime rates.[15] According to a 2015 Gallup poll, for example, 70 percent of the population believed that crime had increased during the previous year, while actual crime rates had again fallen.[16]

Out of this zeitgeist erupted a flurry of retributive legislation that fundamentally altered juvenile justice in the United States. Between 1992 and 1999, 49 states and the District of Columbia enacted new laws that undermined the rehabilitative aims of the juvenile court.[17] These measures fell into three major categories: laws mandating or permitting the prosecution and incarceration of more children in the adult system (45 states); enhanced sentencing, including mandatory minimums, longer terms of incarceration, and "blended sentencing" options (31 states); elimination or erosion of traditional juvenile court confidentiality protections (47 states).[18] In addition, many states amended the "purpose" clauses of their juvenile codes to include such terms as "punishment," "accountability," "community safety," and "deterrence."[19] These new criteria shifted the power in the juvenile court away from the probation officer and judge, who traditionally had focused more on treatment and rehabilitation, to prosecutors who were more focused on punishment.[20] Finally, 22 states expanded the role of victims in juvenile court proceedings and accorded them increased access to juvenile court records.[21]

The New York landscape

Not to be outdone by their compatriots elsewhere, members of the New York State Senate and Assembly introduced juvenile justice "reform" bills during the 1997–98 legislative session. The proposed amendments tracked the national trends and included provisions that would have, *inter alia,* lowered the age for mandatory adult prosecution in homicide cases from 13 to 12; expanded the list of crimes subject to mandatory adult prosecution to include in-concert robberies, attempts, and certain weapons offenses; increased penalties, including incarceration terms, in both juvenile and adult court; increased prosecutorial authority in sentencing; diluted confidentiality protections by expanding fingerprinting of youth and public access to juvenile court records and opening juvenile courtrooms to the public; and enhanced victims' rights.[22]

Despite the broad sweep of these proposals, they were relatively modest compared to those in other states, not because their sponsors were rational but because New York law governing youth crime was already severe. From 1909 until 2017, the age of criminal responsibility was 16, regardless of the nature of the offense charged or the child's previous history.[23] Although recent statutory amendments eventually will extend juvenile court jurisdiction to the age of 18 for youth charged with misdemeanors and some low-level felonies, other 16- and 17-year-olds will remain in the adult system.[24] In this sense, New York is still an outlier; North Carolina, the only other state to prosecute all 16-year-olds as adults, also passed "raise the age" legislation in 2017.

New York also amended its juvenile crime laws governing how and when even younger children are prosecuted as adults in the late 1970s, making them among the most unforgiving in the country. In 1978, a 15-year-old was given a five-year sentence after shooting two subway passengers. Soon after, a 13-year-old with a history of troubling behavior walked up to another boy near the Columbia University campus and shot him. At the time, 13-year-olds could be incarcerated in a secure facility for 18 months before a judge would have to determine whether to keep them there until they were 18.[25] In reaction to these tragic killings, New York hastily enacted a Juvenile Offender Law requiring that all youth between the ages of 13 and 15 charged with certain serious felonies be tried in the criminal courts as adults.[26] Although they face shorter minimum terms of incarceration than adults convicted of similar crimes and initially are incarcerated in youth facilities, every other aspect of these children's treatment within the system is identical to that of adult defendants.

Defenders as policy advocates

Fifty years after *In re Gault's*[27] unambiguous recognition of children's right to counsel in delinquency cases, the country's juvenile indigent defense delivery system is a patchwork quilt of state-wide public defender offices, county public defenders, non-profit organizations, contract attorneys, and assigned counsel.[28] Considerable challenges confront these entities, as juvenile defense is grossly under-funded and not prioritized by legislators, courts, and, sometimes, public defender leadership.[29] Lawyers who represent children struggle with impossibly high caseloads, inadequate investigative and social work resources, and juvenile court systems that have erected seemingly insurmountable barriers to effective representation.[30] Nevertheless, these attorneys and the organizations for which they work have a unique window into the workings of the system and the experiences of the children caught up in it. They are able to evaluate the potential impact of proposed policy changes from the ground up and collect and aggregate critical data to inform policy-making. Their clients' stories put a human face on superficially benign measures and convey the human toll those measures might exact. Because those clients and their families generally lack even a modicum of political power or political access, defenders often offer the only viable avenue for sharing their stories with decision-makers and the larger community.

For these reasons, even over-stretched juvenile defense organizations have an obligation to become policy advocates. Absent an actual conflict of interest with an individual client, and assuming that the organization does not violate its confidentiality obligations, the Rules of Professional Conduct support such activities.[31] National standards that have been developed and revised since the 1970s exhort defenders and defender organizations to participate actively in the policy arena. The Institute for Judicial Administrations/American Bar Association *Juvenile Justice Standards*, for example, require the defense bar to form "committees" to monitor the operation of the system and advocate for reform. The Standards charge these committees with the following tasks:

- Advise, assist, criticize, and evaluate local or regional juvenile justice agencies;
- Publish regular, periodic reports on [their] findings in all appropriate media;
- Draft and disseminate comments on proposals for changes in legislation, rules, regulations, policies, and practices relating to activities of the juvenile justice system;
- Assist and cooperate with the monitoring activities conducted by any other monitoring mechanism to the fullest extent possible while preserving client confidentialities.[32]

The National Juvenile Defender Center's (NJDC) *National Juvenile Defense Standards* impose an even more explicit obligation on both individual defenders and defender organizations:

> Counsel should identify and promote potential issues and strategies that would strengthen and enhance juvenile indigent defense policy and practice, develop leadership, and build the capacity of the juvenile defense bar. Counsel should participate in ongoing policy and reform efforts that will have an impact on youth rights or juvenile court processes.[33]

Fleshing out this general responsibility, the NJDC Standards require defense attorneys to advocate for early access to counsel[34] and a presumption of indigence[35] for all children charged with delinquency and to challenge systemic abuses, including waiver of counsel, racial and ethnic disparities, excessive caseloads, inadequate defense resources, and harmful conditions of confinement for youth.[36] Finally, legal scholars have embraced and encouraged this activist, extra-judicial role for juvenile defenders.[37]

It was crucial, then, for JRD to step into the fray against legislation that would affect its clients in profoundly negative and lasting ways. Developing and implementing a pragmatic and effective advocacy strategy required an organizational commitment, creativity, and coalition-building.

The battle for New York's youth

By mid-1997, it was clear that without a sustained, coordinated resistance movement, New York would go the way of other states in further criminalizing adolescent wrongdoing. The movement that ultimately emerged reflected and drew upon the strengths of New York City's unique system of juvenile defense, as well as its extensive community of youth advocates. At the same time, it struggled to bridge the political divide between the city and other areas of the state, a bridge that was essential if the movement were to have any hope of success. Finally, it capitalized on the political standing and resources of the Legal Aid Society.

Legal Aid, a non-profit organization, is the oldest and largest provider of legal representation to the poor in the United States. Founded in 1876 to offer free civil legal services to German immigrants, the Society rapidly expanded and by 1910 had begun to represent clients in criminal as well as civil matters. Following the United States Supreme Court's 1963 decision in *Gideon v. Wainwright,*[38] Legal Aid's Criminal Defense Division was designated the primary public defender for New York City, a position it continues to hold today.[39] In 1962, five years before *Gault,* the Society created a stand-alone Juvenile Rights Division to represent New York City's children in child protective, termination of parental rights, status offense, and juvenile delinquency proceedings, providing a unique opportunity not only to speak on behalf of almost all of the children who are before the Family Court in New York City but also to develop a robust practice of interdisciplinary, client-centered child representation as a model for the country.[40]

Today, JRD continues to represent 90 percent of the children who appear before the city's Family Courts. State contracts that JRD negotiated over time secure interdisciplinary representation that includes a significant social work staff and access to other mental health professionals, as well as both appellate and "special litigation" attorney positions and a training unit, enabling the organization to engage in highly effective law reform advocacy (often against city and state agencies).[41] Approximately 350 lawyers, social workers, and support staff currently are representing children throughout the city. This far-ranging practice affords JRD's leadership and staff access to extensive data and a wealth of anecdotal and qualitative information, all of which inform and support its policy advocacy, and allows JRD to maintain a significant presence in the city and state legislatures, ensuring that its clients' interests are protected when relevant issues come to the fore.

Although its lawyers often struggle with large caseloads, JRD's size, city-wide presence, non-profit status, relative financial stability, continuing judicial support, and close ties to New York's elite legal and philanthropic circles afford it a level of independence and the resources necessary to engage effectively in the policy arena. From the beginning, the umbrella Legal Aid Society has cultivated relationships with the rich and powerful. Theodore Roosevelt and John D. Rockefeller were early supporters, and the Legal Aid Board of Directors is packed with members of the city's most prestigious law firms. Although some progressives assert that these ties tether the organization to the center, the relationships afford Legal Aid a degree of political clout and agility that is rare among public defender offices (most of which are under-funded governmental entities without political autonomy) and essential to its legislative advocacy efforts.

New York City also is home to countless non-profit advocacy and grassroots organizations with superb political acumen and organizing capabilities. Many of these groups focus on youth justice and children's rights issues but from different perspectives, with different skills, and according to different priorities than those of a large legal advocacy organization like JRD. The law faculties across the State are also filled with JRD alumni who routinely partner with JRD as well as the full range of youth advocacy organizations and foundations for systemic reform. For all of these advocates to work collaboratively and to capitalize on these various pockets of expertise, time, attention, and mutual respect are essential.

In New York, geography has an outsize influence on the shape of public policy debates. The state is divided geographically, demographically, and culturally between the diverse, left-leaning New York City metropolitan area and more homogeneous and conservative "upstate" counties. The State Assembly tends to fall under Democratic control, while the Senate historically has leaned Republican. The governorship veers between the two parties. Frequently, final decisions on legislation are made by what has been labeled "three men in a room": the governor, the Democratic Assembly leader, and the Republican Senate leader. This entrenched division of power requires proponents of legislative change to employ strategies that target members of both parties, particularly those with access to the "three men." Since New York prisons and secure and limited secure youth facilities are located in predominantly rural areas, where they drive local economies, these strategies to target upstate Republicans are especially crucial when juvenile and criminal justice policies are at stake.[42] At the same time, most youth in long-term state custody are from the five boroughs of New York City, creating a deep schism between the two halves of the state. Any legislative advocacy effort has to bridge this divide.

Against this backdrop, in late 1997, JRD and its partners launched an informal campaign to defeat the pernicious pending legislation and, more broadly, encourage progressive youth justice reform. The time was ripe for several reasons. First, although both houses of the State Legislature had passed their respective bills, there were substantial differences between the two and we believed that we could halt the reconciliation process. Second, the tenor of the national debate was slowly starting to shift away from the most inflammatory rhetoric, largely in response to retrograde proposed federal legislation. The Juvenile Crime Control Act 1997, sponsored by then-Representative Bill McCollum (R-FL), and the Violent and Repeat Juvenile Offenders Act 1997, sponsored by then-Senator Jeff Sessions (R-AL) and Orrin Hatch (R-UT), both would have mandated adult prosecution and incarceration of children as young as 13, among other noxious provisions.[43] The House bill passed in May 1997 by a majority of more than two-thirds, but a funny thing happened on the way to the Senate. Newspapers as diverse as the *Tuscaloosa News, Sacramento Bee*, and *The Washington Post* ran editorials and opinion pieces denouncing the Hatch/Sessions bill. A large group of district attorneys publicly opposed it. And, in what was perhaps an unprecedented move, a national coalition of correctional officers, sheriff's officers, and other law enforcement personnel took out a full-page advertisement in the conservative *Washington Times* on June 11, 1999, urging lawmakers to reject the legislation. The ad read, in part: "Lock a Thirteen-Year-Old Up with Rapists and Murderers, and Guess What He'll Want to Be When He Grows Up?"[44]

Despite these glimmers of hope, enactment of the New York legislation remained a real threat. We thus began to chart a course which, we hoped, would not only defeat the pending bills but move the State toward a more compassionate, effective, and cost-effective youth justice system.

The first step was to strengthen and expand existing alliances. The highly regarded Correctional Association of New York had formed a Juvenile Justice Coalition earlier that year, which provided a ready structure for collaboration. In addition to JRD, the Coalition encompassed some of New York City's leading youth advocacy organizations, such as the Center for Alternative Sentencing and Employment Services (CASES), the city's largest alternative to detention and alternative to incarceration program; Citizens' Committee for Children, a policy advocacy organization; and YouthForce, a youth-led coalition of formerly-incarcerated young people, among others. Each of these groups brought a unique perspective to the Coalition, which was to prove essential to the success of the campaign.

The Coalition steering committee, which included representatives from the core organizations as well as several others, recognized the importance of pursuing a policy agenda that was both proactive and responsive. The steering committee developed a detailed list of priorities that included not only defeat of the pending bills but also aspirational goals, such as facility closures, improved aftercare services, expanded alternatives to incarceration, and restoration of previously eliminated educational programs within facilities. It also identified key legislators and other stakeholders who would influence or direct decision-making at the state and city levels, as well as potential allies and antagonists. The steering committee also agreed on certain guiding principles for the campaign. These included firm opposition to building new facilities or adding beds to existing structures; recognition of the importance of data as an advocacy tool; a willingness to "play" to conservatives with fiscal analyses and arguments; and a commitment to highlighting racial disparities. Although Coalition members met and consulted with one another regularly, we did not move in lockstep. Each organization drew on its individual strengths, relationships, and expertise to implement advocacy strategies that were consistent with the Coalition's goals but not necessarily pursued in tandem with those of other member organizations. There was strength in numbers and also in individual actions.

Over the next year, JRD devoted substantial resources to the campaign. Our action plan was deliberately multi-pronged, capitalizing on the organization's longstanding relationships with legislators and legislative staff and utilizing both qualitative and quantitative data gleaned from public sources and our own representation of system-involved children. We also became students of the media in order to influence news coverage and, consequently, public opinion. We began to travel more extensively, not only to Albany, the state capital, but to other upstate locations to pursue our strategies.[45] Our roadmap included many of the fundamental tactics of policy advocacy, including:

Understand and use data effectively: The work of traditional defender offices centers on the interests, needs, and wishes of individual clients. This approach is rooted in ethical considerations; pursuant to the Rules of Professional Conduct, lawyers must "abide by a client's decisions concerning the objectives of representation and … consult with the client as to the means by which they are to be pursued."[46] For reasons of time, resources, and inclination, many defenders do not focus on "big picture" questions or gather, aggregate, and study system-wide data. We knew, however, that understanding youth crime statistics, recidivism, the costs and effectiveness of the full spectrum of responses to youth crime, and racial and ethnic disparities was essential to our legislative and policy advocacy. We thus began to look hard at data.[47] Utilizing our first-generation personal computers, we gathered information about youth offending and arrests rates, admissions to local juvenile detention and long-term placement facilities, the demographics of system-involved youth, the costs of incarceration versus community-based programs, and comparative recidivism rates. We also focused on more qualitative issues that daily impacted our clients, drawing on the direct experiences of the youth we represented. What actually happened to our clients when they were incarcerated? Where did they go, and under what conditions were they held? What were their average lengths of stay? What specific services did the various alternatives to detention and incarceration offer to their participants? What were the programs' reporting and participation requirements and average staff to participant ratios? And, perhaps most imperative in the political context, what were the real short- and long-term fiscal consequences of the various proposals and our proposed alternatives? We then created a set of graphics that conveyed the data cogently and colorfully. These depictions were valuable tools in our subsequent interactions with legislators and the media, enhancing not only our ability to tell the stories we had crafted but also impressing the listeners with an approach that effectively utilized current technological advances. Finally, we learned how to use statistics effectively, to understand their shortcomings, and to anticipate and respond to pushback or seemingly contradictory numbers.

Make information accessible: Lawyers are trained to think and write in a detailed, comprehensive manner. Effective legislative and media advocacy, on the other hand, also requires distillation of complex ideas and information for non-lawyers. To that end, with other members of the Coalition, we developed a series of fact sheets that summarized the relevant issues and statistics, succinctly stated the group's positions, and offered action proposals. We distributed these position papers and the data graphics widely to reporters, legislators, members of the judiciary and executive branch, and grassroots organizations. Because these materials were more accessible and easily digested than anything developed by the opposition, we gained the upper hand in the information debate.

Challenge inaccurate perceptions: Gaining that advantage required some myth-busting. Then as now, public perceptions of crime, incarceration, and community-based programs diverged significantly from the truth. Opinion polls, for example, indicated that even in 1998, after six years of sharply falling crime rates, most people believed that youth crime was on the rise. A smaller majority thought that longer juvenile sentences and trying more youth in adult court would serve as a deterrent and reduce recidivism, while a substantial body of research proved the opposite to be true. The Coalition identified and challenged these myths head-on in our fact sheets and by seeking out every possible venue in which to make our case: community centers, PTA meetings, and women's clubs, for example, as well as the more obvious legislative and media fora.

Cultivate legislative relationships: Legal Aid has longstanding relationships with key state and city legislators, particularly those who chair the committees through which any bills involving its clients must pass and, more important, their staff members. Cognizant of the upstate/downstate divide, we targeted not only members of the New York City delegation but also legislators from other areas of the state who were not natural allies. We cultivated these contacts by submitting written testimony and testifying at every relevant legislative hearing; sharing our expertise and providing informal analyses and feedback outside the context of formal hearings; and, when drafting language for proposed bills. Legal Aid contracted with lobbyists who enhanced our regular presence in Albany by facilitating frequent meetings with legislators and their staffs as well as the Governor's staff and other key decision-makers. Our analyses and written submissions made it easier for staff to adopt our proposals, and the inter-personal interactions encouraged essential trust and rapport.

Develop an alternative argot: Word choice has a profound impact on a reader or listener's interpretation of and emotional reaction to information. The words and images that the media and legislators used to describe system-involved children were negative, disparaging, and harmful, while the argot of the juvenile court was superficially benign. (Children were not "incarcerated," for example, but "placed.") We were determined to shift these linguistic paradigms. We excised the noun "juvenile" from our vocabulary, substituting "child" and "children" whenever possible, and critiqued our language to ensure that it conveyed accurately who our clients were and what happened to them when they entered the juvenile and adult courts and incarceration systems.

Counter "bad news" with "good news": The media's proclivity for sensationalism and doomsday forecasts leaves little room for factually accurate, positive stories. As a result, the public is left with an inaccurate, incomplete, and unjustifiably negative understanding of youth crime and responses to it. Polling data reflects these inaccurate perceptions, leading to unwise and unfounded policy decisions. We decided to tackle this problem head-on by spreading "good news" about declining crime rates, effective prevention and community-based intervention and treatment programs, and progressive legislative and policy initiatives from across the country.[48] A talented JRD paralegal collected the stories, wrote one-paragraph abridged versions, and published them in a one-page, bi-weekly newsletter entitled *Youth Alert*. We distributed the publication to an extensive list of legislators and legislative staff, journalists, non-profit youth-serving organizations, city and state government officials, and attorneys for children in an effort to nudge public opinion into alignment with the data.

Make your own headlines: It was essential for us not only to respond to reporters' inquiries but also to become media activists. We worked with Legal Aid's public information officer and a sympathetic reporter to hone our media skills. We learned how to develop and "stay on" a clear message; how to take control of interviews; how to create effective "sound bites," and how to distill complex information down to plain talk. We combed the papers for relevant stories and developed a rapid response protocol, writing letters to the editor to refute inaccuracies, "spin" the negative, and accentuate the positive.[49] We published longer opinion pieces that were both reactive and proactive.[50] Finally, we made presentations to the editorial boards of the leading newspapers in every quadrant of the state, in which we utilized the data, fact sheets, and coverage we had generated to successfully "pitch" editorials that opposed the pending legislation and embraced our alternative vision of a system rooted in prevention and community-based, developmentally appropriate responses to youth crime. One of the resulting headlines urged lawmakers to "break from the pack" and "focus" on prevention rather than punishment.[51]

Say "Yes" to the press: As discussed above, the television coverage of the late-1990s school shootings was constant and abhorrent. Nevertheless, we took advantage of news programming's typical point-counterpoint format when the cable networks actively sought liberal commentators after each tragic incident. Due to Legal Aid's prominence and Manhattan location, we received many invitations to appear on these shows as "experts" in juvenile justice. After much discussion and soul-searching, we ultimately decided to participate in the media's feeding frenzy. Although we would have preferred to discourage the exploitative coverage, our refusal to cooperate had the potential to exacerbate rather than alleviate the exploitation. We decided to use these opportunities to de-bunk the myths about youth crime and promote our positive agenda. In this arena, like the courtroom and the legislature, silence would only harm our clients.

Engage youth: We were extremely fortunate to have YouthForce as a partner in the campaign. A grassroots organization for and led by formerly incarcerated youth, YouthForce was vibrant, well-respected, and savvy in the ways of politics.

During the course of the campaign, the group organized several Albany "Lobby Days" for their members and other Coalition partners. Prior to these events, adult members of the Coalition helped train the young people on the intricacies of the various proposals and how to interact effectively with legislators. We caravanned to Albany in buses and watched as the youth worked their magic on usually immovable lawmakers. They were passionate, compelling, and persuasive, and they brought personal experience and legitimacy to our collective efforts.

Conclusion: overcoming barriers

Ultimately, our campaign was successful. The legislature failed to reconcile the two bills, and they died with the end of the legislative session.[52] Without question, JRD was instrumental in this outcome.

As the JRD experience makes clear, defenders have a crucial role to play in legislative and policy battles that affect their clients. Most defender organizations, however, face seemingly insurmountable barriers to engaging in this type of advocacy. Most lack the financial resources and staffing levels of JRD. Some are prohibited, either by statute or their status as government agencies, from testifying before the legislature or taking positions in opposition to the executive branch. Elected public defenders may fear public reprisals, and appointed public defenders may fear recrimination or worse by their superiors. The threat of budgetary reprisal is real, as is the possibility of other retaliatory actions, such as re-allocation of resources away from defender organizations and to contract attorneys, who are unlikely to become involved in policy debates.

Although strategies to overcome these barriers must be tailored to each organization's funding sources, administrative structure, and political considerations, the toolbox includes building and nurturing alliances with other advocates, who may not labor under the same constraints and can act as the public face of a campaign; lending expertise to and, when ethically appropriate, sharing client stories with those partners or encouraging clients to develop their own capacities to speak out and create advocacy strategies; speaking "off the record" to educate and provide background information to trustworthy media allies; testifying at legislative hearings and speaking with legislators and legislative staff in one's private capacity; for elected public defenders, addressing policy issues on the campaign trail; developing relationships and advocating informally with key policy-makers or being readily available to answer factual questions for them; and, when possible, challenging harmful policies and practices within the context of the representation of individual youth. Whatever the means, juvenile defenders must lend their unique perspective to bear and raise their powerful voices on behalf of the often voiceless children they serve.

Notes

1 Steven Drizin, *Trayvon and the Myth of the "Juvenile Super-Predator,* HuffPost (Nov. 17, 2013), https://www.huffingtonpost.com/entry/superpredator-myth-lives-_b_3923140.html.

2 Roper v. Simmons, 543 U.S. 551 (2005); Graham v. Florida, 560 U.S. 48 (2010); J.D. B. v. North Carolina, 564 U.S. 261 (2011); Miller v. Alabama, 567 U.S. 460 (2012).

3 Today, the organization is known as the Juvenile Rights Practice. However, we will use "JRD" for purposes of historical accuracy.

4 Barry C. Feld, *Legislative Exclusion of Offenses from Juvenile Court Jurisdiction: A History and Critique,* in JEFFREY FAGAN AND FRANKLIN E. ZIMRING (EDITORS), THE CHANGING BORDERS OF JUVENILE JUSTICE (University of Chicago Press, 2000).

5 Benjamin Weiser, *5 Exonerated in Central Park Jogger Case Agree to Settle Suit for $40 Million,* N.Y. TIMES (June 19, 2014), https://www.nytimes.com/2014/06/20/nyregion/5-exonerated-in-central-park-jogger-case-are-to-settle-suit-for-40-million.html.

6 N.Y. DAILY NEWS (May 1, 1989).

7 In addition to the Central Park jogger case, several other high-profile incidents of youth crime sparked the 1990s legislative attack on children. These included, for example, the 1994 murder in Chicago of five-year-old Eric Morse, who was dropped out of a window by two boys, ages 10 and 11, after he refused to steal candy for them. *See* Jesenia M. Pizarro et al., *Juvenile "Super-Predators" in the News: A Comparison of Adult and Juvenile Homicides,* 14 J. CRIM. J. & POP. CULTURE 84 (2007).

8 MICHAEL J. BENNETT ET AL., BODY COUNT: MORAL POVERTY … AND HOW TO WIN AMERICA'S WAR ON DRUGS 25 (Simon & Schuster, 1996).

9 JAMES A. FOX, TRENDS IN JUVENILE VIOLENCE: A REPORT TO THE UNITED STATES ATTORNEY GENERAL ON CURRENT AND FUTURE RATES OF JUVENILE OFFENDING 3 (1996), https://bjs.gov/content/pub/pdf/tjvfox.pdf (last visited Dec. 30 2017).

10 *Id.* It is worth noting how different this conclusion is from that contained in the 1965 report of President Lyndon B. Johnson's Commission on Law Enforcement and Administration of Justice, *The Challenge of Crime in a Free Society,* which concluded that the solutions for reducing delinquency were to ameliorate the economic and social conditions these children faced and to make the instruments of justice fairer. The latter recommendation is a direct precursor to the Supreme Court's decision in In re Gault two years later. *See* Michael H. Tonry, *Juvenile Justice and the National Crime Commissions,* in MARGARET K. ROSENHEIM, PURSUING JUSTICE FOR THE CHILD (STUDIES IN CRIME AND JUSTICE) (University of Chicago Press, 1978).

11 TIME (Apr. 6, 1998).

12 TIME (May 3, 1999). These headlines notwithstanding, the coverage of the school shootings had a substantially different tone from that of the Central Park case. Rather than the animalistic portrayals of the five boys charged with the attack on the jogger, newspapers and magazines ran photos depicting the shooters as prototypical "boys next door" and focused on such issues as gun control and adolescent alienation in the heartland. The fact that all of the school shooters were white raises obvious concerns about implicit and explicit media bias and its subsequent impact on public policy.

13 Office of Juvenile Justice and Delinquency Prevention, *Statistical Briefing Book* (Mar. 27, 2017), https://www.ojjdp.gov/ojstatbb/crime/JAR_Display.asp?ID=qa05200.

14 Clyde Haberman, *When Youth Violence Spurred the Super-Predator Fear,* N.Y. TIMES (Apr. 6, 2014), https://www.nytimes.com/2014/04/07/us/politics/killing-on-bus-rec/alls-superpredator-threat-of-90s.html.

15 *See* MELISSA SICKMUND & CHARLES PUZZANCHERA, JUVENILE OFFENDERS AND VICTIMS: 2014 NATIONAL REPORT (2014), http://ncjj.org/nr2014/downloads/NR2014.pdf (last visited Dec. 30 2017).

16 Jeffrey McCarthy, *More Americans Say Crime Is Rising in U.S.* (2015), http://www.gallup.com/poll/186308/americans-say-crime-rising.aspx (last visited Dec. 30 2017).

17 A similar federal initiative failed to pass both houses of Congress and was never enacted. Nevertheless, the primary sponsor of the House Bill, Representative Bill McCollum, went on to become the Governor of Florida, where he championed juvenile life without parole legislation later declared unconstitutional by the United States Supreme Court in Graham v. Florida, 560 U.S. 48 (2010).

18 Melissa Sickmund, *Juveniles in Court*, Juvenile Offenders and Victims: National Report Series – OJJDP Bulletin (2003), https://www.ncjrs.gov/html/ojjdp/195420/contents.html (last visited Dec. 30, 2017).

19 *Id.*

20 Franklin E. Zimring, *The Power Politics of Juvenile Court Transfer in the 1990's*, in David S. Tanenhaus and Franklin E. Zimring, Choosing the Future for American Juvenile Justice 47–48 (N.Y.U. Press, 2014).

21 *Id.*

22 *See* Juvenile Justice Accountability and Crime Reduction Act 1998, N.Y. State Assembly Bill A.8179-A (1998) and Juvenile Justice Accountability and Procedural Reform Act 1998, N.Y. State Senate Bill S.2379-A (1998).

23 N.Y. PL § 2186 (1909); N.Y. FCA § 301.2(1) (1982).

24 N.Y. CPL § 1.20(42), (44) (1970; amended 2017).

25 *See Youth Shot 'for Laughing' Dies; 2 Boys, 13 and 16, Are Arraigned*, N.Y. Times (July 7, 1978). One of the authors represented this youth at his subsequent hearings to determine whether he would be released from a secure facility to a less secure facility in order to transition back to the community before his eighteenth birthday. This plan was rejected repeatedly by the court. When he turned 18, with no transition plan or assistance, he was released.

26 *See* Eli Hager, *The Willie Bosket Case: How Children Became Adults in the Eyes of the Law* (Dec. 29, 2014), https://www.themarshallproject.org/2014/12/29/the-willie-bosket-case#.iLpVPM1cc (last visited Dec. 30, 2017).

27 387 U.S. 1 (1967).

28 *See* National Juvenile Defender Center, *State Profiles*, http://njdc.info/practice-policy-resources/state-profiles/ (last visited Oct. 16, 2017).

29 Nat'l Juvenile Defender Cntr., Access Denied: A Snapshot of States' Failure to Protect Children's Right to Counsel (May 2017), http://njdc.info/wp-content/uploads/2017/05/Snapshot-Final_single-4.pdf (last visited Dec. 30 2017).

30 *Id.*

31 *See* Model Rule of Prof'l. Conduct r. 1.6–1.10 (Am. Bar Ass'n, 2014 ed.).

32 Inst. for Judicial Admin./Am. Bar Ass'n, Juvenile Justice Standards Annotated: A Balanced Approach, Standards Relating to Monitoring, Std. 3.2–3.3 (1996), https://www.ncjrs.gov/pdffiles1/ojjdp/166773.pdf (last visited Dec. 30 2017).

33 Nat'l Juvenile Defender Cntr., National Juvenile Defense Standards, Std. 10.1 (2012), http://njdc.info/wp-content/uploads/2013/09/NationalJuvenileDefenseStandards2013.pdf (last visited Dec. 30 2017).

34 *Id.* at Std. 10.2.

35 *Id.* at Std. 10.3.

36 *Id.* at Stds. 10.4–10.8.

37 *See, e.g.*, Katherine Kruse, In re Gault *and the Promise of Systemic Reform*, 75 Tenn. L. Rev. 287 (2008); Mark H. Moore, *Alternative Strategies for Public Defenders and Assigned Counsel*, 29 N.Y.U. Rev. L. & Soc. Change 83, 100–104 (2004); N. Lee Cooper et al., *Fulfilling the Promise of In re Gault: Advancing the Role of Lawyers for Children*, 33 Wake Forest L. Rev. 651, 671–74 (1998); Nevada Law Journal, *Recommendations of the UNLV Conference on Representing Children in Families: Child Advocacy and Juvenile Justice Ten Years After Fordham*, 6 UNLV L. J. 592, 608–09 (2006); Laura Cohen, *Kids, Courts, and Cameras: New Challenges for Juvenile Defenders*, 18 Quinnipiac L. Rev. 701 (1999).

38 372 U.S. 335 (1963).

39 Like JRD, the Criminal Defense Division later was re-christened the Criminal Defense Practice.

40 Jane M. Spinak, *The Role of Strategic Management Planning in Improving the Representation of Clients: A Child Advocacy Example*, 34 Fam. L.Q. 497 (2000).

41 *Id.*

42 Nicholas Confessore, *Official Hopes Prison Crisis May Spur Change,* N.Y. TIMES (December 15, 2009).

43 President Bill Clinton opposed the legislation, but only because it failed to include gun control provisions. The Administration voiced no substantive objection to the punitive portions of the bills.

44 *See* advertisement placed by The Coalition to Prevent Juvenile Crime, THE WASHINGTON TIMES (June 11, 1997).

45 Both authors are from upstate New York and relied on our upstate sensibilities to help influence lawmakers from those areas and their staffs.

46 MODEL RULES OF PROF'L. CONDUCT r. 1.2(a) (AM. BAR ASS'N, 2014 ed.). *See* Kim Taylor-Thompson, Individual Actor v. Institutional Player: Alternating Visions of the Public Defender, 84 GEO. L. J. 2014 (1996).

47 Our use of data during this time also enhanced our ability to convince our state funders to allow us to reorganize the structure of the borough and appellate practices, improving the quality of our representation and deepening our expertise in our various areas of practice. *See* Spinak, *supra* note 40, at 14–15.

48 An important report issued by the Justice Policy Institute in 1998, *Runaway Juvenile Crime? The Context of Juvenile Arrests in America,* facilitated our ability to change the dominant narrative then and in the following years. http://www.justicepolicy.org/uploads/justicepolicy/documents/98–03_rep_runawayjuvenilecrime_jj.pdf (last visited Dec. 30, 2017).

49 *See, e.g.,* Laura Cohen, *Letter to the Editor: Juvenile Justice Bill,* N.Y. TIMES (Aug. 3, 1998).

50 *See, e.g.,* Jane Spinak & Laura Cohen, *Vacco Juvenile Justice Article Misstates Facts, Law,* THE ALBANY TIMES UNION (Apr. 25, 1998).

51 Editorial, *Break from the Pack,* ROCHESTER DEMOCRAT AND CHRONICLE, Apr. 1, 1998, at 9.

52 Several smaller provisions were enacted during later sessions.

Index

abuses 10, 12, 16, 217, 229–30, 237, 259–61, 275; institutional 236–37, 260; physical 53, 256, 260; problems relating to 121; state-sanctioned 194; systemic 227, 275
ACLU 4–5, 193, 259–60; *see also* American Civil Liberties Union
Acts and Regulations 171, 177, 233, 274; *Bill of Rights* 128, 130; *Child Abuse Prevention and Treatment Act* 103, 138; *Civil Rights Act* 170; *Delinquency Prevention Act* 170; *Family Court Act 1962* 88–89; *Freedom of Information Act* 211; *Individuals with Disabilities Education Improvement Act* 121; *Juvenile Justice and Delinquency Prevention Act* 170–71, 181; *Juvenile Justice Reform Act* 95; *Violent and Repeat Juvenile Offenders Act* 277
ADJC 26–27, 229; *see also* Arizona Department of Juvenile Corrections
adjudications 22, 82, 110, 114, 243; hearings relating to 189; juvenile court 177, 189, 191, 244; trial judge's 15; and youthful offenders 155, 161
adolescent development research 51–52, 55, 60, 62–63, 65–66, 68
Adolescent Intervention and Diversion Project 156
adolescents 15–17, 35, 53, 55–60, 67, 126, 141, 155–59, 161, 163, 165, 188, 207, 217, 231, 234–35, 238, 245; and adults 55, 58–59, 67, 156; ages of 201; and the assessment of innocence 31; and behavior issues 24, 58, 121, 189, 202, 206, 209; and brain science studies using 16, 55, 59–60, 141, 155–56; and defence in adult courts 155, 157, 159, 161, 163, 165; and defense council representing 156, 164; development of 24, 26–27, 60–62, 66, 109, 126, 156–57, 190, 202, 206, 212; and improving model of defense representation for 154; incarcerated 233; and policies relating to 195; policing in their communities 163; and the process of maturation 55; and an unprecedented "crime bomb" 271; white 209; younger 58, 68
adult clients 117, 121, 137
adult criminal courts 5, 8, 23–24, 27, 66–67, 82, 107–8, 110, 112, 116–17, 125, 128, 130, 154–59, 161, 163, 165, 279
adult prisons 154, 229, 240, 253–55; resembled 259–60; and systemic racism embedded in juvenile justice 253
adulthood 57–59, 67, 156, 161, 165, 230
adults 6–7, 22–24, 26–27, 31–32, 51–68, 79–80, 82, 92–96, 103, 125–26, 128, 136, 155–58, 162–63, 202, 231–32, 234, 273; black 15, 30, 33; culpable 67; detained 90; low-income 188; and procedural protections 82; for purposes of criminal prosecution 155; for purposes of sentencing 63; young 58, 67–68
advocacy 23, 30, 38, 43, 55, 105, 129, 156, 162–65, 179, 190, 192, 202, 211, 231, 240–41, 262, 281; anti-racist 43; client-centered 206; client-directed 83, 200; dedicated systems reform 171; effective law reform 275; extra-legal 30, 43; in-court 160; individual case 210; informal 242; legislative 156, 163, 210–11, 259; non-legal 30; non-profit 276; paternalistic 83; political 36; post-disposition 191; post-sentencing

161; pre-trial 178; racial-justice 213; skills 176, 178; strategies 278, 281; vigorous 172, 188
African-American youths 40, 44, 106, 109, 131, 253
aftercare services 277
age 7, 15, 24, 31, 37, 53, 56–60, 63–69, 93, 155–58, 161–62, 165, 201–2, 209, 227, 234, 270–71, 273; children's 132, 155; of criminal responsibility 81, 273; differences impacting individual psychosocial factors 57–58; groups 56–57
agencies 115, 118, 124, 172, 175, 235, 240–41; correctional 242–43; policies of 212; protective 164; regional juvenile justice 274; and staff members 241; statewide 173
AID 156, 162–63; lawyers and social workers 160–62; staff 160, 163; teams 157, 159, 161, 164; *see also* Adolescent Intervention and Diversion Project
Alabama 63, 141, 155, 170; and the class action for the desegregation of three reform schools 42; desegregation of all prisons and jails in 41; prisoners 41
Alabama Boys Industrial School 42
Albert, Dustin 57
amendments 170–71, 235, 273; legislative 170; statutory 273
American Academy of Child and Adolescent Psychiatry 238
American Bar Association 55, 137–39, 171, 173, 177, 235; conducts a review of law school clinics, related policies, statutes, rules and regulations in urban, suburban and rural areas 171; conducts an extensive literature review, a national survey, and on-site investigations of public defense systems 171; and the Criminal Justice Section Council 173; and juvenile justice reform 171; and NJDC staff devise strategies to identify juvenile defenders in every state and the District of Columbia 174
American Bar Association Criminal Justice Standards 136
American Bar Association Juvenile Justice Center 171, 235
American Bar Association's Directory of Pro Bono Children's Law Programs 139
American Bar Association's Juvenile Justice Standards 235
American children 95, 99, 101, 105, 113, 118, 129, 133, 141, 171, 181, 270
American Civil Liberties Union 4–5, 193, 259–60
American Juvenile Courts 102
American juvenile justice system 30, 34, 40, 44, 96
American law schools 4, 99, 107, 109, 128–29, 133–35, 137–42, 173, 192
American police 10, 21, 33–34, 68, 79, 86, 107, 140, 191, 199, 203, 207–8, 218–19, 222–25, 244, 270
American Psychological Association 221–23
American youth corrections facilities 256
Annie E. Casey Foundation 229, 237, 256
anti-racist advocacy 43
anti-Vietnam War movement 134
APA 221–23; *see also* American Psychological Association
appeals 4, 8, 15, 21–23, 41, 85, 88–90, 93–94, 101, 110, 118–19, 124, 136–38, 141, 223, 233; administrative 240; bureau 87; rejectection of Beazley's 61; special 87
appellate courts 15, 87, 124, 141, 223
Areen, Judith C. 136–37
arguments 11, 13–14, 54, 101, 109–10, 118, 140–41, 161, 207, 209–10, 277; closing 14, 88, 224; constitutional 264; legal 241; political 31; pre-trial release 207; racial justice 205–6, 212; social justice (of the 1960s and 1970s) 134
Arizona 5, 7, 20–28, 65, 129, 229; children 20, 23, 25–28; economy of 25; forced to respond to the Gault decision 22; and the increase of population 25; juvenile court system 21, 24; juvenile law and children's due process rights 23; and the passing of standardized tests 27; state legislature 22; youth 23
Arizona Department of Juvenile Corrections 26–27, 229
Arizona Juvenile Code 22
Arizona Office of the Courts 23
Arizona Public Defender Association 24
Arizona State Industrial School for Boys 16, 20–22, 227
Arizona Supreme Court 4, 21, 23, 130
Arkansas Training School for Boys 42
arrests 32, 44, 160, 165, 188, 192, 195, 206, 264; first-ever 93; juvenile 230; monitoring of 211; multiple 41; prior for

uncharged allegations 207; rates 181, 278
assessments 31–33, 68, 158, 174, 177, 191; case 157; culpability 31; local workload 173; probation officer's 209; psychosocial 120; state 177, 235; state-based juvenile defense 176
Atkins v. Virginia 61
attorneys 21–26, 83–84, 86–87, 114–15, 122–26, 140–41, 158, 172, 177–78, 187, 189–93, 199–200, 203–5, 210, 235–39, 242, 260, 262–63; appellate 23; court-appointed 24, 26–27, 123; educational 114, 120; fees 44, 190; full-time 88, 123; hiring of 141; immigration 114–15; individual 115; inexperienced 178; new 22, 83; prosecuting 24; senior 117, 125; supervising of 115, 125
authority 30–31, 33, 35, 37, 39, 41–45, 68, 111, 113, 131, 172, 217, 229, 239; black juvenile justice 38, 40, 43; figures 223, 231; governmental 39, 41; investigative 238; prosecutorial 273; supervisory 130; unquestioned 135

Baharanyi, Zawadi 4–17
Banich, Marie 57–58
Banks, Dennis 131
Bar Association 105, 172–73, 205
Barrett, Janie Porter 37, 194
Barrett Prettyman Program 137
Bass, Karen 187
Beazley, Napoleon 61
behavior 55, 59, 121–22, 156, 158–59, 161–62, 188, 193, 200, 209, 237, 273; correcting children's 25; normative adolescent 155, 181, 269; problems 162; youth's 232
behavioral science research 55
behavioral tasks 57
benefits 20, 26, 31, 33, 35–36, 42, 58, 115, 120, 173, 195, 203, 220–21, 243, 259; mitigating 34; political 269; potential 13; public 115, 120, 122; significant 157
benefits specialists 120
Bernstein, Charles C. 228, 258
Bethune, Mary McLeod 39
biases 16, 176, 192, 200–205; explicit 200–201; implicit 192, 200, 203–4; judicial 14–15; own-race 208; policing 211
Bill of Rights 128, 130
bills 39–40, 103, 130, 210–11, 239, 276–77, 279, 281
Black Child Savers 253–54, 264
black children 15, 30–32, 35–38, 40–41, 43, 188, 202
black leaders 36–37, 202
black males 32, 192, 207–8
black parents 36
black schoolchildren 15
black women 36–38, 44
black youth 30–40, 42–44, 181, 189, 199, 207, 209–10, 230, 253–54, 264, 271; advocacy for 30; and communities 40; denigrated 30; incarcerated 37; and the institutional elements of "Jim Crow" juvenile justice 36; portrayed with negative personality traits 209; and racial discrimination 30; and the role of Mary McLeod Bethune 39; and the Warren Court 32
Blackmun, Harry 11–16
blacks 11, 30–32, 35–37, 44, 201
Bolin, Jane 39
Bonner, John 30
boys 6, 14, 16, 21–22, 30, 40, 42–43, 51, 53, 81, 110, 113, 227–28, 253, 270–71, 273; teenage 271; white 30–31; young 52
brain 55, 59–60; development 59; systems 60
Brennan, Justice 11, 15
Brill, Carole 101
Bronx area 86–87
Bronx Corporation Counsel 86
Bronx Family Court 86
Brown v. Board of Education 40–41
Bureau of Justice Statistics survey 256
Burger, Chief Justice Warren 11–12
burglaries 5, 208
Burrus, Barbara 15–16

California 20, 169, 187, 192, 212, 222, 259–61
California Court of Appeals 223–24
California Youth Authority 260
Camp Hill (State Correctional Institution) 111–12
Campaign for the Fair Sentencing of Youth 142
campaigns 142, 192, 212, 260–62, 277–78, 280–81; comprehensive 259; dynamic 264; effective 40; informal 276; issues concerning 39; legal 37; successful 261, 263

capital punishment 53–55, 61, 270
care 37, 85, 103, 106–7, 155–56, 159–60, 164, 203, 230–31, 237, 242, 254, 259; in-home 111; out-of-home 203; secure 254; services 159
cases 10–12, 14–16, 32–34, 53, 63–65, 81–82, 84–92, 94–95, 100–104, 106, 114–16, 125, 129–30, 136–37, 139–41, 156–57, 203–7, 222–25; *Atkins v. Virginia* 61; *Brown v. Board of Education* 40–41; *Crum v. State Training School for Girls* 42; *Duncan v. Louisiana* 11, 13; *Eddings v. Oklahoma* 53, 64–65; *Frazier v. Cupp* 222; *Gagnon v. Scarpelli* 233; *Gideon v. Wainwright* 5, 22, 32–33, 40, 43, 130, 169–70, 275; *Graham v. Florida* 141, 155; *Haley v. Ohio* 51, 65, 223; *J.D.B. v. North Carolina* 65, 219; *John L. v. Adams* 234; *Kent v United States* 5–6, 12, 15–16, 30, 51, 110, 129–30, 132, 170; *Major v. Sowers* 42; *Mapp v Ohio* 5; *McKeiver v. Pennsylvania* 11–12, 14, 16, 132; *Miller v. Alabama* 63–64, 141, 155; *Miranda v. Arizona* 5, 20, 65, 67–68, 155, 191, 225; *Montgomery v. Louisiana* 64; *People ex rel. Wayburn v. Schupf* 92; *Roper v. Graham* 63–64; *Roper v. Simmons* 24, 61–66, 141, 155; *Schall v. Martin* 16, 91, 93–95, 132; *Stanford v. Kentucky* 54–56, 60–62; *Thompson v. Oklahoma* 53–54, 62–63, 80
Casey Foundation President, Annie E. 254
Cauffman, Elizabeth 56–58
Cedar Knoll 118–19
cells 229, 238, 255, 257, 261
Center for Alternative Sentencing and Employment Services 277
Center on Wrongful Convictions of Youth 218
CFSY 142; *see also* Campaign for the Fair Sentencing of Youth
charges 4, 6, 11, 14–15, 22, 24, 27, 52, 80–81, 86, 95, 108, 118, 154, 157, 192–93, 211, 217; adult 112; armed robbery 125; disciplinary 241; felony 137, 154; murder 53, 61, 95, 112, 218, 270–71
Chavez, Cesar 131
Chein, Jason M. 59–60
Chief Justices 181; Earl Warren 11, 217; Roberts 62–63; Warren Burger 11–12
child abuse 103, 106, 143
Child Abuse Prevention and Treatment Act 103, 138
child clients 26, 103, 137, 181, 202
child delinquents 110
child health 39
Child Savers 30, 35, 82, 85, 252
child support 103, 115, 122
child welfare 31, 39, 172, 202; cases 112; clinics 138–39; resources 37; systems 103, 138, 176, 203
childhood 14, 17, 34, 52–53, 59, 69, 193, 195; and adolescence 53, 59; black 34, 40; complex problems of 15–16; healthy 157; innocence 201
children 16–17, 22–27, 51–53, 99–101, 103–7, 118–25, 128–33, 135–37, 139–42, 169–72, 174–78, 180–81, 187–95, 202, 241–45, 260–63, 269–70, 272–75; black 15, 30–32, 35–38, 40–41, 43, 188, 202; constitutional rights of 130; criminal offenses of 26; criminalizing of 187; defending of 120, 192, 199; delinquent 36; dependent 108; detained 24–25; devaluing 179; disciplining 118; educating 104; exposed 95; immigrant 35, 43; incarcerated 25–27, 227, 229, 241, 277; justice for 180, 187; lawyers for 95, 99, 101, 105, 113, 118, 129, 133, 141, 171; neglected 100–101; non-disabled 104; nonwhite 35; punishing mischievous 20; rehabilitate 9; representation of 176; representing 102, 104, 135–37, 139, 218, 275; rights of 23, 27, 81, 104, 128–29, 132, 139–40, 143, 173, 179, 182, 192; voiceless 281; vulnerable 230; well-behaved 36
Children's Court 82–83, 133
Children's Justice Clinic 236
Children's Law Center 111, 141, 259
Chomsky, Judy 99, 101, 105
civil rights 32, 39, 41, 91, 131, 134, 170, 181, 188, 192, 195, 239; class actions 136, 229; clinics 135; crisis 189; enforcement cases 40, 44; era 32–33; federal 91, 239; and federal suits challenging the use of solitary confinement 91; lawyers 32, 40, 44, 100, 192; legislation 31; litigated claims 208; movement 30–31, 44, 131, 170, 192; protests 15, 40, 44, 131; violations 234
Civil Rights Act 170

claims 5–6, 8, 11–12, 16, 34–35, 41, 92–94, 134, 211, 222, 234, 238; clinics 135; colorable 233; constitutional 5; court access 233; federal equal protection 211; juvenile rights 16; legal 128, 234; race-neutral 31; substantive 93
CLEPR 129, 134, 138–39; *see also* Council on Legal Education for Professional Responsibility
clients 83–84, 88–89, 91–92, 100–103, 105–8, 116–17, 120–23, 125–26, 134–35, 157–64, 175–76, 192–94, 200, 202–10, 212–13, 235–42, 274–76, 278–81; adolescent 125; black 201–2, 204; corporate 105; counseling of 204; individual 237, 274, 278; minority 201–2; new 114, 116; under-privileged 142; white 201–2; younger 120
clinical education 129, 134, 138–39, 143; CLEPR survey of 138; courses 140; movement 132–35
clinics 129, 136–39, 141–43; adult criminal defense 138; child welfare 138–39; in-house 137; landlord-tenant 135; legal 129; multiple service 140; out-placement 138; Rutgers 236, 238, 241, 244
coalitions 165, 260, 269, 277, 279, 281; building 210, 258, 260, 275; formal 261; internal 212; local policy 211; national 277; youth-led 277
coercion 190, 200, 225; police 225; state 200
cognitive control system 57
Cohen, Laura 4–17, 21–28, 31–45, 52–69, 80–96, 100–113, 115–26, 129–43, 155–66, 170–82, 188–95, 200–213, 218–25, 227, 227–45, 253–64, 269, 269–81; and Jane Spinak 269–81; and Sandra Simkins 227–45
color 16, 42, 188–89, 199–200, 204, 206, 208–10, 212–13, 230, 254, 258, 270–71; children of 181, 200, 202–4, 206, 208–9, 213; youth of 189, 206, 208–9, 212–13, 230, 254, 258, 270–71
"color brave" 200, 205–6
Columbia Court of Appeals 137
Columbia criminal law 136
Columbia Department of Youth Rehabilitation Services 261
Columbia Juvenile Court 39, 136
Commission on Law Enforcement and the Administration of Justice 43
Committee on Juvenile Courts, Arizona 23
committees 39, 106, 211–12, 274, 277, 279; court reform 212; family court 124; legislative 111, 211; policy 211; rules 124, 212
communities 25, 27, 36, 38, 40, 122, 124–25, 156–57, 174–76, 191–95, 202, 205–6, 209–10, 239, 242, 253, 260–61, 274–75; black 30–31, 36, 39; of children 27; courageous 188; farming 20; impoverished 188; inner-city 208; legal 99, 195; marginalized 131; professional 55; protection of the 95; religious 193; social 162; white 206
confessions 7–8, 51, 65, 106, 218–25, 270; 13-year-old boy's 223; 18-year-old's 225; adult's 224; alleged 8; children's 225; contaminated 224; defendant's 225; final 225; juvenile, false and coerced 217; suppressed 225; uncorroborated 218; uncounseled 217; unreliable 218, 222; videotaped 218
confidentiality 6, 121, 243, 273–74; child's 121; protective 6
confinement 22, 24, 91, 93–94, 115, 123, 191, 209, 228–29, 233–34, 237, 240, 258–59, 261, 275; correctional 229; disproportionate 142; local 212; secure 119; short 234; solitary 80, 228–30, 238, 240–41, 256, 259–60, 263
Connecticut Juvenile Training School 255
Connecticut Youth Prison 255
Constitution 6, 20, 22, 28, 41, 61, 63, 65, 80, 92–93, 96, 190, 231, 258
Constitution of the United States *see* Constitution
constitutional claims 5
constitutional rights 4, 10, 23, 83, 128, 130–31, 191, 194, 202, 263
contamination problem 224–25
convictions 5, 8, 53, 117, 130, 234; adult 112; criminal 155, 158, 161, 234
corporal punishment 42, 228
Corporation Counsel's office 86–87, 95
correctional confinement 229
correctional facilities 119, 170, 243, 259
costs 58, 138–39, 181, 190, 221, 229–30, 257, 278; daily 258; high 131, 258; long-term 221; per pupil 257; physical 220
Council on Legal Education for Professional Responsibility 129, 134, 138–39
counsel 4–5, 7–8, 20–23, 25–26, 31–32, 44, 80–84, 94, 130, 140, 171–74, 177,

180–81, 189–91, 227, 231–33, 235–37, 273–74; assigned 84, 273; assistance of 227; children's right to 199; clients 120, 175; constitutional right to 181; court-assigned 7, 83; full-time legislative 210; guiding hand of 227, 236, 243; law student 134; legal 194; mandated 219; post-dispositional 245; private 84, 259; a requirement for children at every stage of the delinquency process 235; role of 83, 103; skilled 189, 232; waiver of 25, 44, 177–78, 275
counseling 117, 154, 161, 164, 221, 228; increased use of 154; intensive 240; trauma 236; youth 202
counselors 165, 257
court-appointed attorneys 24, 26–27, 123
Court of Appeals 88–90, 93, 118–19
court process 79, 181, 189, 191
court reform 123, 212
court system 9, 67, 79, 84, 165, 187, 189, 191–93, 211; adult 155–56, 158, 161; criminal 157; flawed juvenile 10; juvenile 9–13, 16, 25, 31, 34, 80, 125, 133, 140, 193, 274; nation's juvenile 217; "parent of the state" 22
courtrooms 79, 81, 84, 88, 105, 111, 114, 158, 162–63, 187, 193–94, 199–200, 204, 210, 230, 236, 269, 273; admissions 8; advocacy 156, 213; juvenile 79, 273
courts 4–12, 14–16, 20–26, 32–35, 41–42, 51–54, 61–68, 79–83, 85–96, 105–8, 110–11, 118–19, 130, 132–34, 159–61, 217–23, 231–36, 240–42; appellate 15, 87, 124, 141, 223; and decisions of 21, 62, 132–33; delays requiring additional detention slots 119; and detention orders 87; and the failure to address racial discrimenation 33; federal 22, 43–44, 91, 94, 134, 136, 225; fees 233; fees, *see also* fees; local 134, 173, 179, 212; lower 8, 13, 53, 222, 225; and multiple appearances 157, 189; orders of 85, 87; and parental absence from the hearings of 207; practices of 182; proceedings of 7, 85; refusal to characterize juvenile court proceedings as either criminal or civil 133; rules of 119, 124, 189; and their interest in children's rights 132; and the United States Supreme Court 88–90, 93–94, 137
Crane, Megan 217–25
crime statistics 271–72, 278
crimes 22, 24, 38–39, 51–53, 55, 61, 64, 80, 91–95, 105, 107–8, 110, 128–30, 155–61, 207, 224, 270, 272–73; of murder 53, 61, 95, 112, 218, 270–71; reported 208; serious 220; violent 230
criminal cases 6, 8, 11, 13, 53, 64, 115, 126, 160, 211, 232; adult 7, 13, 83, 130, 136
criminal convictions 155, 158, 161, 234
criminal courts 5, 8, 21, 23, 27, 34, 42, 62, 66, 82, 95, 107, 109–10, 112, 125–26, 130, 154–56, 161; adult 5, 8, 23–24, 27, 66–67, 82, 107–8, 110, 112, 116–17, 125, 128, 130, 154–59, 161, 163, 165, 279; systems of 157; traditional 51
criminal defendants 22, 232; adult 7; represented 117
criminal defense lawyers 14, 82, 85, 94, 103, 138, 191
criminal jurisprudence 65, 67–69
criminal justice 61, 94, 204; jurisprudence 67; policies 276; process 34; reform 258
criminal justice systems 5, 20, 27, 32–33, 52, 66–67, 157–58, 162, 199, 205–6, 257
criminal law 51–52, 66, 68, 88, 130, 135, 138, 156; procedures 32, 68; proceedings 13, 21, 52, 165, 231, 233; revolution 129–30
criminal representation 161, 206
cross-examination of witnesses 4, 8, 36–37, 39, 131, 217, 241, 254, 264
Crum v. State Training School for Girls 42
Cumberland County Court 112
CWCY 218; *see also* Center on Wrongful Convictions of Youth
CYA 260; *see also* California Youth Authority

Darrows, Clarence 101
Dassey, Brendan 217–25
data collection 173, 210–11
Daugherty, Carmen 252, 252–64
Davis, Robert 222, 224
death penalty 24, 52–54, 61–62, 80, 155; *see also* juvenile death penalty; see also capital punishment
decisions 11–12, 21–22, 24, 52, 54–56, 58, 60–62, 66, 68, 92–94, 110, 132, 135, 192, 199–200, 218, 221, 239–41; case-related 200; critical 202; disciplinary 240; important 104, 207; juvenile justice 32; post-sentencing 232; state court

132; strategic 172; Supreme Court 22–23, 85
Defend Children: A Blueprint for Effective Juvenile Defender Service 180
defendants 32–33, 119, 130, 139; adult 273; black 30, 32, 201; criminal adult 7; juvenile 23, 31, 34
defender offices 22, 85, 121, 158, 204–5, 210, 269; funded 190; high caliber 95; largest public 156; organized public 135; primary public 163
defender organizations 269, 274, 281
defenders 52, 83, 115, 120–24, 158, 162, 172–73, 178, 192, 194, 199–213, 220–21, 225, 252, 269, 273–74, 278, 281; court-appointed 121, 205
defense attorneys 26, 51, 122, 158, 179, 201, 206, 223, 225, 235, 261, 274; front-line 223, 225; well-trained juvenile 179
defense counsels 7, 14, 30, 79, 102, 154, 156, 188, 190, 201; juvenile 26, 172, 177, 180; specialized 179
defense lawyers 14, 82, 85, 94, 103, 191
delinquency (*see also* juvenile delinquency) 7, 9, 15, 22, 36, 38, 79, 82, 86, 88, 91, 93, 110, 117, 122, 227, 269, 275; adjudications 8, 243; offense 7, 114, 125; prevention 34, 161, 170, 254; proceedings 130
delinquency cases 8, 13, 16, 31, 86, 105, 110, 115–17, 119, 121–22, 132–33, 136, 138–40, 174, 202, 273; handling of 112; pending 117
delinquency courts 22, 128, 135, 172, 176, 180, 188, 194
delinquency law 129, 133, 136, 139
Delinquency Prevention Act 170
delinquency proceedings 6, 33, 171–72, 176, 189, 203, 235
delinquent children 36
delinquent girls 37
DeMarco, Tony 111–13
DeMuro, Paul 254
Department of Children and Families 255
Department of Youth Services 252, 259
desegregation 41–42, 170; cases 41–44; court's school 32; reformatory 43; seeking 42; total 41–42; victories 42
detention 89, 93, 119, 163, 206, 211; home 10, 21, 38; pre-trial 89, 93, 119, 163, 206, 211; preventive 92–94
detention facilities 41, 115, 122; pre-trial 93; short-term 36
Dewey, John 99
DiIulio, John 269, 271–72
direct appeals 90–91, 93, 231; *see also* appeals
discrimination 33–34, 38–40, 43–44, 210–11; curtailing of blatant 40; racial 30, 32, 34–35, 38, 41–42, 44, 131; systemic 42
District of Columbia Court of Appeals 137
District of Columbia Department of Youth Rehabilitation Services 261
Dorsen, Prof. Norman 4–5, 8, 80, 132
Drizin, Steven 217–25
Due Process Clause 42, 233
Duncan v. Louisiana 11, 13
Duquette, Donald 139
Durden Rush, Gertrude E. 39

Eddings v. Oklahoma 53, 64–65
education 27, 31, 33, 35, 40, 67, 104, 121, 155–56, 161, 165, 202, 205, 238, 241, 244, 252, 257; advocacy 123; appropriate 164, 242; attorneys 115, 120–24; legal 134, 137; Negro 35; special 103, 105, 143, 162–63, 165, 233, 241
education services 115; compensatory 239; special 154, 157, 159, 162–63
educational advocacy 162, 164–65
Edwards, Edwin 262
Edwards, Terry 16
Effective Juvenile Defender Service 180
Eighth Amendment 52–54, 62–64, 91, 130, 263
employees 210, 237
employers 141–42, 244
employment 36, 38, 67, 100, 158, 243–44
environment judges 85
equal protection 30, 40, 44, 189; analysis 92; challenges 40; rights 92; secure 30; victories 32, 40, 44
Equal Protection Clause 34, 41–42, 207
"equal recognition" 30–31, 33, 35, 37, 39, 41, 43–45
evidence 6, 13–14, 30–31, 52, 54, 88, 96, 106–7, 109–10, 178, 188, 192, 203, 209, 211, 220, 222–23, 237; alleged 223; anecdotal 205; explicit 100; false 219; incontrovertible 222; inculpatory 223; medical 223; mitigating 201; ordering 86; physical 115, 270; seized 105; statistical 207; strong 189
executions 53, 55, 61, 270; *see also* capital punishment

facilities 6, 26–27, 40, 80, 118–19, 123, 161, 191, 227–29, 237–38, 242, 252–59, 261–63, 277; adult penal 41, 253; black 42; child welfare 35; dangerous 245; detention 41, 115, 122; educational 41–42; expensive 229; harmful 264; humane 230; juvenile 118, 155, 191, 230, 234, 237–38, 254–55, 258, 263; juvenile corrections 117, 237, 242, 256; juvenile detention 119, 122; lock-down 118; long-term placement 278; maximum security 112; new 259–60, 277; public 41; recreational 41; rehabilitative 261; remote 228; secure 237, 241, 273; state juvenile justice 40; treatment 44, 109; white 42; white juvenile justice 40; youth 254, 273; youth correctional 259
false confessions 190, 218–19, 221–24; cases 223; literature 222; preventing 219; risk factors for 220–21
families 20, 24–27, 116, 122–23, 155, 157, 159, 163–65, 179, 181, 190, 192–94, 200, 202–3, 242–44, 255, 258, 261–63; black 35–36; child's 204; client's 163, 235; dysfunctional 209; loving 157; single-parent 116; stabilizing 165; of youth offenders 244
Families and Friends of Louisiana's Incarcerated Children 262
Family Court 39, 83, 85–87, 89–90, 92, 94–96, 103, 106, 110, 155–56, 164; branches 85; documents 89; features of 91; practices 87, 91; proceedings 90, 122; representing juveniles 91
family court, judges 236
Family Court Act 1962 88–89
Family Law Clinic 136
family members 79, 116, 154, 159, 164, 207–8, 243
family violence 231
farm workers' unions 131
fees 103, 190–91, 258; administrative 190; attorney 44, 190; charged 190; court 233; mandatory 244; processing 190
Feld, Barry 34
felonies 23, 26, 95, 117, 155–56, 201
Ferrere, Eduardo 16, 51, 51–69
FFLIC 262; *see also* Families and Friends of Louisiana's Incarcerated Children
Fifth Amendment 22, 65, 130, 203, 207–8, 220
First Amendment 233–34
Florida state reform schools 41
focus groups 180, 276
Forer, Lois 100
Fort, Judge William S. 133
Fortas, Justice Abe 6, 11, 81, 83, 130, 132, 143, 169, 181, 217–18, 227
Fourteenth Amendment 22, 61, 231, 258, 263
Fourth Amendment 32–33, 68, 130, 207
Fox, James A. 271–72
Frazier v. Cupp 222
Freedom of Information Act 211
Fruchter, Barbara 100

Gagnon v. Scarpelli 233
gang membership 107, 271
Gardner, Margo 57
Gault, Gerald 4–12, 15–17, 21–23, 25–27, 30–34, 40–44, 79–84, 91–94, 99–100, 128–30, 132–33, 135–37, 139–43, 187, 217–21, 225, 227–29, 252–53; and the Court's ruling in *In re.Gault* 44; dispositional hearing process 80; guarantee of access to counsel 42; and the habeas corpus petition 21, 130; insistence on procedural safeguards 34; and the issue of the majority opinion 6; promise of zealous defense advocacy 129; in trial and appellate courts 141; and the years following the Court ruling 31, 133, 140
Gault, Marjorie 169
gays 131, 256
GED 210; *see also* General Education Development
gender and race constraints 44, 135
General Education Development 210
Georgetown clinics 136–37
Georgetown Law Center's Juvenile Justice Clinic 118, 141
Gideon v. Wainwright 5, 22, 32–33, 40, 43, 130, 169–70, 275
Ginsburg, Nancy 154–65
girls 35, 37, 42–43, 108, 237; black 35–37; delinquent 37; little 170, 222; white 108
Goldstein, Joseph 104
Goldwater, Barry 20
Graham, Sandra 57–58, 62–63, 65
Graham v. Florida 141, 155
grants 86, 101, 118, 120, 161, 208; *see also* legal aid
Greene, Judge Harold H. 118
Grisso, Thomas 68
groups 25, 55, 99, 126, 129, 140, 142, 161, 169, 173–74, 177, 179–80, 201,

204–5, 208, 270, 277, 281; age 56–57; juvenile advocacy 141–42; juvenile trial practice 114, 123; large 277; legal 165; minority 85; racial 201; resilient 169; student prayer 271
Guggenheim, Martin 16, 79–96, 137
guilt 14, 110, 207, 218, 222–24, 253
guns 105, 107, 222

habeas corpus action 94
habeas corpus petition 21, 130
habeas corpus process 7–8, 21, 88–92
habeas lawyers 201
Halbach, Teresa 218
Haley v. Ohio 51, 65, 223
Harvard Education Review 104
hearings 5, 7–10, 21, 23, 26–27, 81, 87, 90, 111–13, 118, 164, 173–74, 187, 191, 233, 235–36, 239, 241; adjudicatory 231; disciplinary 115, 240–41; dispositional 232, 235; fair 241; formal 279; initial 114, 177–78; pre-trial 157; preliminary 232
Henning, Kristin 4–17, 21–28, 30, 30–45, 52–69, 80–96, 100–126, 129–43, 155–66, 170–82, 188–95, 199, 199–213, 218–25, 228–45, 253–64, 270–81
Hertz, Randy 4–17
high schools 99, 154, 242–43, 271
Hill, Harry 36
Hills, Lincoln 262–63
Hobson, Mellody 205
holidays 24–25
homelessness 37, 158, 243–44, 270
Hooks, Julia 38
housing 66–67, 115, 122, 189, 244; assignment decisions 240; assignments 240; authorities 122; developments 25; public 243; secure 120
Huerta, Delores 131
Human Services 118, 176

IAT 201, 204; *see also* Implicit Association Test
IEPs 241; *see also* Individualized Education Plan
illiterate inmates 231, 233, 235, 241
immigration attorneys 114–15
Implicit Association Test 201, 204
In re Gault 5–6, 9–10, 12, 17, 20, 22, 28, 128, 132–36, 139, 141, 143, 181; and civil rights 32, 39, 41, 91, 131, 134, 170, 181, 188, 192, 195, 239; and constitutional rights 4, 10, 23, 83, 128, 130–31, 191, 194, 202, 263; and guarantee of access to counsel 42; and the response by Arizona 22; ripple effect of 99, 101, 103, 105, 107, 109, 111, 113; and the Supreme Court's decision in 128
incarcerated youth 229, 231, 234, 237, 239–43, 245, 254, 256–57, 261, 280; attorneys for 243; lawyers for 239–40; and rates of sexual victimization of 254, 256
incarceration 22, 30, 154–56, 160–64, 191, 194, 203, 207, 227, 230, 232, 239–40, 242–43, 252–53, 257, 261, 272–73, 277–79; avoiding 116; long-term 163–64; programs 277; rates 96; systems 279; terms 273; young person's 232
Indigent Defense Delivery Systems 235
Indigent Defense Services 205
Individualized Education Plan 241
Individuals with Disabilities Education Improvement Act 121
Industrial Home for Wayward Colored Girls 37
injustices 16, 126, 187–88, 195; dual 181; racial 34, 44, 205–6, 210, 212–13, 263; systemic 188, 191
inmates 233–35, 240–41, 261; adult 231, 241
institutions 6, 27, 36–37, 39, 42, 103, 170, 235, 252–53, 255, 259; adult penal 35; operated rehabilitative 36
integration 40–41, 43, 134
internal reform 210
Internal Revenue Service 102
International Association of Chiefs of Police 219
interrogation 5, 65, 190–91, 207, 219–24, 231, 270; custodial 219; of Nga Truong 220; post-indictment 232; process 224; recorded 220; reform 218; trainings 220; of Trevon Yates 222, 224; uncounseled 218; videotaped 224
interrogation rooms 190, 219, 270
interrogation tactics 221–22, 225
interrogation techniques 219; child-sensitive 219; pressure-filled 218
investigators 86–87, 115, 125, 154, 156, 158, 173–74, 178, 224
IRS 102; *see also* Internal Revenue Service
isolation 228, 238, 240, 256; punitive 239; use of 228, 230, 238

J.D.B. v. North Carolina 65, 219
jails 6, 9, 21, 38, 41, 66, 109, 117, 155, 253
JDAI 212, 254; *see also* Juvenile Detentions Alternatives Initiative
"Jim Crow" juvenile justice 30, 32, 36, 38, 253
JJABG 120, 124; *see also* Juvenile Justice Accountability Block Grant
JJDPA 170–71, 181; see also *Juvenile Justice and Delinquency Prevention Act*
John L. v. Adams 234
Joseph-Gaudet, Frances 37
JRD 82–84, 87–88, 91–92, 137, 269, 275–78, 281; *see also* Juvenile Rights Division
JSP 115, 122–23; *see also* Juvenile Services Program
JTIP 141, 180; *see also* Juvenile Training Immersion Program
judges 4–5, 12–13, 15–16, 21, 23–24, 39, 79–85, 87–89, 91–96, 105–14, 121–22, 126, 132–35, 137–39, 160–61, 199, 206–8, 217; appellate 110; authorized 89, 91; conviction-prone 16; in delinquency cases 121; dissenting 54; eccentric 13; environment 85; family court 236; federal 61; first black woman 39; incentivizing 220; juvenile court 5, 9, 13–15, 24, 109–11, 133, 135, 217, 228, 242; low level 80; trial 88; upstate 112; weak 85
jurisdictions 23, 67, 80, 89, 118, 130, 172–73, 178, 181, 202, 205, 212, 231, 236, 257; defender's 212; juvenile court's 235; local 172–73, 207, 209; noncriminal 43; rural 217; state 172–73
jurisprudence 51–52, 60–64, 67, 132, 212, 221; criminal 65, 67–69; criminal justice 67; developmentally-appropriate 62; emerging 66; juvenile 51–69, 180; new 62; process 132, 140; reasonable child 65–67; substantive legal 61
jury trials 11–13, 33–34, 130, 135, 206
justice 4, 6, 11, 16, 27, 31, 36, 43, 53, 130, 173, 176, 180, 187–89, 195, 205, 262–64, 271; calls for 171–74, 177, 179, 235; pursuit of 20, 28; racial 42, 199–200, 205–6, 211–12
justice system 38, 43, 52, 82, 96, 142, 169, 171–72, 176, 179, 187, 192, 194, 212, 254; adult 252, 257; and "adulthood" 67; compassionate youth 270; contemporary criminal 200; cost-effective youth 277; criminal and juvenile 32, 192, 269; experts 180; harsh 169; harshest juvenile 95; modern juvenile 227; nation's juvenile 171; and stakeholders 173
juvenile cases 117, 121, 124–25, 136, 138, 172, 174, 202, 207–8; appeals 124; arrests 230; black 38, 206
juvenile clients 83, 88, 114, 116–17, 119–21, 124–25, 142, 210, 212
juvenile clinics 136, 138, 140
juvenile codes 231, 272
juvenile court cases 162, 178, 191
juvenile court judges 5–6, 9, 13–15, 24, 109–11, 133, 135, 217, 228, 242–43; compassionate 12; exhorted to "ensure that effective post-disposition review is provided to each delinquent youth" 236; hostile 112; presiding 23
juvenile court movement 36–37, 253
juvenile court records 6, 272–73
juvenile court system 9–13, 16, 25, 31, 34, 80, 125, 133, 140, 193, 274
juvenile courtrooms 79, 273
juvenile courts 4–6, 8–13, 15–16, 23–27, 37–41, 44, 51–52, 108–10, 112–15, 117, 124–26, 132–33, 135–41, 171–74, 178–79, 187–91, 209–11, 253; of Arizona 23; attorneys 120; bypassing of 82; challenges 117; child-protective 12; children in 22, 124, 174, 190; and the child's misbehavior 27, 228, 230; and the child's misdemeanors 26, 37, 79, 117, 154, 156, 201, 273; complained 140; convictions 172; early 8–9, 35, 37, 51, 128, 130, 169, 253; interventions 243; jurisdiction 66–67, 235, 273; local 39; new 253; overcrowded 170; practices 23, 26, 81, 92, 116, 124, 181; and probation officers 38, 209; proceedings 9, 130, 133, 171, 272; process revolution in 79, 81, 83, 85, 87, 89, 91, 93, 95; processes 26, 179, 274; prosecutors 95; system structure 191; used as a training ground for inexperienced lawyers 178
juvenile crime 112, 269, 271
juvenile death penalty 52–53, 55, 60–61, 141
juvenile defendants 23, 31, 34
juvenile defenders 24–26, 51–52, 55, 60–61, 64–65, 81–84, 95, 122–23, 143, 173–76, 178–81, 187–89, 191–95, 199–202, 205–6, 211–13, 252, 261;

career 126; and defender organizations had unique and invaluable insights 269; funded 190; permanent 120; post-dispositional 240; pushing for a more developmentally appropriate approach to sentencing 54; qualified 187, 191; specialized 125; value of 179; well-qualified 188
juvenile defense 24, 26, 114–15, 117, 119–21, 123, 125, 169, 173–75, 179–80, 182, 187, 189, 191, 193, 195, 273, 275
juvenile defense attorneys 235, 261
juvenile defense community 169, 169–82, 192, 194–95, 199
juvenile defense counsel 26, 172, 177, 180
juvenile defense lawyers 192
juvenile defense systems 171, 176–77, 180–81, 194
juvenile delinquency 88; cases 82, 95, 134; clinics 135, 137–41, 143; courts 130; pro bono cases 173; proceedings 130, 132, 275; work 138
Juvenile Delinquency Guidelines 236
juvenile delinquents 4, 6, 81, 83, 90–91, 140, 155, 164
juvenile detention 119
Juvenile Detentions Alternatives Initiative 212, 254
juvenile dispositions 112, 239
juvenile facilities 118, 155, 191, 230, 234, 237–38, 254–55, 258, 263
juvenile homicides 112
juvenile incarceration 227, 229–30
juvenile indigent defense policies 274
juvenile judge 8–9, 26, 81
juvenile jurisprudence 51–69, 180; reinvigorated 219
juvenile justice 34, 40, 44
Juvenile Justice Accountability Block Grant 120, 124
Juvenile Justice and Delinquency Prevention Act 170–71, 181
Juvenile Justice Clinics 129, 135, 137, 141–42
juvenile justice institutions 40, 42
juvenile justice reform 30, 35, 37–38, 95–96, 171, 173, 259, 261
Juvenile Justice Reform Act 95
juvenile justice system 28, 30–34, 39–44, 79, 81, 83, 104, 108–9, 120–24, 192–95, 203–4, 230–31, 236–37, 252, 254, 256–59, 261, 269–70; American 30, 34, 40, 44, 96; fairness of 81; of Massachusetts 111; of Pennsylvania 109
Juvenile Law Center, founding of 99–113
juvenile offenders 64, 155, 164, 238, 256
juvenile prisons 21, 230, 237, 239, 242
juvenile records 212, 243
juvenile rehabilitation 38
Juvenile Rights Division 82–84, 87–88, 91–92, 137, 269, 275–78, 281
juvenile sentences 112, 232
Juvenile Services Program 115, 122–23
juvenile "super-predator myth" 269–81
juvenile systems 21–24, 30, 38, 44, 137, 199, 206–7, 211–13
Juvenile Training Immersion Program 141, 180
Juvenile Unit 22, 120, 123–24; freestanding 115; holistic 122; and the importance of leadership 123; PDS 115; specialized 114, 124

Kane, Robert 111
kangaroo court 6, 22, 217
Katner, David 138
Keith, Erin 199, 199–213
Kennedy, Bobby 170
Kennedy, Justice 61–62
Kennedy, Pres. John F. 131
Kent, Morris 5, 16
Kent v United States 5–6, 12, 15–16, 30, 51, 110, 129–30, 132, 170

law libraries 233–35
law school clinics 128–43, 171
law schools 4, 99, 107, 109, 128–29, 133–35, 137–42, 173, 192; accredited 135; American 134–35; and the case study 100; curricula 128–29, 134, 143; debt 179; graduates 104; new 177
law students 134, 136, 233; educating 133; local 123
lawsuits 165, 193, 234, 259, 261–63; federal 91; *see also* federal lawsuits
lawyers 4–5, 39–44, 82–84, 86–87, 99–103, 105–10, 115–17, 132–39, 162–64, 169, 174–75, 177, 179–81, 190–91, 202–3, 234–37, 240–41, 274–76; appointment of 190; bad 85; for children 95, 99, 101, 105, 113, 118, 129, 133, 141, 171; child's 95, 121; civil rights 32, 40, 44, 100, 192; court-appointed 174; criminal defense 138; experienced 125; felony trial 114; funded 190; habeas 201; high-quality

private 190; individual 117; jailhouse 233–35; juvenile defense 192; lazy 137; legal aid 99; new 115–16, 136, 141; paternalistic 203; PDS 115–17, 120–21; petitioner's 130; private 141, 174; public interest 134, 190; seasoned 178; senior 116; skilled 136–37; student 137; trained 135, 156, 176; volunteer 106; young 106, 143
Lee, Patti 41
Legal Aid 85–88, 91, 94, 163, 275–76, 279–80
legal aid lawyers 99
legal education 134, 137
legal representation 100, 136, 156, 162, 172, 176, 187, 189, 193, 227, 232, 236–37, 239, 244, 275; continuous 231; effective 171; excellent 95; specialized 125
legal services 99, 176
legislation 26, 138, 192, 210–11, 259–61, 274–77; civil rights 31; enacting of 156, 262; federal 277; federal juvenile justice 170; hearings 111, 261, 279, 281; juvenile 210; pending 276, 280; "raise the age" 273; retributive 272; sponsoring of 260; state 66
legislative advocacy 276
legislators 24, 81, 210–11, 274, 278–81
legislatures 51–52, 64, 66–67, 83–84, 90, 95, 135, 141, 276, 280–81
leniency 219–21; false promises of 220; implied promises of 221–22
Levick, Marsha 99, 234
Lewis, Amelia 4, 169, 234–35
Lewis, Ronald 10, 21
liberty 20, 79, 96, 104, 189–90, 231, 233, 252, 258; civil 5; interest of juveniles 94, 233; pre-trial 93
litigation 31, 40, 44, 88, 93, 118, 137, 205, 234, 258–60, 262; civil 238; equal protection 36, 44; routes 157; skills 123; successful 259
Louisiana state youth correctional institutions 42
Lyman School for Boys 253

Major v. Sowers 42
Mapp v Ohio 5
Margolis, Phil 99
Marrus, Ellen 20–28
Mathis, Judge Charles C. 41
maximum security prisons 112
McDonald, Elizabeth 38
McElhinny, Hannah 114–26
McKeiver v. Pennsylvania 11–12, 14, 16, 132
Means, Russell 131
media 263, 270, 278–79
medical treatment 242, 259
mental health 104, 106, 112, 115, 119, 123, 155–56, 158–59, 165, 231, 240, 242; cases 117; clients 105; and juvenile justice 231; service providers 242; staff 238; treatment 101, 157, 229, 238
Mexican American Legal Defense and Education Fund 131
Michigan Child Advocacy Clinic 139
Miller, Jerome 63–64, 111, 155
Miller, Jerry 111, 252–53
Miller v. Alabama 63–64, 141, 155
minority youth, overcriminalization of 188, 205, 211, 213
minors 53, 104, 155
Miranda custody analysis 66
Miranda custody doctrine 68
Miranda v. Arizona 5, 20, 65, 67–68, 155, 191, 225
mission statements 205, 255
Missouri State Public Defender Director Michael Barrett 194
Missouri Supreme Court 61
Mlyniec, Wallace 128, 128–43
models 117, 120, 125, 139–40, 161, 192, 252, 254, 275; adult criminal justice 178; failed 252, 262–63; representational 156
Monahan, Kathryn C. 57
monitoring 164, 178; service plans 160; and timely intervention 231; the youth's performance in school 163
Montgomery v. Louisiana 64
mooting 89–90
motion 5, 21, 90, 105–6, 110, 112–13, 118, 137, 174, 206–9, 222, 225, 232, 239–40; pre-trial 207; prosecutor's 112; successful 239–40
murder 53, 61, 95, 112, 218, 270–71
murderers 218, 220, 277
Myers, Robert 40

NAACP 38–39, 99; *see also* National Association for the Advancement of Colored People
NACW 37; *see also* National Association of Colored Women
Nanini, Jenadee 30–45
National Association for the Advancement of Colored People 38–39, 99

National Association of Colored Women 37
National Association of Counsel for Children 235
"national consensus" evaluated by the Supreme Court 54, 56
National Council of Juvenile and Family Court Judges 236
National Council of Juvenile Court Judges 133
National Juvenile Defender Center 140–41, 169, 174–77, 179–80, 182, 189, 235–36, 274
National Juvenile Defense Standards 236, 274
National Probation and Parole Association 228
Negro Fellowship League 38
Negro Probation Department 38
Negroes 15, 35, 41; children 30, 42; education of 35; girls 39; inmates 41; juveniles 41–42; women 39
New York 39, 66, 79, 81–83, 88–91, 93–96, 137, 139, 154–56, 160–61, 164, 261, 273, 275–77; Bar 89; City Corporation Counsel 85; City Criminal Justice 161; Family Court 4, 95; law 91, 155, 161, 270, 273; Legal Aid Office 137; legislature 83; prisons 276
New York Times 85
New York University 4, 85, 89, 137
news 199, 207, 270, 280
newspapers 20, 277, 280
Nirider, Laura 217–25
Nixon, Richard 11, 16, 194
non-attorneys 204
non-lawyers 172, 279
NPPA 228; *see also* National Probation and Parole Association

Oak Hill Youth Detention Center 118–19, 261
O'Connor, Justice 54, 62
Offender Rehabilitation Division 117
Offender Rehabilitation Project 120
offenders 62, 155, 170; adult 62; black 37; juvenile 64, 155, 164, 238, 256; minority 34; trivial 112; worst 63; young 96; youth sex 244; youthful 154–55, 161, 217
offenses 4, 6, 21, 24, 26–27, 54, 64, 81, 108, 122, 128, 158, 160–61, 164, 170, 230, 243–44, 253; capital 53–54, 62–63; egregious 160; low level 260; minor 20; non-homicide 62–63, 155; school-based 189, 211; status 100, 108, 210, 275; violent 111; weapons 273
Office of Juvenile Justice and Delinquency Prevention 120, 170–71, 237, 254
officers 20, 32–33, 65, 201, 207–8, 219–21, 223–25; correctional 238, 255, 257, 277; corrections 171; interrogating 225; judicial 24; law enforcement 192; legal services 233; public information 280; school resource 121; sheriff's 277
Ogletree, Charles 116
OJJDP 120, 170–71, 237, 254; *see also* Office of Juvenile Justice and Delinquency Prevention
O'Neill, Judge Jerome 105

parole 61–64, 90, 155, 192, 239; cases 141; compliance 244; eligibility 233; hearings 123, 239; officers 37, 239; programs 67; revocations 233; services 260
PDS 114–26, 210; *see also* Public Defender Service
PDS lawyers 115–17, 120–21
People ex rel. Wayburn v. Schupf 92
Persons in Need of Supervision 86, 91
Phillis, Christina 20, 20–28
PINS 86, 91; *see also* Persons in Need of Supervision
Pittman, Elizabeth D. 39
plurality opinion 11–12, 15
police 10, 21, 33–34, 68, 79, 86, 107, 140, 191, 199, 203, 207–8, 218–19, 222–25, 244, 270; coercion 225; counsel 85; deception 222–23; departments 170, 220; falsehood 222; harassment 208; interrogations 20, 23, 26, 218; misconduct 208; officers 20, 32, 44, 66, 201, 207; practices 165; shootings 207; tactics 221, 225; testimonies 110; violence 207; youth exchange 207
policy reforms 164, 169, 180
Polk, Anthony 220, 222
Powell, Lewis 16
pre-trial detention 89, 93, 119, 163, 206, 211
Prescott, Peter 82, 84–87, 95
preventive detention 92–94
prison reformers 37
prisons 26–27, 38, 41, 63, 111–12, 131, 155, 224, 237, 252–54, 264; adult 154, 229, 240, 253–55; maximum security 112; state youth 260

privileges 4, 7, 22, 42, 80, 243; constitutional 7; distinct 174; lawyer-client 103; optional 181
probation officers 13, 20, 36–38, 79–80, 85, 114, 128, 171–72, 178, 201, 207, 209, 217; black 38–39; and judges 128; and juvenile courts 38, 209
problems 7, 9–10, 13–14, 33–34, 101, 105, 116–17, 140, 142, 180–81, 208, 212, 218–20, 224, 227, 229, 253, 255; abuse-related 121; behavior 162; financial 101; legal 236; school-related 163; substance 121
protection 6, 20, 30–31, 33, 35, 37, 39, 41–45, 92, 119, 130, 132, 176, 188–89, 202, 241, 243, 271; constitutional 130, 134, 187, 189, 264; due process 20–22, 25, 30, 34, 43, 52, 169, 227, 258; equal 30, 40, 44, 189; establishing black child welfare 37; heightened 235; robust 234, 241; seizure 130; skirting due-process 253; statutory 27; substantive 52–53; protests 40, 44, 131; black 33; civil rights 15; peaceful 41; social 40
Pruski, Gina 203
psychologists 24, 55, 101, 141, 228
psychosocial factors 56, 68
public defender offices 22, 24, 26, 126, 135, 165, 173, 178–79, 210, 273, 276
Public Defender Service 114–26, 210
public defenders 24–25, 105, 114, 139, 141, 174, 178, 189–90, 199, 203–5, 273; elected 281; local 260; newly-hired 202, 281; overworked 194; primary 275
Public Defenders for Racial Justice in California 212
public housing authorities 122
punishment 20, 22, 41, 43, 51, 53, 61–63, 95, 125, 130, 202, 217, 252, 272, 280; appropriate 64; disproportionate 62; maximum 6; proportional 62
Puritz, Patricia 169–82

racial biases 16, 31, 34, 200, 203, 205–7, 209, 211; expressed 209; impact of implicit 206, 209
racial biases plaguing 201
racial discrimination 30, 32, 34–35, 38, 41–42, 44, 131
racial disparities 200, 203, 205–7, 211, 264, 277; extreme 42; state-wide 209; unconscionable 269
racial justice 42, 199–200, 205–6, 211–12; advocacy 199, 206; arguments 205–6, 212; initiatives 204; reform 211
reform 4–17, 21–28, 31–45, 52–69, 80–96, 100–113, 115–26, 129–43, 155–66, 170–82, 188–95, 200–213, 218–25, 228–45, 252–64, 270–81; criminal justice 124; institutional 31, 40; legislative 137; movement 259, 261; progressive youth justice 276; sustaining of 252, 264; systemic 124, 194, 205, 210, 276
reform schools 36, 40–42, 119, 253; all-white 40; closed Massachusetts's 111; requiring to desegregate 41; segregated 40–41
reformatories 35
reformers 9, 15, 37, 40, 252, 264; early 8–9; mainstream 35; set out to help children 9; white 36
regional juvenile defender centers 175, 177, 180
rehabilitation 30, 35, 40, 51, 80, 104, 117, 125, 154, 158, 160–61, 165, 170, 202, 217, 252, 255, 272; individualized 80; juvenile 38
rehabilitative 30, 34–37, 40, 42–44, 120, 139–40, 157–58, 210, 229–32, 236, 238, 240, 243, 245, 253–55, 261, 269, 272; approach 255; goals 231; ideals 34, 36, 40, 43, 140, 230, 245; principles 232
Rehnquist, William 16
Reid, John E. 224
relationships 10, 33, 55, 95, 123, 126, 141, 163–64, 202, 206, 276, 278–79; attorney-child 202; attorney-client 204; attorney-social worker 121; caring 258; cultivated 276; developing 281; direct 116; fostered 163; legislative 279; successful 159; temporary 142; trusting 258
reports 57–58, 80, 82, 103, 106, 138, 171, 173, 177–78, 180, 188–89, 208–9, 228–29, 235, 237–39, 254–57, 260–64, 278–80; details of 189; exposing deep fractures in the constitutional protections affirmed for children 189; groundbreaking 171; investigatory 188–89; national 177, 180; referral 80
representation 24, 26, 101, 103, 105, 119, 125, 134, 136, 172–73, 175–76, 189–90, 231, 233, 235–36, 238, 241, 278; adult 202; client-centered child

275; comprehensive 105; effective 106, 116, 189, 205, 274; high-quality 176; legislative 34; meaningful 82, 87; post-dispositional 231, 233, 235–36; secure interdisciplinary 275; single attorney 125; specialized 156, 165
research 39, 55–60, 62, 67–69, 136, 138, 140, 155, 187, 200–202, 206–9, 230, 254, 256; behavioral science 55; brain science 24; contemporary 31; developmental 65, 67, 209; growing body of 156, 230; new 178; relevant 61
residential facilities 118, 188; high-security 118; long-term 230
retributive legislation 272
Rezneck, Daniel A. 132
Richette, Lisa 100
robberies 5, 14, 109, 224, 256
Roberts, Kerry 109
Rockefeller, John D. 276
Rodham, Hillary 104
Roman, Jeff 262–63
Roosevelt, Theodore 276
Roper v. Graham 63–64
Roper v. Simmons 24, 61–66, 141, 155
Russell, John 107
Rutgers clinics 236, 238, 241, 244
Ryan, Liz 252, 252–64

sanctions 43, 79–80, 157–58, 170, 228, 262
Sandalow, Judith 141
Scali, Mary Ann 187–95
Schall v. Martin 16, 91, 93–95, 132
Schinitsky, Charles 82–85, 87, 95
Schiraldi, Vincent 261
school-based offenses 189, 211
school shootings 271–72, 280
Schultz, Lawrence 137
Schwartz, Bernard 99–113
Schwartz, Robert 99
self-incrimination 4, 7, 22, 80, 130, 217–18, 220
sentencing 53–54, 61–64, 67, 92, 155, 191, 209, 232, 234, 273; advocacy 206; appropriate 54; blended 272; decisions 54; enhanced 272; jurisprudence 64–65; juvenile 79; laws 54, 66; mandatory 95; recommendations 209
sexual abuse 36, 237–38, 259, 263
sexual assaults 27, 256
sexual immorality 36
sexual victimization of incarcerated youth 237, 254, 256–57
sexual violence 230, 237
Shapp, Milton 111
shootings 107, 207, 272–73
shoplifting 199, 211
Simkins, Sandra 227, 227–45
Sixth Amendment 11, 13, 130, 219, 231–32
Smith, Clay 136, 233
Smith, Peter S. 136
social-emotional system 57
social services 31, 91, 119
solitary confinement 80, 228–30, 238, 240–41, 256, 259–60, 263; abuses 191; prolonged 238; use of 91, 263; use of at youth prisons 256
special education 103, 105, 143, 162–63, 165, 233, 241
Special Litigation Unit 91–92
Spinak, Jane 269, 269–81
Stanford v. Kentucky 54–56, 60–62
state assessments 177, 235
state courts 22, 42, 44, 64, 94, 136, 207; criminal proceedings 128; decisions 132; forced to take sides on the question of racial justice 42
state legislatures 27, 43, 61, 66, 173, 219, 225, 276
state reformatories 35
State Training School for Girls 42
"status offenders" 100, 108, 210, 275
Steinberg, Laurence 56–58
Stevenson, Bryan 141
Strong, Meghan 128, 128–43
substance abuse 116, 157–58
"super-predator myth" 269–81
Support Center for Child Advocates 106, 255
Supreme Court *see* United States Supreme Court
Swanger, Harry 100

Tallulah Youth Prison 252, 254, 256, 258, 261–63
Taylor, Barry 112
Teitelbaum, Lee 102–3
Terry, Edward 32–33
Texas Youth Commission 237
Texas Youth Committee 237
Texas Youth Council 258
Thames, Jon 136
Thompson v. Oklahoma 53–54, 62–63, 80
trauma counseling 236
treatment facilities 44, 109
Trump, Donald 270
Turner, Ted 272

United Farm Workers Association 131
United States Department of Justice 27, 188, 262–63, 271
United States Supreme Court 4–5, 11, 13–14, 16–17, 21–24, 52, 61, 85, 88, 99, 105, 110, 155, 181, 188, 217, 221–23, 227

Vera Institute of Justice 242
victims 55, 107, 116, 190, 200, 202, 208, 224, 240, 242, 256, 270, 272; alleged 14; dependent 202; enhanced 273
Vietnam War 131
violence 25, 38, 112, 237, 244, 256–57, 269, 271; and abuse 237, 256; domestic 138; drug-related 139; family 231; institutional 229; physical 54, 237; rampant and extreme 237; sexual 230, 237; sustained 159
Voynow, Connie 100
Vukcevich, Steve 228

Ward, Geoff 30–45
Warren, Earl 32, 130, 181, 207–8, 218
Warren, Jimmy 207
Warren Court 5, 30, 32–34, 130
Wedlock, Eldon 136
Wells, Gary 38
Wells, Ida B. 38
white youth 30, 35–36, 40, 43–44, 181, 209, 230, 254, 264; afforded 30; educated 35
Williams, Joseph 87
Wilson, James Q. 271
Womack, Gina 262
Woolard, Jennifer 57–58

youth 24–27, 30–35, 39–44, 51–56, 59–68, 100–106, 111–13, 117–21, 123–25, 155, 161–64, 187–95, 209–13, 230–31, 233–34, 236–45, 252–64, 278–81; accountability 170; at-risk 162; brown 43, 254; Caucasian 230; of color 189, 206, 208–9, 212–13, 230, 254, 258, 270–71; committed black male 253; committed white male 253; and constitution guarantees 51; counseling 202; and crime 112, 161, 273, 278–80; crime 54, 112, 161, 229, 269, 273, 278–80; delinquent 80, 236; deprived 203; detained 123, 162, 199; idealism of 131; immaturity of 62; immigrant 243; incarcerated 229, 231, 234, 237, 239–43, 245, 254, 256–57, 261, 280; incarceration 257, 259, 262–63; and justice 30, 39, 42, 44, 276; justice 30–31, 39, 42, 44, 276; offenders 244; rehabilitation 254; ungovernable 51; unrepresented 238; violence 112; violent 140; vulnerable 229; wayward 178
youth prisons 229, 252–63; closing of 259, 261, 263–64; clothing and food in 255; early 252–53; largest 262; local 261; reforming of 258; and the use of wire fencing 255; *see also* juvenile prisons